WIZARDS AND SCIENTISTS

WIZARDS AND SCIENTISTS

Explorations in Afro-Cuban Modernity and Tradition

Stephan Palmié

Duke University Press Durham and London 2002

Printed in the United States of America on acid-free paper ∞
Typeset in Monotype Fournier by Keystone Typesetting, Inc.
Library of Congress Cataloging-in-Publication Data
appear on the last printed page of this book.

To Doris, on whom I have inflicted this book.

I love you, and I thank you for your patience and kindness.

CONTENTS

ACKNOWLEDGMENTS

This book has been long in the making. In the aftermath of some ten years of reflecting on some of the issues that form its core, it seems to me that it grew—far from effortlessly to be sure—out of some of the contradictions generated by the research on Afro-Cuban religious thought and practice that I undertook in Miami between 1985 and 1989. If so, these contradictions registered not so much in the pages of the book (*Das Exil der Götter*) that resulted from this research as in my own experience. I nowadays look at the project that emerged from these, for me increasingly unresolved, issues as some sort of liability that I had incurred—not just to an academic career, or to myself and my wife Doris, who in many ways depended on the publication of a "second book," but to people to whom I will never be able to exercise the kind of accountability that our, in many ways fortuitous, mutual implication in each others' lives calls for.

For José Luis Rodrigues y Cabriales, there was no reason to extend the kindness and human warmth that he offered to a dollar-heavy *yuma* intruding on his life. To be sure, our chance meeting in front of a tourist art stall at Havana's Plaza de la Catedrál eventually led to my injecting (however fleeting) economic assets into his and his family's domestic economy. Yet his taking me for what I am—someone driven to his island by what friends I had earlier made in Miami diagnosed as a "spiritual affliction" and I, myself, rationalize as unfinished intellectual business—is quite another story. I thank him, not just for sharing my intellectual curiosity for what arguably might be construed as "his" cultural heritage, but for teaching me that *el fula*—that is, the U.S. dollar—does not have the objectifying capacity that one would expect it to exert in the world in which he, Carmen, Michi, Ronald, and Sheila live. The same thanks go to Marisol Serrano Puig and her children, who repeatedly suffered the public stigma of having a foreigner share their private space, and who again and again broke my heart by expressing that they felt they could never reciprocate my puny, but dollarized, contributions to their household. Knowing how much the two of you, José Luis and Marisol, are intellectually ambivalent about, but emotionally attracted to, the religious forms of making sense of that sad world that happens to be yours and forms a subject of this book, I say *alafia* to you: may luck and happiness somehow once more turn your way.

I also cannot omit the debts that I owe to Ernesto Pichardo, a man who—unlike my academic teachers and many of my other informants in Miami—forcefully cued me in to the fact that belief is a political matter. Since we first met in Miami in 1985, I have written several articles about his projects, trials (literally), and tribulations, but I still remember that he once jokingly presented me with the challenge of becoming the historian of his *casa de santo,* which is now a legally accredited American church. Over the years, this has turned into yet another obligation that I feel I cannot, and will probably never, adequately discharge. What I do hope to have accomplished in this book is to suggest that the religion that he practices has not irrupted onto the cultural landscape of present-day North America as some strange African atavism fortuitously preserved within pockets of Cuban immigrant social space left untouched by those processes through which Western rationalism came to understand itself as such.

Thanks of a different nature go to my good friend Bonno Thoden van Velzen, who has read most of this manuscript and has always been a source of inspiration, encouragement, and welcome criticism. This book would surely have turned out better had I had the chance to take more walks through the piney woods of Bosch en Duin with you, Bonno. As it stands, however, it owes more to you than you might think. My debts to Sidney Mintz's pathbreaking work on the integral place of the Caribbean within any history of Western modernity will be apparent throughout much of this book. I am not sure to what extent Sid will agree with the manner in which this book reworks some of his, Eric Williams's and C. L. R. James's insights into a dialogue with Afro-Cuban forms of knowledge, but I at least warned him about what I intended to do. Obviously, I owe many critical insights to the spirited discussions that I have had with many friends and colleagues over the years. To name just a few (in alphabetical order), these include Misty Bastian, David Brown,

Kit Davis, Art Eckstein, Richard Fardon, Bobby Hill, Randy Matory, Dick Newman, John Peel, the late Marie Perinbam, Johannes Raum, Jeannie Rutenburg, Rosalind Shaw, and Ineke van Wetering. None of them, of course, are responsible for the shortcomings of this book.

The list of people whose support was essential to the project of which this book represents the final outcome is long and spans two continents. In Havana, my sincere thanks go to Ruben Zardoya, the dean of the Facultad de Filosofía y História at the University of Havana, to Pedro Luis Suarez Sosa and María del Rosario Díaz at the Instituto de Literatura y Lingüistica, Pedro Cosme Baños and Luis Alberto Pedroso at the Museo de Regla, Ernesto Valdés Janet and the *equipo* of the Proyecto Orunmila, the late Magin Luis Santamaria Hernández, who repeatedly sang me sacred songs that he had first heard in the "cabildo Changó Teddún" on calle San Nicolás half a century before I was born (and that I failed to record), and to Andrés Balais Chenicle, Ángel Fernández, Tomás Spirina, *ocobios y plazas extraordinarios.* All of them most graciously offered their help to an *extranjero alemán* in search of Afro-Cuban culture and history—although saying so cannot do justice to the manner in which many of them, particularly Rosario and Ernesto, extended, not just their time and energy to me, but their friendship as well. In Germany, I thank Berndt Ostendorf for his continued support. It has been a long time since I first presented you, Berndt, with the idea of writing a master's thesis about Afro-Cuban religion in the United States, and in many ways this book is testimony to your encouragement. Further thanks go to Ulla Haselstein and Graham Huggan, who offered helpful criticism of a version of this book that I submitted as a *Habilitationsschrift* to the School of Social Science at the University of Munich.

Fieldwork and archival research in Cuba during the spring of 1993 and the winters of 1994 and 1995 as well as archival research in London, Madrid, Boston, and Washington, D.C., were made possible by a generous *Habilitations-Stipendium* from the Deutsche Forschungsgemeinschaft. Further research in the summer of 1999 was financed by a grant from the Netherlands Foundation for Tropical Research (WOTRO). Finally, a General Research Board summer grant from the University of Maryland allowed me to add the finishing touches to the manuscript.

PROLOGUE

Evidence and Presence, Spectral and Other

When I first began doing ethnographic fieldwork in Miami in 1985, people whom I soon learned to think of as "my informants" repeatedly asked me why I had chosen Afro-Cuban religion as a topic of research. What did I want from them? Why had I come all the way from Europe to study their practices and beliefs? And to what end? I have always felt somewhat at a loss for an answer. My own rationalization of my increasingly frequent visits to their homes as part of a dissertation project seemed a rather weak argument even then, and I cannot say that I have come up with more convincing explanations during the subsequent research that I have conducted in Cuba since 1993. Back in Miami in 1985, at any rate, I was both puzzled and intrigued by an interpretation first ventured by a professional diviner and friend named Cecilia Laca and later—to my surprise—confirmed by another initiated priest of *regla ocha* whom I came to know only as Carlos. The question that both of them had tried to tackle was the following: Given that I steadfastly denied that either I or my personal forebears had any palpable connection with Africa, Cuba, or the Caribbean, how was it that I seemed so obviously compelled to seek information about matters connected with the history of these places? The answer that Cecilia and Carlos came up with was that I had been driven to their doorsteps by the spirit of a dead slave—a solution straightforwardly plausible within the world of Afro-Cuban religion but just about as utterly fantastic within the universe of meaning that I inhabit as the suggestion that a tempest magically unleashed by Shakespeare's exiled duke of Milan had blown me there.

Cecilia's and Carlos's theories explaining my unusual interest in Afro-Cuban religion had, of course, nothing to do with wistful literary metaphorics. They recurred to the spiritist doctrines to which both of them, to varying degrees, subscribed. According to the popular versions of Kardecian spiritism, which, in the second half of the nineteenth century, began to merge with various African-derived conceptions of personalized mystical agents, the dead continue to be present among us as they undergo a spiritual progression from earthbound embodiment to increasing purity and detachment from the base world of matter. Individuals with "developed" spiritist faculties can experience their presence in the form of *videncias, audiencias,* or *sensaciones*—that is, visual, aural, or tactile perceptions. I cannot say that I discouraged these readings of *my* presence in my informants' lives, eager as I was to be introduced into a world in which such interpretations represented common sense. However, I vividly recall my surprise when both Cecilia and Carlos (who did not know each other) independently told me that they *saw* the presence of Tomás: the spirit of an elderly African slave who had lived and died in nineteenth-century Cuba and had come to attach himself to my person, hovering behind me, in the way the dead are wont to do.

Cecilia described him to me in considerable detail: the "muerto detras de mi" (the dead person behind me) was tall and slender and very dark-skinned. He wore a coarsely tailored pair of white pants and a white shirt girded at the waist with a red sash. Tomás's mission was to redeem himself in the spirit world by taking on the task of watching over me so that no harm would come to me as I made my way through a world saturated with both physical and mystical dangers. Miami, as Cecilia and many others had told me, was a dangerous place, and falling victim to a traffic accident or an accidental shooting might not be the worst that could happen. The city abounded with spirits of people who had lived evil lives or died bad deaths. Such "unevolved" spirits seek out the living in the hope that they will help them attain "peace and light." But their tormented state begins to rub off on those to whom they have attached themselves, affecting them with inexplicable sadness, or driving them to erratic and harmful forms of behavior. My spirit guardian was of a more benign nature. Yet had he not, Cecilia would ask, made his influence felt in nudging me toward research on Afro-Cuban religion? Carlos—whose mundane professions perhaps imparted to him a somewhat nonchalant attitude about such matters[1]—simply recommended that, on a day when I felt somewhat depressed, I should sit down in front of a mirror, drink a glass of rum, and smoke a cigar while reflecting on my deepest hopes and worries in life. Surely, I would then gradually see the contours of "my *muerto*" emerging in the mirror. "Try it out," he told me. "Then judge for yourself."

I admit that I tried. Yet, although I never saw Tomás, what I do see today is that the notion of such a presence in my life has levels of significance not exhausted in the literalism implied by such terms as *belief, plausibility,* or *rationality.* Of course, to borrow Francoise Meltzer's (1994, 44) handy phrase, nothing brings out positivism more quickly than what we are talking about here: ghosts. We cannot seem to resist transcribing spirits, gods, or the work of witchcraft into codes that satisfy our deeply held beliefs that stories in which they figure are really about something else: category mistakes, faulty reasoning, forms of ideological misrecognition, projections of mental states, and so on, figments of the individual or collective imagination that may be profitably analyzed in terms of their psychological or social functions but that cannot be taken literally as referents to a reality that is *really* "out there."[2] Yet what if we were to treat Cecilia's and Carlos's accounts, not as the charmingly exotic outgrowth of some sort of shared religious (and therefore irrational, or, at least, mistaken) belief, but as pertaining to a discourse on history merely encoded in an idiom different from the one with which we feel at home?

GHOST STORIES

In a very concrete sense, every form of historical knowledge involves propositions about the role of the dead in the world of the living, shaped as it invariably is by past human existence and agency. Such knowledge lay claims on the past in instantiating, maintaining, or contesting a present world. But it does so in ways not at all captured by objectivist conceptions of historical representation as mere retrieval or correspondence theories of historical truth. This is by no means a particularly novel insight. Histories, Carl Becker pointed out as early as 1932, are themselves historically situated cultural products, even if they do aspire to universal status. Hence, they differ, not just in content, but in respect to the no-less-historical criteria according to which some claims on the past are judged believable, while others are relegated to the realm of the implausible (Becker 1932, 1938). Writing from across the Atlantic, R. G. Collingwood and Michael Oakeshott put the matter in even stronger terms. For the former, historical thought was necessarily driven, not by the accumulation of data, but by the "historical imagination" that constructs empirical givens into evidence rendering varying hypotheses about past events and processes differentially plausible (Collingwood 1994, 231–49). In Oakeshott's (1933, 111ff.) view, knowledge of the historical past cannot be but "a special organization" of a present world of experience *sub specie praeteritorum*. Its object is a construction rather than an empirically ascertainable given, and its truth consists, not in a correspondence between "what the evidence obliges us to believe" and "a past course of events," but in the coherence of the judgments by which "facts" are inferentially constituted with the world constituted by other such judgments.[3]

"Written history," Charles Beard (1934) famously suggested in his 1933 presidential address to the American Historical Association, consequently, cannot be but "an act of faith"—an expression of belief bolstered by evidence not principally different from that by which other interpretative communities (be they composed of Zande diviners, subatomic physicists, statisticians, or practitioners of Afro-Cuban religion) infer, assess, and debate the reality of phenomena and processes inaccessible to "normal" ranges of human sensory perception (cf. Sperber 1982; Danto 1985).[4] Beard was eventually severely castigated by later generations of historians for these assertions (cf. Novick 1988). But he was right—if only because any form of plausibility expressed in a natural language must ultimately rest on horizons of experience and expectation that are historically as well as culturally contingent. Hence Becker's (1932, 235) argument that it should rather relieve than upset us to recognize that "every generation, our own included, will, must inevitably, understand the past and anticipate the future in light of its own restricted experience, must inevitably play on the dead whatever tricks it finds necessary for its own peace of mind." "The appropriate trick," Becker continues, "is not a malicious invention designed to take anyone in, but an unconscious and necessary effort on the part of 'society' to understand what it is doing in the light of what it has done and what it hopes to do." Durkheim (or Marx for that matter) could not have put it more succinctly. Sociologically speaking, no less than religion, history is, ultimately, an assemblage of collective representations positing realities that are—logically—beyond empirical proof.[5] Their consequences, of course, are hardly beyond direct experience. For socially effective constructions of the "historically real"—that is, versions of history that have attained the status of what Marx called *objectively necessary appearances* within specific social contexts—not only tend to underwrite formations of subjectivity, institutional arrangements, and routinized practices in the present, endowing them with a sense of self-evidence and transparency. Rather, the inherently narrative (and therefore inevitably teleological) structure of the historical imagination of particular collectivities can also come to motivate their members to write forward, at times in violent fashion, those unfinished stories that they perceive as their "history." To concede this is not to consign historiography to the status of "mere" discourse (Palmer 1990), a fanciful play of historicizing signifiers on a past the "reality" of which is, and must remain, fundamentally arbitrary. What is at issue instead is what makes certain claims on the past contextually negotiable and dispels others beyond thresholds of credibility that cannot be but historically and culturally specific (MacGaffey 1978; Appadurai 1981; Stoler 1992; Hamilton 1998).

Since at least the eighteenth century, Western historians have constructed their claims on the past on the basis of conceptions of a linear and irreversible growth of unbridgeable temporal distance between past and present realities (Koselleck 1985; Habermas 1987; Kemp 1991; Terdiman 1993). In Koselleck's terms, what this notion enables is the laying out of a *historical space of experience*, or *world* in Oakeshott's sense, in which the dead no longer enjoy the kind of agency that Cecilia and Carlos ascribed to my invisible spirit guide. They are denizens of a world that no longer exists, and, even though we may concede that our world reverberates with the consequences—intended or not—of the actions that the dead once took, the choice whether we want to see matters this way must remain ours. Paraphrasing Marx, one might say that, given this particular structuring of the past in the Western historical imagination, the dead have to be represented precisely because they can no longer represent themselves. We may choose to remember or forget, venerate or vilify them. But they themselves have no say in these matters. In a very real sense, we have to recall them into our present.

This is a proposition without which objectivist notions of truth or factuality in historical representation become tenuous, to say the least.[6] For is not the assumption that the past is over, done with, and hence ontologically sealed off from the present the very foundation of both popular and disciplined quests for the "facts of history" in the contemporary Western world? And yet, not only have philosophers of history long pointed to the fundamental illogicality of such notions (Mink 1978; Danto 1985; Hayden 1973). Rather, as the current multidisciplinary flurry of interest in the phenomenon of memory and the conflictive politics of remembrance and commemoration shows, even within Western cultures there exists an awareness that "the past is not finished and done with, receding ever further into the distance," but remains "imperfect," not just in the grammatical, but also in the ontological sense (Lambek 1996, 246). Finite as the province of meaning of past causes may seem, its content nevertheless leaks into the realm of present effects that become knowable as such only on the basis of hindsight. More paradoxically even, such retrospection not only provides the only basis for discerning structures of past eventuation and causality, but inevitably realigns the past to fit present horizons of historical knowledge and configurations of historical interest (cf. Danto 1985, chap. 8). As soon, in other words, as we think about how to represent the past, we already begin to intervene in its content.

Viewed thus, what is at issue in judging different modalities of constructing what J. G. A. Pocock (1962) calls socially contingent *past relationships* obviously cannot be their relative accuracy or reality equivalence as measured against any putatively absolute or universal standard. It is rather their capacity for generating coherent worlds by rendering the act of establishing relations between past and present a moral endeavor: a "history taking" (*anamnesis*) that interrogates the present in order to reveal its condition as symptomatic of a past, regardless of whether we wish to see such a past as constitutive of our present order, happily superseded, or ultimately irrelevant and "done with." This is so not just because the past itself is available to us only in the form of present phenomena—objects, texts, social forms—whose evidentiary status needs to be recognized as such (Bloch 1953; cf. Ginzburg 1983a). This is so also because the credibility of the resulting diagnostics depends, minimally, on a social consensus about the moral and political consequences of the selection of particular types of evidence from which to spin narratives designed to establish, destabilize, or cancel out certain forms of past relationships.[7]

If so, however, might not my informants' story about my being driven to Miami and Cuba by the spirit of a dead slave simply register a type of past relationship that escapes certain historiographic criteria of facticity but is nevertheless morally all but unrealistic, implausible, or "untrue"? For once we admit ghosts like Tomás to the language game that we call history, does not the man whom Tomás might once have been—an African slave worked to death on a nineteenth-century Cuban plantation—belong to my past no less than to theirs? Might one not argue that thousands and thousands of similar ghosts populate the notionally "remote areas" (Ardener 1989) of the history of that curious entity often called *Western modernity*, an entity known as much through its negatives and absences as through any positively definable characteristics of its own (Gilroy 1992; Comaroff and Comaroff 1993; Felski 1995)? Indeed, might not their invisibility to most of us be more the product of a particular set of beliefs we have come to understand as "history" than a defensible proof of their nonexistence? Is it the proposition about Tomás's presence in our present that is unacceptable, or are we talking about the unlikeliness of his presence in our pasts?

The latter part of this question can be answered only in the negative. As most classical political economists from Locke and Postlethwayt to Smith, Wakefield, and Merivale understood only too well, the brutal exploitation of enslaved and forcefully transplanted African labor in the Americas formed the mainstay of some of the most profitable colonial economies emerging in the New World. At the same time, not only the resulting agricultural and commercial achievements, but also the violence and destruction attendant on them, were substantially entailed in the transformation of Europe into a world of nation-states: political entities increasingly conscious of their separate political-economic identities, their role as competitors within a globalizing theater of capital accumulation, and their agency in forging what by the eighteenth century became thinkable as world history and modern civilization. Despite ongoing historiographic debate about the particulars of the relations obtaining between these processes (e.g., Solow and Engerman 1987; Blackburn 1997), it is undeniable that the modern capitalist world system was erected, at least in part, on the unmarked graves of African slaves whose lives were systematically wasted in the service of what Marx identified as *primitive accumulation*.

Nor has the fate of the victims of these processes escaped scholarly attention. In recent decades, a burgeoning historiography of slavery has provided us with a truly stunning wealth of aggregate data on how human beings very much like Tomás lived and died in New World cane fields and slave barracks. Not only do we have an increasingly clear idea of how many enslaved Africans survived the horrors of the middle passage to be unloaded in regional New World slaving entrepôts. We can pinpoint, with relative precision, their average life expectancy in specific local contexts at certain times; we know their demographic profiles (age structures, sex ratios, birthrates, and mortality); we are aware of how different work regimes and changes in productive technology affected them, what their clothing and food rations consisted in, how they were housed, what diseases they tended to suffer from; we know how often slaves rebelled and how they were punished for it; in some instances we even know what average height they attained or the statistical frequency with which the average slave would have endured the whip. Still, regardless of whatever mixture of zeal, caution, and care went into the compilation and analysis of the sources from which such data were synthesized, regardless, also, of how important some of these findings may prove in correcting previous conceptions of New World slavery, there is an ultimately quite frightening sense of irrelevancy in all this.

For not only are we utterly incapable of disaggregating such data in a way that could illuminate what living through slavery might have meant for more than the minute fraction of its victims whose recollections of life under "the peculiar institution" were ever committed, in one way or the other, to writing. Rather, this mounting heap of abstract knowledge about the atrocities that the *esclave moyen* endured may well contribute to blocking from view what the image of the ghost of a named individual slave haunting the author of this book might be a vivid reminder of. For does not the very idea of the existence of "something" like Tomás (whatever ontological status we may accord him) indicate that there *also* exists a history that largely escapes—perhaps cannot be inscribed at all—into the narratives that we construct from the logs of slave ships, plantation account books, or the diaries of slaveholders? The problem with Tomás, in other words, is not that his existence—somewhere in the Cuban past—is inherently implausible or unrealistic. It is that the person he may once have been remains beyond historiographic recovery because the nature of the evidence we deem admissible simply erases his historical being and subjectivity.[8]

Yet, if there is no place for Tomás within the realm of plausibilities constituted by academic historiographic consensus, might there not be something in the very idea of the spectral presence of dead slaves like him in our present that intrinsically militates against the histories that we have spun from the records his oppressors have left? And might it not be that such ghosts can be "seen" to haunt us precisely because all this writing has not just obliterated the historical reality of their lives, but artificially distanced or displaced it from ours? "The only written thing on slave ships," says Edouard Glissant (1997, 5n), "was the account book listing the exchange value of slaves. Within the ship's space the cry of those deported was stifled, as it would be in the realm of the Plantations." "This confrontation" between the documentary traces of the past and those aspects of it that can be only imagined, Glissant concludes, "continues to this day," and it is not easily resolved in the disciplines with which I myself have cast my academic lot. Elsewhere, Glissant (1989), thus, urges us to acknowledge that "history has its dimension of the unexplorable." And he is right. There exist pasts the reality of which we cannot deny but that we may never find ourselves able to evidence unless we "revalu[ate our] conventions of analytical thought." For the recognition of such systematically obliterated past realities—as well as the recovery of the historical subjectivities of those who lived through them—"has as much to do with the problematics of investigation as with a historical organization of things" (66, 65).[9]

Perhaps echoing Foucault's (1970, 1972) notion of "thresholds of positivity" organizing the generation of what can count as knowledge within a particular "historical organization of things," Glissant's formulation not only opens the door to histories condensed in the image of the ghostly presence of Tomás that might not otherwise find expression.[10] It also takes on critical significance in implying that—as Paul Gilroy (1992, 49) argues—such histories are, not the "special property" of the descendants of their victims, but "part of the ethical and intellectual heritage of the West as a whole." For, to recur once more to Glissant (1989, 66), the very least that a proposition about our being haunted by the spirits of dead slaves might achieve is to relieve us, in Carl Becker's sense, "of the linear, hierarchical vision of a single History," a vision that relegates the violence and dehumanization my "spirit guide" would have endured to a past distant in both space and time.[11] It is not that "this History" has not "roared around the edge of the Caribbean," as Glissant puts it. It has. On the contrary, the Caribbean region provides perhaps clearer evidence of its tempestuous nature than any other site on which European colonization has unleashed Prospero's rationalizing magic. The question rather pertains to what Glissant calls a *subterranean convergence of our histories*. For, arguably, the global historical storm first conjured up in the Antilles in the sixteenth century continues to envelop us all.

In developing this argument, Glissant evokes the image of African slaves thrown overboard on the high seas—an image of human lives sacrificed, not to inescapable exigencies, but to the very ideas and forces that ruled the worlds of their captors and the merchant investors backing their ventures. Nothing, of course, is unrealistic about this, and we know it well. When in 1781 the captain of the HMS *Zong* threw 133 sick and dying African slaves overboard, he did so not merely to be able to collect the premium for which he had insured his human cargo (Fryer 1984, 127ff.). He also affirmed a particular "historical organization of things" in which instrumental rationality and the profit motive—imagined as conjoined in the providential work of the market's invisible hand—had begun to circumscribe a cosmic order that we continue to inhabit. Hinging accountability on amoral (and, often enough, patently immoral) procedures of establishing facticity, this order, I will argue, is a haunted one. Marx clearly saw this when, in the opening paragraph of *Das Kapital*, he referred to his own social formation as an "uncanny" or "monstrous" world of commodities[12] in which massive processes of historical displacement and organized forgetting, not only stabilized social fantasies ("objectively necessary appearances") of the agency of objects, but likewise reduced humans to the status of things. Glissant's image of the economically rational destruction of human commodities, however, points to yet another constitutive feature of this order: the externalization and displacement of the nightmarish excess of its operation beyond the boundaries of the conceptual space occupied by Western modernity.[13] If, in that sense, the victims of the *Zong* left any imprint on this order, it was by involuntarily documenting what Kamau Brathwaite calls a *submarine unity* obtaining, not just within the Caribbean region itself, but between the self-consciously "modern" cores of the capitalist world system and the peripheral spaces of death from which the "West" drew its wealth and confidence in a ghastly dual movement of accumulating capital and knowledge.

"All objectification is a forgetting," Horkheimer and Adorno (1972, 230) once argued in their profoundly disquieting reflections on the immorality and unreason by means of which the West has represented, to itself, its global ascendancy as a "march of reason." And it is such forgetting that, to my idea, Cecilia's and Carlos's vision of a disembodied visitor from an unmarked grave dug in the distant past might help counteract. So let not the language I am using here distract you. Words like *spirit* or *ghost* are merely that: words, elements in a language game different from the one that I am playing as I write these lines. Suppose that we take them to signify a notion about relations between past and present that underlie a contemporary order but remain unacknowledged, unspoken, or even unthinkable within its reigning narrative conventions and definition of the *historically real?* "Haunting," Jacques Derrida (1994, 37) suggests, "belongs to the state of everyday hegemony." It occurs precisely at the moment when that state is thrown into doubt and reveals itself as ridden with "historical excess . . . resisting final codification" (Feldman 1995, 237); when historical "frames" (in Felman and Laub's [1992] sense) begin to fracture; and when an occluded dimension of the past becomes visible through a form of recognition that seizes on its fleeting image before it sinks into irretrievable oblivion, as Walter Benjamin (1968, 257) once phrased it. The feeling of being "haunted" arises when our everyday worlds suddenly appear uncannily bereft of their normalcy and reveal themselves as what they are: collectively instituted and maintained infrastructures of certainty (Castoriadis 1987) built on the systematic (and systemically necessary) forgetting, displacement, and disavowal in time and space of that of which propositions about the existence of spirits like Tomás provide powerfully estranging reminders.

Hence, perhaps, the value of introducing such anecdotal and decidedly flimsy "spectral evidence" as I have marshaled so far into a regime of knowledge that—since Michelet's times (Anderson 1991, 197ff.)—has pledged itself to "speaking on behalf of the dead" but that cannot face the full implications such disciplined forms of necromancy might entail. "Ghost stories," Graham Huggan (1998, 129) suggests, might be considered "as vehicles of historical revisionism, or as means by which repressed histories can be brought back to the surface." For what they render "uncanny" and thereby transform is "not the past itself, but our 'normal,' socialized perception of it." Huggan is concerned with the figure of the ghost or revenant as a trope allowing for the construction or release of versions of history that—irrespective of their moral plausibility—otherwise not just remain "unevidenced" but are actively rendered invisible (Feierman 1999) or unspeakable (Spivak 1988a; Sheriff 2000): not because their relation to the past is merely imaginary, but because such a relation goes beyond the limits of what is representable within the discursive formation that we call *history*.

But "ghosts" such as Tomás are not just figures of speech, and we know that all too well.[14] I have no reason to believe that Cecilia and Carlos did "not really" see Tomás hovering behind my back or merely wanted to humor me. In fact, even to pose such a question may well be already to miss the point (cf. Appiah 1992, 107–36; Fabian 1996, 297–316). Nor is the problem, as David Scott (1991) and Luise White (2000) insist, adequately addressed by carving acceptable facts out of narratives encumbered by patently fantastic, improbable, or, at best, "symbolic" ballast. In his bitter reflections about the murder of twenty-eight black children in Atlanta between 1979 and 1981, James Baldwin (1985, xi), thus, angrily recalls how, in the face of experienced terror, even individual memory can turn into "something one imagines oneself to remember." Baldwin's emphasis on the evidentiary function of "things unseen" is echoed by Karen Fields (1994), who similarly speaks of the sheer moral weight of "things one cannot not remember correctly." What is at issue here is not simply the relativity of the processes and procedures by which knowledge of the past and the pastfulness of the contemporary world is established and expressed. For such "pastfulness" itself is a concession made by—or sometimes painfully wrested from—the present. As Michel-Rolph Trouillot (1995, 16) phrases the matter, the constitution of historical subjectivities is not predicated on an immutable factual storage house of events in various stages of retrievability. Rather, it "goes hand in hand with the continuous creation of the past" by those who aim to predicate their historical being on it. "As such," he adds, "they do not succeed the past: they are its contemporaries."

Afro-Cuban diviners might understand. For, although the majority of their clients tend not to see it that way—eager as they usually are to have their personal life crises resolved—the diviner's craft is an eminently historical one. Guided by the pronouncements of gods or the spirits of the dead who speak through specific oracular signs, they select ways in which the pithy sayings associated with each of them, the accompanying divination verses, and stories about mythological precedents can be applied to the client's present.[15] Diviners in regla ocha take that responsibility seriously, and, even though my metier be different, I intend to do no less. Quite clearly, whatever "modernity" may be ascribed to our—or their—lives, unfolding as they are at the dawn of the twenty-first century, the very possibility of our perceiving it as such must build on pasts that we create. And all too often we do so in a manner that inflicts violence on what the spirit guide my informants saw hovering behind me should be a reminder of.

The question, thus, really is not whether Tomás looks over my shoulder as I write these lines. It is to what extent I will succeed in convincing the reader to follow me in instantiating the possibility of an intersection of my agency as an author with the thoughts and concerns, actions and experiences of people who—given the historical positioning that I enjoy and they endured—must irredeemably remain historical others for me. At a conference at which I presented parts of what became chapter 1 of this book, one of the participants—Timothy Burke—raised the question whether one could ever get the story of people such as the early-nineteenth-century free black Cuban artisan-visionary I talked about "right." Well, how *does* one get somebody's story right? What Burke suggested was that, at times, one is forced to relinquish the notion of being able to reconstruct historical subjectivities and instead acknowledge that—irrespective of one's meticulousness or fidelity to the sources—bringing the past back into the present (i.e., re-presenting it) must involve allowing ourselves to become haunted by it: to turn it into a revenant that neither we nor anyone else can easily shake.[16]

To do so is to estrange and render "uncanny" what Glissant (1989, 64) calls *a highly functional fantasy of the West*, to break the "all compelling frames" of normalized history (Felman and Laub 1992), to counteract the multifarious forms of "narrative fetishism" (Santner 1992, 153) that "exorcise from the body of the West—from its patterns and projects of modernization—the violence, destruction, and human suffering that have belonged to and continue to belong to its history." And, in this respect, the presence of a being like Tomás in my life makes sense to me—if only as a possibility that I feel I need to entertain. Taking Tomás's invisible presence seriously is a moral obligation that I have incurred in my work. If pasts such as his must remain, to varying degrees, "foreign countries" whose citizenship I neither possess nor must endure, they may still be places toward which the spirits of dead people—rather than a mere Shakespearean historical "tempest"—might well have driven me.

A READER'S GUIDE TO *WIZARDS AND SCIENTISTS*

Writing these lines as a member of a department of history who was trained in anthropology, I am only too conscious of the multiple ways in which the resulting book pushes against, and often beyond, the genre conventions of both disciplines. My inclination would be to argue that this, precisely, may be the point. Although I will tell a number of stories, aiming for the comprehensive narrative closure of a historical monograph would, to my idea, compromise the very intent of this book by imparting a sense of transparency to what I want to show is deeply problematic. So would, in my view, an expository strategy modeled after traditional social-scientific conventions of adducing case material to render plausible an overarching theoretical argument purporting to explain a certain—in this case historical—sector of reality. Like all texts that aim to question the epistemological foundations of the discursive formations to which these texts themselves belong, *Wizards and Scientists* will therefore, perhaps inevitably, evidence paradoxical qualities. The endeavor itself may well ultimately be a somewhat quixotic one. Still, given that what Collingwood once called *the historical imagination* is, not a mere deposit of past social experience, but a repository of ways of engaging the present, I take some comfort in thinking that raising questions may be more important, politically as well as epistemologically, than providing solutions.

Yet I realize, of course, that such an answer to the question, What in the world is Palmié trying to argue? is, not just unproductive, but ultimately arrogant. I, too, might be inclined to put down a book proffering little else than what, at this point, must still remain the vacuous promise of being convinced (perhaps against better judgment) by a series of conjurer's tricks. If for no other reason, a brief guide through what the reader might well perceive as a somewhat labyrinthine and centrifugal structure of narrative and argumentation is in order. What follows is a brief methodological reflection and a chapter-by-chapter summary in which I outline major arguments rather than attempting to situate this book within larger theoretical and disciplinary contexts. For the latter, I would refer the reader directly to the introduction.

Wizards and Scientists consists of three chronologically discontinuous but thematically linked case histories or *episodes*—as I would prefer to all them—framed by a theoretical introduction and an epilogue. What these episodes pertain to are moments in the history of the formation of both "Western modernity" and "Afro-Cuban tradition." In stating matters in this way, I am bowing to discursive conventions that I hope to dismantle as I go along. For what I aim to demonstrate is that, far from designating even only typological opposites, the meanings associated with the terms *Western modernity* and *Afro-Cuban tradition* represent mere facets or perspectival refractions of a single encompassing historical formation of transcontinental scope.[17] More for convenience's sake than for any (but the most obvious) analytic reasons, I call this formation *Atlantic modernity.* What I take this concept to refer to is, in part, a set of structural linkages that, since the early sixteenth century, transformed the Atlantic Ocean into an integrated geohistorical unit: an expanding theater of human interaction defined by a vast and intricate web of political and economic relations objectively implicating actors and collectivities on three continents in each other's histories. More important, however, I also intend this term to designate a no less multiply determined, heterogeneous, and historically contingent aggregate of local discourses and practices reflecting on, engaging, and thereby both shaping and transforming this basic structural constellation.

One such discourse is what today we know as Afro-Cuban *tradition.* What I will argue, however, is not just that this tradition emerged from a larger "Atlantic" process of (structural) modernization. My aim, rather, is to show that it is only by disembedding Afro-Cuban religious knowledge from the historical context out of which it emerged that we can juxtapose it to what we have come to designate as Western *modernity.* Whatever else Afro-Cuban religion is, it is as modern as nuclear thermodynamics, or the suppositions about the nature of our world that underlie DNA sequencing, or structural adjustment policies, or on-line banking. For the same reason, I have found it useful to think of Western modernity as a configuration of thought and practices that might profitably be understood as a culturally specific—if nowadays globally diffused and locally multiply refracted—tradition in its own right. What, in this interpretation, came to be thinkable for eighteenth-century Europeans as a universal and open-ended history of human progress represents only one end of an entire spectrum of local models of (and for) the life worlds taking shape within the confines of an emerging Atlantic political economy.[18] In fact, its very pretense to universality ultimately rests on an a fortiori logic that unfolded—and continues to unfold—not on the basis of any transhistorical first principles, but through the global realities of power that it both reflects and reproduces in either subsuming other histories into its own narrative structures or dispelling them into the realm of the irrelevant, mistaken, unreal, or fictitious.

Nevertheless, neither is the result of such processes of overwriting, disfiguration, and dispersal through which a particular discourse on history became thinkable as "universal" fully homogeneous and consistent, nor does it necessarily conceal the traces of its own—oftentimes violent—instantiation. Rather than imagining that such a regime of historical knowledge might be relativized (e.g., as an interested, if structurally normalized, fiction) by simply confronting it with allegedly autonomous (or at least partly independent) alternative formulations,[19] I take methodological courage in exploring its own internal fissures, contradictions, and discontinuities. For let us face the facts: the present book both builds on and contributes to the reproduction of certain—Western, modern, academic, or what have you—discursive formations that have little to do with Afro-Cuban religion per se (even though we may, at times, read something about such matters out of them). My hope is to throw into relief (rather than claim to transcend) the anomalies and conceptual muddles generated by the discourses in which I could not help but phrase my questions. If I manage convincingly to reveal the deep imbrication of the positivities produced by such discourses in their no less systemically generated and ideologically necessary antitheses, I should have achieved a good part of my present goal.

More concretely, I do not entertain the illusion that my limited knowledge of Afro-Cuban religion and its history could authorize my "giving voice" to anything that was *not* mediated by either the nature of the archive at my disposal or the sensibilities and concerns imparted to me by my own historical position as a European man who grew up in the second half of the twentieth century. Quite frankly, to pretend otherwise would be preposterous or, at best, simply foolish. What I seek to achieve instead is to reintegrate a set of seemingly heterogeneous narratives about the making of our present world into their common historical context of origin. I want to reinsert them into what my experience of reading and listening to such narratives leads me to believe is a single, complex historical matrix from which both Western modernity and Afro-Cuban tradition jointly arose and within which they became thinkable *as such.*

In line with these considerations, the introduction opens with a series of reflections on why, up until very recently, the Caribbean region has constituted a marginal field of study for anthropologists and academic historians. Too obviously "Westernized" (and, therefore, culturally "spurious") to generate traditional ethnographic interest, Caribbean societies have similarly been cast as historically inauthentic, their members patients of imperial histories rather than agents of histories of more than purely local significance. The pervasiveness of such perceptions of Caribbean anomaly notwithstanding, this long-standing pattern of scholarly neglect and marginalization arguably has little to do with any "inherent" characteristics of Caribbean societies.[20] It rather relates to the growth of discursive formations through which Western historians and social scientists (along with administrators and economists) came to apprehend the changing role of this region within the emerging geopolitical and intellectual configuration that we tend to identify as *Western modernity.*

The incomplete capture of the Caribbean region by such discourses should, therefore, force us—as C. L. R. James and Eric Williams suggested long ago—to consider that Caribbean and European "modernization" experiences cannot be viewed in isolation from each other. Both arose from a single, integrated processual configuration of transcontinental scope within which economic, social, and cultural processes on both sides of the Atlantic, not only exerted influence on each other, but meshed into an irreducible historical manifold. Once we concede this point, however, we face a categorical muddle: for the denial of history as "purposive movement" (Hegel)—for example, from simple homogeneity to complex heterogeneity (Spencer), *Gemeinschaft* to *Gesellschaft* (Tönnies), mechanical to organic solidarity (Durkheim), and so forth—to non-Western populations in general is blatantly contradicted in the Caribbean case. In fact, the parameters of such definitions of modernization appear curiously reversed in the case at hand: if Western social science has projected such movement as universally leading from tradition to modernity, in the Caribbean modern conditions gave rise to the purposive forging of traditions by collectivities perhaps more uprooted, individualized, and faced with forms of rationality more destructive and dehumanizing than anywhere else at the time.

Of course, the conventional narratives of modernization productive of such Caribbean conundrums represent only a particularly articulate and systemically empowered end of the spectrum of possible recensions of the experience of modernity. For it seems to me that a case can be made for focusing on precisely what they attempt to elide as anomalous in order to safeguard their own conceptual foundations: the absences, silences, and, yes, ghostly revenants from disavowed pasts that are no less constitutive of modernity than any positive statement about its superior degree of rational domination over a world of things. Along with Paul Gilroy, I would thus argue that the "structures of feeling" (Raymond Williams 1980) and vaguely articulated conceptual constellations circumscribed by the term *modernity* bear interrogation from the vantage point of what they aim to repress—namely, the "conceptual hybrids" (in Bruno Latour's [1993] sense) produced by the excesses of the operation of modern forms of rationality and historical agency.[21] Unlike Gilroy, however, I believe that a perspective aiming to redress the balance need not be read out of post hoc recensions of a Black Atlantic "countermodernity" expressed in the work of African American artists and intellectuals. Like Joan Dayan, I am less interested in "how the enlightenment and the philosophers of modernity, whether called Habermas or DuBois, Hegel, or Douglass, crafted their analyses out of the 'brute facts of modern slavery' pressing on 'modernity's ethics of law' " (Dayan 1996, 8–9) than in how the horrific effects of what Horkheimer and Adorno called the *dialectics of enlightenment* were not just experienced but actively analyzed and rendered comprehensible by its immediate historical victims.

This, of course, raises the thorny issues of historical representation, circumscribed, at least for me, by the image of the spirit of Tomás evoked above. I have no intention of adducing any more "spectral evidence" in this book. However, I do not think that "subaltern" historical subjectivities are always necessarily disfigured beyond points of reasonable inference, as some of the more extreme formulations of Gayatri Chakravorty Spivak (e.g., 1988a) imply.[22] Surely, the consciousness of disprivileged, largely nonliterate groups may not be recoverable sui generis. Yet would not attempting to isolate the unalloyed "subaltern voice" from its historical context of enunciation and inscription in itself merely repeat a rhetorical movement that denies the fundamental articulation of the discourses of the dominators with those of the dominated?[23] I explore this issue in a section of the introduction that aims, not only to revise the imagery of homogeneity and single-mindedness so often hastily read into colonial discourses, but similarly attempts to historicize non-Western forms of rationalizing experiences engendered by the operation of what Philip D. Curtin (1955) called the *South Atlantic System*. Confronting conceptions of enlightened rationality with the antitheses that they appear to generate ("African tradition" being a prime example) shows that the two are empirically inseparable. What is more, the distinction depends, epistemologically, on the work of a host of similarly paired oppositions that rather quickly dissolve into puzzling forms of hybridity once subjected to the test of concrete historical situations. Arguing from an example culled from the record on the Haitian Revolution, I suggest that distinctions such as that between African religion and Western rationality are *not* primary givens. Rather, they often enough stabilize only as effects of physical and conceptual violence. The evidence that we have for such discriminatory operations only too often comes down to us in the form of rather uncanny types of historical artifacts: human corpses.

This is patently evident in the frightful levels of violence unleashed in the course of North American "civilizing missions" in Cuba and Haiti, once the Caribbean irrevocably passed into the purview of U.S. imperial power in the aftermath of the so-called Spanish-American War. For, despite the privately sponsored Balch report of 1927 and other government investigations that, in the Haitian case, finally brought the U.S. military occupation to an embarrassing end in 1934 (Schmidt 1995), what it may have meant to live through U.S. Marine counterinsurgency and development measures is hardly conveyed in the—sometimes stunningly vivid—recorded descriptions of the irrational excess that North American civilizers performed in the service of modernization. The point here is not to belabor, once over, mere "mistakes" or "aberrations" that even contemporaries readily conceded, but to expose their systemically determined nature (Bauman 1992). And it is to explore the manner in which even well-meant calls to "reason" essentially served to disqualify—or subjugate, as Foucault (1980) might have put it—other forms of "making sense" of what is morally senseless or qualifiable as outright evil. To access such systematically occluded levels of historical consciousness and experience, I argue, it may be necessary to take recourse to forms of expression—dreams, rumors, and "beliefs"—not generally considered admissible as evidence documenting historical reality. This, if anything, is a major goal of this book: to attempt to delineate the contours of such local, disqualified forms of interpretation and to play them out against the regimes of knowledge on whose terms we have come to understand them as anomalous, irrational, unrealistic, or simply implausible.

Chapter 1 provides the first of three attempts to carve remnants of such disqualified forms of historical knowledge out of the record of their suppression. Set in Havana at a time when Spain's long-neglected Caribbean colonies began to acquire new economic and geopolitical significance, this chapter attempts to exemplify the possibilities (and limitations) of such an approach by focusing on a history told—or rather painted—by José Antonio Aponte (ca. 1760–1812), a free Afro-Cuban artisan known today primarily as the putative instigator of a conspiracy of allegedly islandwide proportions. Aponte lived in a complex and rapidly changing world, marked by what one might call the last great *sugar revolutions* of the Americas. In the early nineteenth century, Cuba was transformed from a stagnant backwater of the Spanish American empire into the world's largest sugar producer and (along with Brazil) the last great devourer of enslaved African labor power. Previously, African slavery had remained an economically (although perhaps not culturally) insignificant traditional institution of Cuban society. With the Bourbon commercial reforms of the second half of the eighteenth century and the destruction of French St. Domingue in the course of the Haitian Revolution, however, the island experienced a furious spurt of modernization. More than anything else, this resulted both in the steady displacement of a previously mixed peasant and ranching economy by a technologically highly advanced sugar industry and in the numerical explosion—and rapidly advancing dehumanization—of Cuba's African slave population. Slavery *may* have taken (relatively speaking) benign forms in Cuba before the beginning of the nineteenth century. By the 1830s at the very latest, it had become a living hell for enslaved human beings regarded as functionally necessary but individually expendable accessories to steam-driven sugar mills and cane fields whose territorial extent was limited only by the buying power and access to productive technology of agricultural industrialists.

This, in a nutshell, was the world at whose making the protagonist of the first chapter of *Wizards and Scientists* was present—although, like E. P. Thompson in his reflections on the "making" of the English working class, I take presence to mean, not just physical "thereness," but presence of mind and moral imagination. For, whatever the truth about Aponte's involvement in a conspiracy may have been (and I reserve my judgment on this matter for reasons that will become clear), he certainly committed his own vision of the history unfolding around him to the pages of a book that he, himself, produced. As fate would have it, this book fell into the hands of Cuban officials anxious to quash what they perceived as an imminent rebellion. After questioning Aponte about its contents for almost a week, making him turn page after page to explain its significance, they finally killed him—perhaps having come to the decision that annihilating its author along with his creation might be a way of making sense of what otherwise appears to have utterly eluded them. Yet, if Aponte's killers thereby inscribed his work into a "discourse of counterinsurgency" (Guha 1983), historians have shown a similar eagerness to disambiguate the mysteries enveloping the man and his book, thus (if unwittingly) silencing Aponte twice over.

By and large, two forms of reductionism have been at work in the historiography on Aponte's case. The first comprises widespread teleological conceptions of the progressive political rationalization of forms of subaltern resistance. In the African American case, these have received their most explicit exposition in Eugene Genovese's *From Rebellion to Revolution* (1979). But they are similarly characteristic of the literature on so-called primary resistance movements, allegedly foreshadowing full-scale wars of liberation in colonial scenarios in general. The second strategy of making sense of Aponte has consisted in accommodating the ostensibly "irrational" symbolism contained in the record into narratives that represent him as an "organic intellectual" turned "vanguardist": a man able to distinguish the discursive registers of modernity and tradition and consciously to deploy this capacity in the service of emancipatory political aims. I do not contend that any of this is necessarily wrong. Nor is my criticism of previous attempts at making sense of Aponte's case aimed at invalidating such interpretations on factual grounds. What I intend to demonstrate instead is the degree to which they have led historians simply to bypass what members of their craft usually consider their major task and scholarly responsibility: close empirical assessment of the documentary record. Like Shelly Ortner (1995), I cannot help but wonder at the studious neglect of the—ostensibly cryptic—content of the more than a hundred pages of documents containing Aponte's own interpretations of his book. Why have we all jumped to conclusions about the man's historical mission without wondering what he himself chose to disclose about it? To be sure, Aponte's ultimate goals in producing the visual record indirectly documented in his interrogations can—to my idea, at least—only be guessed at. Nevertheless, it is far from impossible to recuperate, at least in part, the historical conditions that enabled him to produce (what I believe was) his version of a history of the world.

In attempting to "read" (rather than merely selectively filch) the record of Aponte's interrogation, I begin by identifying the sources on which Aponte documentably drew so as to speculate about the imagistic convention with which he may have been familiar, given his unique historical positioning at what Fredrik Barth (1984) might call the confluence of heterogeneous *streams of tradition*. Gauging the external influences that *might* have shaped Aponte's historical imagination and expressive repertoire, however, is clearly not enough. For not only did Aponte ransack the fragmentary repositories of Western knowledge and iconography that fell into his hands in a highly deliberate, idiosyncratic manner. The visual discourse he condensed out of a variety of disparate media also articulated an essentially independent form of historical and, more specifically, moral analysis. In many ways, the analytic task thus resembles that which Carlo Ginzburg (1992) took up in his study of the case of Domenico Scandella alias Menocchio, a sixteenth-century Friulian miller graced with a similarly exuberant counterhegemonic imagination. Although of related intent, however, my reading of Aponte departs in significant ways from Ginzburg's approach. In particular, I emphatically reject Ginzburg's strategy of resolving the interpretative difficulties presented by Menocchio's case by positing his reading of literate sources as filtered through an ancient oral tradition. For reducing Aponte's individual cognitive achievement to his reading of literate (and, therefore, implicitly Western) sources through the lense of any single African tradition is not just unrealistic. In fact, it appears as much a violation of his historical subjectivity as a priori imputations to his pictorial enunciations of an enlightened and politically manipulative communicative intent.

Even though we may never know what precisely Aponte wanted to communicate (or whether the book held any communicative purpose at all), Aponte's bookmaking activities arguably represented an attempt at theorizing: what he was doing was creating a body of knowledge that may well have been a critical history of an emerging Atlantic world projected from the vantage point of a self-educated Afro-Cuban artisan-intellectual situated in early-nineteenth-century Havana. This can be illustrated by an analogy between José Antonio Aponte and his contemporary and fellow artisan-intellectual William Blake. For not only does Blake's work indicate strikingly similar concerns with developing a coherent moral perspective on such a world. Rather, reducing Aponte to any (African or European) tradition would quite obviously be as absurd as pinning Blake down on any contemporary ideological or imagistic current of turn-of-the-nineteenth-century Europe—or, for that matter, implicating Blake in any insurrectionary political project on the basis of his work. In both cases, unidimensional readings of the documentary evidence cannot but leave us with the spurious clarities produced by evasions of the historical and cultural complexities of the Atlantic world jointly inhabited by these two visionary craftsmen.

What, then, might a perspective imply that defies such reductionist tendencies and deliberately leaves the indeterminacies and seeming contradictions of the historical record unresolved? Genuine aporia may be hard to swallow for those of us who make our living by making sense. Yet, like Fabian (1996), I feel that, in cases such as the one at hand, we are better served with the dissatisfactions of vague and incomplete answers than the invariably overdetermined solutions that we might otherwise concoct. For the question, What culture was Aponte's? may ultimately entail little else than a misleading retrojection of twentieth-century sensibilities, political facts, and commonsense reifications into a historical scenario in which such a question was, ultimately, meaningless. In fact, what Aponte's case speaks to is the need to discard presuppositions about the existence of cultures or traditions of presumably known origins and ascertainable sociological distribution. What I argue for instead are approaches focusing on "ecologies of collective representations" (Wolf 1982a) rather than situations of cultural coexistence, "continua of discourse" (Pocock 1988) rather than isolable semiotic performances and genres. Clearly, what Aponte's (or Blake's) case confronts us with are unstable conjunctures of heterogeneous "streams of tradition" (Barth 1984) within given historical fields rather than processes of confrontation between reified traditions mapped onto people in accordance with their sociological positions.

The usefulness of such conceptual refigurations is not confined to Aponte's—decidedly unusual—case. Chapter 1 thus closes with an examination of the cultural complexity of the social world of three other rebels by default (call them *counterhegemonic activists* if you will) operating in Havana less than a generation after Aponte's death. In all three cases, as well as in that of an early-nineteenth-century Afro-Cuban male street culture whose members were known as *negros curros*, it is clear that the cultural repertoires of the individuals involved cannot be captured by predesigned typologies. Rather, our goal should be to develop a perspective that allows us to approximate how specifically situated actors meaningfully—sometimes aggressively—perform and imagine into being what we, in the aftermath, describe as their identities, cultures, and communities.

Chapter 2 explores the analytic potential of such an approach by focusing on divergent but partly overlapping forms of knowledge and ritual idioms within a larger Afro-Cuban "ecology of collective representations." Ethnographies of Afro-Caribbean religions have often shown internal differentiations to be characteristic of such bodies of knowledge and practice. Best known, perhaps, is the case of Haitian *vodun*, which, as Herskovits (1971) demonstrated as early as 1937, represents, not a unitary tradition, but an aggregate of clearly differentiated configurations of belief and ritual. However, rather than investigating the ways in which adherents of Afro-Caribbean religions maintain such differences and invest them with contemporary meaning, much research has been focused on tracing those differences to the historical conjunction of heterogeneous African belief systems under conditions of New World slavery. While not negating the validity of such approaches in principle, I nevertheless argue that their focus on the putative African origins of locally coexisting New World traditions both obscures the history of such forms of cultural complexity and fails to address the role of representations of difference as a meaningful component of contemporary practice.

I exemplify this with a discussion of the differences that contemporary practitioners of Afro-Cuban religion—and we are really not dealing with just one religion here—feel divide the two coexisting traditions of regla ocha and *palo monte*. Anthropologists have rather consistently sought to inscribe such divisions into narratives about the origins of regla ocha among enslaved Yoruba speakers and palo monte among slaves speaking western Central African Bantu languages. Still, while these narratives are generally known to most contemporary practitioners, they are of rather limited significance within the universe of discourse and practice in which they operate. To them, the differences between what they tend to call *ocha* and *palo* relate to conceptions of the morality of relationships between human and superhuman agents considered possible within, and enabled by, what I suggest are two conceptually distinct but practically intertwined ritual idioms: one foregrounding reciprocal interchange and divine initiative (regla ocha), the other cast in terms of wage labor and payment, dominance, and potential revolt (palo monte).

To a certain extent, this imagery of contrasting forms of sociality between human and nonhuman agents is explicable by a comparison between the contemporary Afro-Cuban "*nganga* complex"[24] and its possible African antecedents: the cult of similar power objects known in several western Bantu languages as *minkisi* (sing. *nkisi*). In both cases, these objects concretize conceptions about relations between human and cosmic spheres. Still, what the Africanist literature tends to represent as an underlying macrocosmos / microcosmos or nature / society analogy appears significantly transformed in the contemporary Cuban case. Here, such contrasts are transposed into a discourse about harnessing morally ambiguous superhuman forces to questionable social ends: what even casual investigation will elicit in the Cuban case are sinister images of coerced or contracted spirits of the dead forced to serve individual goals in a manner strongly resembling conventional anthropological conceptions of witchcraft.

This, however, is a perception that largely derives from the vantage point of regla ocha. For the malign imagery connected with palo monte builds in no small measure on a normalized conception of an ideal of reciprocity in human-divine interaction characteristic of regla ocha. What we are facing, then, is not a mere New World juxtaposition of "essentially" different African traditions—one inherently instrumental, the other expressively oriented. Rather, we are dealing with an aggregate formation in which notions deriving from western Central African minkisi cults and Yoruba-derived forms of worship of divine beings known as *òrìṣà* were jointly conjugated through a single New World history of enslavement, abuse, and depersonalization. In the course of this process, Yoruba-derived patterns of *oricha* worship and western Central African forms of manipulating minkisi objects, not only underwent parallel changes, but also became morally recalibrated in relation to each other. One of the results of this was the transformation of minkisi cults into media for mystical aggression—a process that arguably parallels similar developments in western Central Africa during the early colonial period. Similar to the proliferation of violent types of minkisi within the moral chaos characterizing the Congo Free State, the harnessing of Afro-Cuban nganga objects to projects of slave resistance bespeaks not any inherent or essential characteristic of two variants of a single African tradition. Rather, it points to parallel transformations of social fields within a larger Atlantic economy in the course of which the powers condensed in these objects increasingly became harnessed to purposes of combating perceived evil by similarly amoral means.

Within the context of New World slavery, minkisi cults—to which Cuban palo monte is genetically related—came to take on the significance of what Victor Turner called a *drum of affliction*, thereby, not only defining communities of victims, but politicizing them at one and the same time. This moment is illustrated by suggestive, although admittedly episodic, evidence from the first Cuban War of Independence (1868–78). For, here, groups of maroons who appear to have coalesced around the sacred powers of minkisi-like objects and got caught up between Spanish and insurgent battle lines exhibited patterns of ritual activity that indicate that the manipulation of such objects, for them, represented a form of self-defense. Mystical aggression in this context served to delineate moral boundaries between these communities of former slaves and their callous "liberators" (who often enough swept up such maroon communities only as part of a generalized scorched-earth tactics). At the same time, it counteracted a brutal regime of wartime exigencies by no less violently conceived mystical forms of practical action. Ritual here clearly cannot be seen as anything but a form of historical agency: as MacGaffey (1981, 2000), Guyer and Belinga (1995), and Feierman (1999) have argued, the distinction between ritual and "practical" action bespeaks a fundamentally ahistorical and ethnocentric definition of *the political*. In the moral no-man's-land of the Cuban *manigua* (i.e., the space between Spanish and insurgent battle lines), what we might be inclined to understand as therapy was a continuation of warfare by other means.

Considerations such as the above once more raise the question of why—in relation to regla ocha—practices associated with the Afro-Cuban nganga complex, not just retained their combative character, but are nowadays conceived of as potentially, if not inherently, evil. Obviously, the answer cannot be more than conjecture. Still, rather than tracing such contemporary constructions back to any putatively essential features of the different African traditions that came to coexist in Cuba, a more fruitful way of tackling this problem seems to lie in focusing on the way in which practitioners of the Yoruba-derived oricha cults emerging in nineteenth-century Cuba came to assimilate the nganga complex and the violent imagery surrounding its practices of dealing with spirits of the dead into their own conceptual universe. They did so, it appears, by assigning to the cult of nganga objects a strictly mercenary ethos, thereby ideologically purifying their own practices of moral ambiguity. In the course of this process, the two traditions, not only merged into a larger complex of partly overlapping conceptions and practices, but came to offer functionally differentiated ritual idioms that spoke—and continue to speak—to fundamentally different forms of historical experience and contemporary sociality. What the resulting complex reveals is not just ritual reenacting history or documenting past politics like a scar tissue that continues to testify to past violation. Whatever else may be going on when a *palero* showers a nganga object with abuse in order to incite it to heal a client by attacking his or her violator, his actions reflect present politics conducted in ritual form.

In the end, we thus face a virtual reversion of the question traditionally asked: the problem of internal differentiations obtaining within Afro-Caribbean cultures now is no longer adequately explained as a mere contingency thrown up by structural processes of a wider, Atlantic scope (say, e.g., the dynamics of regional African slave supply and local New World importation patterns). Rather, these divisions became salient, and reproducible as such, only by virtue of their capacity to facilitate meaningful representations and provide forms of practical engagement of the local experiential correlates of such larger histories. No less than José Antonio Aponte, priests of an Afro-Cuban religious formation emerging in the second half of the nineteenth century selectively drew on different and historically heterogeneous cultural resources available within the morally precarious social contexts in which they found themselves operating. And, again not unlike the protagonist of chapter 1, they used such resources both to interpret and to engage the perilous world in which the continuum of discourse and the ritual practice that we nowadays know as Afro-Cuban religion took shape.

If chapter 2 attempts to historicize the differentiation of ritual idioms within an overall Afro-Cuban religious formation, chapter 3 seeks to contextualize the rise of twentieth-century forms of Afro-Cuban religion within a historical framework in which it is not normally placed: the self-conscious modernization of the Cuban state in the aftermath of the U.S. occupations of 1899–1902 and 1906–9. Harking back to the introduction, the first sections of this chapter launch a polemics about the rationality of Western "instrumental reason" as opposed to that of "African witchcraft." My argument is that the rise of science (and similar such indices of modernization) was contingent on the simultaneous suppression or delegitimation of forms of thought and practice retrospectively labeled *irrational:* witchcraft, magic, religion, and so forth. Here, the historical semantics of the term *science* in the everyday parlance of the anglophone Caribbean provides an intriguing illustration. For what the term *science* glosses in this context is a form of instrumental reason that manifests itself in acts of mystical aggression. Today, *science* ironically forms a synonym for *obeah*, a term that entered the English language in the context of the first antiwitchcraft laws passed in the British colonial empire in the aftermath of the 1760 Jamaican slave rebellion. Coming as they did nearly a generation after the repeal of England's "internal" Witchcraft Act in 1736 (K. Thomas 1971, 692), these Caribbean laws, however, provided a foil, not only for the criminalization of subaltern knowledge in other parts of the British Empire, but also for the institutionalization of conceptions of superior forms of Western rationality.

A similar relation obtained in the case of the overtly antagonistic but essentially symbiotic linkages between emerging forms of self-consciously modern Cuban science and the Afro-Cuban religious traditions that consolidated into their present form around the turn of the twentieth century. My discussion takes as its starting point the so-called niña Zoila case of 1904, concerning the—allegedly ritual—killing of a white infant girl by black "wizards." Widely publicized in the contemporary press, this case unleashed a veritable witchcraft panic in post–U.S. occupation Cuba. It also set the stage for far-ranging discussions of the challenges posed to Cuba's attainment of modernity by the cultural and biological legacies of African slave importation, which—despite international treaties—had peaked only in the 1840s and had continued for well over thirty years longer. What was at issue among Cuban elites at the time was not only the stigma of a racially mixed population whose capacity for modern nationhood had repeatedly been cast into doubt by their North American liberators. Cuban modernizers also agonized over a far less palpable legacy: one not of African biology, but of cultural forms, evident, or so it seemed, not only in the behavior of born Africans, but in that of the general populace as well.

Interpretations of early republican Cuban persecution campaigns against practitioners of Afro-Cuban religion have tended to attribute such events to the influence of North American forms of racism in the aftermath of the first U.S. occupation (1899–1902). Alternatively, these campaigns have been explained as expressions of the ideological absorption of idioms of racial otherness into what essentially were processes of class struggle in the postemancipation period (slavery finally ended in Cuba in 1886). Yet the republican witch-hunts were not just expressions of racially structured class conflicts (although they certainly were that, too). They were also, perhaps to an extent not adequately acknowledged, the product of a struggle on the part of Cuban intellectuals and social critics to construe hitherto fairly vague conceptions of cultural Africanity into a social pathogen the extirpation of which would form a precondition for the achievement of Cuban modernity. In their most extreme form, the ensuing discourses on African savagery and witchcraft literally conjured up their own referents: to the extent that a self-consciously modernizing science focused its gaze on the bodies and practices of Cuba's black lower-class citizenry, the indices of wizardry began to multiply, calling forth ever more violent strategies of repression, celebrated in turn as triumphs of science and modernity.

Rather than setting up what might appear a relatively predictable Foucauldian interpretation, I aim to represent this process as part of a struggle far more diversely determined, internally riven, and discursively heteroglossic (in Bakhtin's sense) than might be expected at first glance. For one thing, social and legal reformers aiming to construe manifestations of Afro-Cuban religious activity into incriminable offenses were chafing under the legacies of long-standing colonial persecutory practices. Targeting forms of behavior deemed politically subversive under conditions of slavery, these had left unadumbrated vast areas of subaltern agency now considered symptomatic of social pathologies rapidly spreading from their black contexts of origin into the general population. Yet, paradoxically enough, one of the results of attempts at creating a positive legal basis for crushing manifestations of African savagery was that Afro-Cuban cult groups increasingly came to function as legally inscribed corporations protected under the terms of the Cuban constitution itself. The new Cuban nation, it seemed, was afflicted with a heritage of African cultural forms that, far from representing a fading legacy of a bygone past of slavery, were insinuating themselves into the very structure of the Cuban state and so imperiling the future of the nation.

Short of circumventing the rule of law, one solution to this dilemma came to be seen in an ingenious adaptation of Lombrosian criminal anthropology to the situation of multiracial New World societies. Pioneered in the Americas by the Brazilian Raimundo Nina Rodrigues, and popularized in Cuba in the early work of Fernando Ortiz, theories proclaiming a positivistic solution to the racial and cultural problems impeding Cuba's national progress centered on analogies between Lombroso's conceptions of individual atavism and the collective attribution of deficient moral evolution to members of "lower races." Such reasoning not only allowed for the representation of African-derived cultural forms as physiologically determined racial atavisms. It also rendered them accessible to a discourse on social hygiene that sought to objectify African witchcraft as a transracially contagious social pathogen—something that needed to be, and could be, contained or eliminated only by scientific measures (often explicitly analogized to the yellow-fever eradication campaigns conducted during the first U.S. occupation and generally booked off as a triumph of modern social engineering).

Originating in a single influential monograph authored by the ambitious young lawyer Fernando Ortiz, these ideas experienced an amazingly rapid diffusion into a variety of textual genres and practices of domination and repression: by the beginning of the second decade of the twentieth century, the phantasm of the African wizard conjured up by Fernando Ortiz and others had taken on a life of its own—so much so that the reality of witchcraft increasingly became coextensive with the means by which its supposed perpetrators could be identified and (often physically) eliminated. I illustrate the workings of this logic in the context of two separate cases. The first concerns the "preemptive" fusillade of seven suspected wizards in Matanzas in 1919, undertaken by the national military and rural guard to "save" them (or, rather, to preserve a semblance of the rule of law) from a lynch mob beyond their control. The second deals with the prominent criminologist Israel Castellanos's attempts to concretize the physiological stigmata (in Lombroso's sense) by which "born wizards" could be distinguished from the "normal" black population. Predictably, no such criteria turned up in Castellanos's (fortunately) ridiculously small sample of convicted—and duly garroted—"black wizards." Nevertheless, his monograph achieved considerable acclaim precisely because—or so I argue—it may have epitomized the operation of a largely self-referential logic of knowledge production: one that attained control over its object by discursively producing bodies in need of annihilation.

Despite the pervasiveness of this logic in Cuban public discourse, however, contemporary practitioners of Afro-Cuban religion are ill conceived as inevitably "voiceless" subalterns. Nor were they merely passive victims to the violence, discursive and practical, that their persecutors unleashed. To tell the story of the early republican persecution campaigns without foregrounding the active involvement of practitioners of Afro-Cuban religion in the discourses on Cuba's modernization is to miss—what to me represents—perhaps the most important point. Hence, I show how a group of practitioners of regla ocha, and particularly their major public spokesperson, Fernando Guerra, not just participated in such discourses, but strategically engaged major exponents of witchcraft eradication by involving them in a moral dialogue. At least in the case of Fernando Ortiz, such personal involvement with people like Guerra and his group may well have marked the beginning of a dramatic shift in his perspective on Afro-Cuban culture. For, by the 1930s, this former champion of the scientific eradication of African witchcraft had transformed himself into an ardent advocate of preserving Cuba's African cultural heritage as a key element in projections of national distinctiveness and valor.

But Ortiz was not the only one who was drawn into a network of discursive intertraffic by the intended victims of his persecutory schemes. Examining the public pronouncements of Fernando Guerra in the context of an alleged child sacrifice in Jovellanos in 1913 and the death of his longtime religious associate Silvestre Erice, I argue that Guerra, not only closely followed the development of persecutory discourses, but also managed to harness the rhetoric of scientific modernization to the defense of the beliefs and practices of his coreligionists. Like Aponte, Guerra, not only spoke the language of his adversaries, but was capable of effectively subverting the very discourses originally launched to guarantee the historical marginalization and present domination of people like himself. Proof of this assertion comes from Guerra's main antagonist himself. For, in Israel Castellanos's reaction to a manifesto that Guerra issued on the occasion of Erice's death, we find the prizewinning scholar unwittingly succumbing to the moral logic outlined by the misfits of the modernity that he himself was propagating: in a characteristic giveaway, Castellanos himself unmasked the science that he purported to practice as a form of witchcraft. If, in the end, evil magic *was* being perpetrated in early republican Cuba, its agents were to be found among the advocates of scientific modernism trying to fashion a sense of selfhood from the stuff of black bodies.

In aiming to achieve such—essentially parasitic—forms of selfhood, Castellanos and his similarly minded contemporaries were, in a sense, scripting forward a history long in the making. The modernity they sought to bring about had long (perhaps since the time of Francis Bacon and René Descartes) thrived on forms of conjuration for which such "stuff"—the objectified bodies of human others—had provided a vital resource (Foucault 1978, 139–45). Different, however, from what twentieth-century Cuban witch-hunters seem to have thought, they were not finally catching up with modernity by engineering a Great Instauration of European Reason in a society still plagued with racially induced savage irrationalities. There is a tragic irony here: for what they were tinkering with was magic of self-making that European men had once discovered on the very ground on which they now stood and that Bartolomé de las Casas had denounced as early as 1540 in his moving testimony to what he called the Devastation of the Indies.

As I argue in the introduction, there may be good reasons for seeking the origins of such magic, not just in Lord Chancellor Bacon's study or Descartes's dreams, but in the colonial theaters of accumulation and mastery over a world of things and thing-like humans that had been in the making since the dawn of the sixteenth century. For nowhere, perhaps, did the New Philosophy and the masterful forms of subjectivity that it propagated more readily generate experiential proof than in those New World plantation economies that, since the seventeenth century, had embarked on the large-scale, industrially rationalized wasting of human lives in the service of mercantile profit. Nowhere before had the reduction of human bodies to a mere mechanistic resource—"the controlled insertion of bodies into the machinery of production," as Foucault (1978, 141) puts it—reached greater depth and systematicity. And nowhere before had the fantasy of individuation through sheer utilitarian command over an abject world of matter (including human flesh) seemed more readily attainable.

This book is not the place for a sustained debate on the extent to which the Caribbean and New World slave societies in general historically served as stages on which, not just bourgeois economic morality, but modern formations of racial, class, and gender identities were rehearsed.[25] In closing on some decidedly less than dispassionate reflections, I merely want to note the possibility that the modernity advocated by early-twentieth-century witch-hunters was not just the bequest of a past structured by what Comaroff and Comaroff (1999) call the *violence of abstraction*, but that it rested squarely on a highly concrete, indeed sensory, logic as well. Put differently, this modernity thrived—and continues to thrive—on an order, not just of abstract reason, but of embodied desire focused on historically varying sets of racial and sexual others. As we shall see, in the Cuban case, the perils posed by the phantasm of black wizardry, thus, not only pivoted on a gendered contrast between elderly African men, the perpetrators, and young white women, their supposed victims. Rather, like the dreadful corruptions that other social reformers of the time imagined emanating from *mulata* prostitutes—"infernal fornicating machines," as Benjamín de Céspedes (1888) called them—the real danger posed by black wizardry lay in the seemingly irresistible attraction that such savagery appeared to hold, not just for superannuated ex-slaves, but for the republican citizenry as a whole. If, as Ann Stoler (1995, 192) argues, the cultivation of the bourgeois self (and, I would add, the affirmation of modern rationality) was contingent on a "series of discursive displacements and distinctions" upholding boundaries of embodied race and reason, then the subversive potential of the physiology and social agency of the racial or cultural other consisted, not in the revulsion that it inspired, but rather in its irresistibility.

To acknowledge as much is to raise questions that I am, at present, ill prepared to address. Unlike literary scholars concerned with the part of the world for which I claim (however limited) expertise, social scientists working on the Caribbean have shown themselves singularly unreceptive to approaches theorizing the historical constitution of gendered subjectivities and formations of desire. As Beckles (1999) rightly complains, Caribbeanist historians have tended to deliver unidimensional and ultimately static accounts of the life of black and, to a lesser extent, white women under slavery while remaining virtually silent on the post-emancipation period and skirting the issue of masculinity in its entirety. Anthropologists have fared somewhat better in this respect. But it is doubtful whether anything as subtle as Lowenthal's (1987) or Sobo's

(1993) ethnographic accounts of the contemporary production and reproduction of the gendered Haitian and Jamaican body will emerge from the archive of Caribbean history. Fascinating as they are, Kutzinski's (1993) or Dayan's (1995) readings of literary sources back into the histories that they reflect and refract cannot substitute for what I have aimed to do in this book—that is, to read empirical evidence upward, rather than extrapolating downward from literature. I cannot help, therefore, but confess to the reader a sense of methodological discontent that leads me to clarify, right at the outset of this book, what I perceive as one of its major shortcomings: an inability—conditioned largely by the data at my disposal—to adequately address what Felsky (1995) calls the *gendered nature* of the modernity with which I have been concerned all along.[26]

This strikes me as all the more perverse because the conditions under which I conducted most of my research in Cuba since 1993 hardly ever allowed me to forget what power—in Max Weber's classic sense of getting one's volition enacted by others—the mere physiology of a visibly foreign (and therefore invariably dollar-carrying) brown-haired blue-eyed man in his late thirties could convey at that moment in time and in Cuba's history. Like the European or Canadian sex tourists with whom I (far too often) shared hotel bars and sat next to on charter flights, I was living through situations in which the local utility of the hard currency in my pocket could easily have overridden whatever moral restraints Cubans (of whatever race, gender, and sexual orientation) might have felt toward gratifying foreigners' desires. I still find it hard to abstract from such experiences, but the manner in which they bespoke the global political realities in which both I and these men were operating was, perhaps, most forcefully driven home to me on a flight back to Europe. Then, a particularly obnoxious seatmate told me that he had come to think of paid sex with black Cubans as a virtual necessity. It was, he explained, the only way to "recharge his batteries" for a year of labor and life with a woman whom he called his *girlfriend* and who allegedly would pick him up at the airport. Incessantly chattering away about his sexual exploits all through a long night flight, my seatmate referred to the women with whom he had slept with as "bushbabies," "the blacker the better."

As if to evidence the savagery that he fantasized into the dollarized ministrations these women had performed on his body, he opened his shirt to show me the places where the "black bitches" had bit him—all the while explaining how they had somehow managed to make him spend close to three thousand dollars on them and their families in less than two weeks. When we finally got to Düsseldorf and had missed our connecting flight to Munich, it turned out that he was broke. Since we had the same final destination, he clung to me and my wife, who (for reasons too cumbersome to explain here) had not been seated in our row and only now realized how what I had initially rationalized as an ethnographic experience had turned into a rather bizarre predicament. In the end, I bought him a beer at nine in the morning, gave him money to call his "girlfriend," and then decided to have a drink as well—not just to kill time until that connecting flight would terminate such jarring company, but to swallow a heaving sense of both anger and powerlessness, a sentiment that had been building up all through the airborne night during which our plane, loaded as it was with middle-aged European men, had performed a crazy, indeed, almost laughable, travesty of what historians of slavery call the *middle passage*—in reverse.

No less than Cecilia's and Carlos's diagnosis of my invisible spirit guide back in Miami, experiences similar to this night flight from Cuba in 1993 made me want to write this book, turning it into something of a biographical, rather than merely academic, project. All the more disturbing to me is the realization that the nature of the materials at my disposal has enabled me to address and historicize these aspects of my experience to a highly unequal degree. Perhaps I have lacked the skill—or, rather, the right questions—to uncover, in as much detail as I would have wished, the carnal nature of the modernity that my analysis aims to contrast with Afro-Cuban tradition. The conclusion to this book thus can offer little else than suggestions that I hope might contribute to relativizing—in Sir Trevor Roper's famously misguided words—the unappealing gyrations, not of (what he called) savage tribes, but of the New World Order that this book has sought to denounce. The task as such, at any rate, remains: a challenge unmet, an obligation left undischarged.[27]

In line with my initial speculations about unarticulated pasts, *Wizards and Scientists,* thus, closes on a series of reflections intended to suggest the relevance of the foregoing discussion to the present situation of Cuba—marked as it is by a deep economic crisis and its devastating social consequences. My point of departure lies in observations about the inability of revolutionary Cuban social science to come to terms with the persistent (perhaps increasing) salience of Afro-Cuban forms of religious knowledge and practice to the world in which contemporary Cubans find themselves living. Contrary to its own predictions, the socialist modernity propagated by the revolutionary Cuban state (or whatever is left of it) has not dispelled the phantasms that once allegedly obscured the social relations obtaining in the island's capitalist past. On the contrary, to paraphrase Eckstein (1994), as Cuba returns from its Soviet-financed socialist future, what once could be thought of as the island's past increasingly has begun to envelop the life worlds of its inhabitants.

This is patently evident in the context of Cuba's new post-Soviet role as a provider of leisure services to First World consumers and its implications for the emergence of tourist-oriented economies of prostitution and predation in Havana and other centers of the island's tourist industry. What I suggest is that contemporary Western sex tourism to Cuba may be seen as recapitulating, in a specific historical transformation, long-standing technologies of Western subject formation through the objectification of historically varying others—a theme that has formed a major subtext to the more specific questions addressed throughout this book. I cannot at present[28] pretend to do more than delineate a set of questions pertaining to articulations between Western economies of desire and Caribbean structures of racial and sexual difference as defined within the parameters of a global economy productive of highly unequal distributions of empowerment (in the Weberian sense alluded to above). Arguing from examples culled from the historical record and a small sample of statements by self-identified sex tourists, I merely suggest how a centuries-old dynamic productive of conceptual hybrids and fetishistic strategies of purification may continue to structure the realities through which Cubans lived in the last years of the twentieth century. For the "carnal knowledge" attainable via the medium of hard currency in Cuba at the time of my writing arguably represents yet another effect of the instrumentalization of non-Western bodies in the service of generating Western senses of (male) selfhood.

What I also wish to suggest, however, is that the power that possession of U.S. currency nowadays allows tourists to exercise in Cuba's dollarized economy does not elicit a culturally unmediated response. Just as the projection of desire on the part of Western subjects empowered by such basically economic conditions is historically and culturally prefigured, so is the fulfillment of such desire contingent on the agency and moral interpretations of the human beings who cannot help but become its objects. What we are observing today—and what Cubans are living through—is, thus, the emergence of yet another zone of transcourse, formed in response to a restructuring of the capitalist world system. No less than internet postings extolling opportunities for sexual self-enhancement on the non-Western periphery, Afro-Cuban divination systems nowadays speak to a world in which what Cubans call *el fula*—the U.S. dollar—has become an arbiter, not just of individual morality, but of a global distribution of life chances that renders individual moral choices differentially feasible in the first place. Why this is so is a question that concerns us all.

INTRODUCTION

As Michel-Rolph Trouillot (1992) noted some years ago, the Caribbean is an "undisciplined region." Neither in anthropology nor in history has there ever developed an explicit focus on the Antilles and the odd couple of mainland areas (such as the Guyanas and parts of the Atlantic littoral of Central America) commonly included in standard chorographic definitions of this part of the world.[1] Speaking for anthropology, Trouillot argues that this failure relates to a "basic incongruity between the traditional object of the discipline and the inescapable history of the region" (21). In his view, the all too obvious entanglement of the Caribbean in long-range global historical processes went against the grain of many of the classic fictions on which anthropology built its disciplinary identity. Despite much of the region's conveniently pelagic geographic layout, there is little to be found in the Caribbean that would conform to the classic criteria of an "ethnographic case": no autochthonous populations; no clearly bounded, distinctly organized, and autonomously reproducing social units; no discretely distributed, internally homogeneous, and presumably pristine cultures; no overlap of language, territory, and polity with recognizable ethnic divisions. As an ethnographic site, the Caribbean appears predefined by absences.

The extent to which this region traditionally eluded the so-called anthropological gaze is well illustrated by the plight of the American sociologist James Leyburn, who, in assembling his *Handbook of Ethnography* (1931), saw himself unable to make out more than ten bona fide ethnographic "peoples" in the region. Worse yet, seven of them were already extinct, and the remainder consisted of such questionable entities as "Borinqueno," "Haitians," and "Karif" (i.e., mainland Garifuna). The problem, however, was not just one of taxonomic diffuseness, and Leyburn's *Handbook*—prepared under the auspices of George P. Murdock's incipient Human Relationship Area File project (HRAF)[2]—amply bears this out. Compared with Leyburn's eleven entries for Czechoslovakia or fifty-one for the Philippines, the unfavorable Caribbean case count appears a token, not just of anthropological naïveté and ignorance, but of a specific historical context of knowledge production. While at the turn of the century the scholarly wing of the American occupation forces in the Philippines had duly delivered a vast taxonomy of "tribes" (Drinnon 1980), the Haitian occupation—still continuing at the time of Leyburn's writing—merely yielded degrees of "civilization" among an otherwise undifferentiated mass of "blacks," that is, "Haitians."[3]

Yet it was not just that in the American military administrative perception of Haitians race overrode all other criteria. Whether explained in racial terms or not, Haitians' "difference" was largely envisioned as a matter of relative quantitative absence of "sameness"—as measured against a presumptive "unmarked" white American middle-class standard toward which Haitians (just like African Americans in the United States) had, as of yet, only partly "advanced" (cf. Lewis 1995). It was not the sort of radical qualitative break—a kind of imaginary reversion of the leap from "nature" into "history" that Hegel held as characterizing the modern subject—that made people into ethnographic cases. To be sure, Haitian peasants exhibited exotic features in some areas of life—notably religion and folklore (which, indeed, remained, for long, their only "anthropologically relevant" characteristics). Yet they nevertheless closely conformed to a "social type" that was too much part of the observer's world to be relegated to the realm of genuine ethnographica: the black tenant farmer of the U.S. South, a product of postemancipation history.[4]

This "family resemblance"—characteristically productive of a concern over "race problems" in occupied Caribbean territories—was what perhaps most crucially distinguished inhabitants of the Caribbean from Philippine "tribes." Cubans, Haitians, Dominicans, or canal-building Jamaicans had not suddenly emerged from some kind of primordial Sleepy Hollow—"awakened" and jolted into the twentieth century (or out of existence) by U.S. Marines and Canal Zone authorities. They were part and parcel of a history shared, in a fundamental sense, by object and subject of knowledge.[5] As Fabian's (1983) well-known argument goes, allochronic displacement of the object of anthropology into an ethnographic present separate from the Western observer's rapidly unfolding history was crucial to the distinction between people with and people without history on which the division of intellectual labor between historiography and anthropology came to rest.[6] Yet it should be clear that Fabian's critique fully bypasses the problems posed by Caribbean—and, more generally, African American—social and cultural formations. African American cultures are the product, not of putatively discrete and autonomously eventuating local evolutionary processes, but of a history intimately bound up with the congeries of events and developments generally subsumed under the phrase *European expansion*. As Trouillot (1992, 21) argued apropos of the Caribbean situation, "When E. B. Tylor published the first general anthropology textbook in the English language in 1881, Barbados had been 'British' for two and a half centuries, Cuba had been 'Spanish' for almost four, and Haiti had been an independent state for three generations—after a long French century during which it accounted for more than half of its metropolis' foreign trade." "These were hardly places to look for primitives," he adds. "Their very existence questioned the West/non-West dichotomy, and the category of the native," on which both nineteenth-century historiography and the emerging social sciences rested. Everything to which the term *African American* can be meaningfully applied squarely lodges within the domain of history.[7] More so, it lodges—and in a way that is both crucial and vexingly contradictory—in the midst of the history of that product of several centuries of "occidentalist" thinking (Carrier 1992) to which we tend to refer as *modernity*.

Sidney Mintz (e.g., 1970, 1974, 1996) has repeatedly belabored just this point. Representing, as it does, the historic heartland of African America, the Caribbean might well be regarded as one of the first truly modern localities: modern not only in the sense of the "factory in the fields" character of the slave-labor-driven, although highly rationalized, export economy characteristic of the region since at least the mid-seventeenth century (thus anticipating the so-called Industrial Revolution in the metropolis by more than a century); modern also in the sense in which the sheer scale and rationally calculated nature of the appropriation of commoditized human bodies and their destruction in the service of new forms of production and accumulation, prefigured what in their grim reflections on the "dialectics of enlightenment" Horkheimer and Adorno (1972) would call the characteristically modern "identity of domination and reason"; modern, finally, in the sense of the displacement, rupture, heterogeneity, instability, flux, and incompleteness that characterizes virtually all social projects enacted in the region's troubled past and contradiction-ridden postcolonial present.[8]

Indeed, the Caribbean and African America as a whole provide reasonable evidence that—contrary to some of the most sacred tenets of modernization theory—modernity may well be, not a metropolitan export, but a colonial reimport (Dirks 1992). More realistically, perhaps, it represents a form of sociality and consciousness that, not so much diffused in a linear trajectory from core to periphery, but emerged dialectically from processes of spatial articulation (Cooper and Stoler 1989). What is at issue here is not just the role of New World colonialism, slavery, and its abolition in providing the templates on which distinctly modern ideas about whiteness, freedom, property and its limits, wage labor, or the autonomous subject emerged, as it were, *ex negativo.* The linkages are far more direct and visceral. It is not only (as Eric Williams [1944] argued long ago) that profits drawn from the Caribbean colonial periphery underwrote the Industrial Revolution in the core[9] or that (as Sidney Mintz [1985] has demonstrated more recently) the economic and cultural transformation of Caribbean sugar from an upper-class luxury into a necessity of working-class life provided the caloric fuel for this transition. European and Caribbean modernization experiences meshed on various levels.

Had it not been for the "African foundation" on which—as the British mercantilist Malachi Postlethwayt put it—Europeans built a great "superstructure of American commerce and naval power," what Denys Hay (1968) called *the idea of Europe*—an idea circumscribing both intellectual and political-economic moments—might well have taken a different shape. Although Marx remained uneasy about how to fit plantation economies driven by what, for him, seemed an archaic system of labor exploitation into his dialectics of the transformation of modes of production, he was well aware of their constitutive role for modern capitalism. It was not merely that the African slave trade and New World slavery had been decisive moments of "primitive accumulation" or that they represented vehicles for the extension of the "metabolism of circulation" outward from the European core. Strangely enough, New World plantation slavery continued to play a crucial role at the very core of global capitalist development. "Direct slavery," Marx wrote P. V. Annenkov in 1846, "is as much the pivot of our industrialism as is machinery, credit, etc. Without slavery no cotton; without cotton, no modern industry" (cited in Mintz 1978, 83). Indeed, the very *experience* of industrial growth, economic ascendancy, and overseas political expansion—so crucial to nineteenth-century modernist ideologies of rationality and universal progress—was, at least in part, based on a dialectic of metropolitan surplus appropriation and colonial labor exploitation *as rationalized* within the ideological framework of racial and/or cultural superiority, a dialectic the workings of which intimately linked the civilized identities and progressive histories that European elites projected for themselves to both the economic functions performed and the social roles endured by their enslaved and denigrated victims abroad.

Such considerations lead us to far more pervasive meshing effects attendant to the constitution of modern forms of selfhood and community. The scenario through which Hegel's peripatetic "world spirit" traveled from East to West was defined by both horizontal and vertical coordinates. The dynamics of modern subject formation were not just contingent on the subjection of colonial others but permeated metropolitan contexts, too. Aligned to the political and cultural project of the modern nation-state (the true "subject" of Hegel's world history), such dynamics worked themselves into the structure of European discourses about, and political technologies designed to regulate, the constitution and reproduction of civil society, both at home and abroad. As Lorimer (1978) points out for the English case, the "mid-Victorians, looking outward through ethnocentric spectacles, often perceived race relations abroad in the light of class relations at home" (cf. C. Hall 1992). The reverse also held true. "London," Raymond Williams (1973, 283) observes, "was at one of its peaks as an imperialist city when it created its desperate center of poverty and misery in the East End." It was to such centers of underdevelopment in the core that colonial vocabularies of racial difference returned as if by a law of gravity. They did so in the form of a discourse lifting proletarianization, poverty, and the problem of social control out of the realm of history and into that of biotic otherness. Unintentionally transposing Hegel's world historical directionality to the urban topography defining the class structure of London, Mayhew (cited in S. Jones 1971, 30) mused that, in "passing from the skilled operative of the West-end, to the unskilled workman of the Eastern quarter of London, the moral and intellectual changes are so great, that it seems as if we were in a new land, and among another race." "The Bethnal Green poor, as compared with the comfortable inhabitants of western London," wrote a correspondent to the London *Saturday Review* under the impression of the American Civil War, "are a caste apart, a race of whom we know nothing, whose lives are of quite different complexion from ours, persons with whom we have no contact." "The English poor man or child," the author continued, "is expected always to remember the condition in which God has placed him, exactly as the negro is expected to remember the skin which God has given him. The relation in both instances is that of perpetual superior to perpetual inferior, of chief to dependant, and no amount of kindness or goodness is suffered to alter this relation" (cited in Lorimer 1978, 101).[10]

By the same token, the task of managing the disorderly urban poor and rural proletariat at home had, not just a powerful parallel, but often a precedent in the colonial management of disaffected members of inferior races: "A rural constabulary," Holt (1992) tells us, "was established in Jamaica even before one was dispatched to Lancaster to instruct misbehaving English workers. Schools and prisons, organized on reform principles, were promoted in the colonies almost simultaneously with their development in England" (37). Culminating in Benthamite workhouses, panoptic prisons, and the famous whipping machine, "the new institutional discipline," Holt concludes, bore a "striking resemblance to that of the slave plantation" (38). Indeed, the "dark Satanic Mills" that William Blake denounced on the eve of British industrialization in 1804[11] had already made their first appearance on the other side of the Atlantic. "The industrial discipline," notes Robert Fogel (1989), "so difficult to bring about in the factories of free England and free New England was achieved on sugar plantations more than a century earlier—partly because sugar production lent itself to a minute division of labor, partly because of the invention of the gang system, which provided a powerful instrument for the supervision and control of labor, and partly because of the extraordinary force that planters were allowed to bring to bear on enslaved black labor" (25–26). During Blake's lifetime, according to Fogel, New World sugar plantations still represented "the largest privately owned enterprises of the age" (24). What is more, they had attained a degree of economic rationalization, minutely calculated exploitation of the limits of human physical capacity, brutalization of their productive forces, and totalization of surveillance techniques as yet unrivaled in scope and scale in other sectors of an emerging global economy.[12]

Although an argument for a transfer of technologies of exploitation and domination from the periphery to the core would overstate the case, there is little question that the two scenarios linked up in a cultural dialectic shuttling languages of class and race back and forth between domestic and colonial contexts.[13] Disraeli's image of the "two nations," thus, had a distinctly practical aspect: by the mid-nineteenth century, the cultural project of English state formation (Corrigan and Sayers 1991) had entered into a phase in which the experience of civilizing alien races had begun to provide images "good to think with" at home as well. Neither were the victims of what Miles (1993) calls the *racialization of the interior* unaware of such analogies and the mobilizing value of their inversion into symbols of injustice and degradation (Holt 1992, 21–41). Indeed, to assume that the cultural forms in which nineteenth-century European class struggles came to be cast—from elite evocations of proletarian racial otherness to organized labor's rhetoric of wage slavery, from the Jamaican "Baptist War" to "Captain Swing," from Peterloo to Morant Bay—could be easily divorced from the struggles over slavery and emancipation in the Caribbean is to engage in a form of historical solipsism.[14]

Nor was the case of Britain's modernization unique. As Eugene Weber (1969) has demonstrated, the late-nineteenth-century "nationalization" of the French countryside involved an (often violent) deracination of "savage peasant custom," without which "modern French civilization" might well have remained the parochial concern of a Parisian elite (cf. Chevalier 1973; Balibar 1991; Miles 1993). Yet both the deracination of enslaved Africans shipped to French sugar plantations in St. Domingue and the subsequent nationhood of Haiti, not just preceded the metropolitan moment, but interacted with it in multiple ways. As a slave on the Bréda estate, the man who would become Toussaint-Louverture was no less a denizen of the modern world than at the time he defied First Consul Bonaparte's troops or when he died in Fort Joux, high up in the French Jura, as the prisoner of a nominally revolutionary French state ruled by a man who—in a characteristically modern move—would soon after proclaim himself Holy Roman emperor.[15] If the empire and monarchy of Dessalines and Henri Christophe may be said to have mimicked the imperial histrionics of the grand Corse, they did so at almost exactly the remove that Marx would come to diagnose in the aftermath of 1851. Almost, but not quite. For what Marx derided as the mystifications of a reactionary bourgeoisie parading as a simulacrum of the French Revolution began, at least in Haiti, as non-European (but nonetheless thoroughly modern) authenticity.[16]

FROM MODERNITY TO TRADITION

The predicates that derive from such reflections obviously do not integrate well into the discursive field within which anthropology achieved its formal disciplinary identity at the end of the nineteenth century. Historicity, Westernization, and modernity hardly count among the attributes commonly recognized as appropriate to the subject matter of anthropological inquiry. This, however, relates less to any specific qualities of the phenomena in question than to certain lingering aftereffects of how and under which conditions they entered (or failed to enter) into the orbit of the regime of knowledge that by the second half of the nineteenth century would irrevocably subdivide into the domains of anthropological and historical scholarship. As, for example, Cohn (1981), Kuper (1988), McGrane (1989), and Trouillot (1991) have argued, anthropology derived a conception of its appropriate object from a long-standing European discourse on identity and otherness that premised recognition of the "savage," "primitive," or "native" on a series of negations of Western attributes—absence of "civilized" forms of sociality, religion, or art; absence of individualism, private property, and the state; of change, internal dynamism, progress, and history; of modernity in all its different conceptual shades. Exotic otherness presupposes the attribution of characteristics deemed both essential and unshared. Hence, it is not difficult to see why the kind of double negation implied by the patent modernity and Westernness of African American cultures would have preempted their assimilation into a heuristic mold preorganized in terms of an absolute separation between "the West" and "the rest"—a distinction correlative to the disciplinary division between history and anthropology. African American cultures, we might say, appear to mimic the conventional object categories of anthropological discourse—only then to expose their inadequacy to the task of understanding the products of a chronologically "old" modernity that has taken on the shape of traditions in which, to paraphrase Hastrup (1992, 5), local culture and global history are inescapably "adjective to one another."

By the same token, however, the very *historicity* of African American phenomena that rendered them an unlikely subject for anthropology paradoxically also displaced them from the purview of Western historiography. The surface effect is akin to a structural inversion. The manner in which much traditional academic historiography has, until fairly recently, elided African American pasts as peripheral appendages of European metropolitan or New World national histories converges on an imagery of other directedness, inauthenticity, and contamination similarly "in place" in anthropology. "In the spare moments of a busy life," wrote the long-term colonial administrator Sir Alan Burns (1965, 5), "I have tried to set down the history of the West Indies as I see it. It is mainly the story of the white conquerors and settlers, as the much larger Negro population, during the centuries of slavery, had little to do, save indirectly, with the shaping of events." Presence of history, yes, but of an imported or enforced kind rarely matched by indigenous initiatives amounting to more than a few processual disturbances in the unfolding of alien regimes, a kind of history that—as Trouillot (1995) points out—becomes "unthinkable" in cases such as Haiti, where African American agency turned into a "historical force." This is the kind of view to which John Stuart Mill (1849, 2:230) alluded when calling the West Indies a place where England *chose* to produce sugar by the labor of slaves (just as it chose to produce cloth in Manchester) and that U. B. Phillips (1918) epitomized when referring to the North American slave plantation as an *educational institution*.

We find echoes of this paradigmatic conjunction of historicity with heteronomy in W. E. B. Du Bois's (1997, 38) classic diagnosis of the fragmentation of the African American historical subject in a "world which yields him no true self-consciousness" and restricts African American identity to a "sense of always looking at one's self through the eyes of others." We also find them (albeit in a very different register) in the Trinidadian author V. S. Naipaul's (2001) vituperative criticism of the banality of a foiled Caribbean modernity enacted by "mimic men" whose alienation from their own history keeps them from developing authentic identities and courses of action. It is a fundamental ingredient of the syndrome of "pastlessness" that played such a prominent role in early-twentieth-century discussions of how to conceive of New World black identity (or black social otherness) and that Melville Herskovits (1941) came to subsume under the phrase "The Myth of the Negro Past." Arising out of a conflation of the irreversible with the inevitable characteristic of what one might call the *victors'* perspective on history, such views have always exerted a powerful influence on historigraphic efforts at re-presenting African American pasts. "The Negro in the New World," writes V. S. Naipaul (1977), "was, until recently, unwilling to look at his past. It seemed to him natural that he should be in the West Indies, that he should speak French or English or Dutch, dress in the European manner or in an adaptation of it, and share the European's religion and food. Travel writers who didn't know better spoke of him as 'native,' and accepted this: 'This is my island in the sun,' Mr. Harry Belafonte sings, 'where my people have toiled since time begun.' Africa had been forgotten" (65–66). And yet: Africa was present at the time and place Naipaul wrote. It is not only that we may surely presume lively Shango ceremonies to have been celebrated within earshot while the author sat at his typewriter in a Port-of-Spain hotel room. Being in Trinidad at the height of the Congo crisis, Naipaul noted that the name *Mobutu* was gaining prominence as a signifier for representatives of power. "Anyone in authority, particularly foremen and policemen," Naipaul tells us, "became Mobutu: 'Look out, boy, Mobutu coming' " (84). How people who were obviously following the dismantling of Patrice Lumumba's republic and had come to identify the name *Mobutu* with day-to-day experiences of repressive force could have "forgotten" Africa as a predicate of their identity is something on which Naipaul chose not to reflect.

His failure to do so, however, is no less than symptomatic. Different from Belafonte's renditions of songs reflective of the historical consciousness of a Jamaican peasantry faced with expropriation and proletarianization at the hands of foreign capital,[17] it speaks to a lasting and thoroughly translocal moment of disfiguration and erasure, a movement of the Western mind that displaced a region that had served as both the primordial focus and the long-term fulcrum of European imperial self-production from the purview of the form of inquiry that underwrote the way in which the West came to know itself: history. The issue is far too

complex to be adequately treated here. We are, of course, dealing with an instance of a more systematic process of "muting" (Ardener 1989), dispersing, or rendering inexpressible certain structures of experience and signification—a process integral to the expansion of Western forms of local knowledge into a notionally universal regime of truth. However, it is barely more than common sense to locate the Caribbean's phasing out from the conceptual realm of historiography in two distinct but closely interrelated moments. The first pertains to what Sidney Mintz (1996, 296) calls a *lengthy economic eclipse* into which Caribbean plantation economies entered in the nineteenth century, leading, as Austin-Broos (1997, 23) puts it for the British case, to a "rapid withdrawal of [metropolitan] economic interest" in the region, closely connected, both causally and consequentially, with the abolition of slavery. If Caribbean plantation slavery had once foreshadowed industrial discipline and brought forth modes of existence more thoroughly uprooted, individualized, and deliberately created than those forms of sociality characterizing much of Western Europe, the demise of slavery, the declining viability of sugar on the world market, and the struggle to proletarianize the freed people quickly closed this "modernization gap." "As North American power filled in spaces created by declining European commitment to the Caribbean," Mintz writes (1996, 296), "the relationship of the region to the world outside changed radically. The 'modernization' stopped; as the Caribbean's definition as a key economic area declined, what once had been modern, soon came to be seen as archaic." Excepting Cuba, islands over whose political control European nation-states had—as late as the second half of the eighteenth century—fought major international wars were now rapidly turning, in metropolitan eyes, from prized possessions into liabilities of empire. However one wants to weigh the causal factors involved in the British case, by the mid-nineteenth century the formidable coalition of planter-politicians once known as the *West India interest* had become a bickering but politically inconsequential faction in parliamentary politics. On the islands themselves, the planters' fierce struggle against a backward-bending curve of labor supply engendered by the growth of economies of small-scale independent producers was—as William G. Sewell (1861) observed—fast turning the advent of free labor into an ordeal.

Moreover—and this is where the second moment involved comes into play—by that time "the abolitionists were an ageing group" and "anti-slavery was a dying cause" in British politics (Lorimer 1978, 117). As Nancy Stepan (1982, 1) notes, "just as the battle against slavery was being won by abolitionists, the battle against racism was being lost." The staggered course of international emancipation paralleled a recrudescence of racist ideology. Its target, quite predictably, was those very freed people who chose maximizing marginal utility over selling labor to impoverished and vengeful planters straggling along under the load of foreign debt and a depressed world market for sugar. Echoing as they did Malthus's somber prophecies concerning the reproductive tendencies and voracity of the poor at home, by 1849 Carlyle's (1853) viciously racist remarks on the rights of "Quashee" to either pumpkins or possession of the land on which they grew found their echo in a profusion of rhetorically far more moderate evaluations of the failure of emancipation as a civilizing mission and economic enterprise. As Catherine Hall (1992, 249) argues, by midcentury even the missionary initiative to impart to the freed people civilized wants, industrial discipline, and a sense of perpetually deferred candidacy for social equality was collapsing under the weight of its own contradictions. As early as the 1840s, it was becoming clear that the Christianization of Jamaican freed people was resulting in ecstatic mass movements fully beyond missionary control in both ideological and practical respects. Giving rise to "the strangest combination of Christianity and heathenism ever seen," as the Presbyterian Waddell (1863, 189) admitted, the so-called Myal outbreaks of the 1840s and 1860s doubtlessly represented collective attempts at moral regeneration. But it was not the morality that the missionaries had aimed to impose. Uprooting evil medicine (obeah), and purging the land of death and disease in ecstatic mass processions of white-clad "angels," the Myal bands roaming the countryside transformed Baptist Christianity into an Afro-Jamaican drum of affliction, thus rendering Ranger's (1986) observation that Christianity often entered African societies in the form of a novel witchfinding cult extendable to the New World. Comparable in their political effect to the *mucapi* movements sweeping Malawi in the 1930s (Richards 1935; cf. Fields 1985, 78–90), such emerging forms of Afro-Jamaican Christianity forced missionaries to painfully acknowledge their "own refusal to face the uncomfortable reality that black people might choose to be different" (C. Hall 1992, 249).[18]

In 1853, only five years after emancipation finally came to the remaining French colonies in the Caribbean, the count de Gobineau began to unravel his *Essai sur l'inégalité des races humaines* in the French context.[19] In 1866, the national embarrassment over the investigation into the massacre authorized by Jamaica's governor Edward Eyre at Morant Bay and the imposition of crown government on what was increasingly perceived as a debt-ridden, morally corrupt, and politically irresponsible planter elite and a mass of uncivilizable ex-slaves closed the subject of Caribbean colonial reform in British public discourse. By that time, thousands of East Asian laborers had been funneled into British Caribbean labor markets to depress the wages of those freed people trying to hold onto hard-won land by supplementing surplus marketing with part-time wage labor on plantations. The "moment of the 'poor negro,'" as Catherine Hall (1992, 249) succinctly puts it, "was over." So, too, was the career of the Caribbean—both on the stage of global capitalist accumulation and within a form of historiography whose "theoretical subject," as Chakrabarty (1992) argues, had all along been Europe.

The mismatch productive of the "undisciplined" nature of African American phenomena is, thus, both categorial and systematic. African Americans did not fit what Trouillot (1991) calls *the Savage slot* within which anthropologists had traditionally located the native other. Far from representing exotic remnants of prior stages of human adaptation, the peasant cultures of the Caribbean had been actively reconstituted, to use Mintz's (1974) term, from the human chaos wrought by the slave trade and on the infrastructural debris of a highly rationalized agroindustrial order. The appearance of "primitivity" was a product of "progress": not a symptom of Caribbean peasants' failure to keep their appointment with destiny (Chakrabarty 1992), but a symptom of that double form of factual and discursive disfiguration that Frank (1967) called *the development of underdevelopment*. Yet neither was the history of Caribbean societies amenable to conceptualization within the disciplinary regime of knowledge that European historiography developed in the nineteenth century. If from the eighteenth century onward *history* in European thought came to designate an implicitly uniformitarian and ultimately inevitable passage from tradition to modernity (Koselleck 1985), the Caribbean remained an odd anomaly. The notion of a disruption (i.e., historicization) of a timeless continuum of cognitive and behavioral patterns by the intrusive forces of modernization was—and is—blatantly falsified by this case: "in the Caribbean," Trouillot (1984, 38) notes, " 'tradition,' in any given sense of the word, succeeded modernity."

HYBRID FORMATIONS

The Caribbean and the larger African American world, thus, remained a *remote area* (in the sense in which Ardener [1989] uses the term) but not an exotic one. A place squarely in the West but not of it, afflicted with centuries of modernness but no longer recognizable as a cradle of modernity, thoroughly historical yet possessed of no history of its own. It is this pervasive categorial interstitiality that foils the normalization of Caribbean and, in a larger sense, African American history and culture within the discursive grids of historical and anthropological forms of knowledge. This state of incomplete capture, however, is where the analytic value of occupying oneself with the ostensible banalities of Caribbeana may lie: if "modernist strategies for [categorial] purification and rationalist classification generate their own excess" (Harvey 1996, 27), such excess, once taken, not as a systemic aberration, but as systemically constitutive, has powerful diagnostic properties. As Latour (1993) would have it, the very tendency toward categorial separation—so characteristic of modern attempts to register the world in the form of multiplying binary discriminations—invariably calls forth the "hybrids" that such schemata must disperse or repress. In this sense, one of the aims of this book is to repatriate the seeming chaos, ambivalence, and hybridity of the Caribbean to where it belongs: into the midst of the very forms of knowledge and discourse that produced the distorted image of a foiled African American and, more specifically, Caribbean modernity in the first place.

It cannot, however, be our goal merely to undermine the naturalism of those forms of power and knowledge that produced the scandal (or, in some more recent valuations, spectacle) of Caribbean indeterminacy. Coming from a somewhat different angle, Paul Gilroy (1992) takes the matter a step further. In discussing how contemporary analyses of modernity tend to factor out "traces of black intellectual history" indicative of the existence of what he calls a black Atlantic *counterculture of modernity* (48), he notes a complementary move to "assign to blacks" the history of slavery, as if it were, he says, "our special property rather than a part of the ethical and intellectual heritage of the West as a whole" (49). Arguing that the debate on modernism has been "overdetermined" by "an uncritical and complacent rationalism" and "a self-conscious and rhetorical antihumanism which simply trivializes the potency of the negative" (55), Gilroy identifies the coincidence of racism, slavery, and violence *with* their rhetorical dispersal into premodernity or irrationality as a single key moment in the constitution of forms of modern consciousness.[20] What Gilroy calls for to redress the balance is "a primal history of modernity to be reconstructed from the slaves' points of view" (55). To be sure, Gilroy fails to deliver such cargo in conflating these "points of view" with the *recensions* of slavery offered by African American intellectuals, writers, and musicians. But he certainly is right in identifying the kinds of "subjugated knowledges" (Foucault 1980) that grew out of the experience of slavery—and here one might, with Gilroy, want to insert the experience of slaveholding along with that of enslavement—as a continuous subtext to those forms of modern sociality for which the Caribbean appears to provide a strangely ambiguous and seemingly spurious prototype.

The problem posed by the Caribbean, thus, relates at once to the concrete features of certain places or people and to the way in which their difference and anomaly have been constituted and organized in relation to something else—tacit standards of historicity, criteria of ethnographic relevance, discourses on identity, authenticity, and autonomy, and so forth. Put crudely, the antinomies of Caribbean or African American modernity are, perhaps, less completely contained by strategies of discursive normalization than in other instances and places—including the places or positions from which such strategies were unleashed historically. Long written off as inconsequential anomalies, they perhaps remain, comparatively speaking, "in the raw." If so, attending to Caribbean modernities should offer a venue, not just for rethinking the local worlds to which they pertain, but for theorizing, perhaps more adequately, the political-economic and epistemological regimes that have cast their shadows over the history of modernity as a whole.

In order to exemplify this, let me return once more to the subject of slavery—a foundational feature of Caribbean history if there ever was one. "To be a citizen, to be a slave," Marx wrote in the *Grundrisse* (cited in Corrigan and Sayer 1991,), "are social characteristics, relations between human beings." Speaking with Barnett and Silverman (1979, 4), in the Western tradition freedom and slavery circumscribe systems of social characteristics and representations "already interrelated as parts of a complex totality, in which their existences-definitions are contingent upon one another."[21] Hegel's famous choice of "lord" and "bondsman" as an illustration of the dialectics of subject and object formation is only a late link in a long chain. As Finley (1968) or Morgan (1975) have pointed out, the personal liberties that politized Greek citizens or North American patriots projected for themselves presupposed the presence of bonded objects. The concepts of selfhood, autonomy, and moral personhood they circumscribe emerged—perhaps necessarily so—within social arrangements underwritten by the massive exploitation of an unfree, notionally alien, and systematically denigrated or dehumanized labor force. None of this may be particularly new. But it is rarely explicated—at least in conventional Western intellectual history—that such conceptions represent "reactive objectifications" (Thomas 1992). Their social functionality arose from a capacity to articulate (in both the expressive and the connective sense of the word), not only identity and otherness, but what Simmel (1978) called the dialectics of *objectivity* and *personality* on the ideological basis of a totalizing economic logic defining certain human beings as transactable property while advancing the status of others to that of (if only potential) holders of such (or other) property.

Contrary to overly facile readings of Foucauldian theories of "modern power," regimes of knowledge and domination were never simply structured merely by the serendipitous ingenuity of those defending, or aiming to expand, a momentary monopoly on force or ideological hegemony. Even if not experienced on a face-to-face level, slavery and freedom—these two extreme poles of social existence imaginable within modern Western cultures—were contingent parts of a single complex, perhaps "hybrid" (in Latour's [1993] sense) form of sociality *as soon as* they became thinkable as opposites. Examples from the archive of Western social theory are close at hand. Quoting E. B. Tylor, who in 1881 spoke of the distinction between "freeman and slave" as "the greatest of all divisions," Mintz (1974) notes that this "'greatest of all divisions' involved in every historical instance a way of life, a conception of the human condition, an ideology of society, and a set of economic arrangements, in short a cultural apparatus by which slaves and masters were related" (62). Mintz proceeds to illustrate this by reference to a key element of Western definitions of *personhood:* the capacity for appropriation and propertyholding, including the possession of an inalienable self. "The slave is," Mintz says, "in certain, important senses, the property of his master—as is, for instance, the master's land and the master's mule, though not the master's wife or child. In one way or another, the slave is defined in such a fashion that he is not a person—at least, not a person in all of the senses that a free man is a person in the same society" (64). "But of course," he adds, "the slave *is* a person—and both masters and slaves, in all of the slavery systems of the New World, knew this, even if they were not always willing to admit it or able to say so" (64). Here we have, as if in a nutshell, the experiential paradox at the core, not only of a luxurious growth of a discourse of denigration of racialized human things, but also of historically portentous definitions of personal freedom as contingent on the social capacity to willfully appropriate and dispose of objects, including objectifications of one's own labor power, through commercial transactions.[22] Viewed from Latour's perspective, the ideological denial of the humanity of the slave as an "object-like" factor of production, characteristic as it was of full-blown Caribbean slave regimes, might be a prime example for what he calls a peculiarly *modern* tendency to conjure up quasi objects—unstable mixtures between humans and things or between nature and society—and *then* attempt to think or legislate away their fundamental hybridity. As the diaries of slaveholders tend to evidence, it rarely worked well. For many a master, the "greatest of all divisions" produced experiential realities of extensive ambivalence and dependence—in both an economic and an emotional sense (cf. Morgan 1987; Palmié 1995b).

Still, how the local relations of production and domination, practical and symbolic, on which this form of sociality was based engraved themselves into the experience of the concrete others on whom global Western selfhood built; how their agency, imagination, frustration, or desire, in turn, exerted formative influence on such relations or perhaps even only impinged on them, imparting direction or content to emerging categories of knowledge and domination, is a somewhat different matter. To note the failure of containment is not *eo ipso* to unveil subjugated forms of knowledge. For all its problematic resonances with assumptions about a "true" reality hidden behind the veil of hegemonic discourse, try as one might Gilroy's (1992, 55) "primal history of modernity . . . from the slaves' points of view" will not emerge from the deconstruction of dominant mystifications (however useful such exercises may be otherwise). Rather, it presupposes—as Gilroy rightly puts it—an effort to reconstruct such points of view. The casual neglect of this distinction is a problem only too common to the league of postcolonial critics probing the limits of historical or ethnographic knowledge only to retreat into the comfortable realm of postmodern aporia.[23] To be sure, some subject positions may be irretrievable. The archival disfiguration may be too intense to allow recovery. Still, this is a methodological rather than an epistemological issue. For, the undeniable problems of all forms of representation aside, we cannot afford to disregard out of hand the ultimate fact that both the creation and the "restructuring of *relations* of power, forms of dominance, and social organization," as E. P. Thompson (1977, 266; emphasis in the original) wrote years ago, "has always been the outcome of struggle. Change in material life determines the condition of that struggle, and some of its character: but the particular outcome is only determined by the struggle itself. That is to say, historical change eventuates not because a given 'basis' must give rise to a correspondent 'superstructure,' but because changes in productive relationships are *experienced* in social and cultural life, refracted in men's ideas and their values, and argued through in their actions, their choices and their beliefs."[24] It may sound simpleminded or trite, but I take it that people cannot but experience history, that a good deal of what history is about is experience, embodied and acted on, and that such experience cannot but enter—in some way or other—into the historical process.[25] No less than analytic categories, experiences and their cultural refractions have diagnostic properties. In fact, they are, in many ways, functionally analogous to each other, and it is often not even useful to distinguish between them. True, in both cases, we are dealing with ideological reflections of group interests and social relations, expressive, as Althusser (1971, 162) would have it, not of any extrahistorical truths, but of the "imaginary relationship of individuals to their real conditions of existence." It is too obvious a point greatly to belabor. In fact, it is not even a particularly interesting point. At least in the case at hand a more productive approach might be to question the extent to which such "imaginary relations"—however differently constituted—might exemplify forms of knowledge, practice, and experience that are deeply imbricated in each other. As Hershatter (1997, 26) aptly puts it in another context, in order to escape "the disappearing subaltern impasse, in which any subaltern who speaks loses the right to that status," we may want to "complicate the picture of one overarching discourse, in which subalterns appear only as positioned by their elite spokespersons," not just by "a conception of 'competing discourses' (with its overtones of free-market bonanza and may the best discourse win), but with a recognition that some discourses can be seen only *in relation* to each other." To do so means to refigure, not only the specifics of single cases, but the contours of an analytic field.

ATLANTIC CONJUNCTURES

"It is too often forgotten," the Swiss anthropologist Alfred Métraux (1972, 365) once noted, "that Voodoo, for all of its African heritage, belongs to the modern world and is part of our own civilization."[26] Precisely. And how easy to exemplify. The origins of Haitian vodou lie in the same processes that transformed French port towns like Nantes, Le Havre, La Rochelle, or Bordeaux into thriving entrepôts of the Atlantic slave trade and colonial commerce (Stein 1979; Dupuy 1989). By the time of the French and Haitian Revolutions, St. Domingue generated fully 40 percent of France's foreign trade, producing gross annual mercantile profits close to 100 million livres (Blackburn 1988, 207 n. 1). Genovese (1971, 44) may well be exaggerating when he argues that Caribbean "plantation profits appear to have provided the main source of [French] investment capital from a much earlier point than in the British islands."[27] But it is reasonably clear that the wealth accruing from transactions in both slaves and sugar significantly contributed to destabilizing the ancien régime at home and abroad by adding to "the disparity, the disaccord, the incoherence of the different parts of the monarchy," as a ministerial memorandum to Louis XVI put the matter in 1786 (cited in Blackburn 1988, 165). In part, at least, it was the accumulation of colonial fortunes that, in the words of Jean Jaurès (cited in Fick 1990, 23), "gave to the [prerevolutionary French] bourgeoisie that pride which demanded liberty." The ancien régime not only exploded from within but eroded from without as well (cf. Trouillot 1982).

By the same token, however, the production of the tropical commodities whose circulation within the French Atlantic economy eventually set off these dynamics had been contingent on the capture, sale, and violent displacement of more than 800,000 African slaves to St. Domingue alone. However difficult it may be to reconstruct historically the consolidation of African-derived bodies of religious knowledge and practice among the enslaved victims of St. Domingue's plantation industry, the emergence in the New World of such religions was, ultimately, no less a function of the operation of what Philip Curtin (1955) called the *South Atlantic System* than the ideology behind the aspirations of St. Domingue's planters and their French creditors to attain seats in the Estates-General. Unlike the complex but well-documented permutations that French bourgeois ideologies underwent in the eighteenth century, the ideological dislocations effected by the Atlantic slave trade in the regions of Africa from which St. Domingue drew its slaves, and in the thought of those former residents of such regions as wound up in French captivity, can only be speculated about. Nevertheless, it is clear that much of the cultural knowledge that enslaved Africans carried to the New World had taken shape on slaving frontiers driven into the continent by the labor demands of New World plantation economies. Whatever transformations such bodies of knowledge underwent in the New World, their origins lie not in a—however conceived—primodial African past of timeless traditions. They originated in social contexts characterized by the proliferation of "relations of production and reproduction underwritten by exchanges of neighbors, kin, and dependents for foreign goods" (Miller 1988, 140) or by the wholesale generation of captives through "wars of abduction" fought, as Meillassoux (1991, 158, 162) puts it, "in the same way that fields were cultivated," that is, as a form of social production.

"Africa," writes Lovejoy (1983), came to be "integrated into a network of international slavery because indigenous forms of dependency allowed the transfer of people from one social group to another" (21)—seizure in war being merely a particularly violent mechanism of transfer. It was when, and to the extent that, such indigenous mechanisms became linked to New World social formations where, as Lovejoy notes, "slavery was the basis of production" but "the institutions of enslavement were absent" (276) that the production of slaves in Africa transformed into a mode of social production. Whatever its origins, as a post-Columbian economic complex affecting the better part of the African continent, African commercial slaving was tied to a market that united producers, purveyors, and consumers of human commodities on three different continents in different but functionally closely aligned pursuits.[28] Still, as Shaw (1997, 365) points out, what Lovejoy calls *transformations in slavery* also involved "transition[s] in the political economy of knowledge." In the case of eighteenth-century Sierra Leone, local understandings of witchcraft and its techniques of detection articulated with Atlantic market dynamics in a way that contemporary European observers self-servingly read as an irrational native addiction to witchfinding practices. As Shaw demonstrates, however, such practices, in fact, represented the signs of the workings of a transcontinental economy based on the "production of witches" that fundamentally restructured local "moral economies." Seized by oracular means, its victims were ritually extricated from the moral fabric of kin-based social relations and released onto an Atlantic market for human export commodities. In a different but fundamentally related case, Janzen (1983) has shown how the Lemba cult, a classic western Central African "drum of affliction" or therapeutic association, reworked indigenous idioms of therapeutic ritual and exchange between intermarrying corporations into a new medium "healing" successful traders from the sickness caused by the wealth procured within an Atlantically oriented slaving economy. Called *the sacred medicine of governing*, Lemba's soothing force cut across corporate categories in allowing individual entrepreneurs to knit themselves into a moral community of sufferers, one based on a novel alignment of long-standing discourses on illness, marriage, and exchange that both spoke to and neutralized the moral perils of the slave trade.

In both cases—and they are by no means the only ones that one could cite—it would seem that "capitalist" social relations came to be realized, as Sahlins (1988) puts it, "in other forms and finalities" (5). Yet Sahlins grants far too much historical weight to globalizing versions of Western capitalism and too little to the force of local forms of moral imagination in reading the result of such transitions in local political economies of knowledge as mere symptoms of the emergence of a "world system [that] is the rational expression of relative cultural logics . . . in terms of exchange values" (8–9). Sahlins's own protestations to the contrary, his is a system that metabolizes, in the classic Marxist sense, those forms of sociality not based—or not yet—on its own expansive systemic requisites. As Asad (1993, 4–7) points out, lifting determinism out of the economic sphere only to reimplant it in a logic of cultural process merely reproduces on another analytic level a common confusion of statistical probability *in eventu* with systemic causation discernible only after the event (cf. Comaroff and Comaroff 1992b, 21–22).[29] Given the pervasive, ideologically ill-contained confusion between persons and things the processes in question occasioned even in the Western core (Mintz 1974; Davis 1975; Kopytoff 1986; Carrier 1995), Sahlins's—potentially universalistic—"cultural" teleologies would seem to offer a questionable guide.

Positing a family resemblance between changing structures of opportunity within local African political economies flooded with commoditized imports and the emergence of merchant capital as a social force in early-modern Europe, Miller (1988) seems to provide a more adequate analysis. If the nascent European bourgeoisie captured productive resources in the form of land, African rulers captured such resources in the form of people—both of them hastening "an incipient conversion to exchange and credit by seizing the most productive assets of their respective economies" (137), but doing so on the basis of local cultural contingencies. Comparing early, still weakly capitalized African debt-slaving mechanisms to the "putting-out" system of early European cottage industries, Miller sees both as transitional (but otherwise culturally independent) stages toward full-blown "great transformations" carrying African merchant elites and the European bourgeoisie across thresholds where both systems conjoined in the realization of "forms and finalities" that, *in the aftermath,* can be read as "capitalistic." "Without pushing *the odd contemporaneity* to speculative excess," Miller writes apropos Central Africa, "woolens then flowing out of the British Isles and other London-financed goods reaching Loango and Luanda, slaves from Angola laboring in the cane fields of the West Indies, gold retrieved by Angolan slaves from the hills and streams of Minas Gerais in Brazil, and silver extracted by other slaves from Spain's American mines were transatlantic analogues of the imported textiles and the brass basins that inflated the economies of western central Africa" (137; emphasis added). Analogues, yes, if only under certain historiographic specifications. Homologues, no. What is at issue here is, not systemic determination, but systemic hybridity. Not causality, but complex correlation. Relations of synergy and contingent alignment. The institutions of witchfinding in eighteenth-century Sierra Leone, we might say, had their roots in local conjunctures

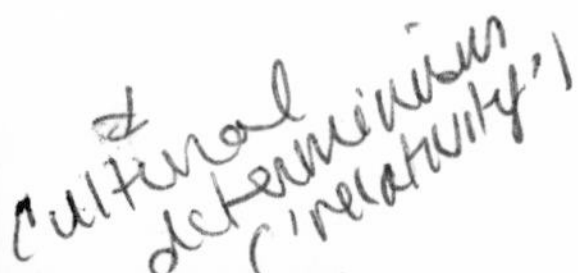

of the same Atlantic matrix that also generated the "West India Interest" in British parliamentary politics or the Club Massiac in revolutionary Paris. Just so, the healing powers of Lemba found their European analogue in the Société des Amis de Noirs and British abolitionism. They were local moments in the constitution of one and the same Atlantic social field, phenomena partly determined by, *but also determinative of,* a larger historical movement that eludes both vulgar economism and cultural determinism. Whatever gulf separated the world of nineteenth-century British industrialists and the slave-trading adherents of Lemba, it is both more than an accident and less than a historical necessity that a pioneer of industrial labor discipline such as Josiah Wedgewood came to engrave the abolitionist call to arms, "Am I not a man and a brother." Whether in the version of Bentham or Mill, utilitarianism was a "medicine of governing" for England's elite. As local responses to options and problems thrown up by processes of extensive scope, the ideology of the *droit des hommes,* Adam Smith's "invisible hand" (cf. Lubazs 1992), Lemba, Timne oracles, and the forms of knowledge underwriting the ritual practices of Haitian vodou all have a common origin in the densely woven mesh of a larger Atlantic modernity.

In fact, there is little reason not to view them as constitutive of each other on an even more viscerally "embedded" level of description. As a report on the execution of a rebel slave during the Haitian Revolution states, in one of the man's pockets "we found pamphlets printed in France [claiming] the Rights of Man; in his vest pocket was a large packet of tinder and phosphate of lime. On his chest he had a little sack full of hair, herbs, bits of bone, which they call a fetish" (cited in Fick 1990, 111). We may, of course, never know what produced or precipitated the conjunction of these objects in the historical situation the corpse of this rebel slave came to index. Even if we had better documentary evidence, the methodological questions involved in getting to the core of the problem suggested by this snippet of archival material are simply overwhelming. On the other hand, is it so counterintuitive to see the contingencies that made for the agglomeration of such seemingly contradictory signs of French modernity and African tradition in the dead man's pockets as symptoms somehow syndromatically connected? If, as Feldman (1991, 4) argues, "political enactment becomes sedimented with its own local histories that are mapped out on the template of the body," the man's corpse represented a rather complex artifact: the sediment of ostensibly disparate histories locally frozen into a seemingly heterogeneous assemblage worn—in this case—on the skin.[30] But are we, in fact, dealing with separable histories? Does not the urge to analytically disaggregate what might be seen as a total—Atlantic—processual field imply the ultimate denigration of the unknown rebel slave's historical subjectivity? Could it not be that the vexing indeterminacy of this single dead body, vested as it appeared to be in a complex intertextuality between signs of both African tradition and Western modernity, results from a vision that rips apart conceptually what is, in fact, a single, seamless historical reality? A reality in which the work of—what we call—*African magic* and *Western modernity*, *vodou* and the *droit des hommes*, may have formed a single synergetic field?

Nor is this merely a matter of situational relativity: of granting the little sack of organic substances ideological force equal to that of the French pamphlets in motivating this man to die in the attempt to reappropriate his person. Much paper has been expended in the famous "rationality debate" over the question of universals in human reasoning (Lévi-Strauss 1966; Horton 1967; Hollis and Lukes 1982) without ever asking why (except by historical a fortiori) Western rationality should have come to be seen as somehow standing outside social arrangements and relations of power. "The belief that the truth of a theory is the same as its productiveness is clearly unfounded," Horkheimer and Adorno (1972, 244) note.[31] What, then, we might ask, was it that Evans-Pritchard's (1937) pathbreaking analysis of the logically impeccable but socially flawed operation of Zande oracles really proved? That knowledge and society are truly separable only in the West, and that this separability is somehow underwritten by an extrahistorically privileged access to . . . yes, access to what? Productiveness? Why compare and contrast African traditional thought and Western science (Horton 1967) without considering the imbeddedness of both in one and the same history?

William Pietz's (1985, 1987, 1988) analysis of the origins and genealogy of the *fetish* concept in Western thought eloquently speaks to this issue: emerging on the fifteenth-century West African coast in a "mercantile cross-cultural space of transvaluation between material objects of radically different social orders," the Portuguese pidgin term *fetisso* had never been part of an African "discursive formation" (Pietz 1985, 10).

Nor did fetishes exist *as such* in any of the societies that European traders encountered along the West African coast. Initially functioning, for European traders, as a totalizing explanation of the "alienness of African culture, in particular its resistance to 'rational' trade relations" (Pietz 1987, 23), the fetish represented a "bizarre phantasm wherein the new forces of the mercantile world economy then reshaping African and European societies alike were read [by Europeans] into a foreign social order and locale" (Pietz 1988, 117). Yet the fetish, not only became a social reality in coastal West Africa, but returned to the centers of rationality simultaneously emerging in Europe. The concept acquired currency in Western discourse through William Bosman's widely read *New and Accurate Account of the Coast of Guinea* (1703)—a key text for the Enlightenment perception of Africa. From there it diffused (with Charles de Brosses's *Du culte des dieux fétiches* [1760] representing an important intermediary) into a host of European discursive genres, reappearing, for example, in the writings of Kant and Hegel, Marx and Comte, Binet and Freud, as a category of universal descriptive or analytic relevance. If so, we might ask, do the semantic functions of this odd transcultural composite within Marxist or psychoanalytic rationalities differ from those performed by the French pamphlets and little sack full of hair, herbs, and bits of bone in the pocket of a Haitian rebel slave? And do we really want to invoke the image of intertextuality (with its implications of two initially separate spheres of meaning) to understand its work?

Saturated as they come to us with historical meanings effaced in the process of rationalization, the discursive work of concepts such as *fetish* implicates their user in a legacy of dispersed or suppressed knowledge.[32] What such knowledge is about are concrete historical interrelations—hybrid worlds of past sociality, thought, and experience—that have vanished into the categorical grid within which they have come to designate universal "facts" salient to a discriminatory logic of "productiveness" culturally cast as "rationality." The hybridity of Caribbean phenomena that some of us are nowadays busily discovering as a new master trope for the postmodern global condition (e.g., Hannerz 1987; Clifford 1988) is, thus, essentially little else but another artifact thrown up by a logic that presumes that subject and object of knowledge somehow—even if only at a certain time in the past or in certain places—could be sundered by some a priori epistemological *cordon sanitaire* (Strathern 1992, 109ff.;

Young 1995).[33] But wait a minute, we might say. What is so new about this? And do we really need to trivialize Caribbean history to make this point? Is it not that as soon as we begin to talk of African traditional religion and Western rationality as contrasts rather than elements of a *single relation* that we turn both of them into the artifice of a discourse that invariably produces hybrids through its very attempts at conceptual separation? Is not discrimination (typological or otherwise) a mere technos for disavowing or mystifying prior facts of mutual implication? Does the problem reside in the contents of a dead man's pockets, or is it a matter of fixing a transcription that turns such metonymic appurtenances into a semantically controllable sign created by an act of violence (Feldman 1991)?

BUILDING ROADS, MAKING SAUSAGES

Nor is this merely an intellectual matter. One paradoxical consequence of what Berman (1982) calls *the melting vision* of modernism may be that attempts to reduce indeterminacy and semantic flux tend to result in the liquidation of people in the service of civilized certainty. The rationalized, technologically enhanced potential of modern forms of domination, not just to mobilize ideological force, but to wreak massive destruction requires us, as Linke (1997) would argue, to rethink terror and annihilation as particularly modern forms of making sense. Schumpeter's view of capitalist entrepreneurialism as centered on processes of creative destruction here dovetails with the most deadly aspects of a civilizing mission that proceeds by culturally marking its object as a thing available for creative effacement and productive consumption (Bauman 1997). Linke and Bauman are primarily concerned with the way in which the German fascist state built on a project of redefining the body of racial others as an object of physical elimination. But a similar logic applies, perhaps even more forcefully, to the project incarnated in Atlantic slavery—a complex of practices and ideas designed to facilitate the effacement of the humanity of commodified labor to a degree where, not just labor power, but the commodified person of the worker became subject to physical wasting in the service of capitalist accumulation and modern self-making (Palmié 1995b, 45–46).

Nor did the mapping out of such histories on the bodies of their victims end with the abolition of those legal arrangements that defined people as commercially transactable goods. Once we begin to attend to the matter empirically, more and more bodies come into play. At times, they do so, not just as thing-like crystallizations of economic potential, but as signposts of cultural value—objectifications, not of productive, but of semantic capacity, taken to gross extremes of concretization. During the U.S. occupation of Haiti, certain native bodies came to signify more than biotic concretizations of the capacity for roadwork or for the spread of infectious diseases—two issues much on the minds of U.S. military bureaucrats commissioned to implement "civilization." When Charlemagne Péralt, the leader of the so-called *Cacos* Rebellion against the occupation, was executed by U.S. Marines in 1919, they nailed his corpse to the door of a Haitian police station—doubtlessly to impress his former followers with the violence they were prepared to unleash. They also photographed the resulting macabre tableau—not so much, one presumes, to record their own savagery (perpetuated, as Kuser [1921, 28–29] and Diedrich and Burt [1969, 40] claim, by Marines in blackface) as to create an archive of terror in the name of order and progress, to document that they, at least, had done their best to ensure that future interpretations of Péralt's martyrdom could be read (if anybody cared to) off the precepts of their own culture. They created a peculiarly prestructured semantic density (Ardener 1989) enveloping a dead human body, thus aiming to authorize a narrative to be told by the stunningly hybridized artifact of a mutilated corpse.[34]

Ten years later, the travel writer Seabrook reported having been told by Haitian peasants about *zonbis* in the employ of HASCO, the Haitian-American Sugar Company, "an immense factory plant, dominated by a huge chimney, with clanging machinery, steam whistles, freight cars. It is like a chunk of Hoboken. It lies in the eastern suburbs of Port-au-Prince, and beyond it stretch the cane fields of the Cul-de-Sac. Hasco makes rum when the sugar market is off, pays low wages, twenty or thirty cents a day, and gives steady work. It is modern big business, and it sounds it, looks it, smells it" (Seabrook 1929, 95). As with so much else in his truly remarkable *The Magic Island,* Seabrook seems to have gathered most of his information on "zombies" in the bar of his hotel (Courlander 1990). But this little detail has the uncanny ring of unwitting authenticity. Speaking about what he feels is a theoretically as well as morally inadmissible distinction between forms of unfreedom generated by legal restraints (as opposed to "mere" market forces) in the case of Haitian *bracero* labor in the Dominican Republic two generations later, Martínez (1996) goes a good way toward disentangling the mystery generated by Seabrook's image of a perfectly rational "chunk of Hoboken" run by a zombified labor force. Both the branding of bracero labor arrangements as *neoslavery* by human rights advocates and the counterargument that such arrangements are being entered on the legal basis of consensual contract, Martínez argues, miss the point. In the Haitian case, structural poverty and political repression render the image of the market as a meeting place of autonomous individuals a particularly cruel phantasm of the neoliberalist imagination (cf. Gudeman 1992).[35] The loss of control over one's selfhood and individual volition characteristic of the notion of the soulless "living dead" at work in the cane fields quite clearly indexes the fundamental alienation of labor power "which is abstract, exists merely in the physical body of the worker, and is separated from its own means of objectification and realization" (Marx 1977, 1:716). Far from representing a mistaken interpolation of archaic fantasy into the rational script of agroindustrial labor relations, the image of the zonbi and the reduction of humans to commodified embodiments of labor power to which it speaks are cut from the cloth of a single social reality long in the making, a reality deeply riven with a sense of moral crisis unleashed by a predatory modernity and experienced, chronicled, and analyzed by its victims in the form of phantasmagoric narratives about how even the bodies of the dead, bereft of their souls, do not escape conscription into capitalist social relations of production.

Like Seabrook's Haitian interlocutors, MacGaffey's Bakongo informants in Zaire in the 1960s seem to have keenly understood the moral derailment at the source of the double fiction of modern individuality and market rationality. They, too, did so in terms that most denizens of the Western world are not easily prepared to concede. In the Bakongo case, we find the idea of a ghastly commerce in "stolen souls" as an explanation for the moral content of the kind of processes all too inadequately subsumed under the bland phrase *development of underdevelopment*. Having legally abolished the trade in human beings decades ago, Europeans continued in the Bakongo imagination to transport dead Africans to places across vast bodies of water where they turned white (as the dead do in their graves) and were made to produce consumer goods—

radios, cars, textiles—for reimportation into Africa (MacGaffey 1968, 1972, 1978).[36] Whether to call it *witchcraft* or *world capitalism* may, in effect, be a choice of words (cf. Palmié 1995b). Like *witchcraft*, *capital* analytically glosses a social relation, although it should be clear that the latter term elides or disfigures precisely the moment of excess, violence, and moral chaos that Bakongo analytics expose.

"Death," Erica Bourguignon (1959) argued in an essay on the Haitian zonbi that keeps hovering on the verge of perceiving just this connection, "may be said to be symbolized in many instances as being 'eaten,' whether by machines, evil gods or other entities" (40). Being of Austrian origin herself, Bourguignon was told that an Austrian immigrant butcher in Pétionville used to hire two shoeshine boys to kill peasants at four dollars a head and that he would then sell the flesh to the townspeople "as sausage and all that sort of thing" (38). Quite in line with the intellectual milieu in which she received her training (i.e., 1950s American psychological anthropology), Bourguignon sought an explanation for this story in a culturally inculcated motive of "oral aggression" relating to the persistent threat of death, illness, and poverty facing the Haitian peasant. She might have looked for a more obvious connection.

As her informants told her, it had become necessary "at the slaughter house to give animals injections, just to find out whether they were really animals" and not humans (Bourguignon 1959, 39). We can, of course, write such rumors into a psychoanalytic narrative indexing fantasies of oral aggression and cannibalistic incorporation. But to do so is to miss the point that, regardless of whatever intrapsychic events and processes may be involved, the referent of such tales of fear and danger lies in the realm of moral relations. Would the military officials administering the roadwork corvée in the service of modernization only a few decades before Bourguignon's arrival in Haiti have exercised similar caution in ascertaining that Haitian peasants were not mere beasts? Or take the organized slaughter of some fifteen to twenty thousand Haitian migrant laborers in the Dominican Republic and in the Haitian border zone by the troops of the U.S.-supported Dominican dictator Rafael Trujillo Molina in 1937—the very year Bourguignon's mentor Herskovits published the first properly disciplined anthropological monograph on Haiti's peasantry. Regardless of Bourguignon's unwillingness to suspend rational disbelief in the case of rumors of ghastly fact-finding operations in the slaughterhouse, it is more than just rumor or folklore that the criterion that Trujillo's soldiers used to select their victims was the inability of *kreyol*-speaking Haitians to pronounce the Spanish *r* in the word *perejil* (parsley). The official code name for the massacre was Operación Perejil. As Fiehrer (1990, 11; emphasis added) puts it, "On 2 October 1937 the armed forces commenced to round up and herd the migrants towards the [Haitian] border. According to a Trujillo apologist, they suddenly *bolted like cattle* into the mountain reaches and ravines, whence the army started to hunt them down with gunfire ('una caseria [*sic*] a balazos')."[37] No injections, one might say, were necessary in this case. The animality of the victims of Trujillo's campaign to restore civilization to the Dominican border zone and remove an unwanted labor reserve had been a foregone conclusion. In the aftermath, and under international pressure, the Dominican Republic agreed to an indemnity of $750,000, or about $30 for every murdered Haitian. Citing sources alleging that the final compensation of survivors amounted to just "two cents a head," Heinl and Heinl (1978, 529) note that, even if the full indemnity had been paid, at that time "a good pig would have brought the [equivalent sum] of $30.00 in the *marché*."

Rumors, as Feldman (1995) points out, are the analytic instrument of local "spontaneous historiography." They are, in Stoler's (1992, 154) words, a "key form of cultural knowledge" diagnostic of what is realistically conceivable, thus "blurring the boundaries between events 'witnessed' and those envisioned, between performed brutality and the potentiality for it." People do get "eaten" by machines, evil gods, and other entities. What Bourguignon was facing, we might say, was a revision of the powerful rumors that, in formally democratic Western states, suggest individual autonomy and inviolability while predicating those very conceptions on the operation of impersonal—and fundamentally amoral—market forces (cf. Fraser 1997). The dispersal of violence, in such instances, is an ideological effect, a result of conceptual separations that Bourguignon's interlocutors seemed unwilling to fully consummate.[38] Building roads and making sausages may appear to be very different activities under certain conditions of action and understanding. Sometimes, however, they converge into the violence attendant on—perhaps even intrinsic to—the keenly felt dangers of a globalizing modernity that collapses into locally experienced "corporal topographies" (Linke 1997) evidenced by the signs of ghastly violation that it inscribes on the "altered" bodies of those who have to live through it (cf. White 1993a, 1993b; Scheper-Hughes 1996).

MIMETIC BREAKDOWNS AND MORAL ARTIFACTS

"Voodoo," then, "belongs to the modern world and is part of our own civilization" in more ways than even Métraux (1972, 365) may have been willing to concede. "The concept of history itself," Feldman (1995, 232) suggests, may well be viewed as "a culturally specific form of rumor, particulary when it is positioned by class, gender, and cultural inequities and discontinuities." It was only in the eighteenth century, Reinhard Koselleck (1985) reminds us, that Western historians encountered—after what then began to seem like centuries of providential story mongering—the "demand, both in terms of techniques of representation and epistemologically, that [they] offer not a past reality, but the fiction of its facticity" (215). Koselleck makes this observation in the context of a disquieting reflection on dreams as forms of historical representation situated "at the extremity of a conceivable scale of susceptibility to historical rationalization" (218) but possessing an incontrovertible facticity within the particular culture of terror—fascist Germany—with which he deals. Unlike Taussig (1987), who explores terror as an epistemological problem, Koselleck travels a rather conventional but therefore perhaps even more suggestive methodological path. "Political and social occurrences are generally illuminated through texts which refer directly to the actions that compose such occurrences," he argues (1985). "Even the leaders of the SS, in the course of their official communications, speeches, and memoirs, made use of a language which is as open as a text to rational examination or ideological-critical examination. Actions and their linguistic articulation here remain open to methodological scrutiny. What happened in concentration camps is barely comprehensible in written form, is scarcely tangible in descriptive or imaginative language" (222). "Representations of dreams from concentration camps," Koselleck writes, "reveal to us a domain in which human understanding appears to give way, where language is struck dumb" (221). In a curious permutation of von Ranke's famous phrase *wie es eigentlich gewesen* (how it really was), he submits that, in the face of such mimetic breakdowns, "we are forced to rely on the metaphor of dreams so that we might learn *what really happened*," to understand how "dreams of terror . . . are, above all, dreams in terror, terror which pursues mankind even in sleep" (220; emphasis added).

This lengthy digression is not meant to insinuate in any way an analogy between fascist terror and the predicament of New World slaves or rural proletarians. Nor is it aimed at endorsing a psychoanalytic reading of their historical experience. Rather, and like Koselleck, I take it to exemplify the possibility of a historical reality constituted beyond the reach of criteria of disciplinary rationalization. To put the matter in different terms, I see the "dreams in terror" Koselleck discusses as evidence for forms of sociality (and, if we accept Simmel's (1950) insight that conflict is a form of consociation, then we should see terror as no less) that defy conventional criteria defining *which* linguistic residues can evidence *what* historical realities.[39] Nor is this to reduce the Afro-Caribbean bodies of knowledge and practice with which the following chapters deal to mere reflections of social realities marked by the clear and present danger of personal violation and bodily harm. It is to suggest that the language of vodun—speaking as it does of such improbabilities as living dead and Austrian cannibal-butchers—or the similarly fantastic idiomatics of the Afro-Cuban discourses that I intend to explore in the following chapters do not necessarily have *any* lesser diagnostic purchase on social facticity within specific historical contexts than do the constructs on which historians and anthropologists build their narratives and explanations (cf. White 2000).

One last example may serve to clarify the issues involved. Consider the following pontifications issued in 1940 by the then high priests of British structural functionalism, Meyer Fortes and Edward E. Evans Pritchard (1970):

> Africans have no objective knowledge of the forces determining their social organization and actuating their social behavior. Yet they would be unable to carry on their collective life if they could not think and feel about the interests which actuate them, the institutions by means of which they organize collective action, and the structure of the groups into which they are organized. Myths, dogmas, ritual beliefs and activities make his social system intellectually tangible and coherent to an African and enable him to think and feel about it. Further-

more, these sacred symbols, which reflect the social system, endow it with mystical values which evoke acceptance of the social order that goes far beyond the obedience exacted by the secular sanction of force. The social system is, as it were, removed to a mystical plane, where it functions as a system of sacred values beyond criticism or revision. (17–18)

Had they been secretly reading Marx? For *sacred symbols* substitute *commodities* (or, perhaps, more precisely, the *exchange value* attached to products of human labor) that come to stand as undecipherable "social hieroglyphics" representing human relationships as relations between things; for *Africans* substitute *producers* or *wage laborers,* and you will get the idea. *De te fabula narratur.* But, what is more, according to Fortes and Evans Pritchard, no less than the capitalist and the worker simultaneously duped by the singular phantasm of the money fetish, "the African does not see beyond the symbols; it might well be held that if he understood their objective meaning, they would lose the power they have over him" (18). Hard to believe though it may be, we are smack in the middle of the discursive space occupied by *The German Ideology.*[40] Hence the never-ending fascination on the part of the ethnographer with ascertaining precisely how the ideas of the ruling class become the ruling ideas within stateless, tribal settings. What, after all, is an ancestor or an initiation rite, exogamy or a classificatory brother, in the classic anthropological sense but a work of culture, an arbitrary semantic excess grafted on panhuman realities, a mystification?[41] To the colonial administrator, however, ancestors and other such execrescences of the native social imaginary were not quite as easily dismissed. On the contrary, they posed the pervasive political problem that Guha (1989) identified as *domination without hegemony:* the chore of having to exercise unroutinized, ideologically ill-contained power, "arterial" rather than "capillary" in praxis (Cooper 1994), violent rather than persuasive, and often attached to little else than the "thin white line" that more perceptive agents of empire at times found themselves incapable of not acknowledging.[42] The "European government can to a great extent replace" the chief, where he exists, in his "secular" capacity as executive of organized force, our crypto-Marxists argue (Fortes and Evans Pritchard 1970, 16). Yet into the "sacred precincts" where his authority is constituted, or where, in the absence of chiefship, the "balanced segments which compose the political structure" are "vouched for by tradition," the "European rulers can never enter. They have no mythical or ritual warranty for their authority."

Yet Fortes and Evans-Pritchard were merely dodging the unspeakable results of the work of a political logic that bore all the signs of extensive "cross-breeding" (Amselle 1993). They did so in the service of what their epistemologically more fastidious colleague Siegfried Nadel (1957) might have called a *methodological fiction*—albeit one with powerful political implications. For, in fact, the "sacred precincts" were full of "European rulers." Dragged there by their own designs and the agency of their subjects, colonial administrators had long been embroiled in a monumental confusion of tongues: issuing witchcraft ordinances, arbitrating traditional law, deciding succession disputes on mythical bases, combating militant native Christianities, or (as in the Haitian case recounted above) crucifying the corpses of guerrilla leaders on doors of police stations—all the while expounding the rationality of civilized forms of domination. Neither did their subjects fail to see "beyond the symbols," although their analyses rarely entered the realm of knowledge discursively available within the semantic field constituted by colonial rhetoric. Again, the analogy to Western ways of divorcing concrete social experience from the discourse on society seems useful. For, on the "level of structured cultural expectation and everyday behavior" (Carrier 1995, 157), colonial domination, as Karen Fields (1982, 574) points out for the case of British Africa, was "the very antithesis of moral community between rulers and ruled. As practice, [the 'civilizing mission'] did not build on institutions by which rulers and ruled ordered a common life. There were none. And its declared purpose was the dissolution of ordered society, as Africans understood it." The same can be said, if in a slightly different register, about the hybrid orders constituted by the Haitian state—or resulting from the constitution of Cuba as a state under North American occupation. Both cases involved a morally unconvincing institutional apparatus created or manipulated by aliens, staffed by native conscripts or collaborators, and operated on ruthless principles of rational domination. And, in both cases, the issue of state terrorism looms large. Contrasting the army (arguably one of the key trappings of modern statehood) of the Haitian republic of 1804 with the *gendarmerie* or *Garde* that replaced it during the U.S. occupation, Trouillot (1990, 106) notes that, unlike the former, "the Haitian *Garde* was specifically created to fight against other Haitians. It received its baptism of fire in combat against its countrymen. And the *Garde*, like the army it was to sire, has indeed never fought anyone *but* Haitians."[43] Much the same holds for the Cuban army and *guardia rural* that, only eleven years after nominal independence, gunned and clubbed down thousands of black peasants during the so-called race war of 1912. They did so in the service of a state underwritten by the Platt Amendment—a unilateral guarantee securing the United States unlimited rights to interference in Cuban internal affairs—and actively reproducing the inequalities of race and class crucial to foreign capital interests in the form of what we, today, would call *national-security* policies. Nor need this surprise us. Along with the predatory states that emerged in Haiti and the Dominican Republic (Lundahl 1992), what Cuban scholars today call the *pseudorepublic* was one—perhaps *the*—New World precedent for a political form increasingly characteristic of the so-called Third World: states whose major function it is to "crush class protests while maintaining economic growth on behalf of multinational interests" (Rejali 1991, 135). Although North American investment in Cuba remained limited before 1898, the vast transformation of Cuba's sugar industry associated with the emergence of the centralized milling complexes (*centrales*) in the last decades of the nineteenth century was firmly linked to the U.S. sugar market, which, by the late 1880s, absorbed fully 94 percent of the island's production (Pérez 1986, 14). This is not the place to chronicle the gradual insinuation of U.S. capital into the Cuban economy during the colonial period.[44] Suffice it to say that, within a decade of the founding of the Republic, North American investment had completely overwhelmed the island, reaching a staggering $215 million in 1911 (Pérez 1986, 74).

By then, the political-economic results of this process were visible to even the casual observer. "Foreigners," wrote Irene Wright (1910), "own, I am convinced, at least 75 per cent of Cuba—fully three fourth of the very soil of the island" (164).[45] "We have then, in Cuba," she concluded, "a country owned by foreigners, the government of which is supported by foreigners, but administered by Cubans, after such a fashion, however (foreigners have not the suffrage), that these Cubans in Office are not answerable to the real source of their salaries for the disbursement of these or other revenues, paid in by foreigners, nor in any legitimate manner can they be obligated to consider the welfare of the country (owned by foreigners) or of the business conducted (by foreigners) within its boundaries" (166). "We have made politics our only industry," Miguel de Carrión would echo a decade later (cited in Pérez 1986, 141), "and political fraud the only course open to wealth for our compatriots." In fact, as de Carrión noted, "This political industry . . . is stronger than the sugar industry, which is no longer ours; more lucrative than the railroads, which are managed by foreigners; safer than the banks, than maritime transportation and commercial trade, which also do not belong to us." "Herein was one of the more anomalous features of the early republic," writes Pérez (1986, 139). "Economic power did not produce political power; rather, political power created riches and an economically powerful class. The state thus served at once as a source and instrument of economic power. For the political class, the state assumed the function of the 'means of production.'" This transformation of the Cuban state into an instrument of economic predation paralleled the disarticulation of economy and civil society in a manner that Fernando Ortiz (1995, 52–53) vividly described as a process of privatization—or, in more contemporary terms, informalization—of power. Speaking about the modern central[46] as a "huge organism for sugar production" "vertebrated by an economic and legal structure that combines masses of land, masses of machinery, masses of men, and masses of money," Ortiz notes that the social sphere defined by such gigantic agroindustrial complexes "is practically outside the jurisdiction of public law; the norms of private property hold sway here. The owner's power is as complete over this immense estate as though it were just a small plantation or farm. Everything there is private—ownership, industry, mill, houses, stores, police, railroad, port. Until the year 1886 the workers, too, were chattels like other property." The consolidation of rural Cuban landholdings into increasingly vast centrales in the first three decades of the twentieth century signaled the final destruction of the Cuban peasantry and its conversion into a seasonally extremely underemployed rural proletariat—"landless, propertyless, wage-earning, and store-buying," as Mintz (1964, xxxvi) puts it. It also signaled the emergence of a political space splintered into local monopolies on organized force usurped by political operatives, answerable, ultimately, to foreign investors rather than the state supposedly legitimating their access to organized force.[47] Under Machado (1924–33), we find the installment of the last element of the full-fledged postcolonial security state: the large-scale expansion of the national army into the institutional sphere of the nation as an instrument of harassment and coercion of civilians. No less than the Haitian Garde, up until 1959 the Cuban army had little function other than to intimidate or attack citizens of the Cuban Republic.[48]

We do not normally think of nations and the state power that is supposed to materialize them as being constituted in what Fortes and Evans Pritchard (1970) call *sacred precincts*—laboratories for the rationalization of power where the symbols securing the legitimacy of domination by cultural means are cooked up. But we should know better (Abrams 1988).[49] That we tend to forget is testimony to a disavowal that circumscribes a peculiarly modern moment, not just in anthropology, but in Western social thought in general (Tilly 1984; Wolf 1988). It is a moment creative of "moral artifacts" (Fields 1985) such as *capitalism* and *native society, chiefship* and *instrumental rationality, nationhood* and *spirit possession, the individual* and *the horse with two heads, ancestor worship* and *socialism*, the *World Bank* and the Haitian *zonbi*, the *Bible* and the *Dow Jones index, witchcraft* and *structural adjustment*. In all these cases, we are dealing with objects of discourse, contingent couplings of signs and referents the empirical materiality of which may seem questionable under certain descriptions. Under others, however, their referents "are present and real, as an arrow or a pistol is" (Fields 1982, 569). They can, in other words, have violent—at times lethal—implications. As Rejali (1991, 138) notes, victims of modern forms of torture present special challenges to the therapist: "Doctors have to exercise tremendous care in the way they speak to and treat their patients, who can no longer effectively distinguish between what is torture and what is medicine." There is no need here to recur to Foucault in order to realize that the sign value of the ministrations of torturers and physicians may be experientially ambiguous. What is healing and what is destruction is often not easily kept apart (Taussig 1987; de Rosny 1985). Simply recall Haitian rumors about injections at the slaughterhouse. The cane field cultivated by zonbis may always be just around the bend in the road.

It is this very potential that opens up such hybrids to *empirical analysis*, although we should be clear about what we mean by this term: analysis by embodied experience. Whatever discursive terms such analyses may be cast in, we must acknowledge their representational validity for what it is—the record of the reflections of people on the moral texture of the world in which they conduct their daily business of being humans in the face of danger. In a fundamental way, the Afro-Cuban traditions that I discuss in the following chapters take their origins, not so much in a distant African past (although they do that, too, in complex and ill-understood ways), but in the historical continuum of Caribbean presents within which they served—and continue to serve—as means of moral analysis and templates for social action. This is why we may want to think of the irrationalities of the "Others" who live through Western rationalities as a form of social diagnosis (MacGaffey 1978, 1981)—a social science that may not only rival ours in analytic acumen but that is hard to separate from it in the first place. The latter, is, perhaps, the decisive point: what the task of a morally responsible analysis may consist in is not to chronicle the multiple distortions produced by the segregation of modern and traditional, global and local knowledge in order to denounce the former. It is to undo such separations.

In what follows, I explore this larger theoretical subject through a series of historical episodes set, and focused, on a single Caribbean island. This is not because I think that Cuba is somewhat more typical or even only particularly representative of issues germane to the history of the Antilles—or African America—as a whole. Cuba clearly is not, and neither are the examples that I intend to marshal. Rather, I think that the local case studies that I explore in the following chapters have a bearing on larger questions that cannot fruitfully be argued through in local detail alone—although such detail must surely form the basis of any significant account. The Cuban scenarios that I discuss are part of a larger picture, and should be seen as such. What they concern are the growth and transformation of distinctly Afro-Cuban forms of knowledge reflective of one might call a state of *incomplete capture*. A state of doubt, perhaps, as reasoned from experience, or simply a feeling of a diffuse but ever-present danger of loss of selfhood, of being submerged in, and perhaps consumed by, somebody else's designs. What the narratives that form the following chapters deal with, substantially, are local conceptions of morality—attempts of historical actors to think through their world—on the premises of the analytic vocabularies available to or conceivable by them. I do not entertain the illusion that such subaltern discourses—for this, arguably, is what they represent—hold a universally valid corrective to the forms of rationality against which my rhetoric will pit them. To do so would be once more to subvert representations of an "other" with whom I myself have become somewhat more intimately involved to an ultimately presumptuous project of autocriticism. I merely wish to entertain the possibility that the modernity we struggle to understand, and perhaps might wish to abandon, is not just ours. It also belongs to those whose physical abuse and intellectual denigration was the price paid for its achievement. Before we decide to exit from whatever it is we find ourselves imprisoned in, their voices should be heard.

1. "FOR REASONS OF HISTORY"

José Antonio Aponte and His Libro de Pinturas

> And if someone, in order to decode a cipher written in ordinary letters, thinks of reading a B everywhere he finds an A, and reading a C where he finds a B, and thus to substitute for each letter the one that follows it in alphabetical order and if, reading in this way, he finds words that have a meaning, he will not doubt that he has discovered the true meaning of this cipher in this way, even though it could very well be that the person who wrote it meant something quite different, giving a different meaning to each letter.—René Descartes, *Principia*

For a few day in late March 1812, the *licenciado* Don José María Nerey stood on the threshold of a strange and incomprehensible world. Before him, on a desk in Havana's fortress San Carlos de la Cabaña, lay a large bound volume of images, partly painted by hand, partly consisting of fragments of engravings cut from books and painted fans and reassembled into bewildering collages of heterogeneous media. This curious book had been secured in the course of a raid on the home and workshop of a free black artisan and retired member of the free black militia, José Antonio Aponte y Ulabarra, who now stood before Nerey as the suspected ringleader of what Nerey's superiors, Judge Rendón and Capitán General Salvador José de Muro y Salazar, marqués de Someruelos, believed was a potentially islandwide conspiracy. Since January of that year, a series of violent uprisings had shaken the eastern provinces of Cuba, and, by early March, rebellions broke out "with major excess" (de Someruelos cited in Franco 1977, 214)[1] on several sugar plantations dangerously close to Havana. Nerey's orders were to find evidence of such a conspiracy, and the volume at hand appeared to contain the key for disclosing what the Cuban authorities feared was a vast subterranean structure of organized insurrectionary fervor.

Such fears were not unfounded. Although sporadic slave revolts had occurred throughout the preceding decades, the present situation appeared a particularly volatile one. For, to anyone aware of the relation between the French Revolution and the slave rebellions that had ushered in the destruction of French St. Domingue some twenty years earlier, the Napoleonic occupation of Spain in 1808, the king's forced exile, the flight of the parliament to Cádiz, and the subsequent waves of nationalist agitation in Caracas, Buenos Aires, Mexico City, Santiago de Chile, and Quito boded ill for the internal stability of Cuba. This was particularly so because, in the preceding decades, Cuba had experienced far-reaching economic as well as social and demographic transformations that were more than incidentally related to the events that had turned the French colony of St. Domingue into the Republic of Haiti. Coinciding with the Bourbon relaxation of trade restrictions in the Spanish Empire, the elimination of St. Domingue as the world's largest sugar producer had hastened Cuba's rise from a stagnant backwater of Spanish America to the position of a booming plantation colony fully integrated into what Philip Curtin (1955) called the *South Atlantic System*. Yet, if the Haitian Revolution had expedited Cuba's economic ascendancy,[2] it also exposed the dangers inherent in the dramatic demographic shifts attendant on the expansion of slave-based colonial plantation economies. If slavery had been an economically marginal institution in Cuba up until the last decades of the eighteenth century, it now rapidly rose to overriding importance and expanded to unprecedented scope. According to Aimes's (1967, 36–37) very rough estimates, Cuba may have imported a total of some 90,000 slaves between 1512 and 1789. Between 1790 and 1810, however, 135,000 Africans entered the port of Havana alone (Marrero 1971–88, 9:28). And, even though Cuba's white population was incomparably larger than that of St. Domingue had been on the eve of the Haitian Revolution, in Havana and its surrounding plantation zones it lost its demographic majority position in the early years of the nineteenth century. Slaves and free Afro-Cubans now made up 67 percent of the city's population (Torres Cuevas and Reyes 1986, 74), and it was clear that most of them were aware, not only of the Haitian Revolution, but of the political turmoil in Spain. What added to the worries of Cuba's colonial elite was the fact that, by the spring of 1812, news about Hidalgo's declaration of slave emancipation in Mexico City in 1810, the independence of Venezuela, and the 1811 debates about abolition in the exiled Spanish Cortes could easily have reached Afro-Cubans through a variety of channels.[3] Quite clearly, the marqués de Someruelos had no reason to take rumors of a black conspiracy lightly. Given the political chaos in Spain and the turmoil spreading across its colonial mainland possessions, the consequences of a well-planned slave uprising were unforeseeable.

The Capitán General acted swiftly. Within a week after receiving information that a conspiracy was afoot in Havana, individuals suspected of involvement in insurrectionary plans had been arrested, their houses searched, and their neighborhoods scoured for potential informers. One of the last who found themselves incarcerated in the course of these measures was José Antonio Aponte y Ulabarra. The circumstances of his arrest are not entirely clear.[4] Aponte, it seems, was denounced by another free black militiaman, Esteban Sánchez, for having participated in secret meetings at the house of Salvador Ternero. Ternero, also a free Afro-Cuban, had had an earlier brush with the police when he participated in the riots protesting the French occupation of Spain that broke out in Havana in March 1809 (Franco 1974, 138–39). At that time, hordes of armed whites and blacks had congregated at the embankment and the Plaza de San Francisco in protest of the "crime of Bayona" and the imprisonment of Fernando VII by Napoléon, loudly asserting their loyalty to the Spanish monarch. Known since then (even though, one might say, for all the wrong reasons) as a seditious character, in 1812 Ternero himself was accused by his free black neighbor Mauricio Gutiérrez of having invited him, Gutiérrez, to participate in a planned insurrection.

Like Ternero, Aponte had a somewhat ambiguous record. His discharge from military service in 1810, it would seem, had occurred under less than favorable conditions. The official documents state advanced age as the reason for retirement, but, as the Cuban historian José Luciano Franco (1977, 12) observes, Aponte's military career may have been terminated by allegations of his association with Capitán Don Luis Francisco Bassave (Basabe) y Cárdenas, the white creole leader of a nationalistic conspiracy known as the Masonic Conspiracy of 1810.[5] Franco makes rather vague references to what he thinks may have been prior seditious activities on the part of Aponte. He thus claims that Aponte dictated an inflammatory proclamation that was posted in Havana in early March 1812 but fails to cite any evidence (Franco 1977, 19). Similarly undocumented are Franco's allegations that Aponte had authored an "extensive" piece of writing inviting Havana's white merchants to join an impending revolutionary uprising that the Catalán merchant Pablo Serra brought to the attention of the Capitán General (Franco 1977, 20). Even if so, however, it is unclear why, almost from the start of the inquest, Aponte was suspected of being the conspiracy's mastermind. To be sure, the book found among his possessions contained images that immediately drew the attention of the Cuban authorities. Most significant, from their point of view, were detailed map-like drawings of Havana and its fortifications but also images of battle scenes in which black and white armies appeared to engage each other in deadly combat. Still, all Aponte himself ever admitted was having had some knowledge of potentially seditious plans that some men with whom he was closely associated were hatching.

Somewhat surprisingly, perhaps, torture seems not to have been applied during Aponte's interrogation, and it is tempting to infer that his interrogators had embarked on a quest for truths they thought could only be gained from the man if they preserved his bodily and psychological integrity. Nerey's task, it seems, was to engage Aponte in dialogue rather than force him to speak. And what Aponte was to speak about was, not some nefarious plan (which his interrogators apparently thought he would never truthfully reveal), but rather the images he had committed to the pages that now lay before them. In three extended interrogations lasting up to eight hours a day, Nerey made Aponte go through page after page of the book and explain the meaning of its pictorial content. For Nerey, it proved a frustrating and ultimately senseless endeavor. Although the interrogators repeatedly felt close to uncovering a cunningly encrypted masterplan, again and again Aponte's exegesis on his own corpus of visual representations foiled their search for strategic intelligence. Rather than clarifying connections between pictorial signifiers and conspiratorial referents, Aponte's reading of his own book, as it were, rendered increasingly opaque and incomprehensible what initially had appeared meaningful signs of subversion. Exploding the ostensibly indexical into a densely allegorical and strangely familiar, although ultimately incomprehensible, form of pictorial semiosis, his vision, it seems, occluded theirs.

Then, on March 29, 1812, the mysterious *libro de pinturas* was closed forever. After a fourth and last long round of futile questions designed to relate the ambiguous symbolism of other objects and representations found among Aponte's possessions to conspiratorial motives, on 30 March Aponte's voice also fell silent—drowned out by the increasing noise of the histrionics of power. No more time would be wasted in probing the bewildering profusion of images conjured up by "the fatuous and heated brain of the *moreno* José Antonio Aponte" (Franco 1977, 217), as the Capitán General phrased the matter. If there was method in this madness—so the high-ranking Cuban officials convoked to interpret the evidence apparently thought—it was better left undisclosed. Indeed, it seems as if the decision to silence Aponte once and for all was an attempt to restore sense by sheer violence. On April 7, without the trial proceedings having come to a conclusion, the marqués de Someruelos, in language ringing with savage pathos, ordered the annihilation of Aponte and eight of his presumed fellow conspirators. Two days later, they died on the gallows, and, in a final display of violence, their heads and hands were cut off to be publicly exhibited in the barrios where they had lived.

Nor would it seem that Aponte's libro de pinturas survived this storm of violence unleashed in the service of order and certainty. We do not know whether it was destroyed along with its creator, filed away and lost in the hurried evacuation of parts of the documentary record of Spanish colonial rule in 1898, or still awaits accidental discovery in some Cuban or Spanish archive, private collection, or other repository.[6] Yet, even though we may never physically recover the product of Aponte's imagination and artistic creativity, we are left with the paradoxical record of an eloquent absence. Created and preserved by the same machinery of power and knowledge production that annihilated Aponte, the archival record has become the medium through which his ghostly voice—warped and distorted, to be sure, by the noise of multiple interferences—now speaks to us about a world of images that we will never see.

OUR MAN IN HAVANA

Ever since the first Cuban War of Independence (1868–78), nationalist Cuban historians have claimed Aponte as a paragon of Afro-Cuban liberation and anticolonial resistance. Not surprisingly, perhaps, they have done so on the same evidentiary grounds on which the original investigators and later colonialist historians constructed what they, too, perceived as a massive threat to Spanish domination.[7] The Spanish historian Justo Zaragoza (1872, cited in Franco 1974, 144), thus, speaks of a "formidable conspiracy" led by a man with "capacities uncommon among his race" but "such perverse disposition of character that it gave rise to the adage *more evil than Aponte* by which villains are designated in Cuba today." And he concludes that, owing to Aponte's "black leadership and the perfectly premeditated and skillfully executed plot, there were certain moments when the island was truly endangered." Writing from exile in the United States only five years later, the Cuban Juán Arnao (1877, cited in Franco 1974, 145), on the other hand, called Aponte "the first Cuban whose dream became the beautiful inspiration of actively rebelling against Spanish domination." With Arnao begins a long tradition of reversing the sign value of what Ranajit Guha (1983) calls *the prose of counterinsurgency* in which Aponte's case was first recorded. By 1940, we thus find the eminent Cuban historian Emilio Roig de Leuchsenring (cited in Franco 1974, 145) elevating Aponte to the status of a "protomartyr of civil liberty and the vindication of the worker." More recently, Levi Marrero (1971–88, 9:34) has spoken of Aponte's case as "the most extensive and best organized conspiracy aiming at the liberation of the slaves that took place in colonial Cuba." And even the most carefully documented study so far (Childs 1998) leaves little doubt that its author concurs with the Cuban authorities' ultimate decision to treat the highly ambiguous information gathered during the inquest as evidence for Aponte's intention to stage an uprising akin to that which had ushered in the Haitian Revolution some nineteen years earlier. Given this massive consensus across time and political positions, Nerey, we might say, had truly wasted his time trying to navigate the turbulent waters of Aponte's imagination. If Aponte's guilt of the heinous crime of sedition had been a foregone conclusion then, his role as prime instigator of an emancipatory project has become so now. What the marqués de Someruelos once called *the products of a heated and fatuous brain* have been transformed into the glorious vision of liberation.

What is at issue here is not just this uncanny but certainly familiar symmetry—so trenchantly explored by Guha (1983) and other members of the Subaltern Studies Group (e.g., Chakrabarty 1988; Spivak 1988a, 1988b). Their strictures target the tendency of both colonialist and post-colonialist historiography to elide the question of subaltern consciousness by assimilating its presumed content to a totalizing discursive opposition defined by historical narratives that merely reverse each other's terms (so that the dastardly deeds of one genre merely mutate into glorious feats, and vice versa). And, whatever quibbles I have with those who do see Aponte as the author of an insurrectionary project, the real problem with their interpretations lies elsewhere. For, apart from the claims that latter-day historians of Cuba have made on Aponte's historical subjectivity by elevating him to the pantheon of martyrs of Afro-Cuban and/or national liberation, his case occasionally draws more generalized attention as well. This is so because Aponte's conspiracy—and I would reserve judgment on whether it was really *his*—appears to illustrate certain far more pervasive problems in conceptualizing the cultural dimensions of African American resistance. In particular, and much like, for example, the conspiracies of Gabriel Prosser (Virginia, 1800) and Denmark Vesey (Charleston, 1822) or the insurrections led by José Leonardo Chirinos (Venezuela, 1795), Charles Deslonde (Louisiana, 1811), and Julien Fédon (Grenada, 1816), Aponte's case seems amenable to analysis along the lines of a typology popularized by the historian Eugene Genovese in his influential *From Rebellion to Revolution* (1979).[8] In this extended essay on slave resistance in the Americas, Genovese argued that the Haitian Revolution marked a historical watershed in terms of the political goals of African American conspiratorial or insurrectionary movements. Surveying the literature on outbreaks of slave resistance before and after the Haitian Revolution, Genovese concluded that earlier rebellions—typically led by a majority of African-born slaves who often appear to have rallied around conceptions of common "ethnic" identity—tended toward what he thinks of as the restoration of an Old World status quo ante in a New World context: slaves ran off into the bush, forming (as in Suriname) corporate unilineal kin groups; they allegedly conspired (as in Mexico City in 1537, Barbados in 1675, or Antigua in 1736) to set up "African" kingdoms complete with enslaved dependents; or they simply marched east (as in the—temporally somewhat anomalous—case of the mutinous African conscript members of the First West India Regiment in Trinidad in 1837), presumably to make their way back to Africa.

Discounting the latter incident, by about 1800, Genovese and those who have followed his lead find, this situation had irrevocably changed. The type of resistance that Michael Craton (1982)—in a particularly inept phrase recently repeated and embellished on by Michael Mullin—calls *rebellions of the spear* now gives way to a new form of outbreak. Previously, Mullin (1992, 40) tells us, African-born rebels "rose up, killed, pillaged, and torched buildings before marching off with their loot, beneath magic banners, into mountain interiors"; "driven by martial drumming, dancing, or ritual oaths," they drank "their foe's blood" and ate "their hearts," even killed themselves "when cornered" in forms "of resistance, whose alien and primitive nature" Mullin—from whom these phrases are taken—finds "hard to convey." After the crucial moment of the Haitian Revolution, a good number of historians concerned with the issue are inclined to perceive a rather different pattern. Although often no less exuberantly violent, the latter-day risings tend to be viewed as spearheaded by creole, that is, American-born, blacks who, more often than not, appear to have been keenly aware of the global political signs of the times. They no longer are the mere performers of "alien and primitive" traditions indelibly imprinted in the consciousness and mechanically reproduced in the actions of African rebels without a world-historical cause. These people have an appointment with destiny, and they know it.[9]

I am, of course, close to parodying the arguments presented by Genovese and those who have followed in his tracks. Nevertheless, they vividly illustrate the moment of systematic incomprehension and active forgetting of the fundamental imbrication of both African tradition and Western modernity so characteristic of the emergence of the Caribbean as a "worlded" space (in Spivak's sense) and so starkly exposed in both C. L. R. James's interpretations of the Haitian Revolution or Alfred Métraux's judgment about the "modernity" of Haitian vodun discussed above. For the juncture that virtually all students of African American resistance have regarded as decisive occurs when, in the summer of 1791, massive slave rebellions in St. Domingue begin to dovetail with the effects of an export of the French Revolution to this colony.[10] There is, of course, no question about the importance of this event. As planters and colonial administrators throughout the hemisphere rapidly understood, after Haiti nothing would ever be the same. And, just as the latter would desperately try to "protect" their local slave populations from infection with ideas about universal rights, so have historians been quick to read symptoms of precisely such infection into the documentary records of African American resistance postdating these crucial events. What they find now are not African rebels seemingly trying to evade the "modernizing" effect of slavery by marronage or other stratagems aiming at the restoration of—or regression to?—what some think of as an "African past." They rather encounter creole revolutionaries heading toward what presumably should have been their goal all along: a decisive plunge into bourgeois modernity effected by doing away, not just with individually experienced unfreedom, but with the institution of slavery itself. Once and for all.

At first glance, Aponte appears to fit such a scenario. His precise date of birth is unknown, but, since we may assume the early 1760s as a probable period,[11] most of his adult life falls within the so-called Age of Revolutions. It is not clear whether Aponte experienced slavery himself.[12] What we do know is that, as a young man, he joined the colored militia troops and, in 1782, took part in the liberation of New Providence (i.e., Nassau) in the Bahamas as part of the Spanish troops under General Cagigal, then allied with the Republican forces in the American War of Independence (Franco 1974, 147). By the time of his discharge in 1810, he had achieved the rank of a first Corporal (*cabo primero*) in the Batallón de Milicias Disciplinadas de Pardos y Morenos (Afro-Cuban militia). Apart from the social distinctions Aponte derived from his military career,[13] his economic position likewise relegated him to Havana's Afro-Cuban elite: a carpenter by trade, Aponte possessed artistic faculties and, after acquiring a house and workshop situated on calle Jesús Peregrino in the extramural section of Havana then known as Pueblo Nuevo or Pueblo Chico, seems to have increasingly concentrated on sculpting. Franco (1974, 146) relates that, toward the end of 1811, Aponte finished a statue of the Virgen de la Guadalupe for a church likewise situated in the *barrios extramuros,* and José Maria de la Torre (1857, 83) tells us that the calle Jesús Peregrino actually acquired its name from a retable of Aponte's making.

None of this is particularly unusual or surprising. Free urban blacks like Aponte virtually monopolized, not only the crafts, but also the sector of artistic production in early-nineteenth-century Havana,[14] and it is quite conceivable that Aponte derived a good part of his income from sculpting religious statuary on commission from wealthy patrons or the Church itself. At any rate, by the time of his arrest, Aponte was an established craftsman, a property owner, a retired officer, and the father of six grown children who had taken up trades such as blacksmithing and tailoring or who worked as store attendants. In other words, he was a highly successful yet by no means exceptional member of Havana's black elite, a man the likes of whom might have been found—although in decidedly lesser numbers than in Havana—in almost any urban center of the Caribbean in the early nineteenth century.[15] Given Aponte's "structural position" as a member of that small but vital sector of Cuba's free black population Deschamps Chapeaux and Pérez de la Riva (1974) designated as *la burguesía de colór*, it is, indeed, tempting to insert him into the mold of the *creole revolutionary:* someone inspired, not by some obscure and hopelessly particularistic African traditional ideology, but by the *droit des hommes.* Aponte was literate, inquisitive, and, in fact, well-read, and there is clear evidence, not only that he knew what had happened in North America, France, and Haiti, but that he was also aware of the 1811 debates about slavery in the Spanish parliament.[16] Possibly he had been involved on the fringes of an anti-Spanish Masonic conspiracy in 1810, and—as Franco thinks—two years later he tried to win the support of certain white merchants for his own projects (whatever these may have been). Moreover, there are good indications that he or his associates may have been in contact with Gil Narcisco, a veteran of the Haitian revolutionary wars then detained in Havana's fortress Casa Blanca. Finally, and perhaps most compromisingly, Aponte was in possession of a small gallery of portraits of New World revolutionaries: Toussaint, Henri Christophe, Dessalines, Jean Francois, and—interestingly enough—George Washington (if Franco is to be trusted). In short, his case appears a particularly apt one to marshal in support of the "from rebellion to revolution" thesis.

And, indeed, most historians have been quick to assimilate him, if not to the typological slot of a Cuban Toussaint-Louverture, at least into that of a Nat Turner or Boukman—leaders of what was once fashionable to call *primary resistance movements.* To mention just a few egregious examples, Philip Foner (1962), not only credits Aponte with having established a "Central Revolutionary Junta (1:92), but also alleges (on the grounds of anything *but* documentary evidence) that he "was strongly influenced by the example of Moses who had led his people out of bondage, and . . . saw himself in the same role for his enslaved brethren in nineteenth century Cuba" (91)—a judgment repeated almost verbatim by Hugh Thomas (1971, 90). More recently, Robert Paquette (1988, 75) has called Aponte's a "conspiracy with revolutionary potential" and illustrative of "new patterns of resistance." Such new forms of counterhegemonic activity, in Paquette's view, no longer "aspired to restore a traditional and hierarchical African or modified-African society in an American setting" but "indicate pollenization from the 'Age of Democratic Revolutions.' " Somewhat more judiciously, Louis Pérez (1988, 99) contrasts Aponte's conspiracy with "common and frequent . . . uprisings born of local grievances, confined to a single estate." While these were "usually brief but violent affairs characterized by widespread destruction of property, the killing of whites, and the subsequent execution of slaves," Aponte's case belongs in a different category of insurrectionary activity: one that "involved planning, coordination, and collaboration among slaves, free people of color, and whites." "Uprisings of this type," Pérez tells us, "were the most feared" because they were "possessed of ideological content and political purpose," whereas—one presumes—the senseless threshing about of mistreated slaves or the depredations on the plantation sector of maroons who "possessed neither the overall unity nor the inclination to end slavery per se" (Paquette 1988, 75) are more properly relegated to what some of us think is the domain of the "prepolitical."[17]

To be sure, there are a few details that do not quite fit the image of Aponte as a man consciously putting his shoulder to the wheel of world-historical dialectics. Somewhat astonishing—although certainly not refutable—is, for example, Franco's undocumented claim that Aponte was of *lucumí* descent (a term scholars have long taken to refer to Yoruba-speaking Africans in Cuba).[18] In a similarly casual fashion, Franco alleges that Aponte carved, not only Catholic images, but African statuary as well. Once more, of course, we are in the realm of sheer conjecture. Yet, even if we granted credence to Franco's—undocumented but by no means unrealistic—assertions, we might equally take them to refer to the entirely rational business decisions of a craftsman aware of the demand structure of the market for wood carvings in early-nineteenth-century Havana. Franco, however, takes the matter quite a step further.

For, if we are to believe his rendering of the events of 1812, there was something about Aponte that diverges rather sharply from the conventional view of the black artisanry growing in the economic interstices of urban slaveholding societies across the Americas. As Franco tells us—again on the basis of anything *but* documentary evidence—Aponte, not just thought of himself as a lucumí (whatever that may have meant in early-nineteenth-century Cuba), but was also a priest of Changó, the imperial deity of Oyo whose cult, not only had traveled in the wake of this Yoruba polity's military expansion across large parts of Yorubaland and Dahomey, but seems to have taken root in the New World no later than the second half of the eighteenth century.[19]

There is some evidence to lend credibility to Franco's undocumented assertion that Aponte's home and workshop were situated close by, or may even have housed, the famous lucumí cabildo de Santa Barbara or Changó Teddún.[20] We also know that raids on the homes of at least two close associates of Aponte's, Clemente Chacón and Salvador Ternero, produced artifacts indicative of African religious practices. Ternero, in fact, appears to have held the position of capataz (headman) of a cabildo of a group designating itself as Mina Guagüí since 1797 (Guanche 1983, 256). While this may throw light on the nature of the secret meetings that had led to Ternero's initial arrest (they may have been accessible only to other Mina Guagüí and could have included rites of an esoteric nature), Chacón's possessions included a box-like receptacle painted red and containing various objects of ostensibly nonexplicable function and import (Franco 1974, 179). For anyone acquainted with the material culture and symbolism of modern-day Afro-Cuban religion—which Franco certainly was—it would have been tempting to interpret this peculiar detail in the light of contemporary ethnography as a precursor to the so-called *batea de Changó*, a sacred wooden vessel containing the *otanes* (stones objectifying the deity) and *herramientas*, that is, "tools" metaphorically articulating the power of the oricha Changó, to whose presence the color red likewise would allude. Contrary to what Franco's account insinuates, however, all this remains sheer conjecture. Nevertheless, that Aponte himself had copied several royal edicts (*cedulas*) pertaining to religious brotherhoods and confraternities and repeatedly chose to claim for himself the title *deputy of the Virgen of Remedios* who counseled his associates to produce flags designed to invoke her intercession in their lives does not quite add fuel to a strictly rationalist interpretation either.[21]

The same degree of indeterminacy surrounds another mysterious detail appearing to link Aponte to still another nascent Afro-Cuban religious culture: with 150 years' hindsight, Franco interpreted certain signs appearing in the papers secured at the homes of Chacón and Aponte as *firmas* or *anaforuana*, that is, as the signatures of *plazas* or titleholders of *abakuá*, a male sodality modeled after a Cross River–type of secret society known as *ekpe* or *ngbe* and initially associated in Cuba with groups of Africans who designated their identity as *carabalí*.[22] Once more, Franco's interpretation seems somewhat suspect since both twentieth century oral tradition and the three most important historical sources on that subject, Trujillo y Monagas (1882), Roche Monteagudo (1925), and Cabrera (1958), concur in dating the emergence of abakuá in Cuba to the year 1834 or 1836. Nevertheless, as Deschamps Chapeaux's (1964) brief but fascinating article about the first documented clash between abakuá and the Cuban authorities in 1839 shows (and I will return to this case), one of Aponte's fellow conspirators, Pilar Borrego, who had been condemned to exile in Puerto Rico in 1812, found himself before the dock again in 1839. This time, Borrego was indicted with complicity in the unlawful reunions of an abakuá *potencia* led by Margarito Blanco, "el Ocongo de Ultán," and was eventually sent to a final exile in Spain. Conceivably, Aponte could have been in contact with members of carabalí cabildos in which the *nsibidi* script proper to ekpe had been in use before being harnessed to the reconstruction of the institution itself.[23] Yet, once more, we simply do not know enough about these matters to concur with Franco's rather flamboyant elaborations on the theme of Aponte's African connections.

Reasonable as some of Franco's speculations may appear, however, they are certainly not serendipitous. For Aponte's putative African background performs crucial work for a particular form of argumentation that champions what one might call an *internationalist* solution. Franco and a number of other Cuban historians have, thus, long insisted on a sort of practical alignment between traditional African and enlightened revolutionary thought as determinative of Aponte's counterhegemonic project. In this perspective—which to some extent parallels the Haitian "noiriste" interpretation of such figures as Boukman or Hyacinthe—Aponte winds up somewhere between the Hobsbawmian "primitive rebel" and the consciously anti-imperialist national liberator: steeped though he was in traditional African culture, Franco (1974, 182) tells us, Aponte nevertheless attempted "the glorious undertaking of doing away with feudalist slaveholding society."[24] Why this would have been so (indeed needs to be so within the genre conventions of the kind of narrative in which Franco was placing Aponte) is spelled out even more explicitly by Franco's predecessor Elías Entralgo (1953, 25), who credits Aponte "with a mentality we might call geometric. He possessed an exact knowledge of the true intellectual and cultural situation of those who continued to suffer under slavery; and, in accordance with [this superior understanding], he used the most convenient and opportune arguments—who knows, perhaps the only possible ones—to capture the will . . . of those human beings whose life was a perennial spiritual asphyxiation." Here, we might say, Aponte experiences another historiographic incarnation as an "organic intellectual" turned revolutionary vanguardist. What Entralgo credits him with is not merely the crucial flash of insight into his own positioning within a larger hegemonic structure (*critical understanding of self*, Gramsci would have called it) and a keen grasp of the mystificatory nature of the symbolic order propagated by the ruling class. Rather, the role cut out for Aponte by these latter-day Cuban analysts demands another ingredient. What Entralgo seems to imply is that, in order to achieve his historical task of uniting what some (e.g., Castellanos and Castellanos 1988, 216–17; or Yacou 1993) think of as a "popular front," Aponte had to be conversant in more than just the discourse of the Age of Revolution. He also needed the capacity to critically engage the terms of what Gramsci (1971, 333) considered a form of discourse "inherited from the past and uncritically absorbed" by the subaltern in everyday life. In Gramsci's conception, this is a rather crucial body of knowledge and communicative practices. For, even though it "holds together a social group," it stabilizes, at one and the same time, "a situation in which the contradictory state of consciousness does not permit any action, any decision, or any choice, and produces a condition of moral and political apathy." Since the enslaved constituency in question in Aponte's case cannot be presumed to have undergone the disillusionary rites of passage attendant on proletarianization (but see

Mintz 1978), this discourse, it would seem, must be none other than that of African tradition—mystificatory, and ultimately regressive, to be sure, but a powerful weapon in the hands of an agitator who can wield it both with credibility and with a transcendent objective in mind. Hence, to capture the will of the masses and force them to the point where their dehumanized, self-alienated state becomes a condition of its own conscious *Aufhebung,* Aponte the vanguardist must achieve the feat of speaking to the global future in a language pertaining to an African past. What we encounter here, in other words, is a Cuban version of what Guha (1983, 37), in the Indian context, calls the image of rebel leaders as "crafty men armed with all the tricks of the modern Indian politician out to solicit rural votes." By a rhetorical sleight of hand, Aponte has turned into Lenin's rationalist operator capable of speaking to the kulaks in a language of the past to usher in a future that we (unlike him or them) already know.[25]

Here then, do we have Aponte's task and consciousness delineated for him by his latter-day ventriloquists: as both Foner and Franco would seem to imply—and as Entralgo spells out—we need (want?) an individual who straddles the divide laid out by Genovese's dichotomy. Not only must our man in Havana master the (necessarily particularistic) discourse of the masses of African slaves whom he is to unite into a "historic bloc." He must perform at least four other tasks as well: reconcile them with each other (torn as they still are, at the time, by African-derived ethnic ideologies); make them bridge the gap between enslaved and free Afro-Cubans; unite them with disgruntled sectors of a racially defined ruling class; and get all of them to feel that they are risking their lives for the common good of humanity. Not a small chore. Fanon (1968), for one, extensively agonized over precisely these issues both in his reflections on the consciousness-raising (in fact modernizing) force of violence and in his no less troubled ruminations about the place of tradition in the making of postcolonial national cultures. And, just as Fanon's conclusions seem rather hopelessly part of a period piece when viewed in the light of the African political realities that Achille Mbembe (1992) has sarcastically subsumed under the label of *the postcolony,* so may we be inclined to think that Aponte functions more effectively in his latter-day recensions than he ever did in life.

I am once more deliberately overdrawing my case. Yet I do so in order to illustrate a rather simple point. For, apart from the tendencies toward rather casually teleological interpretations evident from the quotations given above, one fundamental and really quite astonishing flaw in virtually all treatments of "Aponte's conspiracy" is the equally casual neglect of the central part of the documentary record. Remember that, during three out of the four sessions of the inquest, Aponte was not so much asked about his involvement in the putative conspiracy as ordered to explain the meaning of his *pinturas*. Why then not talk about precisely that? If uncovering the subaltern voice is the historian's business, why have Aponte's latter-day interrogators exhibited such reticence to face precisely that part of the record where we do, indeed, seem to hear his voice? Is the problem to be located in Spivak's (1988a) apodictive pronouncement that the subaltern simply cannot speak through the pages we write? Or does it not rather lie in an unwillingness on our part to face the implications of their expressive agency once they do take the floor, as it were? As I would suggest, this strange silence on the part of Aponte's latter-day interpreters is not accidental. Just as the exuberant indeterminacy produced by his exegesis on his own images appears to have left his original interrogators little choice other than to execute him irrespective of conclusive proof, so have we been keen on performing similarly evasive maneuvers, thereby unwittingly privileging the manufactured certainties propagated by Aponte's killers over the ambiguities, ruptures, and seeming aporia of his own account.

All irony aside, the historiographic situation appears to bear a rather tragic affinity to Graham Greene's novel the title of which I borrowed for this section. In Greene's novel, secret agents keen on discovering military installations in revolutionary Cuba wishfully mistake the financially desperate expatriate appliance salesman Mr. Wormold's hokey drawings of vacuum cleaners for what they all along knew they would invariably depict: Soviet superweapons. In our case, it seems, we are only too keen on performing similar maneuvers on evidence that we simply do not understand but are only too eager to assimilate to what we knew all along should have been Aponte's goal. To phrase the matter once more in Guha's (1983) terms, the result is that Aponte has remained trapped in a tertiary discourse—a register of historiography that not only unwittingly reproduces the categorial apparatus of the prose of counterinsurgency by mere inversion but cannot accommodate—in fact needs to obscure and thereby invariably trivializes—the complexities of the consciousness of those historical actors whom it assimilates to its enlightened narrative of progressive liberation, a narrative that takes the shape of a passage from tradition to modernity, passion to reason, belief to knowledge, rebellion to revolution.

In what follows, I will not attempt to—indeed cannot—redress this balance. Although I will venture interpretations of selected parts of the documentary record, it would be preposterous to advance the claim to be able somehow to reconstitute the content and moral acuity of the vision of his world Aponte committed to a set of images that will forever elude our gaze. This is in part a methodological issue, although it would certainly be trite to elaborate on what truth criteria we might want to apply to a text whose author hovered on the verge of death and whose visual referent has irretrievably disappeared (see Chakrabarty 1988). Beyond that, however, I think that attempts to "pin down" Aponte—much like an exotic butterfly among less ostensibly anomalous representatives of a common species—are deeply misguided precisely because of (and not despite) their endeavors at artificially reconciling what in fact should never have been seen in dichotomous terms. To my idea, the unredeemed promise Aponte's case holds for us concerns the fundamental and unresolvable complexity, not just of his thought, but of the world on which he reflected—a world that produced the record we now have before us. For what the documents reveal to us is what Kaplan and Kelley (1994) call a form of *transcourse:* a record of struggles over the "extension, contradiction, and transformations" of meaning between forms of signification that become constitutive of each other and mesh into an irreducible field of social and semantic relations, even as the signifying agents themselves engage each other in struggles over life and death.

In essence, then, the problems we face in Aponte's case are little different from those posed by a revisitation of the pockets of the dead Haitian rebel briefly discussed in the previous chapter. What if such a pocket contained French pamphlets and African-derived ritual objects at one and the same time? Or, to phrase the question in even more disturbing terms, what if, in fact, they contained *only one of the two,* and we would simply have to infer the other from the structural position occupied by the man into whose pockets, so to speak, we were looking? And would we even want to try and do so? Might not our positing of precisely such clear-cut "antecedents" to the making of the evidentiary situation in front of us violate, rather than clarify, the historical subjectivity of those whose brutal deaths represent a precondition to our knowing them? Would not our willful inscriptions of their thought and action into the interpretative frameworks provided by constructions of African tradition or European intellectual history (the contrast itself is repugnant) represent an ultimate gesture of forgetting what it was they may have died for? The pages of Aponte's book—an intellectual pocket if you will—may well remain forever closed to our inquiring gaze. Yet this may be precisely the point of an endeavor of trying to reread the document that he and the licenciado Nerey coauthored in the spring of 1812. For the impossibility of unambiguously reinscribing Aponte's knowledge and imagination forces us to engage the record in a way that precludes preempting the historical subjectivity of its producer by totalizing retrospective inferences about what "type of history" was being made—or aborted—during those days in late March 1812.

As should be clear by now, the problem really is not whether we are "in fact" facing images of vacuum cleaners or superweapons. To be frank, what intrigues me about the copious record of Aponte's inquest is precisely that, despite its length and detailed nature, it nevertheless leaves us with little more than intimations of a past violently lost. Nothing else but the certainty of this loss is factual about it—at least not in the conventional sense of the kind of certitude achievable by the discourse of evidentiary historical reconstruction. And the documents of his case virtually appear to bristle against being rationalized—"disciplined" if you will—in this way. In reading the record produced by Aponte's eventual killers, one feels relegated to an uncannily dream-like form of knowledge production, a type of inquiry where one can reenvision, but never know, the images to which Aponte's voice spoke and that his interrogators worried over—in that curious *elsewhere* of Europe, to use Taussig's (1997, 4) handy phrase, that was Havana in the early nineteenth century.

Aponte's historical as well as artistic subjectivity are clearly beyond reconstitution from the archive recording his protracted personal annihilation. There is no way in which we could construe from it an impression of transparency that would—in the words so familiar to historians—render the phrase *a window into* Aponte's world fully credible. Aponte and his libro de pinturas are irredeemably gone. Yet the remnants of the strange dialogue in which he and the licenciado Nerey engaged during those four days in March 1812 do afford an indirect, shadowy glimpse of the *contours,* and perhaps even the *conditions of production,* of a body of "disqualified" knowledge and discursivity. For, whatever else it may be taken as evidence of, it is the unwitting document of a disturbance, not just of the normalcy of the political, but—more important, perhaps—of the symbolic order on which the power of Aponte's executioners rested and that they reaffirmed by liquidating (or, in the morally more acute language of modern-day Latin American state terrorism, "disappearing") him along with his book. Part of this gesture of affirmation by violence was the creation of a record that involves us—if we engage it at all—in an almost hallucinatory mission to recover a history that never was and whose creator was killed in the act of its enunciation. For, as I will argue, Aponte speaks to us first and foremost as a self-appointed historian of a past that is, in the true sense of the word, a *vision:* a record of histories rendered impossible, unreal, fictitious, and fantastic by the obliterating agency of a regime of truth that, in a perverse but consistent gesture, preserved the excess of its own operation. What we face in reading the record of Aponte's inquest is the documentary shadow, although certainly not the living memory, of what may once have been imaginable and in reach of expression for someone who was both an intentional agent in and an eventual victim of those processes of global modernization that arguably had begun to radiate outward from the Caribbean long before Aponte was even born.

To paraphrase Gilroy (1992), Aponte's may well be a counterdiscourse of modernity—a rumor, if you will, disrupting the work of the moral artifacts structuring the world into which he found himself cast by forces beyond his control but also profoundly disturbing of those "powerful rumors" that historians have spread around him and his historical personhood. If his interrogation brought such rumors into the open, his death and the likely destruction of his work were but a consequence of the need to silence versions of history that might have been possible to envision yet could not be tolerated in the world in which Aponte lived—indeed seem strangely intolerable to this day. And this—why this was and is so—I think we can speak about.

A CONSPIRACY OF IMAGES: "EL JÚBILO DE APONTE" AND OTHER HIEROGLYPHS

What then was it that set in motion the deadly semiotic machinery to which Aponte was to fall victim in the spring of 1812? Let us begin by observing its operation in the context of the interrogations of the prisoners at the fortress San Carlos de la Cabaña. On the morning of March 26, Nerey confronted the forty-four-year-old former shoemaker turned innkeeper Clemente Chacón with Aponte's libro de pinturas and other materials found in the latter's home. Nerey was taking a pragmatic line: could Chacón, deeply implicated in the conspiracy as he was, give clues to what the investigators at this point believed was a strangely encoded plan of action? Did not the book include meticulously painted charts of the city and its fortifications? And did it not contain images of the most seditious implications? They opened the book and flipped through its pages until they reached the "first of those [pictures] where two armies are depicted in martial action and firing on each other with some blacks mingled in on the right side; and where, on the leaf adjacent to the right, one notices soldiers white and black, one [of the latter] on horseback with the head of one of the former [impaled] on the tip of a lance, and another Negro likewise [on horseback] who carries a severed head from which gushes blood, [and] who find themselves, here, in the situation of having defeated the whites" (Franco 1977, 113).[26] What did Chacón have to say about such images, and how would he explain the one in which "seven blacks were shown in the different costumes of general, monarch, cleric, one of them with sacerdotal clothing and another image of a woman with the insignia RI"? And what about yet another one showing a train of armed black soldiers leading a group of fettered whites? Who were these people, they asked him, and had Aponte—who, as Chacón had confessed, had shown him the book, if only briefly—explained what all this meant? Chacón remained sullen. He did not know what these images meant, Aponte had never shown him just these, or, if he had, he had not explained their content (Franco 1977, 113ff.).[27]

What Chacón did talk about was another set of images that he had seen in Aponte's home, although they were not of Aponte's making. What made these images even more interesting for Nerey and the other officials involved in the case was that, although Chacón had earlier volunteered information about them, a raid on Aponte's house failed to produce them. Aponte himself would later admit to having possessed them, but, in his very last statement on March 30 confessed that he burned them some time ago when he had heard that these engravings (for this is what they were) were on the index for prohibited print materials (Franco 1977, 174). And indeed, their presence in Aponte's house would have been powerfully incriminating evidence. One of these pictures was a portrait of Haiti's emperor Henri Christophe, one of a general "Salinas" (most likely Jean-Jacques Dessalines), one of Toussaint-Louverture (whose name Chacón's interrogators did not remember but who was identified later on by Aponte himself),[28] and a fourth portrait not mentioned in Chacón's interrogation that *may have* represented George Washington, the only white leader of an anticolonial and—at least vaguely—abolitionist insurrection in what may have been Aponte's private pantheon of New World heroes. All of them, Chacón added, Aponte had received from Santo Domingo. Even worse in this context, Chacón recalled that the portrait of Henri Christophe bore the subtitle *cúmplase lo mandato* (fulfill what is ordered).

Of another portrait bearing Aponte's name as inscription and included in the book next to the map of a city, Chacón had equally damaging things to say—if only, perhaps, in the hope of gaining credit by implicating Aponte. It was Aponte's self-portrait, Chacón told his eager interlocutors, and it was meant for people to understand that Aponte was an important personage who, once their projected revolution had succeeded, would be made king (Franco 1977, 114). But matters were rather more involved than Chacón wanted his interrogators to believe. If, as I would seriously doubt, Aponte had, in fact, intended to convey this meaning, he had buried it under a thick layer of allegorical symbolism.[29] Here is how Aponte himself eventually described these images found on pages 24 and 25 of his libro de pinturas:

> In these [pictures] the author of the book is represented with a laurel wreath of fidelity [and] a palm tree for victory in the semblance of a

pair of circles figuring at his breast—on the left-hand side one notices the carpenter's bench on which he fashioned the said book, showing whiteness and youth represented by the figure of a child tied to a column, and in the foreground the face of an old man signifying that the memory of youth goes with old age; one also sees on the bench an ink bottle, ruler, and tins of paint.

Now Aponte proceeded to explain the map, which, as it turned out, related more to his previous biography than to his future plans:

> Likewise on the right side [i.e., p. 25] there appear on the lower part two Indians sustaining the souls, [and then] the city of La Habana as seen from the entrance to Morro Castle in the year 1782 (which is noted above), when the deponent left for the invasion of New Providence, which is painted on the right side with its keys, directly among which are [seen] the ships transporting the companies of blacks that landed at eight in the morning and cleared about a league of the bush on the same key and [then] camped that night at the levee in front of the town until the next afternoon, when we passed the customs pier and set up camp in the Castillo del Fuerte . . . all of which resulted in the [enemy's] capitulation. (Franco 1977, 138–39)[30]

Quite obviously, in these images, Aponte proudly celebrated two cherished aspects of his identity: his role as artist and as soldier, depicted in what appears to have been a remarkable incongruity of styles. The somber allegories of man's fleeting existence transcended by the artist in the act of representation[31] contrast with the straightforwardly narrative rendering of the military exploits of the Batallón de Morenos Disciplinados during the 1782 campaign in which Aponte had participated as a young man. Symbolic elements like the laurel wreath, palm tree, compass, and circle give way on page 25 to cartographic devices, such as numbers distributed across the image of New Providence to indicate buildings or landmarks, and the depiction of scenes and figures. The latter, just as Aponte's explanation of the rendering of a hanged man, are to be taken literally as references to historical events, or, rather, in this particular case, to experience and memory: according to Aponte, this scene depicted a black inhabitant of New Providence who had been sentenced to death for the attempted rape of a local black woman. It was a representation, not of an abstract principle or idea, but of a real person—someone whose ignominious death Aponte had witnessed or heard about.

Such historical elements turn up again and again in Aponte's book, and, from his description, it seems clear that they are intended to document Aponte's own claim to history, perhaps even—as we shall see—to what one would nowadays call *black history,* a collective history vindicating those of his "condition and class": on page 31, for example, we see King Carlos III in the act of laying his hand on the military hat of one of two black soldiers, whom Aponte identified as the Lieutenant Major (Teniente) Antonio de la Soledad and the Lieutenant (Sub Teniente) Ignacio Alvarado, citizens of Havana and officers in the black militia forces.[32] As Aponte explained, Soledad and Alvarado tried to take off their hats in deference to the king, but his majesty forced them to keep them on as a sign of appreciation of their personal and military worth. The next two pages (pp. 32 and 33) include among other personages Captain Juan José Ovando, the first black soldier to wear the cassock of the *milicias disciplinadas* in 1701, and Aponte's grandfather Joaquín Aponte, the officer in charge of the black troops stationed at the fortress of Marianao during the English siege of Havana in 1762. Aponte Senior, who had been decorated for his participation in the Spanish capture of New Orleans under General O'Reilly, is depicted with his sword raised in commanding a tattoo.

Joaquín Aponte appears in another, even more richly elaborated context on pages 18 and 19, which his grandson explained as follows:

> On the left side figures of the god of the winds in front of the entrance to the castillo de Cabañas, [the name of] which is found inscribed below with the sugar mill of Don Gonzalo de Herrera and the tower of the Mariel fortress [and] the Tablas pier figuring in the lower part [of the picture], the sugar mill of Don José María Escobar Callo . . . and a few fishing boats further to the right. The goddess Velona [i.e., the Roman deity of war] in her wagon drawn by two horses indicating the . . . to the battle fought by Captain Joaquín de Aponte, grandfather of the deponent, at the Tower of Marianao against six hundred men and one English battalion who landed there and were all taken prisoners except for the [commanding] lord, who died and is depicted in such condition with appropriate uniform near the bottom of the

> tower, above which is [seen] a frigate that transported them to this spot. Next to the tower and surrounding the dead [commander] are some black soldiers who did violence to him and another one on horseback, who represents the Lieutenant Major Ermengildo de la Luz. Further to the right above some embankments are depicted the Lieutenant José Antonio Escobar and the rest of the black company in the act of leading a number of white prisoners who were those [of] the English who had entered the city at six in the morning and had been brought [hither] by Nicolás Aponte, the son of his grandfather [i.e., Aponte's paternal uncle], who is also shown on horseback near a flag in the paw of a lion the larger part of whose body is hidden in a cavity (Franco 1977, 133–34).[33]

As with the image of the invasion of New Providence, it seems as if we are dealing with a naive and straightforward form of commemorative pictorial representation, comparable perhaps to the popular frescos adorning several public buildings in late-eighteenth- and early-nineteenth-century Havana and proliferating in the rapidly growing barrios extramuros.[34] Yet, after introducing, with the Spanish lion, the first symbolic element, Aponte suddenly switches from a mere narration of the picture's scenic and narrative content to an exegesis of its imagery. He begins with an unfortunately corrupt statement about the meaning of the flags carried by the black militiamen and then continues with the following explication of what he calls *el júbilo de Capn. Aponte:*

> The jubilee of Captain Aponte [directed] to God [and] the King [is] represented by the lion with the flag or the fatherland, which is pictured as an Indian woman [held] in the arms of four other Indians, another woman with two drums, and another [drum?] turned around to face Mairel [Mariel?], which is how this Indian used to be called. The jubilee of Aponte, he [i.e., the younger Aponte] continues to say, is signified in a mute metaphoric *décima* [*décima muda metafora*][35] that should have figured in the upper white [space] that has ten lines drawn out in pencil [but never was inscribed there]; it is shown by the tree blooming forth with flames, painted below in the midst of water. . . . From Aponte love burns upward in live flames to God, the King, and the fatherland. Hidden from your sight by dense smoke, his ardor bursts forth from the waters [like] a strong wall [that] breathes flames.

> The painting that follows above with the moon at its farthest point concludes the tree's allusion with the coat of arms of the city of Havana and an eagle above another tree adorning the configuration. (Franco 1977, 133ff.)[36]

Here, *history* in its conventional post-Enlightenment sense merges with an almost mystical allegoricism, reminiscent in its vividly dramatic imagery of Spanish Counter Reformation baroque while at the same time formally indebted to another popular Cuban tradition: that of the *jeroglíficos,* series of allegorical depictions of the exploits and achievements of deceased members of the elite. In Cuba, such "hieroglyphs," typically bearing inscriptions in verse,[37] were commissioned from largely anonymous (and usually black) artists for obsequies and memorial services and either distributed in the form of printed cards (*tarjetas*) or affixed as large paintings to the walls of a church. Given the fact that Aponte must have been familiar with the formal and stylistic properties of this genre,[38] it may well be that the jeroglíficos represent one source of cultural forms on which he drew in composing this unfinished homage to an important (perhaps apical) ancestor of his own. If emblematic art had come to serve the purposes of linking the temporal memory of deceased members of the mundane elite to eternal principles, why should that same mechanism not be set to work for a man who, in Aponte's eyes, deserved such praises irrespective of the incongruence between his humble social status and his historically transcendent achievement?

We get here a first indication of what Raymond Williams might have called the *mode of practice* informing the production of Aponte's libro de pinturas as an individual, maybe even highly idiosyncratic, project."[39] As the following examples show even more clearly, Aponte does not simply borrow a foreign cultural form in order to replicate its conventional symbolic functions. On the one hand, he appropriates such allogenic cultural material by harnessing the means provided by a representational genre monopolized (although not produced) by the white Cuban elite to the end of celebrating the virtues of an ancestor who—as a mere black militia officer in an increasingly racist society—was destined to social oblivion, regardless of whatever services he had rendered to God or country. Yet, on the other hand, Aponte also expropriates and transforms this colonial form of European mortuary praise along with its (presumably stock-in-trade) emblematic conventions[40] by recontextualizing it in ways that defy the canon of artistic production from which he has drawn. Aponte's description of the *júbilo* of his grandfather, thus, allows the identification of elements of several well-known European iconographic traditions: the Indian female as a motive common to Continental allegory since the sixteenth century; the tree of flames (or perhaps the burning bush) proper to the iconology of Counter Reformation spirituality; the blazing ardor of selfless patriotic love deriving from seventeenth-century emblematic conventions; the lion, tree, and eagle pertaining to aristocratic heraldry; and, finally, moon and water suggesting a darker, perhaps hermetic, sort of mysticism. Once judged from the perspective of European iconology, however, these elements appear fragmented and reassembled in an uneasy juxtaposition, thrown together, as it were, in a manner alien to their contexts of origin and, therefore, damaging to their original symbolic purpose.[41]

And, as Aponte, unbothered by inconsistencies that so confuse his interlocutors (always on the lookout for literal or thinly veiled references to the conspiracy), explains image after image, we are taken on a virtual juggernaut ride through the storehouse of Western iconography and intellectual history:[42]

> Quite fittingly, the book opens with a rendering of what may be taken to represent Aponte's version of a myth of origin with which he, like many other creole Afro-Cubans conversant in the religious idiom of the dominant society, was thoroughly familiar: pages 1–3 detail the biblical Genesis from the creation of the world to the Fall and the expulsion of the primordial couple ("nuestros primeros padres"), but, already on pages 4 and 5, we encounter heterogeneous material: the day pertaining to these images, Aponte explains, is Monday and their ruling sign Scorpio, which he meant to indicate by depicting "a wagon drawn by women who represent day and night."[43] We also see a column marked with the number 18, signifying the midway point in the waters of the Nile at the city of Cairo, which is depicted on the left side of the image, with the waters of the moon held by the sluice gates of a place called Catajipa (Carthage?) figuring on the right. Pages 6 and 7 show the planet Mars, whose influence, Aponte explains, relates to war. We further see the emperor Claudius, "also called Prester

John,"[44] wearing boots made from lion paws, as well as a group of black soldiers referred to as "los cavalleros de San Antonio"[45] and described as inhabitants of Ethiopia ("naturales de Avicinia"). They are embroiled in a pitched battle against the Portuguese, who "discovered or conquered the indicated part of the globe"[46] but are now seen "overpowered and destroyed by the fire."[47] Pages 8 and 9 show the planet Mercury in the sign of Gemini on a cart drawn by two milans and whose influence—as Aponte has indicated by a caduceus—pertains to the achievements of trade. On the left side, Aponte continues, one sees Spring personified and the counsel and force of Trade itself. The sentry of Trade, who tries to impede Contraband, meets his death and fails to stop the latter. In the nearby carthouse, we see a portrait of Godoy, who, Aponte said, had, at the time he composed the book, reached the zenith of his political career.[48] Then there are a number of ships lying at anchor in the bay of Havana, the geographic features of the bay being depicted in realistic detail. Yet—at least this is what Aponte explains to Nerey and his scribe—at the entrance of the port personifications of Avarice and Death are seen jumping on land from a launch sent by the first ship to enter the harbor. Nerey, at this point, obviously disagrees with Aponte's explanation. Why is it, he asks, that the personification of Death carries the caduceus in his hand? Aponte's rather curt answer may betray a lie or, possibly, an indirection. Death destroys only Avarice, he retorts, thus ostensibly exempting Trade, but perhaps obliquely commenting on the moral legitimacy of a regime of bureaucrats serving the interests of sugar planters ("señores de ingenio") and their purveyors of human chattel. Aponte obviously could not have had a clear idea of the quantitative dimensions of the slave trade to Cuba. Yet, one might add with hindsight, the fact that more than sixty-three hundred African slaves entered Havana's harbor in 1811 alone—an average of more than five hundred a month—(Marrero 1971–88, 9:35) may have helped shape his opinion on such matters.

Quite obviously, Aponte had developed a visual idiom of his own; a pictorial language that, while apparently deriving its vocabulary, so to speak, from European sources, neither replicated the syntax of the artistic conventions on which it drew nor reproduced the semantic categories that such conventions served to affirm in their contexts of origin.[49] As Henry Louis Gates (1988, 128) suggests apropos eighteenth-century definitions of a culture of letters, the literary productions of ex-slaves may be read as texts that represent distinctly "impolite" forms of learning. Rather than exemplifying derivative forms of European textual practice, in Gates's view, early black writings constitute themselves, not just within, but against a culture of lettered domination. In his perspective, such writings are first and foremost testimony to experiences of dehumanization and projects of counteractive defilement of the logos that rationalizes the transformation of human beings into things. Whatever else early American slave narratives express, for Gates they represent deeply interested manipulations of alien discourses that rail "against the arbitrary and inhumane learning which masters foisted upon slaves to reinforce a perverse fiction of the 'natural' order of things." Yet does not the same seem to hold true for Aponte's pictorial project? Rather than facing a tertiary replication of colonial recensions of metropolitan Spanish learning—a move "within" a preexisting visual / discursive language (in itself rich with polyvalent sedimentations)—what we encounter in his pinturas likewise appears to have circumscribed a project deeply subversive of the conventions on which he drew.

Aponte's book constituted, we might say, a case of "polite art" mimetically refracted so as to constitute a semiferal system of colonial signification. To explicate this somewhat odd but contextually fitting analogy, what we seem to face is a case of symbolic forms that escaped control and ran away—much like the hogs and cattle imported by the earliest Spanish colonists in the Caribbean—to a future of prolific reproduction, crossing the boundaries of carefully crafted breeds in deliberate translations from one realm of experience to another, and building up semiotic descent lines of their own: genealogies of disruption that ambiguate what Bhabha (1984, 96) calls the *rules of recognition* by which discourses of domination "articulate the signs of cultural difference and re-implicate them within the deferential relations of colonial power." Pocock's (1988, 20; emphasis added) remarks about the deflection and perversion of authorial master languages by the response of the recipient of unsolicited communications (Pocock calls it *verbal rape*) are aposite here: *traduttore traditore*, the "interpreter and *counterauthor* begins to 'read' the text, taking the words and speech acts it contains to himself and reiterating them in ways and contexts of his own selection, so that they become incorporated into speech acts of his own." The ability to bestow order by discourse, we might say, carries within itself the danger of its subversion. The translator of a language game from one experiential context to another may be, not just a surreptitious traitor, but a rebel intent on altering the rules of the game itself. Viewed thus, Aponte's book may well be taken as an attempt at turning, to speak once more with Bhabha (1984, 96), "the discursive conditions of dominance into the grounds for intervention." If so, however, and regardless of whether Aponte was or was not involved in any seditious project, what the records of the inquest disclose is not just Nerey's strained attempt to discover pictorial evidence of a conspiracy physically to overthrow the existing order. Rather, what the documents reveal is—to paraphrase James Fernandez (1982)—a drawn-out argument or, better yet, a conspiracy of images that exploded in the face of Aponte's interrogators with remarkable force.

"We began to study their pictures, read their books, and move near them to learn their secrets"

How, then, can we make sense of this kaleidoscopic swirl of images, this visual cyclone, that Aponte unleashed on the pages of his book?[50] And are we really in a better position to do so than his interrogators in 1812, desperately trying as they were to keep him from turning what they thought were signs of seditious intent into confusing symbols indicative of a disruption not so much of the factual order of domination as of its discursive conditions? It may be wise to pause here for a moment and consider some of the other evidence Nerey had before him. Where precisely, we should ask—and this time in accordance with Nerey—did Aponte derive the cultural stuff that went into his images? Through what channels did such material diffuse into the black barrios of La Habana? And what made him select—as he undoubtedly did—some such materials while discarding others as not germane to his expressive purposes, his experience, or, perhaps, some other referential system the semantic yardstick of which he applied to foreign representations in order to gauge their aptness for assimilation into his project? One set of his sources is relatively easy to identify. For, thanks to the activities of Capitán Juan de Dios de Hita and other policemen who repeatedly searched Aponte's house, we are in possession of at least a partial list of the contents of

Aponte's library. This list of books—"all of them old and used" (Franco 1977, 132)—consisted of the following titles: "descripción de Historia Natural"; "Arte Nebrija"; "Guía de Forasteros de la Isla de Cuba"; "Maravillas de la Ciudad de Roma"; "Estado Militar de España"; "Sucesos Memorables del Mundo"; "Historia del Conde Saxe"; "Formulario de escribir cartas"; "Catecismo de la Doctrina Cristiana"; "Vida del Sabio Hicsopo"; and "tomo tercero de D. Quijote" (Franco 1977, 132). During the interrogations, Aponte further mentioned the following books as having played some role or other in the composition of his own libro de pinturas: "un libro historico"; "Guía de forasteros de Roma" (ibid.: 149); "un libro de la historia general" (ibid.: 149); "el libro de la vida de San Antonio Abad" (ibid.: 149, 155); and "un librito de alabanzas a Maria SSma" (Franco 1977, 121, 149, 155, 158). Some of these books are relatively easy to identify (see the appendix), and it is quite clear that none of them was on the index of works prohibited for export to Spain's American possessions.[51] More interesting is the fact that some of these books cannot be presumed to have been in wide circulation in early-nineteenth-century Cuba. Thus, while the *Catecismo*, the *Librito de alabanzas*, as well as the Cuban *Gúia de Forasteros*, the *Estado Militar de España*, and the *Formulario de escribir cartas* must have been easy to come by, others such as the *Maravillas de Roma*,[52] the *Historia de Mauricio, conde del Saxe*, and, perhaps, also the *Descripción de Historia Natural*[53] and the *Arte Nebrija*[54] were all but common fare. Finally, the biography of Moritz, count of Saxony and Cervantes's *Don Quijote* are not books one would expect to be on the shelf of a black artisan in nineteenth-century Havana. Quite obviously, Aponte was an avid reader, and the heterogeneous and eclectic character of his "library" is perhaps better explained by the difficulties that a free black person in early-nineteenth-century Havana (by no means a center of learning) must have experienced in gaining access to printed material than by any predilection on his part.[55] To speak with Eric Wolf (1982a), Aponte's library, it seems, rather exemplifies a virtually accidental crosscut through the kind of "ecology of collective representations" produced by the emergence of an increasingly all-encompassing Atlantic modernity in a specific local scenario—whether we want to think of it as the Caribbean, early-nineteenth-century Havana, its barrio extramuro Pueblo Nuevo, or indeed, the bookshelves in Aponte's workshop.

Quite clearly, the printed resources that Aponte exploited had been washed into his hands, as it were, by the crosscurrents of much larger political-economic and cultural tides. But it was his agency that made him pick up such flotsam in a deliberate and selective fashion. Once more, Pocock's (1988, 15) remarks about the properties of political "languages" as "objects as well as instruments of consciousness" are apposite here. Although structurally positioned at the confluence of what Fredrik Barth (1984) calls heterogeneous *streams of tradition*—amidst "complex textures of language capable of saying different things and of favoring different ways of saying things," as Pocock (1988, 9) might characterize the situation—Aponte decidedly entered and engaged the complex symbolic universe of the Atlantic world emerging around him on his own terms. For not only the fact that he possessed books at all, and of such variegated nature at that, is surprising: his attitude to what must have been, for him, repositories of knowledge of an alien culture that he tried to master was quite extraordinary as well. To Aponte, these books were, first of all, sources: sources to be exploited, in a very literal, aggressive sense, for their contents. As he himself stated in the last round of questions on March 30, 1812, he literally took some of these books apart to derive from them precious images to be incorporated, at a future date, in his own work (Franco 1977, 171), and it is more than tempting to infer that he pursued reading, too, as a means to the end of gaining control over the representations of a culture to which people of his social standing were normally denied all but superficial access. By devouring every bit of accessible information about the inner workings of this alien culture with which he was daily confronted but to whose secrets he was socially barred, Aponte must have felt that he was closing in on mysteries that held a key to power. The kind of power, perhaps, that energized a society ruled by white men who surrounded themselves with images and printed words: *señores de ingenio*, wealthy *negreros*, priests, and government officials.[56]

Still, for Aponte the printed word or image itself held no intrinsic value or authority endowing it with the kind of sacred quality that such artifacts are often held to acquire in what Goody (1968) calls situations of "restricted literacy."[57] For Aponte, it seems, the medium was decidedly *not* the message. Nor did he elevate such representations as he came about in the printed sources floating through his hands above the realm of what we would call mere hearsay, *mere* rumor. In Aponte's understanding, both printed and oral media apparently were channels—languages, if you will—to be tapped for communications convertible into instruments of knowledge diagnostic, to repeat a point made earlier on, of what is *realistically conceivable,* rather than stamped as "factitious" within the regime of truth to which one finds oneself subjected (much like a slave would receive the stamp of his owner imprinted into his or her flesh). Several times Aponte explains the content or structure of images in his own book by references to what he has merely heard from what he considers relevant sources. His comments on the images numbered 36 and 37 illuminate this particular "economy of information" (Barth 1990). On these pages, he tells us, are depicted "the founding of Rome by its first king, Romulus: the Campo Martio with some victorious soldiers, at the city gates, the houses of the kings, the Colossus of Apollo, the gate of St. Paul, and the tomb of Caius Sextus. Thirty-seven begins with the second [page and] shows Pope Clement . . . with a cardinal and another friar of the Order of St. Benedict, both of them black, the first of them named Jacobo and the second without name and librarian of His Holiness" (Franco 1977, 149).[58]

At what time and for what reason, Nerey asks at this point, did these two black men become cardinal and librarian? He does not know, Aponte replies, for he has only heard and not read about it. Asked, in turn, with whom he had conversations pertaining to such matters, Aponte replies in a much more revealing fashion:

> There having come to this city from Spain a black man whose name he does not know, who possessed a book of general history and instructed him as to the two figures, which is why the deponent found himself composing this picture: [he further stated] that the one who is giving testimony here has read the book about the life of San Antonio the Abbot, where is to be found much that is figured in this picture: and the Foreigner's Guide to Rome, in which is given notice of the church that exists in the middle of the city named San Estéban de los Indianos[59] behind the Cathedral of Saint Peter, which is shown in the upper right part of the number being explained. (Franco 1977, 149)[60]

Nerey was still not satisfied. Why is it that Aponte does not know the name of this black Spaniard, and had he not, in an earlier interrogation, given more detailed information about all the black clerics depicted on page 37? Aponte appears annoyed by the interruption: then why do you not look at the protocol, he retorts. And, besides that, he (i.e., Aponte) has spoken with many people without ever knowing their names. And he proceeds to explain the image. We will skip a few passages and continue with his description of another grouping of clergymen:

> There follow on the right side of the same number 37 the Carmelite father Pereira [and] the Jesuit father Oviedo, who was the prior of the Latin language in Abyssinia. [It] continues with a painting of a cardinal who, with his officer in charge, is [seen] restraining the Jesuit fathers Illescas and Maceo because they were enemies of the Abyssinians. There follows a portal erected by Pope Pius IV and the Church of Santa María del Pueblo, at the entrance of which are [seen] three blacks in clerical robes. (Franco 1972, 151)[61]

Again, Nerey interrupts Aponte with a question that induces him to elaborate further on the channels of transmission of cultural materials into which he tapped in assembling his own visual discourse:

> Questioned for what reasons those [three blacks] were painted with such garments and whether such [black priests] were to be found in Rome, where he had said this church existed, he replied: that they had been depicted there because this was the proper place for priests; and that he is convinced that there exist priests of such [i.e., black] condition because of having heard the reverend fathers Fray Diego de Soto and Fray Rafael Miranda recount, on their return from Rome, that they had seen in a council in which they took part, a black man preaching in the basilica who had been brought there by the General of Abyssinia, who was also present on the occasion; whereas it should be noted that the deponent did not directly listen to the fathers de Soto and Miranda, but to others who conversed about what had been related by the former. (Franco 1977, 151)[62]

For Aponte, there was, of course, no way to corroborate the veracity of such thirdhand information. But it is more than likely that he felt no need, either: people in control of the sacred resources of an alien but familiar religion had been there and had seen it; others had personally heard them talk about it; he had overheard such conversations. Veracity was not the issue here. What counted was the significance—indeed, the moral plausibility and political import—of such communications. To revert again to Koselleck's (1985) somber remarks about the unspeakability of situations where "language is struck dumb" and where rationally unimaginable histories begin to express themselves through seemingly prediscursive genres of signification such as dreams, visions, or bodily experiences, we might say that Aponte's images excavated—visualized—precisely what the discourse on which he was encroaching systematically "muted." What we have here, then, is a case very different from those that Frank Salamone (1982) has in mind when he speaks of post-Conquest Andean writers as "chroniclers of the impossible"—self-consciously bicultural authors of accounts of events (the destruction of a moral universe) that *ought not* have happened. To invert Salamone's phrase, we might rather call Aponte's an *impossible chronicle.* What his book recorded was a narrative chronicling, not of productivity and performance as evidenced by an irreversible sequence of destructive events, but of moral potentiality. For Aponte, it seems, Minerva's owl spread her wings, not at dusk, but at the dawning of a *past* world, still perhaps only dimly beheld by himself. In revising the powerful rumors spread by a regime of truth that he seems to have both admired and deeply distrusted, Aponte authored a form of criticism the compass of which reversed the standard order of reliability and validity in the examination of historical sources. Speaking in terms of Marc Bloch's (1953, 55) famous analogy, we might say that what Aponte was after were, not "facts," but "tracks": signs of past events and situations that could be rendered visible and meaningful—much like the path of a particle within an electromagnetic field—only under certain descriptions. And it was on a methodology capable of generating such descriptions that Aponte seems to have been working when, in the spring of 1812, a train of incidents beyond his control brought him to the attention of the Cuban authorities.

Whether Aponte accepted de Soto's and Miranda's authority (and it seems that he did) is, therefore, another matter. What is important here is, first, that in both cases—book and oral report—Aponte insisted on what Wyatt MacGaffey (1972, 66) calls a *hermeneutical approach:* it was not so much their literal meaning that he was after as their deeper significance—moral, political, mystical—which had to be uncovered, perhaps even induced or created, by exegetical operations. The second point to take note of here is that Aponte, in turn, not only reproduced some of these bits and pieces of knowledge about what, for him, must have been an utterly exotic world from which power beyond fathom radiated outward to Cuba. Rather, such reproduction would, invariably, bear the stamp of his thought as the "counterauthor" of, or at least participant in, an incipient continuum of discourse. Whatever particles of stray information Aponte picked up, he was sure to digest them thoroughly, prying them loose from their contexts of origin, and submitting them to an alien form of semiosis so as to catalyze what, in fact, were new genres of representation and knowledge production. Let me emphasize this point once more. Whatever Aponte decided to include in his book would not simply reappear in unaltered form. Nor would the context that Aponte assigned to the allegorical representations he appropriated into what may have been his very own version of a *summa* preserve their original expressive functions. Something profoundly disruptive of the conventional linkages between signifier and signified occurred between the act of decoding and that of reencoding the European or colonial American representations that Aponte submitted to his *system*.

This much may seem common sense. After all, de Soto and Miranda cannot well be presumed to have intended to conjure up an image of Rome teeming with black clergy, even if they may, indeed, have discussed the curious fact of seeing an African preaching there. The question is, rather, why Aponte chose exactly that piece of information to render—in his peculiar mode of visual transformation—as a part of his book. Quite clearly, this problem is not exhausted by descriptively monitoring what happens if a "man of the people" begins to read.[63] What we would want to know is what Carlo Ginzburg (1992) has called the structure of the *cognitive filter* that Aponte inserted between himself and the texts and visual materials he perused. The reference to Ginzburg is not fortuitous here. For, in his justly acclaimed study *The Cheese and the Worms*, the Italian historian grapples with the methodological problems presented by the case of a historically no less obscure and similarly intellectually omnivorous "folk intellectual" in the sixteenth-century Friuli. Given that these problems closely correspond to those arising in the case at hand, a digression on Ginzburg's attempts to reconcile text and context may help us focus more clearly on what precisely Aponte's counterauthorial agency consisted in and why we should be careful not to inscribe it into some ready-made template of subaltern subjectivity and cultural orientation.

Ginzburg (1992) presents the case of Menocchio, a literate and highly inquisitive sixteenth-century northern Italian miller with a strong bent toward what Ginzburg's compatriot Antonio Gramsci might (if perhaps reluctantly) have called *counterhegemonic* theorizing. Chronicling Menocchio's sad career—he makes such a nuisance of himself that the Inquisition, reluctant though it initially appears, cannot help but kill the man—Ginzburg struggles hard to reconcile Menocchio's exuberantly idiosyncratic cognitive achievements with what he assumes are Menocchio's "roots" in an archaic "oral" and "almost unfathomable" reservoir "of remote peasant traditions" (xiii). Menocchio's heterodox conceptions of the cosmic order, his critical views of Catholic dogma and of the social and religious institutions of his time, Ginzburg tells us, must be perceived as the result of his "filtering" literate information through the interpretative frame of the "oral cultural tradition" of which he was part. "It was not the book as such," he concludes, "but the encounter between the printed page and oral culture that formed an explosive mixture in Menocchio's head" (51). "Printing enabled him to confront books with the oral tradition in which he had grown up and fed him the words to release the tangle of ideas and fantasies he had within him" (xxiv). This approach, at times, generates startling insights. But it is nevertheless astounding that a historian so versed in the social and cultural history of the peasant society of the sixteenth-century Friuli would choose to downplay the fact that its culture was all but uniform and homogeneous and that its *communicative orientation* (if we even want to deploy that term) was by no means pristinely oral. Ginzburg, of course, explores in remarkable detail the stunning complexity of the larger continuum of discourse within which Menocchio's relentless ranting must be situated. Yet, despite the obvious difference in the way in which the various strands of knowledge and discursive practice that interfaced in Menocchio's life and views were institutionally empowered, what Ginzburg seemingly chooses to neglect is the fundamental fact of their mutual imbrication. Ginzburg acknowledges along with Bakhtin the need to consider not just "cultural dichotomy . . . but also a circular, reciprocal influence between the cultures of the subordinate and ruling classes" (xvii). Yet he nevertheless insists on salvaging a conception of their autonomous existence.

This, however, is a deeply problematic move. For, as Lewis (1986) points out in a related context, on closer inspection the implicitly temporalizing—often explicitly teleological—distinctions between "little" (and by definition "oral") traditions and their "great," literate counterparts frequently turn out remarkably spurious insofar as their typological poles can be kept apart only by measures of rhetorical quarantine (see Barth 1989; Lambek 1993, 37–40; Amselle 1998, passim). Moreover, such distinctions are by no means neutral. Often enough, scholars have uncritically accepted the boundaries drawn by socially empowered orthodoxies intent on subjugating rival forms of knowledge and discursive practice. The result, in many cases, is that what appears as a folk tradition is in reality a congeries of divergent ideas and practices held together more by the discursive agency of an opposing elite than by any features inherent in these phenomena themselves. Lewis is concerned here with the sociology of *popular* and *elite* Islam in Africa. Yet his conclusions hold for Menocchio's case as well: just as there is, empirically speaking, no such thing as Islam proper against which local historical deviations could be assessed as pagan survivals, so were Menocchio's heterodoxical discursive productions inseparable from the historical social and ideological context of the elite traditions against which he ranted and within which they become recognizable as heretical.[64]

Peel's (1990, 339) methodological strictures with regard to studies of the interaction between local systems of religious knowledge and so-called world religions are useful here: It is epistemologically unsound, Peel argues, to assume that the effects of the encounter between them "can only be studied *after* we have got a clear picture of the two independent cultural systems" as previously isolated entities. For, in most cases, what we eventually come to know about "traditional religion" is reconstructed from the facts of "impassioned communication" between historical actors already engaging allogenic bodies of knowledge. The contrasts resulting from typological reconstructions, thus, not only impart artificial closure to "traditions" that should initially be approached as fuzzy sets of ideas and practices whose boundedness in social space needs to be established rather than presumed.[65] Rather, in privileging what

Anthony Wallace (1968, 26ff.) long ago called *the replication of uniformity* over *the organization of difference,* such contrasts also tend to preempt considerations of the need to qualify "views of cultures as collective phenomena, of symbols and meanings as public and shared, . . . by a view of knowledge as *distributed* and *controlled*" (Keesing 1987, 161).

If so, however, then, not only oral religious traditions, but religions of the book—perhaps bookish knowledge in general—should be empirically decomposed into what Sidney Mintz (1977) calls patterns of *local initiative* and *local response;* performances of "many mutations in many idioms and contexts, for which the text at times appears little else than the matrix or holding pattern" (Pocock 1988, 27). Coming from different angles, both Michel de Certeau (1984) and Brian Street (1987) have argued that the very constructs *orality* and *literacy* may be predicated on a notion of a nonambiguous, overdetermined universality of meaning (literalism) that betrays the agency of politically empowered communities of interpretation—be they historical religious orthodoxies or contemporary social scientists. This is not to deny the historical effect of what Anderson (1990) has somewhat sloppily designated as *print capitalism.* Still, should we not take into account that seemingly universal bookish knowledge, on a level of local social practice, becomes empirically available only as already implicated in an "indefinite plurality of the 'writings' produced by readings" (de Certeau 1984, 172)? Is writing any more immune to reading than telling is to the multifarious transformative effects of listening? On the contrary, as Lewis (1986, 154) points out, once we move away from artificially homogenized and implicitly evolutionary typological distinctions between local and global, popular and elite, oral and literate cultures, seemingly monolithic bodies of bookish knowledge such as Islam, Christian theology, or Western political theory turn into internally heterogeneous, contradiction-ridden, and fundamentally polyvalent packages "of written compendia that in their catholic [*sic*] profusion facilitate the diffusion and rediffusion of so-called pre-islamic survivals": "traditions" of disqualified knowledge that do not well up from "unfathomable layers" of the past but are entirely comtemporary with, often sociologically driven, and sometimes even produced by the process of confrontation itself (see Amselle 1998, 39ff.).[66]

To be sure, the cognitive filter that Menocchio inserted between himself and the texts he perused was real enough. But we stand little chance of approximating its structure if we content ourselves with the supposition that it must have been rooted in a timeless cultural past. In fact, the "pastful" appearance of certain cultural forms, Lewis suggests, is often a result of their marginalization with respect to elite values translated into a temporal idiom. And it is precisely in the light of this that one wonders why an artificially constructed ancient oral peasant culture eventually comes to stand in for a situation in which various heterogeneous streams of discourse can be imagined as articulating under specific historical—and historiographically traceable—conditions. In the end, perhaps, Ginzburg's oral peasant culture (however much aspects of it may truly be rooted in an ancient past) turns out something of an analytic artifact, a deus ex machina—surprisingly akin to Genovese's African rebels and creole revolutionaries (and their presumed cognitive orientations)—that allows Ginzburg to plead the representativity (and, therefore, social-historical relevance) of Menocchio's case. The problem here is not that such an archaic substratum does not exist. It is that we must start from the assumption that it is heterogeneous and polyvalent right from the start, that it represents little else than a historical clustering within a larger processual matrix of ongoing interaction between politically differently empowered forms of knowledge and discourse, and that the reduction of specific "discursive performances" (in Pocock's [1988] sense) to artificially isolated components of this matrix is both sociologically and historically misleading.

I will briefly return to this issue in discussing the question of Aponte's African connections (which arguably form the analogue to Menocchio's archaic oral peasant culture). Yet, if things were obviously rather more complicated in Menocchio's case, so they are in Aponte's—and not just because locating him within a single tradition is so patently absurd (as is, for that matter, placing him within an alienated vanguardist position). The whole notion of "tradition" and "culture" as something that could be delimitated in time and social space seems threatened by such intellectual nomads and poachers as Menocchio and Aponte. They seem to wander about in complex landscapes of ideas and images. They cross boundaries and invade foreign territory at will, and they return to their hideout laden with loot to be processed into expanding systems of signification more akin to Foucauldian genealogies than to the archives of the hegemonic institutions of their cultural and historical environments.

But let us close this lengthy methodological parenthesis and return to the case at hand. We will, perhaps, gain a clearer understanding of what kind of transformations Aponte wrought on the materials that he appropriated in his peculiar way—shaped as much by his *désir de savoir* as by socially determined limitations of access—by looking at yet another piece of evidence on Nerey's desk: an unbound folder wrapped in oilcloth and containing an amazing variety of images that Aponte had cut from books and other printed matter that, at one time or the other, had passed through his hands. Apart from depictions of heraldic signs of the Spanish nobility, there were engravings of European architecture, landscape, and sculpture; illustrations culled from geometry books and even surgical compendia; portraits of Henry IV, the king of Prussia, the tsar, Prince Charles of Austria, the emperor of Germany (one wonders about whom he is speaking) and his son depicted with Bonaparte; as well as other engravings of European nobility, some of which—like the portrait of the king of Prussia—he had colored in himself (Franco 1977, 171). Several of these images derived from books that Aponte had taken apart. Others, however, as his earlier statements make clear, he cut from fans painted in a fashionable, emblematic way.[67]

In a similar manner, Aponte, it seems, had pilfered the written sources that had passed through his hands, amassing vast quantities of heterogeneous information—*ex omnibus terris ac saeculis*—in a seemingly unsystematic but purposeful way. Then, in a second step, Aponte would fuse or synthesize such raw materials by incorporating them into the visual discourse of his libro de pinturas, thus deriving allegorical or narrative significance from what otherwise was an inchoate jumble of inert elements. For a moment, Aponte's interrogators seemed to have glimpsed some of the mechanisms underlying this kind of mental alchemy, although, in all fairness to Aponte, one must acknowledge that they thoroughly underestimated the extent of his learning.[68]

On page 44, Aponte explained, he had pictured a black king named Tarraco who invaded Tarragona and from whom that city derived its name. Below the image of Tarraco and his black armies, however, one sees another military expedition the standard of which reads "SANA-

GUERIN." This, Aponte said, was meant to show that it was the army of Senaqueril who was smitten by the angel ("derrotado por el angel"). Nerey seems puzzled by this explanation. How did Aponte know of the existence of such a King Tarraco who conquered Tarragona? he asks. Aponte replies that he had read it in the book of San Antonio Abad and in a "Historia universal." He further states that the yellow banners showing black lions and a cross carried by Tarraco's troops identify them as Abyssinians. In what appears to have been an attempt to shame Aponte for his misunderstanding of what Nerey thought was "history," the licenciado now asks "why he mixed the destruction of the army of Senaqueril with the invasion of Tarragona, [events] which had nothing to do with each other."[69] Aponte's seemingly contradictory response is purposively ambiguous. "Although these two events do not go together," he says, "he has nevertheless included that of Senaqueril *for reasons of history*, just like all the other [images] in the book: and [besides that] the two locations are divided by a wide sea, although it appears narrow in the image."[70]

Nerey and his scribe, of course, had no idea that Aponte's knowledge of certain aspects of their own culture exceeded theirs. For the mystery about the apparent temporal incongruity of the fall of Tarragona (to a black king about whom they apparently had never heard!) and the destruction of "Senaqueril's army" is easily resolved by a look at the Bible. A passage in 2 Kings 19 relates how the angel of the Lord smote the army of the Assyrian king "Sanherib" besieging Jerusalem with the plague. Yet it also tells of a black king named "Tirhaka" similarly involved in warfare against the Assyrians. The "Abyssinian connection" appears to derive, ultimately, from Herodotus 2.141, from where it may have filtered through to Pliny or other medieval geographers and, finally, to the "vida de San Antonio" that Aponte admitted to having perused: here, "Sanacheribos" is mentioned as an Assyrian king besieging Egypt, said to have formerly been under Ethiopian rule. In this version, bats gnaw away at the armor of Sanacheribos's troops under the cover of the night, thus rendering their weapons useless. Even "Tarragona" may make sense, for Strabo mentions that the Ethiopian king "Tearco" (Tarcus/Taracus/Taharqa) reached Europe (Snowden 1970, 119), which may have made sense to Aponte, who had read about San Antonio's mysterious removal from Ethiopia to Cataluña (Navarro 1760). However, he might also have known about Tarraco's (i.e., Tarragona's) historical association with

New Carthage, although he was probably unaware of the questions surrounding the "racial" identity of the Phoenicians.[71]

Quite obviously, what Aponte had done was to cross-reference heterogeneous information according to a logic of his own, an "Order of Things" that dissembled the categories and narratives of his interrogators' culture and rearranged their content in configurations they perceived as familiar and disturbing at one and the same time. Yet, even if Aponte had gotten it "all wrong," "mixed it all up," what did he mean by "por razón de Historia," and why is it that, in his exegesis, these elements of Western intellectual history acquire such a conspicuous tinge of "blackness"? Surely, given the degree of control over his sources demonstrated in the last example, we cannot concur with Nerey's assertion that Aponte simply scrambled history in an arbitrary fashion. Rather, what we are facing is the purposeful ambiguation and reinscription of historical narratives, and Nerey seems to have feared as much as well. Why, we should ask—and this time in agreement with Nerey, who obviously worried about these things quite a bit—why all these black saints, kings, bishops, and soldiers? Clearly, what disturbed Nerey was not Aponte's palpable "madness"—the images conjured up by his "heated and fatuous brain." It was the method at the back of it. The uncanny rigor of his procedure. The frightening implication of systematicity. Was *this* history for Aponte?

Any attempt to answer this question must perforce remain speculation. Still, it appears not at all unlikely that Aponte—in a rather realistic manner—perceived the things and personages he read about or saw depicted in the images that he cut from books, fans, and other sources as emblematic semblances or signatures of power. If so, we might argue that, by appropriating and transforming them in acts of both physical and symbolic violence, he authorized a systemic *adikos logos* that he—and maybe some of his associates—regarded as generative of powerful knowledge. Of course, we do not know the particulars of Aponte's ideas about power, authority, legitimacy, and related concepts. It is tempting here to follow Franco's path and short-circuit the obvious imprint that his pondering over such matters left on the pages of his book with modern ethnographic records about similar conceptions in certain West African societies—specifically, of course, the Yoruba. But, at the same time, I think that we would be well advised not to pursue this too far, and not just because the procedure itself is deeply anachronistic. Surely, Aponte *may* have felt that the titles of European aristocrats, the commissions of priests, bishops, and popes, and the semidivine status of Catholic saints and virgins were equivalent to, for example, the Yoruba concept of *oye*, circumscribing, as Peel (1979–80) has argued, the ability (conceived of as independent of the person of the titleholder) to mobilize resources, human or superhuman, in order to achieve morally desirable ends.[72] Yet, at the same time, Aponte may also have been familiar with European ideas of sacred kingship,[73] which, at least formally, still underlay the title of "His Catholic Majesty" Fernando VII, the king of Spain, dethroned though he was in French exile by 1812. Given his historical positioning within an ecology of representations of truly Atlantic scope, biblical as well as African ideas about divine intervention in human affairs, sacred commissions, moral valor, and political authority may have structured his reading of such images of monarchs, priests, and saints. And his mode of typification and contextualization of such received information may have been as much akin to that of Petrarch and Boccaccio, Pico and Ficino,[74] as to that of a Yoruba *babalawo* (divination priest) or even just the modern African popular artist raiding European forms and topoi with gusto and "a grand disregard for the conventions that sustain them" (Barber 1987, 36). And, even if we were to go along with Ginzburg in favoring a "traditional" solution, should we not acknowledge that African tradition—no less than European intellectual history—contains its polyvalences, heterologies, and "unofficial" (Barber 1987, 16) or "critical" (Apter 1992) registers?

In the end, all these reductionist solutions, viable though some of them may perhaps be, direct our attention away from what really was at stake here. Aponte may have been inspired to cut out and rearrange these representations of individuals pertaining to what Mary Helms (1988, 182ff.) identifies as the conceptual category of *power-filled strangers* for quite a number of reasons and according to quite a number of rules. To pin him down on any single cultural template is to entrap once over his historical subjectivity in the deterministic conceptual snares generated by the reductionism inherent in tertiary discourses. What we do know, however, is that—at least this is what Aponte chose to tell us—the intended addressee of his libro de pinturas, the one person with whom he wanted to share his insights, was the (then-exiled) king of Spain. It was to his Catholic majesty that he had ultimately intended to present the book through the mediation of the Capitán General and the Ayuntamiento of Havana. Why this was so, Aponte never really explained. When asked what he had expected to gain or achieve by doing so, he answered that he desired only such reward as his majesty would see fit to bestow on him (Franco 1977, 144). Nerey probably thought that Aponte had lied to conceal the true purpose of the book as a strangely encoded blueprint for insurrectionary action or simply wrote it off as the naive fancy of a free black suffering from delusions of grandeur. Yet, for us, this detail provides ground for a number of intriguing speculations: Why would Aponte choose to address the Spanish sovereign in order to, so to speak, cash in the "symbolic capital" that he had been accumulating for years? What—if indeed he had not lied—did he expect from such a transaction?

Had Aponte—conscious of *history* in the sense of the legitimacy or even power that the past can bestow on the present as he undoubtedly was—intended to recover by means of word and image the dignity and moral authority of which he and his fellow Afro-Cubans had been deprived? Their past had been obliterated by forces radiating outward from the faraway continent of Europe, forces shaping their very existence as black people in a society increasingly structured by racial slavery and impinging on their daily lives in the tangible form of legal as well as extralegal forms of social exclusion, exploitation, repression, and abuse. Although unleashed by what we now think of as the emergence of the modern capitalist world system, such forces and the contradictions that their impact engendered were experienced—by their perpetrators as well as by their victims—as concrete, sensual manifestations of power, whether in institutional, corporate, or personal guise. And it may well be that Aponte had reacted to such experiences by beginning to theorize about the nature and origins of such power: by appropriating representations likewise issuing from this *axis mundi* (whether conceived of as located in Madrid or Rome), might he not succeed in uncovering—in what would appear a strikingly modernistic move—similarly obliterated, perhaps even secret sources of power on which Europe drew but that, in fact, were originally African? There is no telling to what extent Aponte was aware of the foiled Napoleonic invasion of Egypt. Yet, although it is reasonably clear that he did not have access to the comte de Volney's

Voyage en Egypte et en Syrie (1787) and *Les Ruines* (1791), Baron Denon's *Voyage dans la Basse et la Haute Égypte* (1802), and the monumental *Description de l'Égypt* of the Commission des Sciences et Arts d'Égypt, the first volume of which appeared only in 1809 (what, one wonders, could he have achieved had only a couple of its volumes fallen in his hand?), Aponte undoubtedly partook of a long-standing European discursive tradition that located the source of superior knowledge in or beyond the African floodplains of the lower Nile.[75]

Had not King Solomon once invited the queen of Saba into his temple, just as black men were now seen preaching in the cathedrals of Rome?[76] Had not the black "caballeros de San Antonio" once vanquished the Portuguese? Had not King Tarraco come down from the Nubian hills to conquer Tarragona? Had not the people of Cataluña implored San Antonio to come to their aid?[77] And then the Seven Wonders of antiquity that Aponte depicted at various places throughout his book: were not the pyramids or the library of Alexandria situated on the African continent? And, closer to home, there was the black Virgen de Regla, patron of the bight of Havana, whom Aponte depicted in a truly extraordinary image.[78] Aponte shows her on a pedestal surrounded by the "caballeros" of San Antonio, Prince David,[79] Moses,[80] San Benito of Palermo, Jesus Christ, and the personifications of Faith and Justice—the former being crowned and defended by two blacks, the latter shown without arms "so as not to receive anything with them."[81] In the background, this time, were, not the fortifications of Havana, but Mount Ararat and the Ark, from which life had spread forth over the earth after the deluge. And, as if intended as a warning, the same image showed a congregation of black saints, one of them, San Felipe Martín, wielding a sword that he had received from the archangel Michael to decapitate a white king for the sin of blasphemy.[82] Was this not powerful knowledge?

Had Aponte perhaps targeted the Spanish sovereign as the recipient of such communications because he felt that knowledge as powerful as that which he had uncovered could be shared only with a person possessed, not only with the most exalted power, but also with a moral authority that transcended that of the abusive and morally corrupt Cuban elite? Had they not slighted the valor of his ancestors who had bravely fought for God and the fatherland? Had not the Cuban authorities unjustly terminated his own military career despite his loyal service at New Providence? Was it not obvious that—as he had shown in his libro de pinturas—Avarice and Death had descended on this island from ships lying at bay in the same harbor that the Virgin of Regla protected? And had not the Spanish Cortes—as Aponte and his associates, like many other blacks in Havana, knew—debated liberating the slaves and granting legal equality to the "gente de color"?

It is tempting here to see Aponte's project in the light of baroque theories of the moral power of images. José de Maraval (1986), thus, characterizes the baroque use of visual media as technologies of affective movement through sensual means ("resortes"). Calderón de la Barca succinctly expressed this moment when he asked whether the "mute rhetoric" and "noble deceipt" of "painted words" did not possess greater evocative powers than that of rhetorical suasion in "inciting affects" in the social world: "For even though one knows that a painting is only a linen stained with minerals and liquids, it induces one to believe . . . that the historical is made present, and the unimaginable made real in front of one's eyes" (cited in Curtius 1936, 92). There is a "phatic" moment in baroque representations that lends reality to the pintorial vision *in so far as* the image comes to serve as a mediating agent. For, in affecting the mind of the beholder and guiding him or her to act on the experience (*afecto* in Calderón's terminology) so engendered, the image itself realizes (rather than merely visualizing) the pictorial content (Bauer 1969; Stoichita 1995).[83] The patent convergence with the morally evocative functions of "traditional" African art forms should not go unnoticed here. For, to recur once more to Yoruba ethnography, Aponte's project arguably resonates just as much with baroque theories of artistic evocation as with the Yoruba genre of *oríkì*—a highly stylized, nonnarrative form of commemorative discourse that, as Barber (1991, 15) argues, functions as a

> principal means by which a living relationship with the past is daily apprehended and reconstituted in the present. They are not "history" in the sense of an overview or attempt to make sense of a sequence of events, but a way of experiencing the past by bringing it back to life. They represent the "past in the present" (cf. Peel 1984), a past which they have brought with them and which can be reopened and reacti-

> vated by their agency. But they also represent the "present in the past," for through all the stages of their transmission they do not lose their relationship of contemporaneity to the events they refer to.

Here, too, "the historical is made present, and the unimaginable made real." Just like the mute power of the *picta poiesis* crystallized truths beyond full narrative rationalization, so are oríkì performances only partly open to the "explanatory hinterland" (Barber 1991, 28) of what the Yoruba call *itan*—fully developed, often explicitly legitimatory narratives *about* the past. In both cases, we encounter "metahistorical" (White 1973) or "historiological" (Fabian 1996) conceptions that—regardless of their activation in linguistic or pictorial media—speak to a relation between past and present that is the ground, not merely on which strategies of identification, constructions of community, and legitimations of power rest, but on which they become contestable as well.

Hence, toward whatever source—African, European, or neither—Aponte himself may have traced the sense of moral authority that he unquestionably vested in his pinturas, their political function as a "resorte" (in Maraval's sense) would remain the same. Once more, we are reduced to guesswork. Was Aponte's book intended to "engrave"—as Gallego (1972, 93) puts it, referring to the political functions of emblematic literature—his "advice most deeply into the monarch's memory," thus obliging his majesty to take cognizance of the evils unveiled by his pictorial analysis? If so, instead of couching moral advice in a pictorial language designed both to delight and to educate the sovereign, Aponte's imagery seems threatening rather than seductive. Might he have wanted to insinuate that, just as images could reflect the blinding splendor of power, so could they turn into "resortes" affecting, not states of illusion ("engaño"), but states of disabusement ("desengaño") as well? The caduceus in the hand of Death certainly would suggest as much. But so do Aponte's images celebrating the virtues of Aponte Senior and the forgotten splendors of Ethiopia and Egypt. If, once again to switch cultural vocabularies, the "dead remain, in *oriki*, perpetually and potentially present" (Barber 1991, 134), might not Aponte's imagery have raised the possibility of an insurrection of the victims of monstrous histories of the "creative destruction" of dehumanized African bodies, which a regime of slaveholders backed by his Catholic majesty sought both to perpetuate and to repress? We can be quite sure that Aponte did not have unmediated access to the Bible, but secondary recensions of Exod. 21:16 seem to ring through his images. "And he who stealeth a man, and selleth him, or if he be found in his hand," reads the King James version, "he shall surely be put to death." Had not San Felipe Martín received the sword that he wielded against a Christian king from the archangel himself? Was death at the hand of the abused not the just reward for such blasphemy? Although the site of such crimes may have been divided by wide seas, such seas signified distances in space and time that, as Aponte phrased it on March 29, could become "narrow in the image": once a conception of Africa, Europe, and the Americas as a single historical space of moral interrelations became thinkable for Aponte, such distances simply collapsed.

Regardless of the mysteries surrounding the book's communicative purposes, it is clear that Aponte was on the verge of devising a comprehensive *theory* about what was happening around him. A theory, we might say, based in part on false premises, perhaps even on a good dose of what some would call *false consciousness.* But a theory the essential rationality of which is hard to deny.[84] In a very concrete sense, what this theory—expressed in a pictorial medium rather than a discursive one—achieved was precisely such a "narrowing," a synthesis of heterogeneous information, various histories, and doubtlessly personal experiences into a single body of powerful moral commentary and critique. Given his day and age, given his social position, and given the knowledge available to him—always subjected to his own frame of interpretation, changing as it probably did in the course of what must have been years of collecting, cutting out, sorting, pasting, and painting—what more could Aponte have achieved? He had identified one crucial source and modality of power and its generation—the mechanisms that Marx would, some half century later, begin to diagnose as the necessary side effects of primitive accumulation—and he was approaching its mysteries, getting closer to them day by day. No less than for the famous Rhinelander working away in the British Library, analyzing the phantasmatic workings of power within his own social formation, for Aponte, too, piece after piece began to fit in as he "studied their pictures, read their books, and moved near them to learn their secrets."

There is, of course, another possible, although not necessarily contradictory, interpretation. For Aponte's conspiracy of images may have had more than accidental affinity to the "Bible of Hell" projected by his contemporary fellow craftsman and "Ingenuous Practitioner in the Art of Symmetry" William Blake. Like Aponte, Blake was a man who, although situated on the other side of the Atlantic, deeply worried about the fearful transoceanic "symmetry" productive of the evils spewing forth from the West India docks at the Isle of Dogs in his native London. Like Aponte, Blake knew of the "well-timed wrath" with which "Africa" had "cut his strong chains&overwhelm'd his dark Machines in fury and destruction" in St. Domingue (Blake cited in Erdman 1977, 429). And, like his ignominious Cuban counterpart, Blake was a master of exploiting the polyvalences of the language games constituting the continuum of discourse in which he took part—both as reader and as author. Nor was Blake unacquainted with the other side of that violent Atlantic modernity dawning in the Caribbean during his own lifetime. Between 1791 and 1793, Blake engraved some of the illustrations to Captain John Gabriel Stedman's *Narrative of a Five Years Expedition against the Revolted Negroes of Suriname, In Guiana, on the Wild Coast of South America; from the year 1772–1777*, published in 1796 (see Stedman 1988) and only after extensive censorial intervention. Blake's thought is not usually accorded more than local British significance or (for that matter) translocal inspiration. Yet his personal acquaintance with, and work for, this agent of (and in many ways victim of) Atlantic history allows us a glimpse of the concerns—utterly disjoined as they appear by a transcontinental hiatus—that he and Aponte may have shared.

Stedman was a mercenary, and his friend Blake knew it. Stedman had made a career of sorts as a professional soldier turned slave catcher in Dutch service. He had been commissioned to hunt down the large groups of maroons that had consolidated in Suriname's interior since the late seventeenth century. For Stedman—who came both to loath slavery and to keep slaves himself (including his enslaved lover, Joanna)—this assignment turned into a tormenting psychological ordeal out of which he seems to have tried to write himself in the *Narrative*, parts of which Blake undoubtedly read while he was composing his *Visions of the Daughters of*

Albion.[85] By the same token, however, Stedman's ordeal was one, it seems, into which Blake consciously engraved himself when designing plate 71 of Stedman's book (the only one of the sixteen plates that he never signed). It depicts "The Execution of Breaking on the Rack" by an enslaved executioner (whose deeply troubled gaze upon his victim Blake masterfully captured). The victim in this case was yet another free craftsman, a black carpenter who had killed a plantation overseer, and the image illustrates one of the most bizarre moments in Stedman's horrendous confession of silent complicity in civilized monstrosities.

After the executioner had chopped off the victim's left hand with a hatchet, "Blow After Blow he Broke to Shivers every Bone in his [victim's] Body till the Splinters Blood and Marrow Flew About the Field," and Stedman imagined the man dead. Yet the man regained consciousness and sang "two Extempore Songs, With a Clear Voice taking leave from his Living Friends & Acquainting his Deceased Relations that in a Little time more he Should be with them." Moreover, he found the strength to utter a series of remarks that made Stedman recoil with "Shudder" at "the Bloody theme": "Observing the Soldier Who stood Sentinel over him biting Occasionally on a piece of Dry Bread he asked him, 'how it Came that he a *White Man* Should have no meat to eat along with it' *Because I am not So rich* said the Soldier. 'then I will make you a Present first pick my Hand that was Chopt of[f] Clean to the Bones Sir— Next begin to myself till you be Glutted & you'l have both Bread and Meat which best becomes you' " (Stedman 1988, 547).

At that point, fully three hours into the execution, Stedman flees the scene in horror. We can perhaps imagine why Blake could never bring himself to sign the engraving visually rendering this moment illuminative of the almost hallucinatory terror reigning in what Stedman called this "Blood Spilling Colony," why Blake chose not to affix the plate in question with "the Cypher by which each master knows his Property"— as Stedman (1988, 534) puts it on a page facing another one of Blake's images. This time the engraving represents a "Family of Negro Slaves from Loango" in a "State of Tranquil Happiness." And yet, the father bears Stedman's initials—J.G.S.—branded on his chest "as we mark furniture or any thing else to authenticate the property" (175): a sign of truth inadvertently prefiguring the mechanical agency of the executionary apparatus in Kafka's "Penal Colony" that makes the captive realize the reason for his bodily destruction by the act of inscribing the conviction into his flesh. "From different Parents, different climes we came / At different Periods," says the frontispiece to Stedman's *Narrative*, which depicts a runaway slave dying at the foot of a European soldier. "Fate still rules the same. / Unhappy Youth while bleeding on the ground / 'Twas *Yours* to fall—but *Mine* to feel the wound" (3). Image making, we might say, can be a violent act, implicating the maker in truths too horrible to be consciously contemplated, and inflicting wounds that violate all parties involved. We may well imagine an enslaved blacksmith sorrowfully fashioning the branding iron that would stamp such "marks of property" on the breast of Stedman's contented possession. Yet had not Blake's friend come to be haunted—possessed, perhaps—by a history of such nefarious proprietorship?

If Blake chose not to authenticate his artistic property in the case of "The Execution of Breaking on the Rack," the "voice of slaves beneath the sun, and children bought with money, That shiver in religious caves beneath the burning fires / Of Lust, that belch incessant from the summits of the earth" (*Visions of the Daughters of Albion*, as cited in Erdman 1977, 234), would instead begin to ring through Blake's work, railing as he was—like Aponte, one wonders?—against Urizen: Your Reason, the kind of chrematistic rationality that, not only energized the dark satanic mills of Blake's foiled Jerusalem and drove billowing clouds of Atlantic war into the mouth of the Thames, but—in truly "fearful symmetry"—simultaneously disembarked at the port of Havana in the form of Avarice and Death. As Blake wrote in 1793 (Erdman and Moore 1977, 113),

> Though born on the cheating banks of the Thames
> Tho his waters bathd my infant limbs
> The Ohio shall wash his stains from me
> I was born a slave but I go to be free.

Havana's rio de Almendares, we might say, held no such promise for Aponte. The baptismal passage afforded by the waters of the bay of Havana was one toward slavery and the auction block for human chattel. For Aponte, it seems, those very waters were polluted by greed and immoral power. And, in a curious geographic inversion of Blake's imagery, for whom the faraway banks of the Ohio River demarcated a boundary between living death and worldly redemption, for Aponte the river

Nile came to stand for the threshold between histories of slavery and freedom. Once more we can only wonder about those charts of Havana in Aponte's book that so aroused the interest of the Cuban authorities. Like Blake's native London washed by the "cheating waves of charter'd streams," Aponte's Havana had undergone a series of brutal transformations in the lifetimes of the two artists, exposing the horrible costs in human misery occasioned by the agency of merchant capital. If Albion labored at the mill with slaves, might not the caduceus, for Aponte too, have been the sign of the beast? "Is this the land where the life of men has a fixed price?" Jacinto de Salas y Quiroga rhetorically asked in his reminiscences of a visit to Cuba at the height of its development as a plantation colony. And, in a manner that Aponte would have understood immediately, he added another question that he himself eventually answered in the positive: "Is this that terrible city that feeds on gold and corpses?" (Salas y Quiroga cited in Ortiz 1986, 193).

Still, no matter how misleading it would be to construe Aponte into a creole revolutionary (who would seriously reduce Blake to Jacobinism?), we should not forget that Aponte had been in the possession of portraits of Henri Christophe, Dessalines, Toussaint, and Washington. Moreover, among his papers there had been found an image of vipers crawling over a broken scepter and crown. This, Aponte said, he had received at the time of the French Revolution from a man who had come from France, but, by 1812, such imagery would have enjoyed wide diffusion all across Spanish America. There are, further, many unclear references linking Aponte to persons and groups of politically ambiguous, if not outright revolutionary, character. According to Franco (1974, 130ff.), in the winter of 1795–96 Aponte may have been among the members of Havana's black cabildos preparing a welcome ceremony for the Haitian revolutionary heroes Jean Francois, Biassou, and Narcisco, then in the service of the Spanish crown about to evacuate its troups from the failed attempt to reconquer the rebellious French colony St. Domingue. Although their arrival in Havana had been kept secret, word had gotten around in Havana's black barrios, and the authorities, fearing further spread of information about the Haitian Revolution, prevented the landing of the Haitian brigadiers.[86] As we have seen, by 1810 Aponte appears to have been implicated in the so-called Conspiración Franco Masónica headed by the wealthy white Masons Román de la Luz, Joaquín

Infante, and Luis Francisco Bassave (or Basabe) y Cárdenas, the latter of whom apparently had made contacts, not only with the black inhabitants of the "most humble barrios of the capital" (Franco 1977, 11), but with officers of the Batallón de Morenos as well.[87] Masonic ideas and imagery—such as would, in the 1820s, inform the conspiracy of the "Soles y Rayos de Bolívar" or the "República de Cubanacán" (see Ponte Dominguez 1951; Morales Padrón 1972)—might, by 1810, quite conceivably have entered Aponte's visual vocabulary. Yet we must be careful here. Regardless of the powerful role that Masonic lodges played in creating a network of ideological interchange between nationalistic movements in Latin America and connecting these movements to the much wider, transatlantic discursive contexts of the Age of Revolutions, Masonic ideas, first, were all but unambiguously revolutionary, and, second, may have appealed to Aponte for a variety of reasons—not the least of which may have been the epistemological promise that yet another hermetic system of knowledge production may have held for him.

Furthermore, there is little evidence in the records to the effect that Aponte considered himself a *revolutionary* in the "modern" sense of the term; that is, as the agent of a universal, irreversible, and irredeemably accelerating process progressing along a single—and, since Copernicus and Newton, literally stellar—path of world history along which pasts began to change in alignments with projected futures (see Koselleck 1985, 38–54). If the young Marx (cited in Tucker 1978, 597) thought that the "social revolution of the nineteenth century" could not "draw its poetry from the past, but only from the future," and if the historical message of revolution coincided with the biblical injunction to "let the dead bury their dead," then Aponte's mission was an entirely different one. His project was to disinter the dead, to conjure up and redeem their spirits through a poetics of the past designed to dispel the "nightmare on the brain of the living" to which their lives and memory had been sacrificed. Although in very different ways, not only Calderón and Blake, but also Barber's Yoruba informants in twentieth-century Okuku might have understood.

This, however, does in no way discount the possibility that Aponte might have availed himself of the discourse of the Age of Revolution to project his vision. That he did not elaborate on exactly those matters during the interrogations might be expected. He had already burned the set of images implicating him in such matters because he knew their potential for unleasing the most brutal of sanctions. Why would he choose to implicate himself even further? Once more, we can only speculate. When cutting images from books about Europe—this exotic and utterly remote part of the globe from which there nevertheless issued laws and political decisions that structured his own world—might not Aponte conceivably have had in mind that he could not just "re-member" the pasts that European learning dispersed into the realm of the impossible without bringing into being what was unthinkable within such forms of knowledge? Even though I do not find much of the evidence conventionally adduced to implicate Aponte in a planned uprising of major proportions convincing, we cannot discount that he was contemplating what might have been a radical move from text to life: not only to redress a violated past, but to "make history" in the present, much like the Haitians had done only a few years before. Aponte knew of a black king in Haiti, and he may have known that an emperor preceded him. He also knew that, not only his immediate social environs, but the world of those faraway European rulers of a colony of slaves and sugar barons was rife with contradictions.[88] Could he have contemplated the possibility of, not only envisioning, but actually bringing about an alternative version of history? Was he, as his interrogators (past and present) presumed, on his way from icon to action?

This question must, of necessity, remain unanswered. If there existed a conspiracy (which is quite probable), and if Aponte was involved in it (which cannot be ruled out), we will still never know its ideological content and pragmatic aspirations. Whatever seditious plans were then afoot in Havana, and to whatever degree Aponte was involved in them, we will never know what the conspiracy associated with his name would have resulted in had it ever come to fruition. What we do know is that some of Aponte's associates actively manipulated—conjured with, if you will—symbols of the Haitian Revolution. One of the potentially seditious characters among Aponte's acquaintances, a free first-generation African and former resident of Charleston, South Carolina, named Juán Barbier who considered himself a "congo," certainly seems to have taken a decisive step in the direction of escalating forms of symbolic violence into embodied ones. As it turned out during the inquest, on repeated occasions Barbier had assumed the identity of a "Juán Francisco." Barbier denied this, claiming that another one of the accused, Juan Lisundia, had proposed this change of names and that he himself had refused to go along with it. The portent of this change of names became clear only on March 25, when Clemente Chacón confessed that, when Aponte and Barbier came to his house, Barbier said that he had been an admiral of the revolutionary troops in Guarico (i.e., Haiti) and "that he had come to conquer this land [i.e., Cuba] for the colored people as they had done in many other countries" (Franco 1977, 104).[89] Barbier, in other words, had taken on the identity of Jean Francois, one of the famous generals of the initial phases of the Haitian Revolution.

It is unclear whether Barbier—or any of the others—could have known that Jean Francois had meanwhile died in Spanish exile, just as Toussaint had met his death in France. Yet as in the case of the mysterious black general said to be waiting for a sign of attack in the fortress Casa Blanca[90] or the five thousand black warriors hidden in an equally mysterious place called "the mountains of Montserrate,"[91] the relation between the signifier *Juán Francisco* and its referent need not have been an indexical one. It is tempting to rationalize Barbier's posing as a Haitian revolutionary hero as a strategy to mobilize popular support or allay fears of the potential failure of an insurrectionary project. But we surely can think of other forms of embodiment than role-playing and strategic dissimulation—ones in which the mimetic process engenders, not purposeful deception, but profound slippage between metaphoric and metonymic modes of alignment of terms and in which the distinction between "instrumental" and "symbolic" practices cannot but obscure the experience of those who deploy and engage them (see Jackson 1990). As Lynn Hunt (1984) has pointed out in considerable detail, to construe the death of Louis XVI as a logical outcome of—rational—revolutionary politics is profoundly to misunderstand the nature of the "symbolic forms of political practice" at work in revolutionary France. Given that the symbolism of power prevailing during the ancien régime revolved around the king's person—indeed, his very body—it was equally logical that the person of Citizen Capet had to be physically destroyed or (as an engraving reproduced on p. 108 of Hunt's book shows) literally *consumed* by the equally personified revolutionary populace.[92] Both Jacques-

Louis David and Maximilien Robespierre—men hardly accusable of suffering the defects of premodern irrationality—apparently saw little in such actions and images that conflicted with the Revolution's "cult of reason." In fact, as Robert Darnton (1968) has shown, Enlightenment reason was shot through with conceptions and practices the fantastic character of which has become obscured and defaced "by our own cosmologies, assimilated, knowingly or not, from the scientists and philosophers of the nineteenth and twentieth century" (43–44). If Newton's discovery of mechanical physics had been part and parcel of a larger alchemical project, Marat's ceaseless pamphleteering about invisible fluids, Lafayette's ardent mesmerist convictions, and even Robespierre's brief flirtation with the mysteries of electricity are not as easily put aside as aberrations as it would seem. As Darnton puts it, at the very moment when our retrospective teleologies would expect enlightened Frenchmen to have done away with irrational beliefs, their view "opened upon a splendidly baroque universe, where their gaze rode upon waves of invisible fluids into realms of infinite speculation" (44). Rousseau and Cagliostro, Franklin and Mesmer, Swedenborg and Saint-Simon, were not just contemporaries. They were participants in a single, complex continuum of discourse that held room for political economy, universal rights, and scientific experimentation, just as it did for copulating planets, invisible fluids, and spiritistic communion with the dead.

What then, we might ask in the light of this, might Barbier have lent his body and person to? Again, it would seem moot even to pose the question of what kinds of ideas about the merging of persons (or spirits?) might have informed what looks like the first-generation African Barbier's becoming or incarnating Jean Francois.[93] As Hunt (1984, 67) argues, the French revolutionaries "took up their symbolic cudgels with a rationalistic vengeance," effecting a powerful and irreducible convergence of imagination and action, representation and reality. Neither is it an accident that, long before Hunt, Emile Durkheim (e.g., 1995, 212) repeatedly invoked the example of the French Revolution to express the reality of what Kramer (1993), following Lienhard (1961), calls states of *passio:* being overwhelmed by forms of experience that originate outside the self. "Feeling possessed and led on by some sort of external power that makes him think and act differently than he normally does," Durkheim (1995, 220) writes, the ritual actor:

naturally feels he is no longer himself. It seems to him that he has become a new being. The decorations with which he is decked out, and the masklike decorations that cover his face represent this inward transformation even more than they bring it about. And because his companions feel transformed in the same way at the same moment, and express this sentiment by their shouts, movements, and bearing, it is as if he was in reality transported into a special world, entirely different from the one where he ordinarily lives, a special world inhabited by exceptionally intense forces that invade and transform him.

Might not the conspirators of 1812—if they were such—have aimed at a similar merger? If, on the morning of August 5, 1789, the members of the French National Assembly could not justify to themselves that they had, in fact, ratified the destruction of the ancien régime the night before, would it even have mattered to Aponte's plotting friends that Jean Francois had meanwhile died in exile? Given his chance, Barbier might, in fact, have turned into a Jean Francois, thus transposing the Haitian past into a Cuban present and dispersing the question of "true" identity and "strategic simulation" into the realm of factual irrelevance. Enacting an insurrectionary drama in which the past comes alive to impassion and overwhelm the present, we might say, was an option less irrational than—in retrospect—simply not feasible under the given circumstances. But all this, too, will necessarily remain guesswork of dangerously teleological character.

OF SENSIBLE SHOES, MIMESIS, AND APPROPRIATION: SITUATING APONTE

What, then, does a close reading of the documentary evidence in Aponte's case leave us with? Certainly neither an African rebel nor the kind of creole revolutionary born from predesigned typologies and ventriloquistic exercises. Taking the documents of Aponte's inquest seriously is to walk on precariously thin ice. Nowhere does this become more evident than when we entertain the question of the historical and sociological significance of his case. For, once we steer clear of the Scylla of facile typology, are we not up against the Charybdis of having completely to individualize the man and his project? Do we not face a situation in which all that we can say about Aponte and his libro de pinturas is that the case represents a mere idiosyncratic quirk fortuitously exposed by the record? An instance of exceptionality impossible to reinscribe into a social history of Afro-Cuban culture once we have shorn it of the spurious claims to representativity concocted by historians mongering interested tertiary accounts? Yet does rejecting reductionist solutions really leave us with no better choice than to singularize Aponte and his book in a manner reminiscent perhaps of post-Enlightenment Western stereotypes of artistic genius or the autonomy of aesthetic production? Hardly. For to phrase the problem in such terms is once more to set up an artificial dichotomy that is not so much unhelpful as positively obscuring of the meshing effected by the Atlantic modernity that shaped the world in which Aponte lived, thought, and painted.

Quite clearly, the problem at hand is not so much an empirical as a conceptual one: it is not just factually wrong but simply wrongheaded to presume that typological distinctions—such as African / creole, free black / slave, artisan / laborer, religious functionary / rationalist conspirator, rebel / revolutionary, oral tradition / literate culture, ethnic particularism / enlightened universalism, and so forth—would unequivocably indicate the joints along which to carve up Aponte's world. For, if significant additions to the corpus of data on which such judgments have been traditionally based should leave us more perplexed than before, might not some analytic housekeeping be in order? Polemically stated, Aponte's case exposes the affinity of such categories to the proverbial "sensible shoes" that mid-twentieth-century English-speaking mothers commended to their daughters. They get you somewhere, but is it where you want to go? It may be apposite here to recall E. P. Thompson's famous attack on both vulgar Marxist and Parsonian conceptions of *class* in the opening remarks to *The Making of the English Working Class* (1968, 9–15). For, from Thompson's perspective, it is rather clear where the shoe pinches in the case at hand. There is no question that the sociological attributes of individuals as defined within the power structure of early-nineteenth-century Cuban society—say, their being black rather than white, Africans rather than creoles, free people rather than slaves—had tremendous bearing on their life chances and potential range of experience. Yet it is a gross methodological error to deduce the content of their consciousness (as, e.g., rebellious or revolutionary, African or Western, traditional or modern, religious or rationalistic, etc.) from the status positions, role sets, or places within the relations of production that they occupied. This holds true on both individual and collective levels, and it pertains, not just to issues of class consciousness, but to such phenomena as ethnicity, cultural orientation, and even racial identification—none of which is simply structurally determined, and all of which can come to underwrite the historical transformation of what Max Weber called structurally determined *communities of fate* into *communities of intent*—although certainly not in any predictable way.

This is a problem often simply obliterated by a sociologistic vocabulary that proceeds from notions of *collective representations* or *elective affinities* without reflecting on whether the collectivities in question really represent self-defined or otherwise distinct social units (instead of mere artifacts of typological procedures); whether such representations actually signify even only roughly similar things for the members of such social aggregates; and whether any of this corresponds to whatever "objectively given" social conditions they may share (Peel 1990).[94] Once more, the Caribbean situation would seem to throw into relief what tends to be more easily obscured in cases where the peripherality of local worlds appears to suggest, not just their social closure, but their cultural "rootedness"—to use Ginzburg's phrase—in unfathomable layers of endogenously generated traditions. For what is at issue here are not just what Thompson (1991) elsewhere calls *overconsensual* representations of the cultural repertoires of subaltern collectivities or the romantic "sanitizing" (Ortner 1995, 176ff.) of their internal politics by privileging the great divide that separates them from dominant social sectors over their own internal conflicts and "struggles for the real." The question rather is in which sense and to what extent such collectivities are more than the products of analytic procedures that slice up the "social cake" according to predesigned carving rules. Before we entertain such Platonic maneuvers, should we not ask ourselves how much leeway we are willing to concede to actors' strategic manipulation of the cultural forms circulating in their historically specific social contexts—contexts the scope of which may be far more extensive than the local settings of face-to-face interaction would suggest? And might we not want to consider the extent to which our attempts to repatriate historical actors into symbolic universes of *our making* represent a perpetration of symbolic violence *post festum?* Late guests that we are, what right do we have to subject the indeterminacy—perhaps deeply felt uncertainty, ambivalence, and vacillation—that marked the lives and thought of those who died in negating the certainties on which our own world is built to forms of determinism that replicate (if through conscious inversion) the certainties of their executioners?

There is no need here to add to the discussion in the previous chapter. For, if anything is clear about Aponte's case, it is that there was nothing particularly ancient, rooted, homogeneous, or even only local about the local world in which he lived and painted. On the contrary, as I have tried to show, the better part of the cultural resources at his disposal were, not just heterogeneous, but allogenic: their origins, quite obviously, lay elsewhere, and their circulation in Havana owed as much to local agency as to the larger political-economic currents that tied Aponte's Havana into the South Atlantic System. Neither was the symbolic milieu (for lack of a better term) in which Aponte operated restricted to his immediate social environment in Pueblo Nuevo, nor were its contents even temporally homogeneous: it extended from Paris to Port-au-Prince, from Madrid and Cádiz to Mexico City and Caracas, from London to Kingston and Philadelphia, from Havana to the Bights of Benin and Biafra, deep into the hinterland of Angola, and—by Aponte's own imaginative extension—onward to Egypt, Rome, Ethiopia, and the Holy Land. It included contemporary information as well as knowledge produced in the distant past and transmitted to him through both written and oral channels. This world of data swirling around his home and workshop in Havana's calle Jesús Peregrino was energized by the circulation of people—representative of European merchant firms and their Cuban staff, priests and government officials, sailors and slaves, booksellers and pamphleteers, foreign spies and nationalist agitators. And what integrated it were printing presses and the stencils of engravers just as much as merchant ships and men of war, rumors circulating at the dockside and the markets of Havana as much as proclamations issuing from the governor's palace at the Plaza de Armas or the groans and curses emerging from its bottom floor, which, during Aponte's lifetime, served as Havana's city jail ("thus affording a practical exposition of government and a novel piece of architectural morality," as the English visitor Jameson [1821, 63] put it). It was in Masonic ceremonies, Catholic processions, slave auctions, patriotic demonstrations, or conspiratorial meetings that this condensation of global streams of discourse became palpable. But it also did so in a profusion of no less diverse African-derived practices ranging from public dances performed in front of Catholic churches and market squares and formal meetings of the cabildos de nación, to rituals staged behind the closed doors of initiatory chambers, nightly sacrifices performed over graves or directed toward beings inhabiting uncultivated spaces on the outskirts of town, and secret acts of furtively committed mystical aggression.

Aponte's case, in sum, exposes not just a body of data resisting easy assimilation into the procrustean categories that continue to plague the literature on slaves and other "invisible people." It also indicates the need to shift our focus away from conventional emphases on intgration, homogeneity, boundedness, and seemingly passive "endemic" reproduction of social and cultural forms and toward perspectives capable of analytically accommodating constellations of heterogeneous but contiguous, perhaps overlapping, forms of knowledge and practice: "syndromatic" clusterings of cultural materials whose distribution in local social space at specific temporal junctures need coincide neither with their historical origins, nor with structurally identifiable collectivities, nor even with the boundaries maintained by self-identified social groups. In fact, as Thompson (1968) argued so forcefully, we might want to see such collectivities *themselves* as historically mutable patterns of social alignment discernible only over time and only through observation of the manner in which their constituents make use of specific cultural forms in enacting their relations, expressing their interests, and creating institutions responsive to the experiences that they may have come to share for historical reasons and that they sometimes *come to understand* as shared (see Wolf 1982a, 387; Wolf 1988).

All this obviously militates against Europeanist conceptions of popular cultures as timeless reservoirs of intensely local folk tradition.[95] But it also does not sit well with the colonial scenarios in which anthropologists have rightly begun theoretically to relocate a good part of their casuistry. What I am referring to is the voluminous body of writings on how the contemporary ethnic and cultural phenomenology of much of the Third World reflects, not just the penetration of previously autonomous local worlds by capitalist market forces and alien colonial states, but the interplay between the colonial reifications of social units ("tribes") and cultures ("custom") and the ethnic identities and traditions objectified or "invented" by subject populations in response. What Melanesianists came to designate as *kastom* some twenty years ago—a pidgin word signaling indigenous attachments to cultural arrangements that originate, not in a traditional past, but in a process of feedback between colonizer and colonized (see Keesing and Tonkinson 1982)—has nowadays come to haunt ethnographers worldwide. Still, views of the constructed nature of social and cultural difference in colonial and postcolonial scenarios often only push the idea of local ethnic and cultural specificity (not to say authenticity) backward to a point where, as Amselle (1993, 25) puts it, "the loss of the conditions under which utterances [i.e., representations of cultural practices, social identities, forms of community, institutions, and so forth] were produced" allows us "to apprehend as structures those classifications" that most dramatically depart from what V. Y. Mudimbe (1988) might call local borrowings from the *colonial library* or other alien repertoires.

The analytic artifice of the "invention of tradition" literature presupposes a state when things were not invented (or not yet) or—differently put—still authentic. Logically, however, suppositions of such a prelapsarian state can thrive on little else than the fact that nothing can positively be known about it—and that holds true for both Europeanist and Africanist anthropological retrojections of data into an undocumented, "prehistoric" past. It is precisely this moment of illusory regress that is at work in Franco's strained attempts to pin Aponte down on a Yoruba identity (of which we know little else than that it did not exist *in Africa* at the time). What this allows him to do is to shift the focus away from the dizzying indeterminacy of Aponte's recorded utterances and toward a more stable point of collective tradition that can take the place of Ginzburg's cognitive filter in the making of an organic intellectual turned revolutionary agitator. One cannot help here but notice how Franco's interpretative travails seem to prefigure more recent anthropological attempts at capturing what, for example, Kramer (1993) and Taussig (1993) theorize as a dialectic between mimesis and alterity in non-Western appropriations of those strategies of Western self-making that lay at the roots of colonial domination. Speaking about the Mami Wata cults so conspicuous today in much of Western Africa, Henry Drewal (1996, 306) compares the omnivorous appetites of such cults for

Western symbolic matter to nineteenth- and twentieth-century Western modes of appropriating the exotic in the form of museum specimens or primitivistic inspirations for artistic projects. "While Mami Wata followers possess a certain awareness of foreign ways," he argues, "they do not use alien objects primarily to analyze or understand the ideas or values of the Other, but rather to examine and construct themselves and their own society."

To be sure, in imitating African sculptural aesthetics by gluing a bicycle handlebar to a bicycle seat after a visit to the Musée de l'Homme, Pablo Picasso did no less. Yet, although eminently intriguing, Drewal's analogy with Western primitivism is nevertheless flawed in the case at hand. For the issue here is not whether Aponte emulated alien strategies of creating historically grounded selves in order to access powers in whose grip he felt himself (in inverse analogy to the way in which Westerners fashioned their contemporary colonial subjects into timeless primitives in order to give meaning to their own modern predicaments). The real question is where would one locate such alterity in Aponte's case. Can there be mimesis in a world that never contained an Archimedean point of formerly unproblematic selfhood from which to launch such endeavors at incorporating the exotic other? Can there be "modernity" in the absence of "tradition"? Notwithstanding the violent expansion of slave-based plantation agriculture in nineteenth-century Cuba or the multiple forms of social exclusion that free urban blacks like Aponte surely experienced, in a world composed of allogenic symbols, practices, and forms of knowledge—a world where everything (or nothing, if you will) is strange—would not all forms of *cultural* difference (as distinct from social inequality) have to be generated on the spot?

This holds true not just for the fragments of European traditions that Aponte painstakingly appropriated into his own symbolic repertoire over the years. It was true also for the similarly displaced elements of African cultures that reached Cuba and had begun to recombine into New World complexes of knowledge and practice the local social distribution and salience of which waxed and waned even during Aponte's own lifetime. As Roger Bastide (1978, 47) writes in respect to the—in many ways analogous—Brazilian situation, "Time, in the long run, would erode all [African-derived] traditions, however firmly [they came to be] anchored in the new habitat. But the slave trade continuously renewed the sources of life by establishing continuous contact between old slaves, or their sons, and the new arrivals, who sometimes included priests and medicine men. In this way, throughout the whole period of slavery, religious values were continuously rejuvenated at the same time that they were being eroded." "We know little about Afro-Brazilian religion in those distant times," he admits with a candor that would become some contemporary historians of African American culture, "but we should certainly give up the notion of cult centers surviving through the centuries down to the present day (something that slavery precluded) and think of a chaotic proliferation of cults or cult fragments arising only to die out and give way to others with each new wave of arrivals." Bastide's strictures against scholarly imputations of historically unwarranted continuities in Afro-Brazilian traditions certainly ring true for Cuba as well. In both cases, the bodies of African-derived knowledge and practice that congealed into genuinely Afro-Cuban and Afro-Brazilian religious formations in the course of the nineteenth century and the early twentieth were in good part the product not just of the local agency of transplanted holders of originally African forms of knowledge (although they certainly were that, too). They also were resultants of erratic shifts in the larger Atlantic matrix that temporarily linked places like Havana or Salvador da Bahia with specific African source regions. And it was this matrix that generated what, at times, must have been stunningly diverse patterns of circulation of heterogeneous African cultural forms in single New World localities.

Aponte, we must presume, was acquainted with—although not necessarily directly involved in—more than one of the many African-derived cultural formations caught up in various stages of aggregation and decline in early-nineteenth-century Havana.[96] Yet, although possibly eclipsed in his work by the importance he seems to have placed on representations issuing from European (or, better perhaps, bookish) sources, the contrast between these and originally African cultural resources could not have been a simple, unmediated one.[97] Irrespective of whether Aponte himself may have identified with any single emergent Afro-Cuban ethnic or cultural formation, we know that friends and acquaintances of his—such as the creole Clemente Chacón and the first-generation Africans Salvador Ternero and Juán Barbier—certainly did. Ironically, however, this fact alone should dissuade us from trying to displace the question about a cultural bottom line to Aponte's interpretations of European cultural materials toward some specific African tradition. For, even if we accept Franco's claim to Aponte's lucumí descent at face value, had not the men who repeatedly met in his house chosen what appear to have been rather different ethnic identities? Was not Ternero the headman of a *mina guagüí* cabildo? And did Barbier not claim a *congo* identity? We will, of course, never know what precisely these ostensibly ethnic identity referents meant in the historical context in which these men deployed them. Nor is it clear to what extent such "onomastic emblems" (Amselle 1993) referred to exclusive definitions of social belonging and whether the African-derived cultural formations present in early-nineteenth-century black Havana were in any way socially congruent with, let alone restricted to, such groupings (Palmié 1993).

As I will argue in the next chapter, it would be a mistake to reify locally coexisting cultural complexes (whether their elements be traceable to Europe *or* different regions of Africa) by overestimating their individual separateness and neglecting the fact that their multiple articulation with each other must be seen as part and parcel of the process of their differentiation—which may be better understood as an ongoing process of working off each other than as a process of discrete speciation (see Handler and Linnekin 1984; Thomas 1992; Fardon 1995). At this point, however, I am more concerned with the question of agency in the production and reproduction of such cultural aggregates. For, in a fundamental sense, the contours of social or cultural difference and identity, selfhood and otherness, are never mere natural givens—somehow preceding their cultural construction and social deployment (a point that feminist critics have amply made clear). And the degree to which they are socially carved out of what otherwise would be a field of generalized "indistinctiveness" (Amselle 1998) needs to be historically ascertained rather than assumed. This often becomes a sufficiently pressing analytic concern only in cases of patently complex social worlds, and, once one chooses the Caribbean as a field of study, one cannot but talk about just that: cases where one is forced to take seriously the potential of actors to *select* symbolic forms from a number of sources, thereby actively or reactively confirming, contesting, or reformulating historical arrangements of power and identity associated with the use of such forms.

Aponte's case reveals clearly that the process of the production and reproduction of what we tend to call *traditions* is not one that could be modeled after seemingly natural (e.g., evolutionary) ones. Rather, it is an eminently political process in which attempts to control the distribution of specific forms of knowledge and symbolic practice (on whatever level) may lead to situations of hegemonic saturation ("redundancy of ideological communications," as Wolf [1982a, 388] puts it) and the objectification of cultural representations of social relations as bounded entities—corporations, ethnic groups, religious cults, social classes, and so forth. By the same token, however, such processes of differentiation by which identity and otherness come to be naturalized through the control over representations of past or present social realities are never complete. At the very least, they do not rule out extensive border traffic, poaching and contraband, or simply the leakage of symbolic matter that comes to be comprehensible only within larger social fields.[98] However real the social entities resulting from political maneuvers designed to reduce flux and indeterminacy may appear in practice, to prioritize their separateness is already to espouse parts of the Whiggish interpretations against which I have been arguing all along.[99] On the contrary, once we shift our attention away from nominalist notions of social identities or cultural differences and toward processes of identification and differentiation, what comes into view are rather different phenomena: complex "ecologies of representations" (Wolf 1982a), "continua of discourse" (Pocock 1988), or conjunctures of "streams of tradition" (Barth 1984, 1989) the emergence and transformation of which can no longer be reduced to origins (let alone essential characteristics) but must be studied as a matter of social practice under identifiable historical conditions.

MAKING DIFFERENCE

To turn to questions of individual cultural-resource access, interested choice, cultural loyalty by default, and retrospective misprision is, thus, not to invoke the specter of methodological individualism. It is a step in the direction of specifying the historical factors at work in conditioning the options that historical actors *perceive* in furthering their goals by choosing to appropriate certain cultural forms while rejecting others (even if their perception of alternatives is objectively constrained). It is to pose the question why they appear to privilege some interpretations over others in their attempts to make sense of the worlds into which they were thrust by processes beyond their control. And it is to situate their utterances—behavioral, verbal, or pictorial—not just in relation to their concrete referents (be they mundane individualistic goals or collective bids for power, particularistic rebellions or universalist revolutions), but in relation to what Bakhtin (1986, 22) calls "other utterances within the limits of a given sphere of communication." Quite clearly, we would not want to assimilate Caribbean slave rebellions to the similarly unpredictable hurricanes that devastated prosperous plantation colonies from time to time (but see Craton 1982, 293). Yet, even if we did, we would be well advised to adhere to metereologic common wisdom: even the most localized storms represent products of the articulation of what often are vast weather fronts with local topographic and climatologic conditions. Given Aponte's uniquely inquisitive disposition and his historical positioning as a free black man in early-nineteenth-century Cuba, it would be naive to presume that monothetic attributions of cultural loyalties would exhaust either the sources of or the modes of reaction to allogenic representations available to him. His orientation was, to say the very least, dialogic—although we cannot be sure of exactly what conflicts and alignments, symbolic as well as concrete, intended or accidental, the heterologue productive of his libro de pinturas might have embroiled him in.

A final excursion into the world of three Afro-Cuban "conspirators"—Margarito Blanco, León Monzón and José Inocencio Andrade—active about twenty-five years after Aponte met his sordid fate may help underscore these points. In the evening of July 11, 1839, the police arrested a group of seven free black creoles engaged in a suspicious gathering in the house of the free black dressmaker Dominga Cárdenas in the barrio extramuro of Jesús María. In the course of the raid, they secured several documents bearing inscriptions in a strange language as well as pictographs of equally mysterious nature. What their significance was became clear two days later, when the police likewise arrested the twenty-five-year-old free black coachman and dockworker Margarito Blanco, in whose home similar papers were found. This time, however, they contained a sufficient amount of Spanish vocabulary to allow for their decoding: they addressed the "Ocongos of Obane, Ososo, and Efó" and invited them to assist at the constitution of a new corporation named "Arupapá." Blanco had not only signed them with his name but added his title "Ocongo de Ultán" and a pictogram that—we now know—was a *nsibidi* sign signifying the *firma* or signature of a titleholder of *abakuá.* The word *Ocongo* (or *mocongo* in current usage), Blanco explained during his examination, signified the office of "head" or "captain" and collector of funds.

A whole wave of arrests followed. The next victims were the fifty-four-year-old captain of the battalion of Morenos Leales, León Monzón, a decorated officer who looked back on thirty-five years of active military service, together with five other black officers. In the course of another raid, four free black artisans and one slave, José Inocencio Andrade, were arrested—almost all of them creole inhabitants of the barrio of Jesús María. What is more, evidence found at Blanco's home clearly indicated that there existed connections between at least two of what initially had appeared to be several distinct groupings: one of the officers arrested together with Monzón, José Nemesio Jaramilla, had signed one of the documents in Blanco's possession, thus linking Monzón's group of black officers with Blanco's abakuá *potencia, tierra,* or *juego.* Moreover, Victor Villegas, one of the young creoles arrested in the initial raid on Dominga Cárdenas's house, turned out to be none other than the Ocongo of the potencia Efó, whom Blanco had invited to join in an *enlloró* or *llanto*—a type of mortuary celebration directed to deceased members of abakuá—to be held, in this particular instance, on the occasion of the initiation of a new chapter of abakuá.[100]

Yet, while the judicial authorities involved in the case obviously did not grasp the meaning of Blanco's papers or his statements to the effect that he had intended to form a "mutual aid society such as had been founded in the town of Regla" (Deschamps Chapeaux 1964, 105),[101] there was no question about the materials found with Monzón: this decorated military officer, who in 1832 had received official permission to open a school for the religious and literary instruction of "the young ones of his station" (Deschamps Chapeaux 1964, 102),[102] had been found to possess such unequivocally subversive materials as a proclamation entitled "Liberalismo Constitucional del Batallón de Pardos de la Habana" and a pamphlet entitled "Libertad y Tiranía" in which the phrase "No hay patria sin libertad" specifically caught the eye of his interrogators. Andrade, finally, seems to have headed a group of apparently quite different character and cultural orientation. Among his possessions were materials that—again in the eyes of the judges, knowledgeable about the impact of Masonic ideas and symbols on Cuba as well as revolutionary Latin America—must have made at least some sense: there were papers relating to topics like a "Sublime Puerta," the "Serenísimo Señor," and the rules of an association entitled "Nueva Constantinopla, Habitantes de la Luna, Hijos del Sol y Academía Nuestra Señora de los Dolores."

Viewed superficially, we thus get three—culturally—quite distinctive manifestations of Afro-Cuban modes of counterhegemonic practice coexisting within the same barrio of Havana since at least the mid-1830s: two early juegos de abakuá framing their collective identity and activities within an African idiom, a group of disillusioned officers for whom the discourse of the Age of Revolutions seems to have provided an appropriate rallying ground, and a third type of association thriving on the more esoteric intellectual currents of the Enlightenment. Yet such typological interpretations are just as misleading as those for whose rejection I have argued in Aponte's case. In fact, none of these groups were *either* African *or* European, traditional *or* modern, in orientation. They were both and neither. But let us turn to the evidence. If we begin at the apparently most Europeanized, most rational, progressive—in other words, revolutionary—end of the spectrum, that is, Monzón's band of mostly elderly disgruntled officers, we register a first sense of contradiction in the fact that one of them, José Nemesio Jaramilla, had signed a document instrumental in the founding of a tierra or potencia de abakuá, that is, a seemingly "traditional" African corporation. Yet the interrogations of Monzón's associates yielded information even more damaging to neat typological schemes: in a manner not altogether dissimilar to Aponte's penchant for exotic imagery and surely reminiscent of the symbolic repertoire of Andrade's group, members of which styled themselves as "católicos, apostólicos, y romanos" as well as "sons of the sun" and "inhabitants of the moon," there existed, in Monzón's group, offices like that of a "Grand Visir" and "Grand Selim." Moreover, according to the testimony, Monzón, this seeming model of a rational, alienated, creole revolutionary, apparently had himself crowned "Pope" in a ceremony held at Pilar Borrego's house. He also presided over an "Academía de Irlandia" in the function of Reverend Father "Gregorio Benedicto," while one of his associates, José del Monte del Pino, presided over a similar "Russian Academy" under the title "Alejandro III."

This, however, is only where our problems start. For at the other end of the spectrum—Margarito Blanco's abakuá potencia—we encounter even more astounding evidence. Here, we should remember that the people arrested in the course of the raid on Dominga Cárdenas's house were *exclusively* young black creoles—a fact that likewise puzzled the judges concerned with the case. For, while they may not have known that, only a few years prior to the event, the first autonomous Cuban branch of a male secret society of the ekpe or ngbe type had emerged from nearby Regla's "cabildo de los carabalí brikamo apapá efí," they could not help but note that these young creole dockworkers, bricklayers, and quarrymen were trying to "imitate the habits and customs of Africans."[103] In other words, Blanco's grouping did not fit their conception of a cabildo de nación, that is, an association of Africans integrated by what white Cubans (as well as many modern scholars) thought was the common ethnic origin of its members. I will not dwell here on the problems surrounding what may be called *New World African ethnicities* (see Palmié 1993), yet, whatever the organizing principle of the cabildos de nación had been, it is clear that, while abakuá emerged from the cabildos of the "nación carabalí," its own organizational structure no longer resolved around ethnic allegiances. Instead, its mode of incorporation was based on ritual ties established by initiation, a fact that endowed abakuá with a unique capacity for autonomous reproduction. All that had been needed for abakuá to emerge was the initial establishment of a ritual infrastructure of titleholders capable of swearing in a new chapter, and this unique constellation of personnel had apparently come about in the cabildo de los carabalí brikamo apapá efí in Regla in 1836. From then on, abakuá reproduced itself independently, and it was fewer than twenty years after Margarito Blanco's arrest that another creole, Andrés Facundo de los Dolores Petit, initiated the first *white juego de ñáñigos.*[104] Blanco and his unknown predecessors had laid the groundwork for this by transforming the African organizational model of a Cross River–type secret society into a New World institution well adapted to the social demands of the rapidly changing society of urban Cuba. By the second half of the nineteenth century, abakuá had formed tightly organized ritual and economic networks in several port towns of western Cuba, controlling, among other things, the labor market at the docks of Havana. By the early twentieth century, it would begin to infiltrate the union movement and become actively involved in electoral politics.[105]

Yet we still have not quite exhausted the complexity of the ecology of representations existing in Havana's black barrios in the early nineteenth century. For there was at least one other uniquely Afro-Cuban universe of discourse with which Aponte may have been familiar, although he most likely was not involved in the social practices that generated and sustained its cultural forms. What I am referring to is a vibrant and colorful male street culture that had emerged on the social and economic margins of black Havana and whose participants were collectively known as *negros curros* or *curros de Manglar*. The origins of the curros are unclear. By the early nineteenth century, however, the term *negros curros* had come to refer to what was not so much a self-identified or internally cohesive Afro-Cuban grouping as a set of social practices—a distinctly black lifestyle associated in the mind of the Cuban elite both with highly specific forms of gendered personal comportment and active engagement in Havana's exploding urban economy of crime.

Like many other American port towns linked into the South Atlantic System, Havana had long hosted a large population of socially marginal participants in informal, and often extralegal, venues opening on the fringes of an Atlantic economy: "masterless men" (and women), to use Christopher Hill's expression (cf. Scott 1986), whose lives expressed some of the central contradictions of the regimes of value extraction and forms of domination to which they were collectively subjected. Divorced from the means of legitimate production in a society increasingly based on slave labor, Havana's masterless people included casual laborers, peddlers, beggars, prostitutes, smugglers, fencers, petty thieves, burglars, and paid assassins. In part, this renegade population recruited itself from the ranks of deserters from various naval and military bodies, escapees from metropolitan prisons, defrocked members of the priesthood or monastic orders, and sidelining members of the military and urban militias. More important, however, its constituents were drawn from the vast numbers of free but unskilled people of African descent and the many hundreds—perhaps thousands—of escaped slaves who either stole their way from the surrounding plantation areas into Havana or headed from the confines of the old walled parts of the city into the sprawling and largely black barrios extramuros that, as Deschamps Chapeaux (1983, 14) aptly puts it, had begun to resemble a "vast urban maroon camp" by the time of Aponte's death. Drifting in and out of various semilegal and illicit forms of economic pursuits in trying to maintain themselves outside a formal economy that increasingly conflated productive labor with slavery, these men and women formed a volatile mass that contemporary elites perceived in terms strikingly similar to the images of "dangerous classes" proliferating among European elites at the same time. "Every kind of vice can be found in Commercial Towns," wrote Jamaica's governor, Lord Balcarres (cited in Scott 1986, 33), about analogous conditions existing in Kingston in 1800: "Turbulent people of all Nations engaged in illicit Trade; a most abandonned class of Negroes, up to every scene of mischief, and a general levelling spirit throughout, is the character of the lower orders in Kingston." Such judgments were echoed by colonial administrators situated all along the Atlantic littoral of the Americas (see Scott 1986, chap. 1 and passim). While booming colonial export economies were generating profits that led to spectacular patterns of embourgeoisement among the local elite, their base in slave labor (which dominated, not only the productive, but the distributive sectors as well) generated no less spectacular patterns of *encanaillement* among those not reduced to human chattel or actively resisting such debasement. By 1812, free Afro-Cuban men less fortunate than Aponte and his largely free, largely skilled seditious associates had little choice but to enter what Redicker (1988, 236) in a related context calls an economic world that "was essentially picaresque, brimming with those whom the upper classes never tired of calling rogues, rascals and tramps, and who swarmed with restless movement." "Police records and sugarmill reports of the period," writes Moreno Fraginals (1976: 139) apropos the Cuban situation, "fulminate with indignation against the mass of people without known occupation, living off gambling or prostitution or as petty hangers-on or middlemen, always flatly refusing to bury themselves eighteen hours a day in the sugarmill." Although the early nineteenth century certainly saw the expansion of a black artisanal petit bourgeoisie in Havana's barrios extramuros, Moreno likewise draws attention to the rapidly increasing growth of a heterogeneous "lumpen" population much akin to that which inhabited the most poverty-stricken areas of London, Paris, or Seville.

To be sure, we need to be careful here, lest in following Moreno we repeat Engels's famously confused vacillation between a view of delinquency as a protorevolutionary expression of popular "contempt for the existing social order" (Engels 1969, 159) and its denigration as a defining characteristic of the lumpenproletariat—that "passively rotting mass thrown off by the lowest layers of old society" (Marx and Engels 1967, 92; cf. Bailey 1993). If "subproletarian" heterogeneity represents a problem for Marxist analysis in the metropolitan core (Stallybrass 1990), one should expect no less with respect to the colonial periphery. A closer look at the phenomenon of the curros de Manglar bears this out. Forming part of the extramural barrio of Jesús María in the southwesternmost corner of the bay of Havana near the wharves of Tallapiedra, by 1812 the slum-like area of "el Manglar" (lit., "the mangrove swamp"), where the subculture of the curros allegedly originated, no longer represented a literal swamp to Havana's concerned elite but a figurative one. Like much else of Jesús María, the miserable hovels of el Manglar had been destroyed in a massive conflagration in April 1802—an event that, as Chailloux Cardona (1945, 100ff.) argues, represented the calculated destruction of lower-class housing situated on real estate the property value of which was rapidly increasing owing to the expansion of the harbor.[106] Nevertheless, throughout much of the nineteenth century, the toponym *el Manglar* continued to impart the meaning of a social cesspool onto which respectable Habaneros projected fantasies of vermin-like social parasites whose animalistic depravity not only passively bred filth and disease but also transgressed the boundaries between the legitimate and the illegitimate city in the form of violent predatory forays.[107]

I will explore latter-day permutations of this discourse assimilating cultural difference and the effects of social inequality to conceptions of dangerous biotic otherness more fully in chapter 3. Here I am less concerned with elite representations of the "Other," than with the question of how subaltern "signifying practices" (Comaroff 1985) functioned as strategies of differentiation. For, however much the public image of the curros—as the literary productions of contemporary Cuban writers have preserved it—appears to speak to nineteenth-century bourgeois ideas about urban dereliction (see Stallybrass and White 1986, 125–48) and even modern conceptions of criminal subcultures, there was more to it. Thanks to the efforts of Fernando Ortiz,[108] the negros curros represent one of the better-documented nineteenth-century examples of a local

African American street culture, complete with all its moral ambiguities, expressive brilliance, and creative verve.[109] The curros, Ortiz (1986, 40) tells us, were part and parcel of what he calls the *hampa afrocubana*—a teeming black underworld that formed a counterpoint to the economic parasitism and ostentation of the white elite in its equally parasitic economy of crime and a consciously elaborated culture of conspicuous symbolic subversion. The curros, he writes (50),

> were decidedly bent on showing who they were. This [attitude of] boasting and exhibitionism was characteristic and essential to them. . . . The black curros distinguished themselves from other mortals by a multitude of details. Their figure, their hairstyle, their gait, their shirt, their trousers, their footwear, their hat, the pieces of cloth they wore, their [filed] teeth, etc., all [of these] denoted the curro. There was not to be observed in him any mimetic adaptation to the social environment in which he grew up; much rather he seemed set on struggling to separate and distinguish himself from all other individuals, so that they might recognize, admire, or fear him.

As Ortiz seems to have understood, the curros' bodies were not just surfaces off of which contemporaries unilaterally read signs of grotesque subversion. That surface was a consciously crafted one, and the practices that constituted it aimed, not just to communicate "contempt for the existing order" in the sense of disrespect for the legal inviolability of personal property, but to signal a form of defiant self-possession. By itself, engagement in criminal activities—ranging from petty thefts to mercenary killings—was not a privilege of free Afro-Cubans. Havana's highly mobile urban slaves frequently engaged in criminal ventures as well and not infrequently acted on commissions from their masters. Yet, as Ortiz points out, what really distinguished the subproletarian world of the curros was that it bore specific markers expressive of their defiance of the norms of a society structured by racial slavery. Readable through forms of bodily comportment and individual agency, the flamboyant emblematics of male bravado and lawlessness that characterized the negro curro were, not just "displays of his vanity," but signs of "the luxury of his liberty, the obvious proclamation that he was his own master and that he would proudly defend such mastery with a dagger if necessary" (Ortiz 1986, 186). If, for free black artisans such as Aponte and Chacón, carpenters' knives or shoemakers' awls and reamers represented legitimate insignia of freedom and modest economic independence, what separated their curro contemporaries from the mass of urban slaves was their right to bear arms—and make use of them if necessary—both as tools of illegitimate trades and as the potentially deadly means of producting self-possessed personal identities.[110]

Yet a cultivated air of fierceness, masculine prowess, violent defiance, and "authoritative individuality" (Breiner 1985–86, 37) was not all that rendered the curro visible as a social type. Here is a contemporary description of the physical appearance of the curros at a time when their distinctive style of life and comportment may already have been in decline:

> The curros had a physiognomy of their own, and seeing them was sufficient for identifying them as such: their long strands of plaited curls falling over their face and neck in the manner of great "mancaperros,"[111] their teeth filed in the manner of the carabalí, the embroidered cotton shirt, their pants, tight at the waist and very wide at the bottom, almost always white or with colored stripes, the low cut shoes of hemp cloth with silver buckles, the waistcoat made of "olancito" with short and sharply pointed tails, the wide-brimmed straw hat adorned with pendants, fringes, and tassels of black silk, and the heavy golden earrings from which hung hearts and locks made from the same metal constituting a style of adornment found only among them; besides that they were known for their swaggering gait, swinging their hips and moving their arms back and forth; for the singular inflexion they imparted to their speech, for their vicious argot, and, finally, for the peculiar manner in which they expressed themselves—so excessively rhetorical and absurd that, at times, it was difficult to understand them. (José Victoriano Betancourt cited in Ortiz 1986, 36)

As David Brown (1989, 34–39) has argued, such descriptions of the curros as are found in the writings of Cuban *costumbristas* (local color writers) invite comparison with modern accounts of what Roger Abrahams (1983) calls *patterns of performance* in the West Indies or the expressive culture of African American "streetcorner societies" in the United States. In Brown's view, concepts like *reputation, rudeness, noise,* and *nonsense*—as employed by students of African American performative cultures (see, e.g., Abrahams 1983; Wilson 1969; and Reisman 1970)—are crucial for understanding what he sees as a consciously cultivated style of subversion of values associated with "high-variant" performative codes. Even though the linguistic analogies underlying much of the literature on which Brown draws are not unproblematic, his discussion of the available evidence on the curro subculture along such lines is certainly intriguing.[112] Yet it is a different problem that I would like to touch on briefly in concluding this chapter. For, as Ortiz's meticulously researched catalog of possible Old World sources for single items of the curros' expressive repertoire shows, any attempt at construing clear-cut derivations in terms of categories like *African* or *European* is bound to fail. Speaking about their mode of personal adornment, Ortiz (1986, 49) suggests, for example, that, even though they may have partly responded to African aesthetic antecedents, the expressive force of the curros' self-presentation was inevitably directed toward a New World context of interpretation: it "aimed to signify *a distinct social condition,* superior to the common one in the social milieux in which they lived."

Ortiz's own attempts to untangle the resulting complex of strategies of elaborating and projecting versions of Afro-Cuban selfhood by what essentially were philological means are strikingly naive.[113] Nevertheless, they are, in principle, instructive. Consider his discussion of the noun *cheche* and the adjective *chévere:* both connote qualities of male bravado, prowess, sharpness, flashy appearance, the ability of giving quick repartee, etc. and were formerly used to designate the male curro—even in tautological combination as a "cheche muy chévere." Yet, as Ortiz's often rather questionable philologistic attempts at using etymology to trace the cultural origins of these concepts and their associated semantic values demonstrate, they point into a variety of linguistic and historical directions: in his view, the Yoruba terms *ṣse* (to happen, do, achieve, make come to pass, etc.) and *agbára* (strength) and the Efik *sebede* (to adorn oneself profusely, to dress well) seemed to provide as likely candidates as did the French term *chevalier* (knight, man of honor) filtered through the Haitian kreyol term cheveré (Ortiz 1924, 166ff.; Ortiz 1986, 23). In the end, Ortiz's strained attempts to trace the curros to any African antecedent known to him seem to have resulted in the massive categorial confusion from which, by the early 1940s, his pathbreaking concept *transculturation* would emerge (Palmié 1998b). As in the case of the "bell-bottom" pants worn by the curros, their use of cloth adornments, their plaited hairstyle—more reminiscent perhaps (as Brown has suggested) of Rastafari dreadlocks than traditional African coiffure—Ortiz came to opt for the conjunctural convergence of heterogeneous elements, in both morphological and semantic terms, on an essentially new expressive complex inseparable from its local historical context of enunciation and interpretation.

This realization may have been one of the first steps that Ortiz took toward seeing Africa and Europe as ineluctably conjoined in the constitution of the kind of historical (rather than essential) Cubanness ("Cubanidad") that he eventually came to propagate as a model for that island's nationhood (see Ortiz 1995). Yet, reasonable as this solution may be, it leaves us—just as in the case of Aponte—with the problem of explaining the articulation of the components of heterogeneous bodies of knowledge and practice into relatively coherent aggregates of thought, action, and expression that, in turn, articulate with other such cultural formations on a higher level of sociological abstraction. This is a question only too easily obscured in its historical dimensions (rather than as a mere matter of synchronic morphological description) by references to concepts such as *bricolage* or *creolization*. For what both suggest are templates that essentially lie outside the concrete processes of reflection, communication, and struggle by which individuals attempt to forge forms of selfhood and moral community in interaction with their historically given social and cultural milieux: the first by insinuating determination through preexisting organizations of thought and perception, the second by imparting a false sense of determinability to the contingencies of the appropriation and deployment of cultural resources. As I have tried to show in the case of Aponte's libro de pinturas, the bridging of disparate universes of discourse and aesthetic traditions does not occur randomly, nor can it be divorced from the agency of actors whose historical positioning enables them to unproblematically adopt, strategically appropriate, or forcefully wrest the cultural resources variously distributed in a given ecology of representations or continuum of discourse from their forebears, from similarly positioned contemporaries, or from those who wield power over them.

As Brown suggests, the curros may have forged an expressive style signifying the value system and marking the boundaries of what the

British sociologist Dick Hebdige (1979) terms a *spectacular subculture*. The curros achieved the crucial identity-productive "unnatural break" (Hebdige), not only by appropriating what seem to have been prestige symbols of both African and European cultures, but by recontextualizing them in a consciously outrageous manner.[114] But saying so much may already be to exaggerate the specificity of what may well have been little else than a particular set of strategies of identification and differentiation available to, and variously deployed by, free Afro-Cubans in early-nineteenth century Havana. As in the case of Hebdige's youths in 1970s Britain, labels such as *punk*—and, for that matter, *curros* in nineteenth-century Havana—may suggest temporally cohesive identities and groups where there may, in fact, exist only transitory, intersecting, and multiply compounded techniques of individual differentiation.[115] Once more, the mere existence of onomastic emblems does not relieve us of investigating the role of agency in the making of historical patternings of action and consciousness—whether in the case of the English working class, that of renegade subcultures (the label itself is misleading), or seemingly decontextualized activities fortuitously exposed by the documentary record. Constructions of individual agency and collectively representative forms of consciousness, we might say, always turn precarious if viewed historically: the one may always mutate into the other. How patterns of practice congeal into traditions or dissolve into fading memories or personal idiosyncracies is obscured rather than elucidated by anthropological conceptions that—in harkening back to the days when concepts such as culture change or acculturation still sufficiently blanketed the historical processes in question in this particular discipline—obfuscate the very realities that historians who eagerly appropriate them are trying to uncover.

The curros' multiply outrageous recontextualization of diverse symbolic matter into an aggregate of signifying practices advertising and celebrating authoritative individuality is, thus, only an instance in a much wider spectrum of counterhegemonic activities in early-nineteenth-century Havana. For, irrespective of his role in a conspiracy, did not Aponte wreak similar symbolic damage—although perhaps with quite radically different intentions—on the representations that he absorbed from the variety of sources at his disposal? Did not Monzón, Borrego, Jaramilla, and Andrade fuse the droit des hommes with popular European orientalist exoticism and the symbolic repertoire of abakuá? And, finally, did not the group of young creoles coalescing around the Ocongo Margarito Blanco—*apapás chiquitas* as they called themselves to distinguish themselves from their African forebears—similarly invent (or, at best, reinvent) for themselves a cultural style suited to the chances and demands that they perceived as relevant to their existential options as actors positioned at a specific juncture of several streams of tradition confluent within the complex world of nineteenth-century black Havana? They all may have experienced the contradictions of this world in a different manner; they made different choices, to be sure, and they elaborated on the representations that they appropriated in their own peculiar way. Aponte, the former militia officer, "deputy of the Virgen de los Remedios," and alleged Changó priest, was no curro, and it would simply be foolish to underrate the distinctions that separated him from a bricklayer aspiring to be integrated into Blanco's prospective abakuá potencia or a curro making a living on the criminal fringe of Havana's underground economy. Yet, while valid sociologically, the question about their typologically salient characteristics as Africans, creoles, men of letters, dockworkers, officers, criminals, members of Afro-Cuban cult groups, participants in Catholic church life, etc. is moot when it comes to investigating their cultural repertoire.

"People," writes Fredrik Barth (1989, 130), "participate in multiple, more or less discrepant, universes of discourse; they construct different, partial and simultaneous worlds in which they move; their cultural construction of reality springs not from one source and is not of one piece." Rather, as Eric Wolf pointed out quite some time ago, and as I hope to have shown in the foregoing, it is crucial for us to recognize that people may "straddle more than one cultural adaptation" (Wolf 1971, 173). How they come to do so is a question of historical nature, and it has to be attended to, not in constructing types (however useful such a procedure may be for primarily heuristic purposes), but by close differential diagnosis of concrete historical symptomatologies thrown up at the conjunctures of intersecting forms of both material and symbolic production. It is this issue—so far discussed only in a perfunctory manner—that I intend to take up in the following chapter. Granted the multiplicity of symbolic codes articulating in the continuum of discourse from which what we, today, know as Afro-Cuban religious traditions originated, how are we both to conceive of the distinctiveness of the components of an overall Afro-Cuban religious formation and explain the mechanisms that integrate its various streams of discourse at one and the same time? The answer that I will venture in the following is once more a historical one. This time, however, it is geared less toward questions of the origins of a particular ecology of representations than toward the processes of synergy between heterogeneous components of a continuum of religious discourse in the construction of senses of selfhood and otherness that vertebrate historically specific moral communities.

2. GENEALOGIES OF MORALITY

The Afro-Cuban Nganga as Wage Laborer, Slave, and Maroon

Although often obscured by simplistic notions of culture contact between monolithically conceived Christian and African belief systems, the internal differentiation of regional African American religious formations[1] has long been noted in the anthropological literature. Since Herskovits's early attempts to deal with the composite character of the non-Christian elements observable in Haitian vodou (1971), the prevailing analytic strategy has been ethnographically to isolate African component traditions and to interpret their coexistence as the result of the selective transplantation of elements of originally disparate African source cultures to single New World localities. The demographic dislocations effected by the slave trade and the arbitrary enlistment of enslaved Africans into New World plantation societies, thus, tend to be represented as resulting in a compression of African cultural geography: according to such reasoning, in certain New World settings the lower Zaire nowadays abuts southwestern Nigeria. I call this the *theme-park approach*.

Best known, perhaps, is the case of northeastern Brazil, where practitioners distinguish various types or brands of *candomblé*—such as candomblé Nagô, Jeje, or Angola. These qualifiers not only denote differences in ritual style and ideas about the divine. They also refer to conceptions of origin associated with the concept *nação*—a term formerly used by slaveholders to designate the putative provenance of enslaved Africans as well as by slaves to express ethnically framed aspects of their New World identities. In keeping with this indigenous terminology, students of Afro-Brazilian religion have tended to correlate such distinctions with the observable clustering within distinct social settings (i.e., cult groups) of cultural forms traceable to different African source cultures. Hence the syllogisms on which much Afro-Brazilian scholarship thrives: Nagô : Yoruba :: Jeje : Ewe / Fon :: Congo / Angola : western Central African Bantu speakers and so forth. In a similar vein, the Haitianist literature reflects a long-standing tendency to transpose ritually salient distinctions between groupings of deities into a discourse on cultural origins.[2] Haitian ideas about the so-called *rada lwa*, for example, have usually been traced to Dahomean cultural influences. Conceptions of the so-called *petwo lwa*, on the other hand, have variously been interpreted as deriving from western Central Africa or as representing creole phenomena and, hence, New World creations.[3] Analogous, if perhaps even more complex, divisions have been recorded in the Cuban case. Here, cultural-historical fault lines are said to obtain between at least four different Afro-Cuban religious traditions: the Yoruba-influenced regla ocha; the *reglas de congo* such as palo monte, *mayombe*, *vrillumba*, *kimbisa*, etc., seen as based on western Central African cultural sources; the Adja-derived *regla arara;* and, finally, abakuá, a male secret society thought to relate historically to similar institutions in the Cross River region of southeastern Nigeria.

Such interpretations are by no means invalid, particularly when phrased as testable hypotheses about the relation between cultural forms and the history of their social enactment. Much too often, however, have they taken the form of presuppositions about the formal determination of contemporary African American religious practice by forces of tradition" or similar empirically elusive dei ex machina.[4] As transpositions of a practitioners' discourse salient to a religious present into an academic discourse on cultural origins, they evoke numerous epistemological problems. The most obvious one is that, by locating the sources of present-day African American conceptions of difference in Africa, the theme-park approach generates, not only questionable cultural history (for such distinctions could have become salient only in a New World context). Rather, as we have seen in Aponte's case, it also obfuscates a question that should be given logical priority: How exactly are such distinctions generated in social praxis, and what is their significance for those who make use of them? Not surprisingly, in both the Brazilian and the Haitian cases, conventional anthropological attributions of cultural-historical salience to indigenous constructions of religious difference have recently been subjected to harsh and by no means unwarranted criticism.

As, for example, Dantas Gois (1985, 1988), Sjørslev (1989), Richman (1992), Matory (1999), and Harding (2000) argue, the conjunction of and interaction between indigenous and scholarly conceptions of *traditionality* and *African purity* have engendered considerable discursive slippage. In both northeastern Brazil and Haiti, practitioners seized on the potential of anthropological inscription, not only to confer prestige, but to buttress political agendas. By cultivating strategic relationships with ethnographers, single priests and cult groups have managed to gain variable degrees of control over the public representation of what constitutes "authentically African," hence "orthodox," and therefore legitimate praxis. At times, such collusion occurred at the expense of other cult groups lacking strategic public linkages. At others, it formed part of more extensive attempts to manipulate relationships between different social categories within a larger collectivity of practitioners. The latter tendency is exemplified in Richman's (1992) reconstruction of the emergence in Haitian vodou of supposedly "African" relationships between increasingly professionalized male priests (*gangan ason*) and female initiates (*ounsi*) whose labor became subject to priestly appropriation within new ritual contexts—duly inscribed by anthropologists as traditional. The former can be observed in the creation of a "public canon" of Afro-Brazilian traditionality based on definitions of African purity launched by a few anthropologically well-connected *candomblé nagô terreiros* in Salvador de Bahia (Dantas Gois 1988).[5]

Similar points about the interaction between scholarly and native essentialisms can be—and have been—raised in the Cuban case (see Palmié 1995a). However, it is not the potentially misplaced concreteness on which such attributions thrive with which I am concerned here. For one thing, they provide a poor substitute for a historiography of Atlantic cultural transmission,[6] let alone New World modes of demarcating and socially organizing cultural difference. The second major problem with this line of inquiry is no less crucial. For it cannot deal with—and, indeed, obfuscates—the significance of diversity in contemporary practice: the ways in which practitioners invest the distinctions they draw between the components of a particular religious aggregate with practical and moral salience. In what follows, I will attempt to locate a set of notions about African origins within the semantic space they occupy in actual New World practice—a space from which they tend to be rhetorically displaced both by ill-conceived academic shortcuts to cultural history and by a native discourse highly responsive to cues provided by the former. With this in mind, I now turn to representations of the relation between two Afro-Cuban religious complexes—regla ocha (popularly known as Santería) and the so-called reglas de congo (an aggregate of cults within which further distinctions of mainly ritual significance are recognized by the practitioners themselves). Partly, my aim is to delineate the contours of what might be called an *indigenous sociology of religious forms*—one that transmutes a (scholarly) discourse on origins into a discourse on the morality of human-divine interaction. But I also suggest that practitioners' tendencies to moralize constructions of difference—persistent as they are in contemporary Cuban discourse about the relation between Yoruba- and western Central African–derived religious forms—might fruitfully be viewed as linked to more generalized images of sociality arising out of specific historical experiences.

Both regla ocha and the reglas de congo initially emerged from processes entailing the transplantation of African aggregates of knowledge in the course of the slave trade and their successive transformation into and indigenization as relatively coherent sets of social practices and beliefs under conditions of Cuban slavery and its aftermath. At least in the better known case of regla ocha we have some indications of the time frame within which these processes occurred.[7] Since the beliefs and ritual activities of practitioners of regla ocha evidence remarkable similarities to the ethnographic record on comparable phenomena among the (modern) Yoruba, its emergence in Cuba has usually been traced to the period postdating the first massive slave imports from the Bight of Benin into Cuba (i.e., the early nineteenth century), after which Yoruba-speaking slaves can be presumed to have been shipped in large numbers to the expanding sugar plantations of western Cuba.[8] As regards the reglas de congo—the formal characteristics of which indicate strong influences of western Central African cultures—the chronological picture is much more diffuse. Speakers of western Central African Bantu languages were imported into Cuba as early as the sixteenth century, and there is evidence that Cuba drew on this source population up to the very end of the illegal slave trade in the last quarter of the nineteenth century.[9]

While this chronology implies that we should reckon with the intermittent existence (although probably not continuity) of western Central

African–derived cults throughout the period of Cuba's involvement in the slave trade, it is clear that today's reglas de congo show considerable influence of Yoruba-derived religious forms.[10] As Romulo Lachatañeré (1992) was first to point out, these may have been grafted onto an older stratum of Bantu-Cuban cultural forms in the course of the late-nineteenth- and early-twentieth-century expansion of Yoruba-influenced cults from their original areas of inception in urban western Cuba to eastern parts of the island that had remained largely untouched by the nineteenth-century influx of slaves from the Bight of Benin.

Regardless of their different origins and the far from adequately explored history of their eventual conjunction,[11] Yoruba-Cuban and Bantu-Cuban traditions nowadays form part of a spectrum of religious forms that intersect in the religious lives of many, if not most, practitioners of Afro-Cuban religion. The way they do, however, has little semblance to conventional notions of syncretism as a blend or hybrid of originally separate elements. Particularly in the ritual sphere, but also as regards institutional aspects such as priestly roles or networks of initiatory kinship, clear-cut distinctions are maintained. These translate into complex techniques of spatial and temporal segregation of matters palo and ocha.[12] While I cannot adequately discuss this subject here, a few points bear mentioning.

Cult objects related to the Yoruba-Cuban regla ocha are usually prominently displayed in practitioners' homes. The sacra pertaining to a regla de congo, however, tend to be tucked away in closets or converted pantries or—if the owners' situation permits such a solution—housed in a shed in the backyard or garden.[13] Similarly, ritual activities in both cults are subject to strict temporal segregation. Unlike some forms of Haitian vodou, where ceremonies may switch from a rada to a petwo mode (McCarthy Brown 1989), rituals in regla ocha and palo monte never overlap or even only succeed each other in close sequence. Partly, this is so because the priestly personnel necessary to stage one type of rites would rarely match the set of officiants necessary for the performance of the other—although many of them may, indeed, be initiated practitioners in both religions. More salient, however, are deep-seated ideas about a fundamental incompatibility between the mystical addressees of such rites and less clearly articulated but nonetheless powerful notions about the moral implications of interacting with them.

On one level, self-identified practitioners of regla ocha tend to represent the relation between "their religion" and that of "the paleros" in terms of a fairly straightforward dichotomy echoing conventional social constructions of nature and culture. In contrast to ocha, palo is said to be more crude ("rustico") but also very powerful ("muy fuerte"), violent but fast and effective ("violente," "trabaja rapido," "muy efectivo"); it is associated with the dead instead of divine beings ("cosa de muerto") and with the uncultivated landscape ("cosa del monte") instead of humanly inhabited, and therefore socialized, spaces. Differences in ceremonial style, and particularly in the dramaturgy of possession, would seem to underline such representations: possession by an oricha will generally result in a stately display of divine personality. Individuals possessed by a *nfumbi*[14] (*spirit* in the reglas de congo) present an image of violent motor behavior, uncouth speech, and generally "uncivilized" demeanor.[15] While a person possessed by an oricha notionally takes on a role circumscribed by images of awesome royal authority, the medium of a congo spirit is represented as an embodiment of brute force. To a certain extent, this opposition between refinement and crudeness, civilization and wildness, has a gendered dimension. Although women fulfill ritual roles in both types of cult, palo tends to be represented as a "cosa de hombre." In contrast to regla ocha, which counts a large number of homosexual adherents (sometimes euphemistically referred to as *overly refined*), palo cult groups are characterized by a pronounced homophobic atmosphere, and many women have told me that they dislike the machismo that pervades social relations within a "casa de palo."

On a theological level, this dichotomy finds expression in a strictly regulated order of initiation. Although many practitioners of regla ocha are also initiates of one or the other reglas de congo (and may have become so because Yoruba-Cuban divinatory methods indicated the need to *rayarse*, i.e., undergo the rites of initiation into palo monte or a cognate cult), initiation into a congo cult must precede initiation into regla ocha. Sometimes this is explained by reference to the idea that the oricha into whose cult a person was previously initiated would not tolerate the body of its initiate receiving the ritual cuts (*rayamiento*) attendant to the initiation into a regla de congo.[16] At other times, I was told that to go from ocha to palo would signify a spiritual regression. While the initiation into ocha established a link to a divine entity, the purpose of the rayamiento was to relate the initiate to a being of a decidedly lower order: the spirit of a dead human.

The latter rationalization—although probably influenced by spiritist doctrine about the progression of souls in the afterlife—provides a clue to another dimension of the dichotomy that practitioners of Afro-Cuban religion set up between the cult of the oricha and the reglas de congo. At least within the Yoruba-derived traditions, ritual dealings with the dead are fraught with ambiguities. Although the priestly dead of one's religious line of initiatory descent as well as familial ancestors must be propitiated in the course of every ritual undertaking, the *muertos* as such—particularly if not connectable by initiatory or biological kinship—are a potential source of danger. While the oricha may act out of vengefulness for neglect or inflict harm to enforce their will, they are generally benignly inclined toward their human "children" (one term for initiates in regla ocha is *omo oricha,* "children of the gods"). So are, in general, the priestly and ancestral dead. "Alien" muertos, however, are regarded, not only as morally ambivalent, but as potentially malignant. Within the idiom of regla ocha, to work with the dead—*trabaja con los muertos*—signifies witchcraft, and it is telling that the two orichas said to "work most closely" with the dead (*son muy muerteras*), the female deities Yemayá and Ochún, are described as the only oricha who will, at times, tolerate their powers to be put to amoral ends.[17]

To a large extent, such conceptions do not derive from ascriptions of an inherently amoral or evil nature to the spirits of the dead but relate to theories about the nature of the relationship that humans can establish with different types of nonhuman agents. And it is here that the conjunction of heterogeneous bodies of knowledge—articulating as they often do in the daily life of single individuals—becomes salient. Ocha and palo work off each other in at least two ways. On one level, they are treated as functionally differentiated ritual technologies. Different problems, people will say, require different solutions. At the same time, however, palo and ocha circumscribe images of sociality that, though part of an aggregate of knowledge that embraces both complexes, stand in a relation of crass opposition. The tension between these images expresses and, to a certain extent, renders palpable the contradictions of dependency and individuation in a social world where objects at times take on the role of social actors and people mutate into things.

Whether thought of as personalized divinities or forces immanent in natural and social processes,[18] the oricha are regarded as entities whose volition is fundamentally independent of the agency of their human counterparts. Unless angered, oricha will generally see after their human children. Still, they must be cajoled into granting specific favors and may, indeed, refuse to do so. Initiation is thought to establish a particularly close bond between a devotee and his or her oricha (symbolized by a series of ritual operations linking the initiate's head with vessels containing the objectified presence of the deity in question). This allows the person to participate in the oricha's powers to a certain extent (expressed as the ability to "work with the oricha"). Nevertheless, an oricha may refuse to grant consent to particular undertakings or even turn against the devotee should he or she persist in divinely unsanctioned behavior. Moreover, and in keeping with the symbolism of kinship implicit in representations of the ties established through initiation (oricha as parent, devotee as child), the interchange between devotees and their gods is often conceptualized as a process of nourishment based on notions of generalized reciprocity. Gods must be fed (i.e., sacrificed to), and the image of feeding condenses a whole array of notions about exchange as a medium binding humans and oricha into enduring moral relationships. Once established by metonymically installing the deity in the initiate's head and bringing its objectified presence into the person's home (quite literally rendering the deity a member of the household), such relationships cannot be terminated by either party and must be maintained in what is thought of, ideally, as a chain of reciprocal prestations. These take the form of sacrifice and other kind of ritual attention on the part of the devotee and positive influence on the part of the god.[19] In practice, the god appropriates the devotee's ritual labor by consuming its products in the form of sacrifices or ceremonies. And, indeed, initiates sometimes complain about how demanding their gods are, what hard work working with the oricha actually is.

This is particularly so in contemporary Havana, where general scarcity combines with the rapid dollarization of the market in nonrationed consumer goods and the state's attempt to access the foreign currency flow within an emerging informal sector of prostitution, illegal money changing, theft, and other activities generating tourism-related hard-currency revenue (see the epilogue). Indeed, since in many cases only a visit to the state-controlled dollar stores (popularly known as *chopin*, i.e., "shopping") will satisfy an oricha's demand, the Cuban government may be said to have entered an unholy alliance with the gods. Although both the socialist state and the oricha increasingly fail to reciprocate, the latter enjoy a somewhat ironic advantage: unlike the state, the moral salience of which is increasingly being undermined by the deprivations that it forces on its citizens, the gods are viewed as not having received their dues themselves. Nevertheless, a human-divine moral economy would seem to hold. People may threaten to withhold ritual attention and even bargain with their oricha. Yet they remain in the position of supplicants who must—and usually do—count on the reciprocal nature of the ties that bind them to their divine patrons.

An entirely different symbolism characterizes the relationships between practitioners of Bantu-Cuban cults and their mystical alters. To begin with, whereas the oricha are considered to initiate the relationship with their devotees by "claiming their heads" (e.g., through a series of misfortunes or—more typically—an illness that divination discloses as the expression of an oricha's intervention), human agency is the key to the establishment of relations with a mystical entity in the congo cults. Although nfumbi spirits are sometimes inherited (mainly when this is prescribed by divination), the characteristic route to acquiring a ritual relationship with one of these beings is by commissioning a priest (*tata nganga* or *marenkisi*) to fashion an object known as *nganga* or *prenda* (Spanish: "jewel" or "treasure").[20] The priest, whose consent to initiate the candidate must be won and whose ritual labor must be paid, will then establish contact with the spirit of a dead human being and ritually install it in a container—the nganga object. More so than the actual rites of initiation (rayamiento) that establish the right of a person to own and interact with a nganga and that formally integrate him or her into a series of social ties to the initiator and his or her religious kin, it is this highly complex object that mediates and concretizes a mystical relationship between the spirit and its human counterpart, a relationship often described as a pact or bargain entered into (*pacto, trata*) and surrounded, not by images of domestic nurturance, reciprocal exchange, and beneficial dependence, but by symbols of wage labor and payment, dominance and subalternity, enslavement and revolt. Similar to the relationship between a devotee and his or her oricha, a tata nganga and the spirit with

whom he interacts stand to each other in a relation of dependence. Yet, if the former might be seen as partly modeled on naturalized conceptions of mutual obligations between offspring and parent, this validation appears reversed and perverted in the congo case: the human "father of the nganga" (tata nganga) is a mystical entrepreneur commanding a labor force bound by contract or capture.

THE AFRO-CUBAN *NGANGA* COMPLEX

Despite the somewhat confusing terminology, Bantu-Cuban nganga objects are New World variants of a western Central African type of sacra known in Kikongo (and the—largely Bakongo-based—anthropological literature) as *minkisi* (sing. *nkisi*). Just like Kongo minkisi, Afro-Cuban ngangas are highly complex aggregates of heterogeneous materials the conjunction of which is thought both to contain a spiritual presence and to render its power—in concretized and functionally channeled form—accessible to human manipulation. While an adequate comparison of the cis- and transatlantic features of minkisi/ngangas is beyond the scope of this chapter (see Palmié 1991, 395–436), a few correspondences must be established.

Most obvious, perhaps, is the symbolic emphasis on the composite character of these objects. Like Kongo minkisi, Afro-Cuban ngangas are complex assemblages of heterogeneous objects (*bilongo*) that are assigned specific symbolic valence in relation to each other and together acquire a "systemic" character.[21] Luc de Heusch (1971, 182ff.) may have been the first to suggest that the ordering of ingredients of Kongo minkisi can be understood as based on a functional distinction between substances that metonymically condense and concretize the nkisi's power and substances that metaphorically circumscribe its mode of operation and effect. In a similar vein, Thompson (1983, 117–18) speaks of "spirit-embodying" and "spirit-directing" materials. While grave earth, white clay, pebbles, or human bones serve to objectify a spiritual presence,[22] other types of bilongo—mainly plants and animal remains—impart functional specificity to the total assemblage of matter and spirit. Laman's (1962, 91) description of how the ingredients of a nkisi of the kula (pursuer) type metaphorically qualify its mode of operation may serve as an example:

> Apart from the general medicines [i.e., Thompson's "spirit-embodying" materials], I have found in Kula (a large bundle), inter alia, the following: a hen's foot, foot of a partridge, hoof of the nkabi-antelope, claw of a giant lizard, head or fore-feet of shrew-mouse, mpingi-mouse, kanza and mpidi snakes and other venomous snakes. These represent the qualities of the animals in question, such as e.g., swiftness, the ability to dart into the smallest hole, pugnacity, ability to kill quickly and so forth, all of which qualites are needed for Kula to be able to pursue the evil spirit to the grave.

Within the nkisi object, these ingredients obey various principles of internal organization, such as a hierarchical ordering based on precedence and defining the "seniority" of bilongo introduced earlier over later additions to the total corpus (Jacobson-Widding 1979, 40ff.; MacGaffey 1988, 1991), or functional organizing principles based on physiological analogies specifying the role of bilongo as differentiated organs or limbs of the nkisi (Laman in Jacobson-Widding 1979, 134). But the nkisi object is not simply a self-contained objectification of power the compositional logic of which is expressive of a desired social effect. Once assembled and therefore introduced into the social sphere, minkisi enter into relationships with human actors, establishing, as MacGaffey (1988) has pointed out, yet another chain of metonymic signification that wreaks havoc on commonplace Western distinctions between persons and objects. Minkisi thus incorporate parts of the physical being (hair, fingernails, bodily effluvia, etc.) of initiates, clients, or intended victims. Likewise, they force a discipline of proscriptions on their users (significantly referred to by the same term used to denote their component elements—*bilongo*), thus imposing an order, analogous to their own internal "disciplines," upon the very body of their human manipulators. Finally, minkisi literally penetrate the boundaries of human selves by restoring the physiological integrity of patients' bodies or by destroying that of their victims. Similar to ancestral graves, masks, and the bodies of chiefs, minkisi enter the social process as mystical catalysts—part personalized medicine, part objectified actor—binding ordinary mortals into relations in which subjects and objects of mystical action merge in the transformation of bodily states and/or social arrangements.

Astonishing correspondences to these conceptions have been recorded in the Cuban case. A nganga (i.e., Afro-Cuban nkisi object), writes Lydia Cabrera (1983),

> is constructed, "mounted," or "charged" by the brujo [lit. "sorcerer," i.e., religious specialist] with a dead [i.e., spirit of a dead person], a kiyumba [i.e., skull], branches from the bush, vines, nfita or bikanda [i.e., herbs], earth, and animals. By rule of association, the vessel containing the supernatural forces that are concentrated in the bones, sticks, plants, earths and animals and that are utilized by the brujo [ritual specialist] is called *nganga, nkiso,* or *prenda.* It is into this mixture of diverse materials that the spirit enters when called on. It is where he lives. (118)

Similarly, the following description of the construction of an Afro-Cuban nganga object leaves no doubt that we are dealing with cis- and trans-atlantic elaborations on a single theme:

> First one traces a cross with white chalk or ash on the bottom of a new cauldron and puts a Spanish silver real on the center and the four end points of the cross. Then [continues her informant] I put powdered chalk, candle wax, a bit of ash, and a piece of tobacco [inside the cauldron]. On one side I place a piece of cane filled with seawater, sand, and quicksilver, stopped up with wax, so that the prenda will always be alive like the quicksilver, light and mobile like the sea, which never rests, and that the nfumbi [i.e., spirit] will gain the ability to cross the sea and cover vast stretches of territory. Above these substances one puts the dried cadaver of a small black dog so that it acquires a keen sense of smell and picks up tracks. (123)

Here, it seems, we have much of the conceptual ingredients to the making of a Kongo nkisi: metonymically valorized substances such as chalk, ash, and wax (recalling, in their whiteness, the Kongo spirit-embodying substance par excellence, *mpemba,* or white kaolin) combine with metaphorically active ingredients such as the charged piece of cane—itself, a minuscule metaphoric machine generating associations of expansive mystical energy—to synthesize a new entity, part inhabited microcosm, part personalized agent.

"A prenda is like a little world unto its own," Cabrera quotes an informant elsewhere (1983:131), "and it is through it that you gain power. For this reason, the ngangulero [somewhat unusual term for ritual specialist] fills his cauldron with all [kinds of] spirits: within it he has the cemetery, the bush, the river, the sea, lightning, the whirlwind, the sun, the moon, and the stars. A concentration of forces." Similarly, a Miami palero told me that his ngangas contained little amounts of "all there is in the universe, and which also is found in your body," that is, among other things such minerals as gold, silver, zinc, and aluminum but also organic substances such as plants, bones, and protein. This, he maintained, facilitated "direct access" to the forces of nature and, thus, allowed him to cure "much more rapidly than the santeros," who, after all, had to implore the oricha for help and even then could not guarantee their cooperation. Again, as a priest in Havana succinctly told me, palo is "nada menos que el encuentro del hombre con la naturaleza"—nothing less than the encounter of man with the natural world, mediated by the nganga object, but by the same token bared of social constraints. If ocha tends to be represented as imposing a civilizing process on an unruly world whose powers are made to enter domestic ritual space (*ilé ocha* or *casa de santo*—i.e., house of the gods) as divine kings, palo prescribes an obverse directionality. It notionally leads ritual actors out of the human oikos and into physically as well as morally unsocialized terrain. Manipulating a nganga is, quite literally, an errand into the wilderness.

UNNATURAL RELATIONS

More so, perhaps, than the Bakongo image of the essential ambiguity of the powers wielded by persons with access to superhuman forces—be they *banganga*, or chiefs who are expected not only to execute criminals in daylight, but to devour kinsmen at night (MacGaffey 1970, 1977, 1986)—the way paleros gloss their manipulation of the ngangas that they command as a "return to nature" speaks to the fundamentally "unnatural" character of their relationship with the spirits contained in these objects; unnatural, that is, from the perspective of regla ocha. While all practitioners of Afro-Cuban religions acknowledge the role of the muertos as agents in a social universe comprising more than just living human persons, the quality of the relationship obtaining between paleros and their spiritual counterparts is alien to the understanding of proper relations between humans and nonhuman entities prevailing in regla ocha.

Once more, the initiation of a relationship between human and nonhuman actors in both cults provides a pertinent example. After an oricha has unequivocally stated (usually through divination) that a person must be initiated into his or her cult, the initiating priests will go in search of the so-called *otanes*—stones that will later form the core of the oricha objects the novice receives in the course of the initiation ceremonies. This is done by questioning stones found in suitable locations (usually pertaining to the natural domain ruled by the oricha in question) as to whether they are the oricha. Once extracted from nature, these objects are then subjected to ritual processes paralleling the procedures later performed over the initiate's head and cast in an idiom of gestation and eventual birth (see Brown 1989). The initiation itself, thus, essentially circumscribes the parallel *nacimiento* (birth, or, more literally, "coming into the world") of a new priest and a new set of ritual objects, both conceived of as vessels of the god.[23] In the case of palo monte, the origin of a new nganga object and its relationship to its human owner lies, not in a "natural" process of procreation, but in a deliberate act of appropriation. Cabrera has described the initiation of a relationship with a nfumbi as based on the establishment of possession over substances metonymically connected with the personhood of a deceased human—that is, the extraction of skulls, bones, bone fragments, or simply dirt from a grave, an act socially valuated, not as the appropriation of a natural substance, but as theft. "The brujo," she writes (Cabrera 1983, 121), "gains control over a 'muerto' by appropriating his bones." For "the soul . . . remains tied to the body, 'it customarily goes in search of what is his' as long as [bodily] remains subsist." In classic Frazerian terms, the act of acquiring control over a fragment of, or a substance associated with, what was once a human being establishes mastery over his or her spiritual essence. In somewhat different terms, I was told that the key to the successful performance of this operation was to "con a spirit who wants to get out of the grave."[24] Since a spirit need not always dwell in the immediate vicinity of the grave, it is necessary to attract it—by means of songs and offerings of liquor and other substances—to the remains of its former body. Once this is achieved and the spirit's willingness to enter into human service is confirmed by a gunpowder oracle, a payment consisting of a few coins is deposited at the point where spirit-embodying materials are taken from the grave.[25]

But it is not only that a payment initiates the link between the muerto and its human alter. A contractual symbolism pervades all interchanges between tata ngangas and the spirits they command. Oricha and muertos connected through kinship usually receive ritual attention in order to assure their blessing of and cooperation in important ventures and projects.[26] Contrariwise, apart from certain regular offerings of tobacco and hard liquor designed to maintain their proper functioning and loyalty, ngangas are usually fed after the completion of a specified task. They work on commission as it were, and, while the appropriation of their mystical labor defines a relationship expressed in an idiom of exchange, it would seem to conform far more to Marxist notions of social relations mediated by the transaction of commodities than to a Maussian image of gift exchange. Particularly in Miami, there exists a rich—and sometimes rather ghastly—folklore about the kind of recompense that ngangas receive for their labors. One story about a nganga named *avisa me con tiempo* (warn me in time)[27] dealt with a drug dealer who began feeding his nganga lines of cocaine—not only to enhance the spirit's vigilance, but to bind him ever more closely into a relation of dependency. The stratagem backfired. The nganga began to demand more and more cocaine, joining his owner in a vicious circle of economically fatal overconsumption, until the latter was eventually done in—not by the police, but by his suppliers / creditors.

Although meant, on one level, as a comment on the vicissitudes of dealing a drug to which one is addicted oneself, this narrative links up with an imagery concerning the necessity of separating the identities of mystical entrepreneurs and their spiritual labor force: feeding a nganga drops of one's own blood is said to enhance its effectiveness immensely. This, however, may result in the spirit acquiring a taste and eventually undoing its master.[28] By turning one's blood into the object of commodified exchange, one risks falling victim to the wants of a fundamentally alienated, because literally thing-like, consumer: the nfumbi. Dehumanization through the agency of things is, thus, but the flip side of the fantasy of total control gained through rendering objects extensions of the self. "I don't like to work with these pots [meaning nganga objects]," a practitioner of regla ocha told me in Miami, "they eat you alive"—expressing, it would seem, his unease with the tendency toward dissolving conventionalized boundaries of identity between persons and objects that historically characterizes the western Central African minkisi complex but that also figures prominently in European folklore about Faustian bargains and man-made familiars, Iberian versions of which can be documented in Cuba. Yet his comment also accentuated—if perhaps unwittingly so—a different series of no less historically determined signifiers pointing toward rather more concrete New World histories of violence and dehumanization, histories centering around the consumption of commodified human beings by a plantation economy based on slavery.

For, on yet another level, this need to evade excessive closeness to one's spiritual alter—sharply contrasting, as it does, with the striving of oricha devotees to deepen the intimacy between themselves and their deities (and, it would seem, Bakongo ideas about merging the identities of minkisi and banganga in ritual action)—appears to relate to ideas of dominance and control that resonate, not just with the contradictions of wage labor, but with those of slavery. This is patently evident in ritual symbolism—such as in the practice of verbally abusing, beating, spitting on, or flogging the nganga object in order to activate it, "drive it to work." "The 'brujos' themselves," writes Ortiz (1958, 851),

> customarily say to their "prenda": kotina ngua ko, which is an offending comment about "your mother"; [they address it as] nkenta muya nkala or "lesbian," if the spirit thus conjured is that of a woman; mpangui manganone y mpangui nkoya or "sodomite," if it is a man; and [they use] other similarly insulting terms, both in the African language and in Spanish, while they simultaneously spit on or beat it [i.e., the nganga object] to drive it on so that it gets to the point; just as the slave driver used to in order to make a slave work for him.

As Ortiz's further remarks indicate, this practice may combine ideas about the abuse of "sold souls"—widespread in Europe as well as West Africa, although modified in the present case by the historical experience of a system of chattel slavery—with Bakongo ideas about the activation of minkisi, particularly of the *nkondi* or "hunter" type. Just as nails and other sharp metal objects are driven into nkondi to incite its wrath and send it on errands of vengeance, so do other forms of abuse stimulate the Afro-Cuban nganga.[29] "When asked why he insulted the enkise and threatened him with a beating," Ortiz continues, "he [i.e., the priest] answered us 'in order for it to heat up and start moving, so that it [begins to] work.' In other words, not in order for it to react angrily against his abuser, but so that it gets excited, enraged, heated up, as if it were a machine that had to be under steam to function or an electric battery that had to be charged with energy." As David Brown (1989, 375 n. 71) was the first to point out, the Afro-Cuban term for the verbal abuse showered on the nganga, *puya* (nowadays also used for more "respectful" taunting songs intended to incite the oricha to come down during a possession ceremony), can be etymologized not only toward the Spanish meaning of the pointed tip of a weapon (such as the picador's lance) and, figuratively, a piquing comment. It also directly relates to the Bakongo practice of "nailing" minkisi of the nkondi type, about which Laman (1962, 90) writes as follows: "Sharpened sticks, knife-blades, iron pins (luvuya, plural mpuya) etc. may be hammered into Nkondi in order to make him more effective, for as soon as he is wounded he acts like a human being, who recoils and wonders what it can be. He at once understands the connection." In the Cuban case, however, the imagery of force and coercion extends further than just that. If the western Central African minkisi complex dissolves the distinction between objects and persons in the creation of personalized medicines (or "medicinalized" persons, in the case of ancestral graves and the bodies of chiefs), the Cuban equivalent circumscribes a less indeterminate but at the same time more ambivalent conception of the relation between people and things: one akin to the historical social fantasy—characteristic of New World plantation regimes and amply attested to in the discourse of enlightened proslavery economists—that the productive consumption not only of alienated labor, but of the objectified laborer him- or herself represented a desirable social end. Many of the ritual activities associated with the activation of Afro-Cuban ngangas resonate with allusions to a history of New World slavery. During possession rites in the reglas de congo, the medium whose body incorporates the nfumbi's presence (called *ngombo*[30] or *mbua,* i.e., "dog"[31]) speaks in a linguistic register identified by the practitioners with *bozal,* the creolized speech of African slaves in nineteenth-century Cuba. He likewise is expected to, and indeed tends to, address the tata nganga as *mi amo,* "my master." Underscoring this analogy in another register, the onset of possession is marked by a ritualized march of the medium along the perimeter of the ritual space, termed—according to Cabrera (1979, 142)—"making a round of the sugar mill" (*dar vueltas por el ingenio*). Finally, many of the nfumbi invoked and incorporated in such rites are, in fact, thought of as *being* the spirits of slaves. Often addressed by (what are nowadays regarded as) stereotypical slave names combined with terms descriptive of the type of nganga that their spirits inhabit ("Francisco Siete Rayos," "María Chola Wengue," and so forth), their brutish and violent possession behavior—countered by no less violent ritual action—enacts a present-day reading of nineteenth-century slave experience.

CANNIBALS ALL

But the nfumbi is not merely the abject slave of his human master. A different stream of tropes represents him as the apical character in another hierarchy, a structure of command and submission that subjects Bakongo conceptions of the principles ordering the relations between medicines and spirits within minkisi to a historically cogent twist. "All these animals [contained in the Afro-Cuban nganga]," Cabrera (1983, 131) tells us, "each one according to its character, are the slave gangs ('sometimes they revolt') that assist the spirit in his workings. 'The ngangulero [, says one of her informants, is] the master [who] commands the spirit; the spirit who is the slave driver gives orders to the animals and branches that are his slave force.'" The indication of a possibility of revolt is not serendipitous. Just like historical systems of New World slavery were beset with chronic social contradictions arising out of the fact that the complete dehumanization of the slave as a mere factor of production remained an unattainable goal, so does the Afro-Cuban nganga complex condense historical experiences, not only of control and brutalization, but of resistance and violent retaliation as well. Indeed, part of the danger of manipulating nganga objects—often expressed as *manejarlos,* "to steer or drive them"—is that "revolts" may radiate outward to endanger the whole structure of command. If treated improperly, ngangas may be rendered ineffective. But they may also turn against their owners, consuming their persons in a phantasmagoric transformation of the Hegelian image of the dialectics of dependence between master and slave.

If we can believe Miguel Barnet's rendering of the centenarian ex-slave Esteban Montejo's autobiography,[32] such contemporary imagery may represent not just latter-day recensions of a historical reality. The violence condensed into the symbolism of the Afro-Cuban nanga complex may, in fact, stand in a direct referential relation to a history that was experienced, by its protagonists, as a deadly struggle to wrest control over one's human subjectivity by depriving others of it. Talking about his life on the plantation Flor de Sagua in the early 1870s, Montejo recounts how slaves engaged in a kind of mystical warfare against abusive owners. His account of the *juego de mayombe* (mayombe ritual)[33] on this plantation entails a fantastic reversal of roles in which slaves assert their collective personhood by seizing, objectifying, and ultimately undoing their master:

> During mayombe drums were played. A nganga, or great cauldron, was placed in the middle of the courtyard [i.e., the place enclosed by the slave barracks]. In this cauldron were the powers, the saints [i.e., mystical beings]. And the mayombe was a useful undertaking. They [i.e., the slaves] started to drum and sing. They brought things for the nganga. The blacks asked for health for themselves and for their brothers and that harmony would reign among them. They made *enkangues*, which were [ritual] works with earth from the graveyard. With this earth they made little mounds in four corners to signify the [cardinal] points of the universe. Into the cauldron they gave *pata de gallina*, which was an herb, together with cornhusks to protect the people. When the master punished a slave, the others took a bit of earth and put it into the cauldron. With this earth they resolved whatever they wanted [to achieve]. And the master would fall sick, or some misfortune would befall his family. For, as long as the earth was in the cauldron, the master was imprisoned in it [as well], and not even the devil would be able to get him out of there. It was the revenge of the *congo* against his master. (Barnet 1984, 34–35)[34]

This remarkable account of mystical slave resistance invites speculation about the historical continuity, not only of the form of such practices, but of the conceptual universe within which they become salient. It thus seems not overly far-fetched to read these passages in Montejo's recollections as evidence for the transatlantic salience of highly specific sets of notions relating to the social uses of *minkisi mi nloko*, or "cursing charms," which, as MacGaffey (1986, 156) notes, "healed by attacking the witch responsible for the affliction." Relating to the modern Hispanicized verbal construction *enkangar* as well as to the Kikongo verb *kanga* (both meaning to tie or bind a person by mystical means), the term *enkangue* and the practice of victimizing a perpetrator of evil by symbolic seizure and incorporation into the structure of a nganga / nkisi bespeak a notion of the master, not only as an author of suffering, but as a witch, someone whose extraordinary powers and actions are judged to be evil by a self-defined collectivity. As MacGaffey (1977; 1983, 140–47; 1986, chap. 6) has pointed out, among the Bakongo (as in much of Central Africa), the definition of incidents of mystical aggression as witchcraft—and not, for example, as the exercise of chiefly power—is a matter, not of intention or effect (both are thought to kill or result in other forms of depersonalization), but of the social valuation of its ends. "Approved and disapproved violence," MacGaffey writes (1986, 160), "are the two complementary values of the struggle to control others and to escape from control." Homologous with witchcraft in both form and effect, the powers of chiefs and elders are endured as legitimate means to keep greater evil in check (MacGaffey 1986, 163–64). In the absence of legitimizing authority, however—as, for example, was the case after the colonial unmaking of Bakongo chiefship[35]—the fundamental ambiguities of such conceptions come to the fore. The result, in a sense, was akin to a militarization of social arrangements in which healing could proceed only by counterattack. Hence the proliferation of increasingly specialized minkisi in the area affected by the ravages of *Bula Matadi* during the early ethnographic period.[36] European observers tended to read this state of "mystical free enterprise" as a degeneration of religion into magic. What had occurred, however, was the destruction of an indigenous system of allocating authority by an invading state that, not only blocked the channels through which institutionally validated violence had previously flown, but itself exhibited the features of a regime of witches (see Axelson 1970, 263–66). Under such circumstances, then, the balance of power shifted from larger corporate cults centered on the figure of sacralized persons (chiefs) to those centered on the relation between sufferers and personalized sacra (minkisi). If politics had always been a continuation of religion by other means, ritual now turned into a mode of combat. The function of minkisi mi nloko in this context is obvious: to remove affliction by wounding the aggressor, to release the victim by seizing the captor.[37]

This, in turn, clearly links up with the copious evidence—ranging from the seventeenth century to the twentieth—of how Africans perceived the Atlantic slave trade as a system of cannibalistic consumption. Fears of being eaten by white captors are widely documented among Africans traveling along the horrible route from initial enslavement, through the middle passage, to the final insertion into the workforce of a New World plantation.[38] Prominent as they figure in the documentary sources on the Central African slave trade, references to such fears of falling victim to cannibalism are more usefully interpreted as pertaining, not to conceptions of the literal ingestion of human body matter, but to ideas about the victim's loss of personhood through sorcery or other evil machinations designed to augment the sorcerer's wealth and power. The Kikongo verb *dia*, thus, not only signifies factual acts of consumption—to eat up foodstuff, to spend money, and so on—but also refers to the wasting of human beings (*dia bantu*) through nefarious sorcery or mystical vengeance (Laman 1962, 216). If witchcraft figuratively transformed people into walking meat traded and consumed by witches in an ultimate perversion of normal social relationships, the Atlantic commerce in human flesh literally turned Africans into personified goods, human commodities exported overseas and duly wasted by the plantation economies of the New World.

This analogy was not lost on some contemporaries (Monteiro 1968, 1:56) and was still very much present to MacGaffey's Bakongo informants in the 1960s. In their recensions, the trade in coerced labor (then centuries old and only barely abolished) took the form of a commerce in stolen souls. These were smuggled out of the country in man-made vessels and forced to work on plantations and factories in the land of the dead (Mputo): a parallel universe variously identified with Portugal, Belgium, or America and thought of as the wellspring whence consumer goods produced by the labor of dead / depersonalized Africans would, in turn, issue forth onto African markets (MacGaffey 1968, 1972, 1978; cf. Axelson 1970, 264–65). Such conceptions were not of recent origin. Peschuel-Loesche (1907, 361) observed in the late-nineteenth-century Congo that the local use of minkisi seemed to transpose the struggle of everyday life in a blighted and war-stricken region onto a mystical plane. As the ravages of disease, famine, and slave raiding under the reign of Bula Matadi increased, so did the functional specificity of minkisi employed to battle concrete and unseen dangers. Neither was it fortuitous that the term *nkisi* came to be applied to the storehouses of the European factories (Ekholm 1991, 56), where the objective products of coerced African labor miraculously mutated into wealth and power; or that the Kikongo term for Europeans, *mindele*, connotes distinctly nonhuman features that corresponded, in several ways, to the characteristics of witches and malign spirits (Axelson 1970, 289ff.).

That conceptions of the evil nature of the South Atlantic System also informed the outlook of those caught up in the Cuban sector of this economic complex is more than likely—even though (or perhaps *precisely because*) some of them may have found themselves in captivity as victims of witchcraft accusations.[39] There, plantation slavery entered its most brutal phase only in the early nineteenth century, when working slaves to death and replacing them by importation came to be seen as the economically most expedient way of reproducing the plantation labor force. Already in 1766 Agustín Crame had referred to African slaves as "machines employed in the cultivation of the land" (cited in Moreno Fraginals 1978, 2:13–14).[40] Yet it was not until the early nineteenth century—when Spain finally opened Cuba to free trade in sugar and slaves, thereby plunging the island into a hectic process of plantation development—that such fantasies of total instrumentalization of slaves as machinery in human shape became a horrific social reality. "Considered as equipment," writes Moreno Fraginals (1978),

> the slave lost human significance. He was devoid of personhood. Therefore, his birth and death or his purchase and sale entered the daily accounting ledgers as the gain or loss of an asset. Although they bore different names for reasons of identification, the congo Luís or the gangá Pedro were equally human machines, typified productive equipment, acquired in the market, and they were attributed a determinate productivity per harvest season and a median durability given their submission to standardized exertions and their adequate maintenance. (2:14–15)

"As with all other equipment," he continues, rational planters "calculated the depreciation of the blacks, which, in the years of the height of barbarism, was [generally] estimated at an annual 10 percent" (2:15).[41] Yet, if the calculations of enlightened planters turned slaves into hybrids between humans and things, the economic practices in which they engaged likewise took on a hybrid character. As Moreno notes elsewhere, the mills—now increasingly mechanized, steam driven, and run according to sophisticated methods of calculating productive efficiency—"were like huge grinders, which chewed up blacks like cane" (Moreno Fraginals 1976, 143), an image that recalls Erika Bourguignon's twentieth-century Haitian informants' conceptions of being "eaten by machines, evil gods or other entities." It certainly would have reflected an experiential reality under conditions where the average annual deathrate of workers stultified by chronic sleep deprivation, malnutrition, and physical overexertion may at times have approached or even exceeded 10 percent.[42] Although the drying up of the illegal slave trade in the mid-1860s after a last furious wave of African imports (Pérez de la Riva 1979; Eltis 1987, 245) gradually led to an improvement of living and working conditions on Cuban plantations, it is obvious that the "old congos" whose mystical practices Montejo reports had lived through the horrors of both increasingly vicious forms of enslavement in Africa and the most violent stages of the Cuban plantation regime. And it is not unlikely that the idiom of witchcraft may have provided them, not just with an explanation of their predicament, but—by its very logic—with a means of identifying the author of evil and returning the attack. If so, what the slaves on Flor de Sagua were engaging in was resistance to an abusive and dehumanizing system of labor extraction by mystical means. Countering witchcraft with violent sorcery became a political means of restoring moral balance.[43]

PRECARIOUS STATES

But Montejo's statements seem to indicate yet another sense in which the use of early Afro-Cuban minkisi objects may have served political purposes. Acts of mystical aggression presuppose, not only a definition of victimizers, but a definition of victims as well. Once invoked, subjectivities become mutually defining, even in the case of the unilateral abrogation of personhood to an objectified other (Leach 1977). Montejo's prefacing of his account of mystical vengeance perpetrated against a master by the slaves' invocation of collective health and harmony, thus, suggests that the harnessing of minkisi to the goal of vindicating maltreated slaves *eo ipso* defined a local collectivity of victims; a group whose collective proneness to abuse translated into an incipient consciousness of representing a moral and, therefore, political community. As Montejo (Barnet 1984, 42) wistfully reminisces in a passage that seems to evoke Fanon's conception of therapeutic violence (see Perinbam 1982), "If you think about it well, the *congos* were assassins. But if they killed somebody it was because they had been harmed themselves." Sundering victims from victimizers, the violence emanating from the scene of ritual action, thus, both is productive of a moral consensus and demarcates its limits, limits beyond which social interaction potentially turns into sheer predation.

In this sense, the ritual manipulation of Afro-Cuban minkisi may, at least in some cases, have represented, not only a formal, but functional analogue to western Central African "drums of affliction." As Janzen (1983, 21) has argued in his magisterial treatment of the history of the Lemba cult, there may be some grounds for arguing that the emergence of such ritual complexes both was preconditioned by the same factors and served similar purposes, as processes of state formation. MacGaffey (1993, 80) likewise notes the eminently political functions of certain types of minkisi in situations lacking clearly defined structures of centralized authority. In his view, chiefship, here, represents "a collective affliction cult and a commission, rather than an institution" (MacGaffey 1986, 139). In another context, Werbner (1979) speaks of related phenomena as "personal security cults" that precipitate the forging of moral communities among individuals and groups not linked by clear-cut loyalties pertaining to ideologies of descent or otherwise integrated into a coherent polity.[44]

This, however, is precisely what we may presume to have been the case on mid-nineteenth-century Cuban slave plantations. There, widely fluctuating populations of initially totally estranged first-generation Africans were haphazardly integrated into a brutal labor regime in the field and a fragile structure of everyday cooperation in the slave barracks. Some scholars, such as Moreno Fraginals (1983), have argued that the Cuban plantation regime systematically inhibited the forging of meaningful social relations among slaves in order to ensure their degradation to a state of mere embodiments of labor power. We know, however, that, aside from "creole" complexes of social relations—such as shipmate bonds and the kinship structures that tended to evolve from them under certain circumstances (Mintz and Price 1992; Besson 1992, 1995)—there also emerged social units based on New World constructions of African ethnic identity, often integrated by collectively salient conceptions of the relation between sacred knowledge and social power (Palmié 1993). Although we have no clear indications of the role that minkisi-like objectifications of power may have played in the internal structure of the so-called cabildos de nación (voluntary associations of first-generation Africans condoned by the Spanish colonial state), it is quite possible that the hierarchical organization of these associations—headed as they usually were by elected "kings" and a staff of titleholders (Ortiz 1921)—may have been vertebrated by conceptions akin to those operative in the context of the early-modern Bantu-Cuban cult groups that evolved from congo cabildos. "The Casa Nganga [i.e., cult group]," states one of Cabrera's informants,

> "which is also called Casa Mundo [house of the world], comes to be like a tribe: there is the chief or king with his vassals. There is the wife of the king, of the foremost father [meaning tata nganga], the Mfumo, who is like a queen. This principal Padre Nganga is addressed as master. Primary master. Below him in the structure of command comes the Mayordomo, or his two Mayordomos, and the Madrina ["godmother"] of the nganga—fundamento [another term for nganga]—the Ngudi Nganga, and the Gajo's madrina, the Tikantika or Nkento Tikantika Nkisi. Then there are the Nkombos or Ngombes, Mbua, the children or dogs of the Nganga, those which are mounted by the Fumbi" (of whom the spirit of the dead person serving the Taita Nganga takes possession), "and the Moana." The Moana are all who belong to the house [i.e., cult group] of the nfumo.[45] This is the same description that, in a profane sense, is given to us by those who knew the old and now vanished "Cabildos de Congos." (Cabrera 1979, 130)

If Cabrera's latter assertion has a basis in fact—and there are indications that it does—minkisi not only structured certain kinds of slave resistance, thereby transforming mere collectivities of fate into collectivities of intent. Perhaps even more fundamentally, such objects may have engendered social relations among their users that were characterized by differentiated allocations of sacred authority. Minkisi, in other words, generated forms of social power hinging on ritual roles. Given the correspondences, in both ritual form and conceptual elaboration, between the Central African nkisi complex and contemporary practices in the Afro-Cuban reglas de congo, the assumption that the knowledge "stored" in minkisi objects, as it were, could bring forth certain social arrangements seems not implausible (see Guyer and Belinga 1995). Although African bodies of knowledge pertaining to individual types of minkisi may have been regionally specific enough not to have led to the emergence of transplanted cults of affliction in the New World, it is possible that a sufficiently generalized conception of the—potentially politicizing—role of such objects in the social process may have empowered the formation of American slave collectivities organized around objective sources of authority. Such New World cults of affliction—or, in other words, incipient polities—based on a notion that, no less than the allocation of sacred authority to human persons, things could bind people into relations of power and dependence may be hidden by the scant documentation we have of the cabildos of people who styled their diasporic identity as congos (see Ortiz 1921; Palmié 1993). But the principles on which they were founded do seem to surface more clearly in another context.

As David Brown (1989, 373–74) has speculated on the basis of an imaginative reading of the visual evidence, the imagery of the contemporary Afro-Cuban nganga object—usually an iron cauldron packed with a variety of sacra but prominently crowned with an array of *palos,* that is, wooden sticks jammed into the structure—may be read, not only as a miniature "forest" or "wilderness" (*monte, manigua*), but as an analogue to the stockaded settlements (*palenques*) of nineteenth-century Cuban maroons. Viewed thusly, the fundamental ambiguity of the relation between object (spirit/slave) and objectifier (priest/master) in modern Afro-Cuban practice appears in a different light: in keeping with the precarious nature of subjectivity in the ritual interaction with Afro-Cuban ngangas, the spiritual slave driver may well turn into a rebel captain, the symbolic plantation into a maroon camp. This transformation is certainly suggestive of the mercenary relationship between the contemporary tata nganga and his nonhuman counterpart. But perhaps it is also indicative of yet another level of historical experience that may have gone into the making of the modern Afro-Cuban nganga complex.

In a fascinating passage in his dissertation, David Brown (1989, 376) quotes one of his New Jersey informants styling himself as an urban warrior-priest conquering alien territory by incorporating it into the "world" enclosed in his nganga. "The Prenda," the man told Brown, "is like the whole world, there is something of everything, wherever you are, you have to put something in it: if I go to New York to establish a point, I have to take something back from there and put it in the Prenda. You see, we are like warriors. When an army conquers a country, they leave an occupying army. I live in Union City; if I go to New York to 'work' I will have to leave scouts or guards, build a perimeter, a fortress." In the following, Brown's informant unravels an amazing imagery of ritual skirmishes, forays, and retreats in the spiritual combat zone on both banks of the Hudson River; he talks of spies and sentries posted in a twelve-block perimeter of his own house, warning him of enemy movements, of spirits in the enemy territory of Manhattan whom he tries to draw on his side by strategic deposits of sacrifices, and about his image of himself as the master of a mercenary army under the command of the nfumbi. When Brown asks him, "Is there a right or wrong, a morality in the work?" he answers: "Whatever you pay it to do, it will do, it's not like the Santeros."

While such grisly imagery may well correspond with some Bakongo conceptions of the nightly errands of minkisi of the mi nloko or avenger type, there are sources of comparative data closer to Brown's material both in space and in time. For the knowledge enabling this urban warlock to operate in what he portrays as a spiritual no-man's-land along the shores of the Hudson River might conceivably represent the outgrowth of a series of transformations of a complex that had taken shape in the human as well as physical wilderness of the Cuban *manigua* at no later date than the third quarter of the nineteenth century. Although the term *manigua* and some of its more figurative significata have prior applications, it refers, here, to the geographically fluctuating no-man's-land between the operational territory of the Spanish troops and the precarious space wrested from the former colonial regime by the ragtag army of "Cuba Libre" during the so-called Ten Years' War of 1868–78.[46]

As part of the popular campaign to malign the Cuban insurgents, in 1875 a Spanish periodical published what remains the earliest unambiguous visual evidence for the existence of minkisi-like objects in Cuba.

In an article aiming to cast the Cuban independence struggle as a race war fought by barbaric savages, the magazine *La Ilustración Española y Americana* ("Isla de Cuba" 1875) depicted an anthropomorphic wooden sculpture that had been captured by Spanish troops in the course of an assault on a black rebel camp. Already the general stylistic features of this object are reminiscent of western Central African sculptural traditions. Yet the fact that the central part of the figure's torso bore a cavity packed with medicines[47] strongly suggests that this so-called *matiabo* idol represented an Afro-Cuban version of a nkisi. This is corroborated by the author's comments on the use of another object depicted at the side of the matiabo idol—a cow horn, the opening at the base of which bore an inserted mirror. The insurgents, we are told, "suppose that when the tip of the horn . . . is applied [to the medicine-filled cavity in the figure's body], a little mirror within the opening of said object will reproduce the shapes and movements of the Spaniards in close pursuit of the insurgent group possessed of such a treasure" (2). This account leaves little doubt that we are dealing with a direct precursor of the so-called *mpaka* horns used in contemporary Bantu-Cuban divination.[48] As the author further states, when the Spanish troops confiscated the objects, one of those taken prisoner fell to his knees and implored the soldiers in tears: "Kill me, your mercy, my Lord! But do not touch this greatness of the forest" (2).

Another contemporary account from the first Cuban War of Independence corroborates this tactical use of minkisi in military operations: here a nkisi enclosed in a goat skin induces trance in a female member of a black maroon settlement (palenque) turned insurgent camp. As the Cuban soldier who witnessed the scene recounts, the medium fell down, tossing about on the ground, while the other members of the camp continued chanting at her: "Then taita Ambrosio directed himself to the afflicted one, touched her head, and asked her: Ma so-and-so, where are the troops? Troop very close, in such-and-such a place—answered she, without stopping to toss. And this place was invariably at about ten or twelve leagues' distance" (cited in Ortiz 1973, 112). We are dealing here with episodes from a brutal and drawn-out guerrilla war in which Afro-Cuban minkisi had become harnessed to the goal of military reconnaissance. More so, particularly the first source indicates that what the imprisoned maroon called *esa grandeza del monte* may well have been more that just a technical device, or weapon, used to evade Spanish attacks. It may have been the central force integrating a community at war.

Thus, aside from the technical aspects of sending spirits into enemy territory to reveal vital intelligence—which it is tempting to read into these quotes—it is perhaps more useful to ask what kind of warfare these *matiabos / matiaberos* (i.e., users of matiabos) were involved in. Cuban nationalist historians have generally been inclined to cast Afro-Cubans in the role of ardent supporters of the independence struggle, and, indeed, there is evidence to support such a view. Still, it is sufficiently clear that, despite de Céspedes's initial emancipation of his own slaves and the continued public declaration of an antislavery stance on the part of the revolutionaries, insurgent leadership vacillated on the issue and displayed all but a consistent line of action in the theater of military operations.[49] While their scorched-earth tactics with respect to plantations were designed to wreak maximum damage on Spanish economic interests, they also invariably released large numbers of former slaves into a legal as well as a social limbo. Slaves initially welcomed their liberators, and many fled from still-functioning plantations into rebel territory. However, as Franklin Knight notes (1970, 162), there is little evidence in support of the view that the cause of Cuba Libre united blacks and whites in a common struggle for freedom. White commanders displayed considerable unease about integrating the so-called *libertos* into their troops, and military necessity at times forced rebel leaders to reinstitute a regime of forced labor. Freed people invariably bore the brunt of such wartime measures, often being reassigned to the same plantations from which they had been liberated or fled (see Scott 1985, 45–62; Robert 1992). By the early 1870s, their rate of desertion from insurgent units suggests that many of them chose life in the manigua—with its considerable dangers of falling victim to the increasingly ruthless depredations of Spanish troops, loyal Cuban *voluntarios,* and rebel forces alike—over participation in an anticolonial war effort.

De Céspedes's declaration of freedom to inhabitants of palenques, that is, runaway settlements established during colonial times, hardly revolved the ambiguities surrounding the halfhearted commitment of Cuba Libre to the cause of emancipation. There is certainly no question that many, if not most, palenques existing within the combat zone were swept up in the revolutionary war, as Franco (1973, 115) states. There is also considerable evidence that many of their inhabitants, at one time or other, found themselves integrated into the struggle for independence—although less often within the combatant units (*fuerza*) than as part of the *maja*, the train of civilians, often inhabitants of destroyed villages, that invariably trailed, and often impeded, the former. Surely, many erstwhile *apalencados* fought valiantly on the rebels' side. Still, there is at least incidental evidence that the encounter between blacks and whites in the manigua may at times have driven home to the former that they had, in a sense, remained human objects that were simply caught up in a process of exchange from one legal owner to another.

In one of several memoirs of his insurgent life in the manigua, the Cuban writer Ramón Roa, thus, recounts in chilling detail an encounter between his rebel unit and a group of about ninety matiabos, whom Roa (1950) describes as "a devilish and mysterious sect of ignorant and ultra-vicious men that, in those days, were hunted down at gunpoint to force them to offer their services to the Republic since they had passed from being miserable slaves to the status of free citizens" (100). Roa's callous sarcasm leaves no doubt that the legal fact of (provisional) emancipation did not translate into a redrawing of the boundaries of a moral universe. Far from cooperative, the matiabos were dragged from their settlement and—according to Roa—eventually proved themselves "such a fatal and dangerous plague" in the eyes of their liberators that executing their priest and leader, Tata Ezequiel, and destroying his bush shrine appeared the royal road to the integration of these maroons into Cuba Libre. Forced to march along with Roa's unit, the matiabos nevertheless continued to hold divinatory rituals—only that now their prognostications seemed to direct the insurgents into a Spanish ambush (100–105). As Roa adds elsewhere, at a later stage of the revolutionary war, such groupings of matiabos were "dissolved"—either by "the extreme forms of justice mandated by the [Cuban] council of war or by the swift action of those ordered to persecute these sectarians" (128).

Whatever else these contemporary accounts tell us about the social history of the Cuban insurgent struggle, they give a fairly precise picture of the role that objectified sacred knowledge played as a political resource among people who could not define themselves as anything but communities at war. This, we should recall, may have been true regardless of which side of the combat zone they found themselves located on. And we should not forget that, although many of these communities had come into being as a result of the internal turmoil of the revolutionary wars, a good many of them had formed in the course of a more generalized warfare that had, for centuries, pitted maroons against a slaveholding colonial state. Whoever the matiabos were—and regardless of whether this label points to concrete historical social units—the model of minkisi-based cults of affiction that seems to have characterized the social organization of some such groups was carried on beyond their physical destruction at the hands of the colonial or republican state.

GENEALOGIES OF MORALITY

By the early twentieth century, we find evidence of the employment of minkisi-like objects in the police records generated by waves of persecution of practitioners of Afro-Cuban religions in the wake of the first U.S. occupation of Cuba and the so-called niña Zoila case[50] of 1904, discussed in the next chapter. Revolving around the alleged sacrificial killing of a white girl, the niña Zoila case unleashed an outburst of racist terror geared toward ridding Cuba of its legacy of African savagery, bequeathed to the young nation by its slaveholding past. Culminating in the so-called race war of 1912 and the lynching of five presumed sorcerers in Matanzas in 1919,[51] this "witch-hunt" affected practitioners of all forms of Afro-Cuban religion. No less than nganga objects, oricha shrines found in the course of raids on the homes of Afro-Cubans were subjected to wholesale destruction or confiscation. In effect, these purges violently dramatized the conjunction of two ideological complexes that had reached a certain stage of maturation at the end of the nineteenth century. As I will argue more fully in the following chapter, these were, on the one hand, the civilized superstitions of a self-consciously postcolonial elite about the genetic predisposition of Africans toward religious fanaticism and other types of disorder: an ideology predicating scientifically informed national progress on the disciplining and political muting of a racially defined labor reserve located largely beyond the limits of civil society. On the other hand, these civilizing projects found their counterpart in Afro-Cuban notions of spiritual combat directed against the witchcraft of a neocolonial state that once more relegated black Cubans to a role of dependent suppliers of labor to the (now largely American-owned) sugar mills. In this sense, the surge of racist violence in the aftermath of the founding of the Cuban Republic may provide yet another historical foil against which contemporary representations of difference between single Afro-Cuban religious traditions might fruitfully be assessed. Yet it does not satisfactorily explain the way palo and ocha eventually came to be inserted into a relatively coherent universe of discourse within which their respective modes of operation circumscribe highly disparate and morally charged images of sociality.

Why, in other words, did ocha come to occupy a semantic position in the Afro-Cuban religious imagination that appears to signal a moral opposite to the imagery of violence, terror, and depersonalization that palo condenses? It is patently counterfactual to presume that the "founders" of Yoruba-Cuban religion somehow escaped the historical experiences from which palo may have derived the warlike and, indeed, predatory ethos that Afro-Cuban religious practitioners ascribe to it today. If shorn of its romantic idealization of the "folk," Bastide's (1978) old hypothesis that the "less faithfully preserved" Bantu religions of Brazil more easily gave in to the pressures of the values of an individualistic urban modernism—thus disintegrating into a socially atomized regime of magic—is intriguing but most certainly wrong. But Africanistic interpretations, that is, that Central African religious orientations may have preconditioned enslaved Africans from that region to certain cognitive responses—as, for example, Schuler (1979) and Karasch (1979a) have argued in the Jamaican and Cariocan case—likewise remain intriguing but historically unsubstantiable conjectures.[52]

Although my own hypotheses will necessarily remain as tentative as theirs, I am much more inclined to view the result—the casting of palo as an instrumental regime of magic, opposed to a largely expressive regla ocha—as a consequence of the social history of the aggregation of these two complexes, uneasily conjoined, as they are, in contemporary ideation and practice. Regardless of that—and the historical speculations I offer in the following—it is important to note that, within the discursive possibilities generated by the symbolic universe of a larger Afro-Cuban religious formation, palo serves as a medium for the expression of experiences that are emphatically not just "of the past." The mercenary ethos ascribed to the tata nganga circumscribes a specific model of human sociality that has lost none of its relevance of expressing the moral derailment of social relations in the world inhabited by contemporary practitioners of Afro-Cuban religion. This is so because ascriptions of morally ambiguous exercises of what Cubans call *interés*—forms of ruthless self-interest invasive of relationships conventionally cast in terms of trust and mutuality—find a particularly vivid expression in the ambiguities of the discourse deployed in characterizing relations between tata nganga and the nfumbi that they command. The contrast between palo and ocha, then, is not just the result of the accidental conjunction of two African traditions under the conditions of Cuban slavery. Irrespective of its history—to which I now briefly turn—this contrast enables what we may call a form of *indigenous* Afro-Cuban historiography and social analysis that stands on its own, a language of practice, we might say in the case of palo, that makes use of recensions of a past of slavery but resolutely speaks to the present.[53]

We know that, by the turn of the twentieth century, Yoruba- and Bantu-Cuban religious formations were well on their way to at least practical integration. What may have been previously separate "streams of tradition" (Barth 1984) now increasingly began to be carried forward in time (and space) by the religious activities of individuals who had begun to draw on elements of both complexes in formulating differentiated personal religious routines. Apart from some documentary evidence, there are good oral historical indications that single Afro-Cuban priests—such as, for example, the famous Habanero Andrés Facundo de los Dolores Petit, founder of the intentionally syncretic "Regla Kimbisa del Santo Cristo del Buen Viaje"—had come to achieve such an integration of heterogeneous bodies of knowledge into coherent systems of practice well before the end of the nineteenth century (Cabrera 1977). By the early twentieth century, however, their conjunction had become an irrevocable social fact. We do not know when the aggregate of heterogeneous notions and practices that we currently associate with the term "Afro-Cuban religion" attained relative stability (or whether, indeed, this impression of relative stability is not just an artifact of ethnographic reporting, tending as it does to flatten out the temporal dimension in its frequent uncritical evocation of tradition). Yet there is ground for speculation on how a present discourse transmuting divergences in cultural form into an idiom of moral difference may have originated from the ways in which practitioners, themselves, came to define a division of cultic labor.

From what we know today, it is clear that the large waves of importation of Yoruba-speaking slaves from the Bight of Benin in the first half of the nineteenth century crucially affected the further development of Afro-Cuban religious formations. At least in the western regions of Cuba, the nineteenth century represents a watershed, marking the increasing displacement of older—ethnographically unknown—Afro-Cuban religious cultures by an emerging priesthood of evolving Yoruba-derived cults. To be sure, a New World "congo royalty" associated with the institution of the cabildos de nación (and probably underwritten by the power of minkisi objects) survived into the twentieth century. By that time, however, social relations between individuals who constructed their identity with reference to diverse bodies of knowledge had become intense enough to lead to the partial reinscription of the relations between priestly manipulators of Afro-Cuban minkisi in an idiom of equivalences between categories of minkisi and conceptions of divine entities salient within the evolving discourse of what came to be known as *regla ocha*. This interaction—syncretism if you will—may have been accelerated by the catalytic effect of spiritism, diffusing into an Afro-Cuban universe of discourse from its original white upper-class entry point into Cuban society to certain segments of the Afro-Cuban population at roughly the same time. Defining a generalized scheme of progressive evolution in the afterlife, Kardecian spiritism may have contributed to easing the intellectual integration of heterogeneous conceptions about the dead in the two major Afro-Cuban religious traditions. For it offered the concept of a moral continuum along which nfumbi, alien muertos, the ancestral and priestly dead of regla ocha, and even the oricha themselves became classifiable as specimens of more or less obscure or enlightened stages in the ontogeny of numinous entities. For many a practitioner, elements of spiritist doctrine nowadays function as a kind of euhemeristic glue that holds his or her individual belief system together. Paleros, in this sense, simply work with darker, tormented, and potentially malicious beings, whom they subject to morally suspect treatment—buying, capturing, exploiting, and abusing them, instead of "giving them peace and light" (the standard spiritist phrase for proper interaction with "unevolved" entities). Yet, while most contemporary practitioners of Afro-Cuban religion will agree with the spiritist judgment of one of my Miami informants that "the dead are a bridge between good and bad," this does not provide a full answer either.

Indeed, I would suspect that such cannot be found in a single predisposing cultural scheme analytically construed to match observable facts (such as Bakongo ideas about witchcraft, Yoruba notions of royal authority, or the speculations about Central African conceptions of morality adduced by Schuler). Given the current state of affairs, it seems more likely to suppose that neither ocha nor palo could have evolved to their present phenomenology and moralized positions along a spectrum of differentiated ritual idioms without the presence of the other within the same social framework. To be sure, this is a question most fruitfully pursued in the analysis of individual religious careers—how do people come to integrate their existence as kinfolk and devotees of the oricha with the role of ruthless mystical entrepreneurs prescribed by their simultaneous commitment to the cult of a nganga object? Yet the complex itself might, perhaps, be better approached from another angle. How, to rephrase the question posed at the beginning of this chapter, do ocha and palo complement each other in the definition of a symbolic universe that seems to satisfy practitioners' needs for a body of knowledge enabling them to operate in a mundane world saturated with disparate and partly contradictory mystical referents? Where, to fully reverse the traditional course of inquiry, does a conception of human subjectivity as constantly endangered by violent negation fit into the scheme of the beneficial interpenetration of human and divine selfhood exemplified by the logic of initiation and sacrificial exchange in regla ocha?

The pragmatic answer to this question is easy to see. It is easy to elicit support from practitioners for the view that ocha and palo stand to each other like religion and magic, expressive and instrumental forms of human-divine interaction. Ostensibly working off each other like nature and culture, generalized conceptions of what the two religious complexes stand for reinforce a tilting of moral balances in ocha's favor. Palo is thereby transported to the limit, if not beyond the bounds of a moral topography structured by consensual notions of idealized sociality. Although ultimately anchored in the system of coordinates laid out by ocha, this mapping device also charts a good part of the moral terrain within which self-identified paleros move. Their self-conception as mystical entrepreneurs and mercenary healers is, at least in part, objectified in specific opposition to ocha. Hence the universally felt need for physical segregation of matters ocha and palo—a stratagem literalizing an ideological discontinuity by projection onto real social space. Still, however credible the results of such dialectical constructions have become for everyone involved, they merely suggest absolute divisions where there are, in fact, at best relative ones.

Viewed closely, the bonds between oricha and their "children," at times degenerate into exploitative relations of divine patronage masked by gift exchange. In contemporary Havana, where nearly everyone undergoes experiences of deprivation, the gods have turned into a ragged royalty, haggling with their subjects over issues of food, and consuming a good deal of their livelihood in the form of ritual dues. Conversely, in Miami, the oricha have embarked on a lavish course of conspicuous consumption, visibly marked by increasingly stunning ritual displays (cf. Brown 1993; Flores Pena and Evanchuck 1994)—readable, and, indeed, at times read, not just as documents of the orichas' redistributive powers, but as self-objectifications of an entrepreneurial elite. But these are really only the outcome of the differential play of an independent variable: just as the ritual kinship networks linking "godchildren" (*ahijados*) of a single initiator in regla ocha occasionally turn into conduits for accusations of witchcraft, so are such moral ruptures, at times, conceived of as mediated, not by the sinister presence of a nganga object, but by the greed and zealousness of the oricha themselves. Changó may reveal himself a loudmouthed braggart, Ogún may turn into a wanton destroyer and Ochún into a fickle prostitute willing to sell her affections to the highest bidder.[54] The tremendous pharmacopoeia of regla ocha consists of preparations designed, not only to heal, but also to establish control (see Cabrera 1983), and, if an idealized conception of regla ocha defines the oricha as the only site toward which humans can legitimately extend their selfhood, these divine others, at times, not only condone, but encourage maneuvers aiming at the expansion of the self to the detriment of human others. After all, few divination specialists in regla ocha would deny that, apart from seeking help in health crises, the desire of their clients to assert control over the sexuality of a present or potential partner or to attain economic goals at the expense of others secures the better part of the income that their gods derive from their "children's" oracular practice.[55]

At least under certain circumstances, then, the oricha themselves take on mercenary characteristics. Hence the distinctions between palo and ocha's alleged instrumental and expressive orientations—much written up in a literature that casually draws on what, in fact, is bad indigenous sociology of religion (e.g., Wetli and Martinez 1983)—crumble, ultimately returning us to purely pragmatic native considerations that, by themselves, do not explain much: palo works faster, it can guarantee results, but it entails dangers to the self that working ocha will not pose.

It is important, however, to recall that the ranking of palo and ocha along a moral hierarchy rests on definitional criteria derived from the theology of regla ocha. Ocha, in this sense, lays out the coordinates of a "value space" on which instances of ritual practice are differentially mapped. But, if ocha marginalizes palo within a moral topography derived from its own idealized projections of human-divine sociality, it also prioritizes palo along a temporal axis. Apart from the order of initiation, there are other symbolic facts that underline a concept of the temporal primacy of palo. "Muerto pare al santo"—the dead give birth to the gods—practitioners of regla ocha will say, usually referring to the obligation to honor deceased priests and family members before commencing a ceremony involving the oricha, or to clarify certain euhemeristic notions about the origins of the gods themselves. But, as noted above, the term *muertos* points to an ambiguous category of beings. Despite all spiritist influence on the conception of the afterlife, the dead remain entities whose moral characteristics can be ascertained only in the course of interaction. The realm of the dead is literally a wilderness, a kind of primeval preserve into which people venture to domesticate or colonize its denizens. Such forays may be undertaken to assert kinship ties and bind the dead into enduring moral relationships. But the realm of the dead is also a reservoir of mystical labor and may turn into a theater of slave-raiding operations.

And, in this sense, I think, current representations of the relation between palo and ocha may be historicized in yet another, perhaps more adequate, way. Given the contemporary evidence, it appears not unlikely that the partial syncretism between ocha and palo occurred in the form of the appropriation, not only of originally Bantu-Cuban mystical techniques, but of a whole ideological complex relating to the dead by the priesthood of a Yoruba-influenced Afro-Cuban religion emerging in the course of the nineteenth century. The absorption of locally preexisting Bantu-Cuban forms and the partial superimposition of Yoruba-style conceptions of the divine on a—largely intact—complex of ritual intercourse with the dead would, thus, appear as complementary aspects of the same semantic move. On the one hand, it resulted in a stratagem of displacing an imagery of violent depersonalization and heteronomic control over human selfhood (prefigured as it seems to be in conceptions of witchcraft common to both modern Yoruba and Bakongo) into the construct of a universe of discourse that, from the perspective of early Yoruba-Cuban priests, may have appeared both allogenic and autochthonous—the preexisting cults of Afro-Cuban minkisi. On the other hand, this "externalizing" shift would have been countered by an acceptance—perhaps even strategically motivated—of a hegemonic value scale defined by an ascending Yoruba-Cuban religious discourse. The latter, thus, became increasingly purified (on, at least, a rhetorical level) of its darker components but increasingly weakened, ritualistically, by its emphasis on idealizations of images of sociality hardly in touch with the realities of a world structured by a political economy that continued to predicate the individuation of Cuban selves on the subjugation and exploitation of African others.

THE PAST IN THE PRESENT

The latter qualifiers—*Cuban* and *African*—ought not to be seen, here, as unambiguously referring to racial constructions. Rather, they circumscribe historically volatile and synchronically fluctuating collectivities within which individuals come to be positioned (Riley 1988; Guillaumin 1995)—whether they find themselves forcefully recruited into categories reducing their selfhood to the markers of difference that they appear to embody within a specific discursive regime or are "ideologically interpellated" into constellations of practice and privilege (as Althusser might have it). Particularly if we proceed from conceptions beholden to the North American historical experience, language is apt to play tricks on us here. At least since the time of Martí's visionary pronouncements on the transracial foundation of Cuban nationhood, the imagined community that would become the Cuban Republic in 1902 was predicated on the ideological disavowal and discursive subsumption of racial difference under a project of ostensibly hybrid cultural homogeneity (see Martínez-

Echazábal 1998). Almost inevitably, the result was a situation that Lancaster (1992, 230) describes as the presence of racial ideologies in the absence of corporate races. Yet, if the specifying play of the color sign on the Cuban body was individualized in a way delegitimizing racial otherness, the subsumptive (while simultaneously differentiating) power of a self-consciously modernistic national cultural project brought Africanity and Cubanness into pronounced disalignment, all the while the two conceptual domains began bleeding into each other.[56] In fact, as in so many other situations where postemancipation situations demanded ideological reconciliation, not only with a racially heterogeneous vision of nationhood, but with what Segato (1998, 130) calls the "insertion of bearers of African culture in . . . particular national settings," the leakage of meanings between racial and cultural domains, in the Cuban case, generated forms of indeterminacy and semantic excess that threatened to expose a fundamental arbitrariness in the relation between bodily signifier and cultural signified, thus prodding attempts at (often violent) resolution (see O'Malley 1994; Appadurai 1998). As a result, and irrespective of the structural facts of Cuban forms of racism,[57] representations of cultural difference tend to function as the most insidious devices for demarcating the boundaries of internally pacified social spaces—particularly since their meanings can be, and at times certainly are, conflated with notions of origin and descent.

Still, different from the wider public spheres of both contemporary Miami and Havana, *Africanity* and *blackness* are not coterminous in the world of Afro-Cuban religion. Nor have they, for what must surely be a long time, more than partially overlapped in complex and ill-understood ways. "Today we know," Teodoro Díaz Fabelo (1960, 16) wrote shortly after the Revolution, "that the most knowledgeable and well-respected [titleholder of] abakuá is white.—There are many cult houses [of regla ocha] in which blacks do not enjoy an elevated position. Most of the initiations performed are undergone by whites. Santería and all the other cults of African origin live off the whites, particularly [white] women . . . What is more: of the fifteen persons most knowledgeable in this respect in Cuba, five are whites." Díaz Fabelo was an Afro-Cuban secondary school teacher from Regla, a town across the Bay of Havana, who was recruited as an ethnographer by Fernando Ortiz. And he knew what he was talking about. Regla had long enjoyed the paradoxical reputation of a predominately white town that nevertheless represented a crucial site both for the history of the cult of ifá in Cuba[58] and as a bastion of the male secret society abakuá. The most-knowledgeable and well-respected abakuá to whom Díaz Fabelo refers was the formidable holder of the *Iyamba* title of Regla's powerful abakuá potencia Enlleguelle Efo, Manuel de Jesús "Chuchu" Capaz, who was soon after to emigrate to the United States.[59] At the time of Díaz Fabelo's writing, socially white Cubans had documentably been members of abakuá for more than a century and had probably occupied priestly ranks in ocha for two generations.[60] Different from ocha, where priestly genealogies function as a major authenticating device in contemporary practice, the picture is less clear as regards the history of palo. Yet there is little reason to doubt, a priori, that the current "racial" distribution of the reglas de congo in Cuban (and Cuban-American) social space originated in the early twentieth century—a period during which, as we will see in the following chapter, the meaning of both *race* and *Africanity* within the Cuban public sphere underwent crucial transformations.[61]

Such complications of commonsense linkages between race and Africanity notwithstanding, both in Miami and in contemporary Havana images of blackness *are* being deployed to signify the break-off points of moral consensus. And, not surprisingly, such tendencies articulate with the ocha/palo distinction. In the forefront of the 1993 U.S. Supreme Court decision on the legality of animal sacrifice, Ernesto Pichardo, president of the Church of the Lukumí Babalu Ayé and eventual victor in the case, repeatedly complained to me about the witchcraft his political opponents in the Hialeah city council were perpetrating against him. To him, there was no question that much of the spiritual adversity with which he was battling came from "the palo camp." Moreover, in his view as well as that of other phenotypically white Cuban-American *santeros,* the incidence of witchcraft in Miami had increased, not only because of the thriving drug trade, but also because of the advent of the "antisocial scum from the black barrios of Havana" in the course of the so-called Mariel exodus of 1980.[62] Pichardo's suspicions, however, should not be construed as implying a simple equation between palo, blackness, and evil. Although partly expressed in racialized (or, better perhaps, potentially racializing) terms, his claims to being victimized by witchcraft emanating from his political opponents must be interpreted with some care.

Being himself, not just a priest of regla ocha, but the possessor of several nganga objects, Pichardo was well aware of the implications of the charges that he leveled against the members of Hialeah's city council, none of whom (and like Pichardo himself) even faintly qualified as black by North American standards. Indeed, if the trope of blackness figured in the confused and deeply antagonistic dialogue that ensued in South Florida's exile community over the place of an African-derived religion within the American public sphere, it was played out according to North American, rather than Cuban, conceptions of race. Still, as I have detailed elsewhere (Palmié 1996), Pichardo's own reading of the events that led to the eventual downfall of Hialeah's mayor Raúl Martínez involved a conception of the oricha's retributive power based, ultimately, in Pichardo's ongoing oracular communication with the divine. In his ruthless and ultimately futile opposition to the orichas' will, Hialeah's mayor—so divination revealed—had taken recourse to immoral means of deploying superhuman powers. The most likely conclusion appears to have been that what was at play was palo.

Divination appears to have confirmed it. Through the intermediary of qualified but unscrupulous priests, Hialeah's city government had begun to send out vengeful nfumbi. As for other practitioners of Afro-Cuban religions, palo provided Pichardo with a language for expressing what ocha, by itself, cannot articulate, although it may well contain it in practice: the possibility of fundamentally immoral forms of rationality entailing a reduction of the value of human beings—including dead ones—to the ultimately impersonal equivalent suggested in the payment received, or coercion endured, by a nganga for the execution of its nefarious commission. Regardless of the manner in which the lines of battle were drawn in the mundane political contest that eventually culminated in front of the U.S. Supreme Court, Pichardo's perception of it as the surface effect of a drawn-out mystical battle imbued it with an invisible—indeed, literally spectral—dimension in which past politics informs present ritual and ritual becomes thinkable as present history. Although social whiteness undoubtedly played a tremendous role in the political arena within which Pichardo was maneuvering as an American citizen pressing a class-action suit, it clearly was not an issue within the symbolic universe that linked him to a lengthy genealogy of oricha priests going back to an enslaved *ara takuá* (i.e., Nupe) priest in nineteenth-century Cuba and a chain of nganga objects from which his own specimen descended. Nor is the matter adequately explained by reference to the far more generalized misgivings that the predominantly white Miami exile community bears toward its country of origin—which, owing to the population drain of the last three decades, is blacker today (at least by North American standards) than it has been since the late nineteenth century. The linkage obtains at a deeper level. And it is to some of its possible historical matrices of origin that I now turn in order to conjure up yet another set of ghosts from disavowed, but hardly superseded, pasts.

3. UNA SALACIÓN CIENTÍFICA

The Work of Witchcraft and Science in Cuban Modernity

> Upon other *Obeah-men*, who were apprehended at that time, various experiments were made with electrical machines and magic lanterns, but with very little effect, except on one, who, after receiving some very severe shocks, acknowledged that his master's *Obi* exceeded his own.—Bryan Edwards, *The History Civil and Commercial of the British West Indies*

In an article published in the disciplinary augury *Annual Reviews in Anthropology* a few years ago, Sarah Franklin (1995) notes that, regardless of the acerbic polemics characterizing the so-called science wars of the 1990s, many of the issues on which contemporary critical science studies seem to turn implicitly reproduce the foundational logics of the knowledge practices on which such studies focus. In her view, much of the current debate about "the nature of nature" or "the reality of reality" (166) tends to obscure its epistemic and operational basis in a culturally specific mode of knowledge production. Both realist and relativist parties to the exchange, Franklin argues, essentially partake of a critical tradition in Western scholarship—one that remains internal to the regime of truth that it aims to perfect and sustain. Caught up as the debate is in the discursive and institutional tangles of this tradition, the potential for radical critique is largely preempted by the specifications of possible utterances and admissible statements within the language game that is Western science. By the same token, Franklin invests rather sanguine hopes in the capacity of anthropology to shine light into the dark recesses of an "invisible" and presumably "culture-free" zone of "Euro-American [scientific] certainties." What she has in mind are, not the kind of lab ethnographies that have revealed some of the mechanisms by which scientific knowledge is socially constructed, but the more thoroughgoing enterprise of relativizing science *as* culture. Only by laying an axe to the roots of the "perspectival techne" underlying both Western science and scientized Western common sense will we expose the discursively submerged mechanisms that "black box" or unmark the work that conceptual artifacts—say, *nature, society, the market, mechanical causality,* or *empirical truth*—perform in the service of knowledge practices that are as globalizing in their centrifugal penetration of alien intellectual space as they are local in origin, positionality, and intent. Anthropology, Franklin feels, is uniquely suited to this task—not just because of its traditional focus on the relativity of thought systems, but because "the sustained critique of its own practices . . . has kept it 'in crisis' since mid-century," such a state of uncertainty and unsettlement presumably enabling its practitioners "to draw on a recent history of great transformations in their own discipline" (179–80)—doubtlessly to the advantage of us all.

Despite the wedge of irony I cannot help driving into Franklin's smug assessment of anthropology as "a better, more inclusive, less naively Eurocentric and even more objective [!] form of scholarly inquiry" (1995, 179) I find myself in fundamental agreement with much of her argument. Recall, for example, the role that anthropology—or perhaps the Azande as delivered by E. E. Evans Pritchard—played in the so-called rationality debate a generation ago. Much of the ethnographically enhanced criticism of logical positivism unleashed in the course of this controversy nowadays looks, not just stilted, but politically suspect. Part of this has to do with the discipline's new sensitivity to the arbitrariness of the ethnographic sign. To mention just one rather painfully obvious defect of this enterprise, none of the participants in the original debate ever seems seriously to have entertained the idea of questioning the social and cultural foundations of the descriptions under which non-Western cognitive practices were transformed into ethnographic facts. The line, we now understand, between ethnographic authority and authoritarian ethnography was thinner than our modernist elders thought. Sadly, but consequentially, Robin Horton might well find himself accused today of "orientalizing" African traditional religion, and "occidentalizing" Western science at one and the same time, of matching Western recensions of the colonized other against the colonializer's reading of his Western selfhood in an unwitting exercise at intellectual omphaloscopy. To be sure, dealing in typology has become increasingly dangerous business since Max Weber's time. Bowing to the language eman from Chicago these days, we might say that totalization and totalitar ism now increasingly stand to each other as modernity to its malcontents.

Viewed thus, we currently observe—at least arguably so—what with Edwin Ardener (1989) we might call a *hiccup of demodernization* with respect to a core contribution of anthropology to the old rationality debate. A case in point is the resurgence of anthropological interest in witchcraft—a subject once thoroughly spoiled by modernistic excesses such as social strain theories or psychological functionalisms. This situation has changed dramatically in the last few years. Repressed from the list of career-generating topics for some two decades, witchcraft has returned with a vengeance. Divorced from moribund structural-functionalist fictions of normalcy and deviance within closed social systems, "spectral stories" about the "immoral economy" and "poetics of predation" of witchcraft (Comaroff and Comaroff 1993, xxv–xxvi) are now part of a different agenda, one that is very much alive. It is an agenda that still foregrounds the signifying potential of the witch—in a way that translates, however, not into symptoms of contradictions endemic to delimitable social arenas, but into those of a pandemic of sinister signification[1] born from attempts at "coping, imaginatively and practically, with the encounter between local and translocal worlds" (Comaroff and Comaroff 1993, xxvi). As Jean Comaroff and John Comaroff (1993, xxix) formulate the new consensus, witches "embody all the contradictions of the experience of modernity itself, of its inescapable enticements, its self-consuming passions, its discriminatory tactics, its devastating social costs."[2]

PROSPERO'S MAGIC

So do, of course, scientists. And not just in the self-consciously paramodern discourse of contemporary popular cultural criticism. Citing Marcuse, Stanley Tambiah (1990, 146) speaks of technoscience as a "vehicle of reification," productive forms of political domination that leave the individual "subject to an objective rationality that is both uncontrollable and mysterious." As scientific rationality spills over from its proper domain into other areas of life, it suffuses them with a sense of vulnerability to external control and transparency to power that most of us find, if not frightening, at least morally vexing. Popular representations of the moral derailment of science have flourished in Western cultures since at least the times of Mary Shelley (or Marlowe, for that matter). The mad scientist is with us still. New reproductive technologies, genetic engineering, the emergence of virtual worlds with their as of yet largely indeterminate potentialities as arenas for subjection—all these appear to loop backward, in some forms of the Western imaginary, to a stage where fair turns foul and Trobriand deep-sea fishing magic might just be what the situation calls for. Malinowski to the contrary, however, magic and science do not stand to each other as tradition to modernity, nor is the equation reversible in such terms. It is trite to point out that the terms themselves were always analytically inadequate, and not just because modernity is a myth (Comaroff and Comaroff 1993) and science both "ordered technique" and "rationalized mythology" (Bernal cited in Hill 1986, 293). What is at issue here is not just the ethnocentrism of uniformitarian fictions of utility and rationalization and their retrospective teleologies, and it is not enough to assert that the very vision of a passage from the mystical to the mundane is part of a self-making scenario by which the West fashioned itself against the rest. Rather, the conceptual separation on which these distinctions build already derives its intelligibility and seeming descriptive value from a prior submersion below the level of discourse of the mutually constitutive character of magic and science.

A brief look at the grand twentieth-century interpretations—from Robert Merton to Michel Foucault—of the seventeenth-century shift from signatures to representations, from magical to rational means of explanation, prediction, and control in Western thought amply bears this out. If Newton was the last of the magicians, whom would we want to call the first of the scientists? And on what grounds other than the authority by which royal academies retrospectively invented a tradition of rational inquiry, forcefully patriating undisciplined thinkers within the genealogical charters of politically conservative scientific disciplines? One is reminded here of seventeenth-century notions of real artificial magic, of Newton's vast unpublished alchemical writings, or Descartes's inspirational dreams and flirtations with Rosicrucianism, all of which were conveniently policed away in the annals of rational science. Hildred Geertz (1975, 76) put a finger on this moment of the dispersal of inopportune knowledge into newly opened conceptual reject bins in her critique of Keith Thomas's overtly Malinowskian theory of the historical dynamics of English magic and religion. "It is not the 'decline' of the practice of magic that cries out for an explanation," she argued, "but the emergence and rise of the label 'magic.'" This has an apt parallel in Wyatt MacGaffey's (1981, 230) assertion that, in contemporary social science, religion "has become an affliction that *other* people have, a bizarre form of discourse for which . . . only bizarre explanations come to hand."[3] Hence our peculiar incapacity to deal with the politically highly rational aspects of religious fundamentalism. Would we concede the possibility of an Islamic science (see Asad 1993)? If, as Homi Bhabha (1984, 97) puts it, "hybridity is the sign of the productivity of colonial power," then magic and religion (unless it is civil) are signs of the productivity of science. They display, to quote Bhabha again, "the necessary deformation and displacement of all sites of discrimination and domination."

But what about science as an affliction of the mind? A globally anomalous, historically specific, and, therefore, truly local excrescence of the Western social imaginary? False religion? A belief system like any other, wholly explicable in terms of something else—say, social structure, individual needs, anxiety-reducing functions, or anticipatory affirmations of prosperity and plenty? Domination is certainly a powerful candidate on the list of potential explananda. As Frances Yates (1964) has shown so vividly in the case of Giordano Bruno and his contemporaries, well into the seventeenth century the distinction between the Neoplatonic magus or hermetic operator and the natural philosopher and scientist was likely to be moot. The two figures had to be torn apart by a rhetoric hedging in politically acceptable forms of rationality. "The mechanical philosophy yields no security to irreligion," Joseph Glanville pronounced the British Royal Society's political credo in 1644 (Hill 1986, 287), thereby enchanting the halls of science and mechanizing God in one and the same discursive move aimed at preempting the counterhegemonic potential of hermetic speculation. Even in Counter Reformation Rome, infringement of the rationalized disciplines of theological knowledge elicited violent reactions.[4] But nominalism and the very real effects—including physical terror and deadly violence—that conceptual separations can bring forth are not the only issues at stake.

Magic, science, and religion are not merely artifactual of each other in an intellectual or discursive sense. Karen Fields (1982, 1985) has made a splendid case for the mutually constituting role of British indirect rule and Central African witchcraft in a fantastic—or, shall we say, phantasmagoric—collusion perpetrated in the service of a business-as-usual moral fiction of legitimate domination that makes Macbeth look like a staunch bureaucrat. Although this is rarely acknowledged, I think that Fields actually led the way toward an interpretation that Giordano Bruno's case still lacks. That the modernity of witchcraft—in fact, the deep imbrication of colonial development economics with the very phenomena that it was predicted to supplant—was first discovered in the early 1990s in Africa was probably fortuitous, but not accidental. In a rather audacious variation on themes by Max Weber and Eric Williams, Ralph Austen (1993) has argued that the connection may have been there all along. In his view, the African slave trade, New World plantation economies, and the eighteenth-century European consumer revolution represent the global crucible in which *both* African witchcraft beliefs *and* European rationalities were forged at the expense of historically variable others. Prospero's magic worked both ways. MacGaffey's (1968, 1972, 1978) data on Bakongo theories of European economic growth and export capacity well illustrate the point. Rather astutely, his informants pinpointed the exploitation of the disembodied labor power of Central Africans killed by sorcery as the motor of unequal development. In terms of accounting for the history of the lower Zaire and its role in the so-called South Atlantic system as an exporter of commodified humans, the rationality of such theories is hard to deny. At the very least, they compare favorably to the patent failure of the predictions ventured by that particularly obnoxious branch of Western export knowledge usually referred to as *modernization theory.* White (1993a, 1993b, 2000), Meyer (1995), and Scheper-Huges (1996) offer more timely analogies. As the latter notes with respect to organ-theft rumors centering on notions of an unequal exchange of biotic materials—and, hence, life chances—between First and Third Worlds, it is not enough to assert that such "stories are metaphorically true, operating by means of symbolic substitutions." "In the violent everyday encounters in shantytowns and squatter camps," Scheper-Hughes (1996, 5) continues, "the metaphors are materialized in the grotesque enactment of medical, economic, and social relations which are experienced at the immediate level of the violated and dismembered body."

CALIBAN'S SCIENCE

As a Caribbeanist, I cannot resist mentioning the well-established but very insufficiently understood semantic link between the terms *obeah* and *science* in British West Indian popular parlance. Both, arguably, represent Old World imports into the lexicon of presentday West Indians.[5] But, contrary to appearances, there are good grounds for arguing that the contemporary conceptual content of the former owes at least as much to a British colonial legislative tradition going back to the first anti-obeah laws in the aftermath of the 1760 slave rebellion as to whatever African traditions went into the making of the practices initially (or subsequently) so classified (see Götz 1995). Conversely, while ethnographers working in the British Caribbean since the 1940s tended to give "science" or "book magic" short shrift as a symptom of acculturation, the few descriptions that ever entered ethnographic texts arguably support comparisons with the burgeoning literature on neotraditional witchcraft in Africa.[6] I have long thought that a solid business history of the Chicago-based DeLaurence Company—the major, if not the sole, purveyor of Western occult literature to the Caribbean in the early twentieth century (Simpson 1956; Hogg 1961; Smith 1965; Elkins 1986)—would provide a key to the region's religious history more revealing, perhaps, than the outmoded West African ethnography usually adduced for similar purposes. In the hands of a competent "scientist," the pages of compendia of Western magic such as the *Petit Albert* or the *Sixth and Seventh Books of Moses* begin to vibrate with ostensibly weird, but morally acute, and wholly contemporary resonances. As in the case of the Bible in the hands of a Rastaman, it is a move back from text to life, comparable to those performed by contemporary African reversionists who pore over colonial ethnographies in search of an African past yet to be enacted (Palmié 1995).[7] And it is a move comparable to those of Renaissance systematizers similarly in search of a future in an eclectically constructed past. What these disparate instances of the pursuit of knowledge share is a fundamental rationality that is hard to deny and a similar history of disfiguration and displacement performed by dominating discourses—

including, in this case, anthropology and its disciplinary fetish of authentic cultural difference.

As early as 1961, Donald Hogg noted in a brief communication on the differentiated character of Jamaican occult knowledge practices that his ethnographic materials indicated

> that some of our fondest ideas about magic may be ethnocentric and faulty. That which we call "magic" is not necessarily mere superstition, but may be the product of intelligent, careful searching for knowledge. . . . Magicians are not usually charlatans, nor do they rest secure in traditional knowledge or beliefs—they pursue their work sincerely and many of them search constantly for better ways of aiding their clients. Thus the application of the term "science" to some practices usually considered magical may not be entirely inappropriate. Obeah men, so to speak, may be Scientists too.

And he concludes, most significantly, that,

> on the other hand, the suspicious attitudes which motivate their skepticism and experimentation suggest that our own sense of "science" could perhaps stand close examination, and that it might not be unprofitable to investigate the incentives of persons that we call scientists. Some of them may turn out to be Obeah men. (5)

Be that as it may, the science a handful of self-consciously literate propagators of a knowledge born out of 350 years of global commerce in slaves and sugar—such as the Haitian physician and occultist Artur Holly (whom Zora Neale Hurston eagerly befriended), his Trinidadian predecessor Myal Djumboh, alias Cassecanarie, or the far more radical authors of *The Holy Piby* (Robert Athlyi Rogers), the *Royal Parchment Scroll of Black Supremacy* (Fitz Ballantine Pettersburgh), and *The Promise Key* (Leonard P. Howell)—confined to printed tracts and books since the turn of this century still awaits discovery as a reflection of, to speak with Bhabha (1984, 97), "strategies of subversion that turn the gaze of the discriminated back upon the eye of power." What we face, in other words, was arguably an Afro-Atlantic analysis of the witchcraft of modernity. An analysis, I should like to add, more penetrating, perhaps, than anything Paul Gilroy (1992) has mustered in support of his black countermodernity thesis.[8]

What makes this subject particularly relevant to a concern with the interaction between different systems of knowledge and rationality is the unexplored possibility that colonial British West Indian legislative experiences with obeah provided the precedent for the witchcraft ordinances enacted all over British Africa under indirect rule. If this were so—and there are a few indications—might we not entertain the hypothesis that the cultural knowledge that enslaved Africans undoubtedly carried to the New World was transformed into African American traditions in close articulation with an emerging regime of legal reconnaissance and control that was subsequently reexported to British Africa in the course of a nineteenth-century intra-imperial transfer of technologies of power?[9] Could it be that the colonial officers–cum–lay ethnographers who drafted witchcraft laws in the early years of the twentieth century unwittingly wore Caribbean spectacles? And, if so, what might this tell us about the possibility that many of the classic colonial African ethnographies not only reflected "traditional" realities partly produced by colonialism but were themselves products of a reading of African colonial realities in terms significantly prestructured by powerful analogies to American (and, of course, Indian) colonizing experiences? We now know how colonial technologies of documentation, surveillance, and control significantly shaped the realities they purported to reflect or deal with.[10] As Bhabha (1984) and others have argued, what the colonizer knows is always already a hybrid formation. But we have hardly begun to question the extent to which the diffusion of colonial knowledge across imperial space served to construct—and, thereby, factually restructured—some places in the image of others (but see Cohn 1981; Appadurai 1986; Fardon 1990). That Sir Arthur Gordon went to Fiji from a post in Trinidad may well speak to the subsequent history of Indian plantation laborers there. Just so, the fact that the judge who investigated the 1915 Nyasaland rising found himself presiding over the trial against Leonard Howell and the other early founders of Rastafari in Jamaica in 1934 (Hill 1981, 67 n. 42) may tell us something about the way in which John Chilembwe's ghost may have hovered, not just over the Jamaican courtroom, but over Kingston's prophet-ridden squares and squatter settlements or the island's mushrooming rural millenarian encampments.

Viewed from the other side of the fence, however, this process by which colonial knowledge practices actively inscribed themselves into their object—including the filling of such multipurpose categories as *native unrest, slave insubordination, rebellion, idolatry,* and *witchcraft* with locally specific content—found its counterpart in the simultaneous appropriation and reconstruction of European culture within the practical and speculative knowledge of colonial subject populations.[11] In this respect, the critical issue is not only that specific technologies of control may have contributed, in significant ways, to shaping the forms that resistance against them would take. It is also that the practical exigencies of day-to-day rule led to the absorption of the hybrid forms emerging from such processes into the cultural realities within which both colonizers and colonized came to know and deal with each other (cf. Spivak 1988b; Bhabha 1984). In this sense, both obeah and science as well as—say—Christian witchfinding movements in Africa like Bamucapi or the drilling practices of Songhai Hauka adepts (Kramer 1993, 134–37) and Herero Otrupa companies (Werner 1990; Hendrickson 1996)[12] form part of a larger Atlantic social and intellectual space; a formation the structure and dynamics of which elude analyses conceived within the geopolitical units European colonialism imposed upon it but that neither become fully accessible to Gilroy's rather superficial focus on intertextual currents in Black Atlantic literary and musical production (see Cooper 1996). It is within the context of such an analytic frame that we might begin to re-member, on a conceptual and moral level, what, not just the growth of global capitalism, but its dominant systems of knowledge production have dismembered (see Linebaugh and Redicker 1991, 2000). What is more, by thus refocusing our lenses, we might begin to see how the sinews of empire interlock with the ligaments of resistance and in what sense Prospero's magic and Caliban's science are, not just complementary, but constitutive of each other, albeit in highly complex and often unpredictable ways.

THE CUBAN REPUBLIC AND ITS WITCHES

The aims of this chapter, however, are more restricted. In what follows, I intend to take a look at an episode in the formation of a "moral artifact" (Karen Fields 1982) born from a strange symbiosis between Afro-Caribbean religion and Western science in early-twentieth-century Cuba. The emergence of this artifact spelled physical danger to practitioners of Afro-Cuban religions caught up in a "zone of transcourse" (Kelly and Kaplan 1994, 129) that provided the stage for a period of at least two decades of massive, often violent repression, beginning in late 1904.

In November of that year, a twenty-month-old female toddler named Zoila Díaz disappeared from her parents' homestead in Güira de Melena, a rural town south of Havana. Within days, confidential information received by the mayor led to the arrest of three elderly Africans—Domingo Bocourt, Julián Amaro, and Jorge Cárdenas—members of a cabildo or voluntary association of Africans and their descendants who had chosen the name Congos Reales as a referent to their collective identity. Initial questioning as to their having abducted the child brought no results, and the prisoners were soon released owing to lack of evidence—amid public outrage fired by Eduardo Varela Zequeira, a correspondent with Havana's daily *El Mundo*. Like others, Varela was keen to perceive analogies, if not connections, to another murder of a ten-year-old white female committed in Havana in July and conveniently pinned on a twenty-seven-year-old illiterate black soil peddler with a police record named Sebastián Fernández alias Tín-Tán. A fortnight later, shortly before Fernández faced his death sentence on December 4, the second girl's body was found near the house of her parents in a state indicating violent mutilation, including removal of the heart and—as the pervasive rumor had it—pickling or salting of the corpse. By mid-December, Bocourt and his associates found themselves in jail again, together with two other Africans and nine native Afro-Cubans. They were charged with having assassinated and disemboweled the child—by now pervasively named *la niña Zoila*—for sacrificial or curative purposes. The theory about the nature of the crime emerged early on and, although it was never factually proved in court, led to the eventual execution of Bocourt and his alleged accomplice, the creole Victor Molina, in early 1906, life sentences for two others of the accused, and prison terms ranging up to fourteen years for three more.[13] Being a "locally known" *brujo* or African wizard, Bocourt, so the reasoning went, had aimed to cure an African woman named Juana Tabares of a magical harm (*daño*) done to her by the whites in the period of slavery, which had led to the successive deaths of her nine children. The therapy of choice, it was argued, consisted in the application of the girl's blood. In all likelihood,

Tabares and her children were suffering from tuberculosis, a major killer of slaves even in the comparatively "ameliorated" stage of Cuban slavery near the advent of abolition in 1886, and a continuing scourge of Cuba's poor in the postemancipation period—an explanation that, of course, hardly exhausts the semantic spectrum of the Cuban term *daño*.[14] Selected to procure the victim, Molina had killed the girl and extracted, not only the blood, but various organs from her body, which he intended to fashion into charms to be sold commercially (ANC, Audiencia de la Habana, leg. 627–10).

In itself, the story is as fascinating in its dramatization of themes pertaining to the abuse of dehumanized bodies for economic purposes—a key feature of slavery if there ever was one—as it is obscene in its political implications and concrete results. In his moving oral history of the events that led to the lynching or otherwise ill-accounted deaths of six presumed brujos in Matanzas in 1919, Ernesto Chávez Álvarez (1991) counts eight supposed ritual child murders between 1904 and 1922. I have not scanned the whole extent of the contemporary press, but I think that three times that number would easily come closer to the truth. Incidents involving the death of children interpreted as victims of *brujería and* brought to court in such terms occurred in 1908, 1913 (twice), 1914 (twice), 1915, and 1919 and repeatedly elicited, not just vociferous bursts of public outrage, but mob violence and attempted or consummated lynchings of assumed black brujos. In public discourse, the term *brujería* soon came to flourish as a highly inclusive category, metonymically condensing a variety of practices by means of a superimposed metaphoric scheme in which Afro-Cuban cultural otherness and the violent murder of children interacted to form a novel complex exhibiting stunningly expansive tendencies.

Between July and December 1904 alone, Fernando Ortiz (1973, 186–208) clipped thirty-seven newspaper articles referring to highly diverse events interpreted as manifestations of brujería. Referring to the eastern provinces a decade later, Havana's chief of police Rafael Roche Monteagudo (1925, 215) argued that "brujería augments daily in geometrical progression." Indeed, brujería proliferated—if in the form of a growing ubiquity of signs newly perceived as symptoms of its presence or created in the course of measures to eradicate it. Particularly in the aftermath of the so-called race war of 1912—the violent military campaign to smash the Partido Independiente de Color[15]—Havana's urban police increased raids on Afro-Cuban cult groups in an attempt to stem what was felt to be a rising tide of African witchcraft complementing black political unrest in a dangerous manner. In what *El Mundo* (June 30, 1913) called a long overdue "crusade against brujería," the chief of national police, General Armando Riva, gave order to the captains of local police stations to find out which persons in their precincts "dedicated themselves to the practices of brujería." Provisions were to be made to establish close surveillance over them and—if possible—to confiscate their ritual paraphernalia. By that time, Havana itself seemed virtually under siege—not just by a vast network of rural wizards converging on the city from the countryside, but by an amorphous underground system of urban ritual activities, difficult to bring to light by the hit-and-miss tactics of the police.

In Havana's working-class neighborhoods, "where misery and ignorance is encountered in sad company," wrote Roche Monteagudo (1925, 177), "it is neither rare nor unusual to frequently find, particularly in the early morning hours, bundles or packages, or more generally a dead bird thrown into the public way or on the thresholds of houses, containing an *embó* [magical preparation] composed of hair, ashes, teeth, bones, human excrement, toasted corn, seeds, the peel of fruit, buttons, black beans, disgusting rags, herbs, feathers, claws and crests of roosters, money, nails and brads, shells, fishhooks, coconut oil, etc." Once interpreted symptomatically, such sporadic irruptions of "matter out of place" into the public sphere indicated a sinister process insidiously unfolding behind closed doors or under cover of darkness. Aided by denunciations from neighbors or reports from plainclothes detectives, the police occasionally broke through this veil. But each new case of mass arrests of "fetishist congregants" under doubtful legal auspices only added to—as a headline in *El Mundo* on December 12, 1914, put it—"what one does not know about contemporary Havana." Nor was the sense of danger brewing beneath the civilized surface of urban life restricted to the native Cuban elite. "If these things venture into the public," the long-term North American resident Irene Wright (1910, 95–96) shuddered, talking about what she called "male humans whose condition certainly warrants removal from the public thoroughfare," then what of such even more horrendous human objects that civilized imagination suspected to be lurking "hidden in the poverty and uncleanliness of the unlighted, unventilated cells in the tenements that present their sometimes rather handsome fronts (they are occasionally the ancient palaces of old families) to Havana's principal streets, leaning now against some leading commercial establishment, or, again, beside some fine and modern apartment house."[16] By the time of the second U.S. occupation, the American forces could not help but face up to the problem. In the wake of the so-called niña Luisa case in Alacranes (province of Matanzas) in 1908, the commanding officer of the U.S. occupation forces in Matanzas saw fit to report to his superiors the results of his confidential investigations into the beliefs and practices "responsible for most, if not all, of the child-murders that so frequently occur in Cuba." Somewhat confused about the difference between the male secret society abakuá and brujería proper, Colonel O. J. Sweet concluded that "on [*sic*] of their beliefs is that the blood of a child is a sure cure for some diseases. The higher and nobler the birth of the child, the greater and surer the efficacy of its blood" (NA RG 199, Prov. Govt. Cuba, Conf. Corr. 1906–9, case file 248). While a similar investigation launched by the occupation forces in 1900—this time through the "Havana Detective Bureau"—had merely disclosed fairly inocuous folk healing and divination practices common among "the colored people, and those of the lower classes" (NA RG 140, Mil. Govt. Cuba, letters received, 1899–1902, 1900:4163, box 105), by the time of the second occupation Cuba seemed to be overrun with demons. As Fernando Ortiz (1973, 103) summed up the consensus that had emerged by the time the Americans returned in 1906, the diligent labor of reporters like Varela had uncovered "that the disappearance of children in the countryside is not a rare occurrence, although it is not always reported to the authorities for fear of reprisals from the delinquents; that the country wizards are veritable savages and capable of every imaginable crime; that in abducting children, one of them rides on horseback carrying a large sack in which to put the victim and to quickly asphyxiate her by covering her with coarse fabric; that they cure sterility with the viscera of children, etc."

To be sure, Ortiz (1973, 105) thought that the viciousness of Cuba's black brujos had not—or not yet—reached the degree that it had reportedly attained in Haiti or Jamaica, where notorious Victorian travel writers such as the long-term British consul to Haiti Spencer St. John had "uncovered" the endemic nature of child sacrifice, cannibalism, and other abominations as early as 1883 (see Dash 1988; Lawless 1992; Palmié 1998a). Nevertheless, Ortiz (1973, 106–7) warned, "after the happenings in El Gabriel [i.e., the niña Zoila case], their introduction to Cuba by the African brujos cannot be doubted, in part at least, although it is not as frequent as in those countries." Fears were to increase in the years to come as the number of labor migrants from those islands to the American-owned plantations in eastern Cuba and the region of the old fortifications of La Trocha—dangerously close to Havana—steadily rose throughout the first and second decade of the century.[17] To paraphrase Chávez Álvarez (1991, 35), during the decade of the 1910s the white civilized west of Cuba steadily raised its defenses against a barbarian tide of black plantation workers in the eastern sugar regions, where the grand-scale exploitation of cheap commodified labor secured the "dance of the millions" that characterized Cuba's export economy during the First World War.

In any case, what was significant about the Antillean connection was that it seemed to explain—although only in the aftermath and not in entirely satisfactory terms (for the massive influx of Caribbean migrant workers had not commenced in earnest at the time of Zoila Díaz's murder)—why a wave of ritual crimes had broken out in the republican period. Writing about the Zoila case, Ortiz (1973, 103) put his finger on the problem of timing when arguing that "the crime has taken [the Cuban public] by surprise less for the viciousness exhibited by its authors than for the unexpected discovery of the cancerous fanaticism that corrodes the ignorant strata of our nation. For, in effect, a similar case had not occurred, or had not become known, since the time of slavery."

In fact, excepting a single thirdhand report about alleged serial killing of slave infants[18] on a plantation near Aguacate that neither provided a fitting precedent nor stated a suitably magical motive (and, besides that, was quite obviously fabricated by an eager journalist at the height of public excitement over the niña Zoila trial), Ortiz apparently found himself unable even to pinpoint the origin of such practices in the period of slavery. Hence a vexing paradox that occasionally surfaced in the highly inconsistent and often patently contradictory public discourse on the issue: if no continuity or tradition of the present irruptions of African savagery could be established with the period of slavery and Spanish rule, what exactly was it that had brought such monstrous practices to an untimely fruition under the auspices of republican government? And what did such ominous signs of the *Gleichzeitigkeit* of what should have been *ungleichzettig* portend in terms of Cuba's general prospect for civilizational progress? As Ortiz's pregnant metaphor of a "cancerous" growth appeared to indicate, a mysterious pathogen seemed to be corrupting the feeble moral fiber of the nation's ignorant working class and even threatened to infiltrate the "higher organs" of the Cuban body social in the form of brujos ministering to the white elite. If an image of communicating vessels seemed to explain the "frequent, almost inevitable" tendency of lower-class whites "who find themselves in constant communication with African natives" to regress to their level of "ideas, superstitions, and prejudices" and compared well with Tyler's authoritative remarks about the effects of colonial exposure of whites to "negro ideas" in Africa, this explanation stopped short of revealing the true extent of the damage (Ortiz 1973, 174). For it was not only that "the inferior classes of Cuban society . . . had commerce with the brujos," Ortiz noted, but, "particularly in the past, not a few persons of brilliant social standing, more removed, at any rate, from an intimate psychological communication with the blacks, stealthily consulted the brujo for advice and assistance. 'This very day, wrote me a juridical authority who had been involved in a modern case of witchcraft, can I cite [the names of] distinguished ladies of good society who resort to the brujo and who lend themselves to his nauseating rites, usually by inspiration of jealousy'" (175). Once more following a Tylorean argument, Ortiz argued that the "tendency to fear the magic of the priests of nonconfessional cults manifested itself also among the white Cubans, all the more so since, in truth, the brujos [do] practice witchcraft; hence the fact that for reasons of atavism there are incredulous and relatively cultivated people who manifest a certain anxious respect for the embós [magical preparations] and oracles of the most savage African witchcraft" (169–70).

Ortiz, we might say, came close to realizing the extent to which brujeria was an affliction, not of concrete people, but of the republican mind; a hybrid formation, not just in the literal sense, but also in terms of the way in which it seemed to disfigure the identity of the *clases responsables* of the neocolonial republic in what Bhabha (1984, 97) calls a "strategic reversal of the process of domination through disavowal." But it was not until more than two decades later that Ortiz broke through the smoke screen of a discursive regime within which the signifier *brujería* worked to produce its own referent. As we shall see, in the early years of the century, the lure of the prefabricated discourse of Lombrosian criminal anthropology instead led Ortiz to fetishize the phantasm of science as the supreme vivisector of the body social. In fact, his first book—entitled *Los negros brujos*—was to turn into a canonical text establishing the rules of recognition for republican witch-hunting, much like the *edictos de fe* had done for the Spanish Inquisition. But let us first turn to some interpretations of more ostensibly immediate relevance to the events on the ground.

THE POLITICAL ECONOMY OF REPUBLICAN *BRUJERÍA*

Of course, it is not difficult to see what class interests the construct *brujería* served in the new Cuban republic. As several authors have noted (Chávez Álvarez 1991; Helg 1995, 1996), the Zoila case marked a historical watershed in terms of both the social construction of Afro-Cuban religious practices and the practice of their persecution. Helg (1996), thus, argues that the construct *brujería* and the techniques of repression that it suggested held four principal advantages for a new white Cuban ruling class bent on avoiding having to address the problem of persisting racial inequality under a nominally color-blind constitution. In her view, allegations of brujería thus served first, to besmirch the image of black Cubans as heroes of the independence struggle; second, to justify the social hierarchy of the postwar era and legitimate the failure to implement social policies benefiting all Cuban citizens; third, to endow the members of the republican elite, politically as well as economically dependent on the United States, with a sense of moral and cultural superiority; and fourth, to impede the political self-organization of black Cubans by emphasizing cultural divisions between a black petit bourgeoisie and the mass of an illiterate black working class with persisting cultural loyalties to Africa. Similarly, Chávez Álvarez (1991, 33) argues that the niña Zoila case dramatizes, in symbolic form, the turn from the "violent mechanism of slavery" to the "violence of racial discrimination" vital to the political-economic order characterizing the U.S.-sponsored first Cuban Republic. In his view, brujería focused and thereby rendered more effective general strategies of racializing social inequality.

In addition, Chávez argues, following Pérez de la Riva (1979, 29), that even more specific interests were involved. As regards the controversial issue of Antillean labor migration, for example, government officials instrumentalized the stereotype of the alien black sorcerer in raising the price for presidential permits issued to employers keen on exceeding the ridiculously low official immigration quota. As the United Fruit Company and other large-scale employers sought to buy out comparatively expensive Cuban labor, the graft-ridden governments of Gómez and García Menocal happily acceded to their demands for Haitian and Jamaican workers who, on entering Cuba, found themselves, not only subjected to crass exploitation, but reduced to harbingers of evil in the imagination of native Cubans, both white and black.[19] Public fears and the interests of international capital, thus, conspired in helping to line the pockets of republican cleptocrats.

Helg and Chávez are certainly right in situating the case within its larger political—and political-economic—context. In practically all post-emancipation plantation societies in the Americas the "mills of inequality" (Wolf 1982a) switched gears, from a system of production and domination based on the appropriation of the coerced labor of racial others by means of legally instituted property rights in persons, to (usually)[20] less clearly formalized systems of strategies aiming to create and stabilize a racialized rural proletariat deprived of access to the means of production, social equality, and political participation. And, in practically all cases, this switch called forth or exacerbated divisions within the black population. Although largely based on unequal access to education and wealth among black workers and the Afro-Cuban "middle class," these rifts tended to become socially visible in the form of symbolic practices evaluated within the total societal context as indicators of unredeemed Africanity or civilizational progress and hence, as diagnostic of the social worth of the individuals or groups in question as citizens of the republican state (see Scott 1985; Holt 1992; Trouillot 1990; Morrison 1999).[21]

Likewise, as Helg and Chávez argue, the important role that U.S. interference in the economic and political affairs of the Caribbean region played in this process can hardly be underestimated. With respect to Cuba, it is moot to speculate about just how the transformation of slave (or apprentice) labor into nominally free agroindustrial surplus labor would have proceeded had the second Cuban War of Independence not found its unintended consummation in the Spanish-American War and the founding under North American military auspices of what Cuban historians nowadays refer as the *pseudo-Republic.* As in Puerto Rico and the Philippines (see Drinnon 1980; Rafael 1993), the official rhetoric of an American duty to come to the aid of heroic insurgents against the tyranny of Spain—luridly stereotyped in the contemporary U.S. press as a racially inferior and morally corrupt European power that had seen its day—rapidly changed under military occupancy to one foregrounding the burden of a civilizing mission to people "little other than," as one contemporary U.S. observer (quoted in Helg 1995, 92) put it, "turbulent and illiterate negroes needing the government of a stronger race, indisposed to industry and quite unsuited for that independence for which they had been fighting." As had become clear even before the conclusion of the war—the vicious slander directed against General Antonio Maceo certainly being the most blatant evidence[22]—U.S. endorsement of an admission of Cuba to the family of nations would not be secured but on the grounds of a transfer of North American post-Reconstruction technologies of racial exclusion. The civilizing mission included a lesson in disciplined racial typology. Although the all-white Estrada Palma government quickly acted to institute U.S.-style electoral laws aiming to exclude large segments of Cuba's black population by literacy clauses and property requirements, the fact that it could not but grant franchise to veterans of the disbanded Liberation Army—a large contingent of which was of undeniably African descent—may have precluded colonization by a nation that, at the time, was busily engineering the systematic exclusion of its black population from civil society. Yet, regardless of Cuba's failure to become a de jure dependency of the United States, Rafael's (1993, 136) remarks about the cultural template on which the American liberation of Spain's ultramarine possessions proceeded ring true in the Cuban case as well. "While colonial rule may be a transitional stage to self-rule," he writes, "the 'self' that rules can only emerge by way of an intimate relationship with a colonial master who sets the standards and practices of discipline to mold the conduct of the colonial subject. The culmination of colonial rule, self-government, can thus be achieved only when the subject has learned to colonize itself." Despite Theodore Roosevelt's repeated bouts of irritation with "that infernal little Cuban Republic," self-colonization was high on the agenda of Cuba's republican elite. Part of this process—soon to become one of its driving forces—consisted in the attempt, on the part of self-consciously national politicians and intellectuals, to rid Cuba of its racial stigma by discursive and / or physical means.

In this respect, Chávez's and Helg's interpretations of the niña Zoila case and its successors ring true as well. Sharing important structural features with the North American obsession with the sexual defilement of white women by black men (see Helg 2000), the image of the disemboweled body of white female children sacrificed to African deities for the sake of healing illiterate ex-slaves provided, as Chávez (1991, 29) puts it, Cuba's "worst republican interests with the weapon they needed." Its power derived not only from the invocation of a symbolic inversion of the projected future of the Cuban nation—suggesting the ravage of white republican progeny as an attonement for the clinging evil of a slaveholding past. It also constituted a national embarrassment with respect to Cuba's accreditation as a civilized state. The construct *brujería*—that is, a manifest instance of deviance from Western norms interpretable in terms of African-derived belief systems—provided fuel to the fire of those who saw the systematic de-Africanization of Cuba as the key to its national and international future. Ever since the 1820s, critics of slavery such as Antonio Saco had branded as shortsighted and misguided Spain's policy of building up its last prosperous colony by condoning the illegal import of Africans instead of white metropolitan laborers and discouraging internal economic diversification. Now, it seemed, the Cuban Republic labored under the lasting heritage of a problematic colonial demographic development scheme and its unintended social, cultural, and—most painfully for contemporary nationalist thinkers—biological results.

In this respect, the discourse on African wizardry had its antecedents in an apocalyptic vision of biotic contamination outlined with particular clarity, as early as 1888, by the social reformer Benjamín de Céspedes in a diatribe against Havana's burgeoning market in Afro-Cuban sexual services. Arguing that, recent emancipation notwithstanding, the "colored race" was more than ever enslaved by its own "indolence, vices, and depredations," Céspedes (1888) ominously warned that, "far from destroying itself" in its own "putrefaction," the sexual profligacy of its women—forced (as he dimly recognized) to prostitute themselves by economic conditions and restricted access to marriage—would soon infect the body social to a degree where "the race originating from our shame will also have to serve as the instrument of our misery, and what yesterday was guilty and covetous exploitation will, for the dominating race, have to turn itself into humiliating expiation. Abandoned between two forms of solitude, concubinage and prostitution, and without anyone attending to her betterment, licentiousness and Africanism in public custom will spread like a terrible moral epidemic" (174). "What better revenge" he concluded, "could ever be consummated in the historical destiny of our people in favor of the wronged race than the slow but sure corrosive infusion of all its vices and wretchedness into the core of the social organism?" If Cuba's progress toward "civilized modernity" had been achieved through the savage exploitation of African slaves reduced to machine-like appurtenances of industrial sugar mills, its present order was haunted by the specter of this past reappearing in the form of the mulata prostitute's seemingly irresistible sexuality. Visibly embodying a history of unequal sexual exchange, for Céspedes the free mulata had become the instrument of the "sweet revenge of the slave woman of yesterday": an "infernal fornicating machine driving a great part of the present generation toward madness and enervation" (177) and corrupting the physical and moral body of postemancipation society.

To be sure, by 1888, Céspedes could (and undoubtedly did) draw on a rapidly expanding international repertoire of social hygienicism. Echoing representations of the pernicious tendencies of socially marginalized groups to transgress, not just "the boundaries through which bourgeois reformers separated dirt from cleanliness," but also those "of the 'civilized' body and the boundaries which separated the human and the animal" (Stallybrass and White 1986, 132), he certainly situated himself within a discourse that included the writings of Parent-Duchatelet and Mayhew, Zola and Engels, Sue and Tarnowsky (see Gilman 1985; Corbin 1987; Walkovitz 1992). Prefigured as it was on the colonial periphery toward which such modernistic discourses gravitated in the concrete experience of the multiply conditioned sexual availability of racially marked women, the collapsing of black female sexuality into an imagery of predatory promiscuity characterizing late-nineteenth-century representations of prostitutes undoubtedly was a foregone conclusion. Describing the red-light district of the calle de Montserrate in the 1880s,

Céspedes, thus, anticipated, in good measure, the hermeneutics of suspicion that was to grip the Cuban public imagination in the aftermath of the niña Zoila case: "At nightfall, one sees beings like formless mollusks emerging from some holes, their sex difficult to ascertain were it not for their cynical attempts at exhibiting it through the holes in the tattered rags that serve them as garments. They are generally black or mulata women who live in colonies like the fungus that collects on green water and who surrender themselves on the floor, in a chair, and the more wealthy ones in a grimy bed" (Céspedes 1888, 157).

All the more stunning, then (but perhaps not surprising), is the structural transformation of this older, and essentially exogenous, discourse on biosexual transgressions into a uniquely national obsession with the mysterious agency of elderly black men, physically as well as socially incapable of siring miscegenated offspring, but mystically compelled to disembowel the youthful white women on which the nation's future was unmistakably pegged. The incessant colonial fornication performed by "infected" white male bodies on racially indeterminate females whose similarly questionable "womanhood" could be ascertained only through gross genital exposure thus found its republican equivalent in the sterilizing ritual embrace of the elderly black brujo of its youthful white (or sometimes not so white) female (or sometimes not so female) victim. While the former scenario identified a colonial heritage of rampant miscegenation, illegitimacy, and venereal disease as the prime debilitating factors, the latter projected a violent asexual detritus into a future forever beholden to the sins of "Spanish slave traders who had inundated the island with Africans," subjecting Cuba to an "invasion of savages," as the nationalist author Manuel del la Cruz put it in 1895 (cited in Pérez 1999, 92). As republican ideologues began groping their way toward conceptions capable of representing a racially heterogeneous Cuban nation in terms of José Martí's vision of citizenship transcending the "accident of color," the specter of boundary transgression, thus, came to be recoded along the lines of gender and culture: if, as Kutzinski (1993) has argued, the mulata eventually became a sexualized postcolonial icon of transracial homosocial reconciliation, the African (or Africanized) male body turned into a site of violent—at times deadly—contests between different forms of knowledge and competing conceptions of modernity.

Quite apart, then, from the fact that the political-economic seeds of

U.S. capital planted (or rather refertilized) during the occupations of 1899–1902 and 1906–9 luxuriously germinated in the progressive economic marginalization and social exclusion of Afro-Cubans in the republican period, the very presence of an African and African-descended population within the social and political space defined by the new Cuban state posed a vexing ideological problem. As in many other Latin America nations, the reception of European scientific racism and positivistic social thought by local intellectuals and the political elite since the late nineteenth century had created an obsessive awareness, not only of the existence of an African population, but also of the racially mixed status of the better part of the national population.[23] Particularly in contrast to the United States—a contrast often, and self-consciously, invoked (see Nina Rodrigues 1977, 5–11)—where long-standing antimiscegenation laws and postemancipation legal segregation safeguarded national racial prestige, Latin American nationalist thinkers of the late nineteenth century and the early twentieth faced an excruciating dilemma. How to imagine and credibly represent political communities whose racially tainted character, not only threatened to preclude claims to a respectable position within the "family of nations," but also cast serious doubts on their ability to live up to international standards of modernity and progress?

For the young Cuban lawyer Fernando Ortiz y Fernández, the answer came in the form of a series of ingenious conceptual linkages for which the Brazilian forensic scientist Raimundo Nina Rodrigues had earlier cleared the way in the Brazilian case. Expectably, these linkages pivoted on the kind of organicist conception of race flourishing in scientific circles in both Europe and the United States at the turn of the twentieth century. Due to the "special nature" of Latin American nationhood, however, the way in which Nina Rodrigues and Ortiz came to localize diagnostic representations of their own social realities around it deflected the work of core discursive authority from the polities within which the peripheral scientist positioned himself while reflecting it in his own vision of social progress at home. Unlike U.S. theorists of the results of an "unthinking decision" taken by British colonists in a distant past, what Nina Rodrigues and Ortiz saw themselves faced with was, not a "Negro problem," but an "African problem" squarely lodged in a national present and threatening to corrupt the American futures that creole local elites were claiming for their nations. If it took Herskovits pains even to raise the issue of "African survivals" in the twentieth-century U.S. public sphere to a level of disputability, in Cuba or Brazil Africa had never receded to a location distant enough to have to be resurrected discursively or to which it could once and for all be relegated as irrelevant to the politics of culture in undeniably multiracial societies.

Much as he seems to have regretted the fact at the time of his writing in 1906, Ortiz was well aware that the 1899 census undertaken by the U.S. occupation forces in Cuba still enumerated some thirteen thousand native Africans (Ortiz 1973, 222) soon to be endowed with legal citizenship in the new Cuban Republic. Moreover, at the turn of the twentieth century in Cuba, Africans were not just an abstract statistical presence. A leisurely walk of no more than ten minutes would have taken Ortiz from his law office on the corner of the fashionable calle San Rafael and Galiano to the teeming black working-class barrio of Colón, which had grown on the former site of the barracoons of the slave market of Havana and General Tacón's old city jail, famous for being the largest structure of its kind in the Americas. As a consequence, Cuban and Brazilian scholars did not discover the Africanity of a racially othered sector of their respective nations in the manner that Herskovits did—that is, in the course of a sojourn to the Suriname bush akin to those that, for a long time, had allowed European travelers to cover spatial expanses in the pursuit of humanity's past.[24] To them, Africa began at their doorstep: in the rapidly growing slums and tenement complexes of their cities; in the barracks of increasingly industrial sugar mills; and in the very bodies of an extensively racially mixed national citizenry.[25] They merely found new vocabularies for the discursive transformation of Africa from a vaguely conceived social residue—the all-too-vivid heritage of a slave-importing colonial/national past—into a domain for the application of scientifically conceivable measures toward national progress and social control. A major constituent of these vocabularies was that of race: a rapidly internationalizing and—because of its biologistic foundations—universalistic discourse on the "natural" determination of culture and sociality.[26]

Here, then, was a second arena in which the niña Zoila case and its successors came to perform cultural work. No doubt, Chávez and Helg are right in arguing that the early-twentieth-century "witch-hunts" served the overt political purpose of discrediting Cuba's black electorate and justifying the manner in which landless rural Afro-Cubans wer shuttled back into coercive labor regimes different from slavery only in the formal legitimating structure undergirding their exploitation. But to say as much is to stop short of the larger analytic task of relating concrete technologies of repression to the ideological templates that not only inform them but within which instances of repression, in turn, come to function as cultural performances reproductive of situated projections of identity and moral community. As I shall argue in the following, the concept *brujería* acquired its tremendous power as a device for constructing overtly racialized notions of Cuban national selfhood precisely at a moment when Cuban versions of European science came into their own. The conjuncture was not fortuitous. The vision of social progress and scientific control of human affairs that animated Cuban intellectual life in the early republican period was deeply imbricated in the construct of an atavistic other whose very body—indeed, its anatomy and viscereal structure—would serve as the theater within which apprentices of an international sorcery such as the young Ortiz would perform their cures of the Cuban national organism.

AFRO-CUBAN RELIGION INCORPORATED

One of the obvious problems connected with brujería was its legal intractability. Talking about his inability to encounter precedents for the niña Zoila case in the forensic literature of the colonial period, Ortiz (1973, 103) noted that "it would be futile to turn to the juridical statistics of Cuba for [an answer]; when they exist, they hardly do anything other than classify the facts according to the conventional legal casuistry without descending to the level of the particular and explicating the sui generis nature of crimes such as the one mentioned." Indeed, one of the critical defects of the old Spanish criminal code—still in force in the early republican period—was that it failed to provide for legal measures to be directed against the evil that Cubans now found themselves facing. While the Spanish colonial government had outlawed the male secret society abakuá as a seditious and criminal organization since 1876, thereby rendering its ceremonies acts of "unlawful association," no such legal grounds existed for the persecution of practitioners of other Afro-Cuban religions at the time of Zoila Díaz's death. Moreover, the Cuban constitution of 1902 had explicitly guaranteed freedom of religion and peaceful association for legal ends, thus, among other things, prolonging the lease on life of many of the old cabildos de nación (see Palmié 1993). Although subjected to the Law of Associations since 1887, many of the old African cabildos simply transformed themselves into legally inscribed mutual aid societies—a purpose that, along with their religious functions, they had served anyway since at least the seventeenth century (Ortiz 1921, 22ff.). By 1909, more than twenty such legally inscribed associations explicitly linked to African-derived cult practices existed in Havana alone,[27] and, excepting a law prohibiting the use of African drums issued (or rather renewed) under the first U.S. occupation, there was little the police could do to impugn their legitimacy other than declare their members *ñáñigos*, that is, adherents of abakuá, in order to charge them with unlawful association.

The injunction obtained by the licenciado Angel Fernández Larrinaga in defense of thirty-one prisoners who had been arrested along with twenty-eight others on May 21, 1902, on such charges provides a good example of the legal difficulties involved. Arguing that the defendants had merely congregated to celebrate the proclamation of the Republic on that day, Fernández Larrinaga went on to explicate the contorted legal reasoning underlying the case against his clients:

> Peacefully enjoying themselves on account of the solemnity of the day, they were surprised by the police, who accused them of pertaining to a grouping of the ñáñigos on the grounds of nothing other than the malicious suspicion of the officials who formulated the accusation; for neither did they find lists in which their [i.e., the defendants'] names appeared as individuals pertaining to what was claimed to be an illicit association, nor does there exist the slightest evidence for believing them to be so affiliated or for qualifying them as ñáñigos.
>
> Second: the fact of having encountered them in the patio of the said house without [their] actual commitment of any illicit act does not constitute a crime of any sort and even less so that of unlawful association as defined in numbers 1 and 2 of article 186 of the penal code, in combination, as it is argued [by the prosecution], with articles 413, 414, and 415 of the same (the reason for an invocation of which I have not succeeded in comprehending), and of which [the defendants] are gratuitously supposed to be the founders. Because in order for that [to

be legally admissible] it would be indispensable to have previously established the existence of the association and the commitment of acts indicating the intent of realizing the crimes of parricide or murder or [alternatively to submit] that there still existed slaves in Cuba, [these two stipulations constituting] the only conditions under which the provisions expounded in article 415 could find application. (ANC, Audiencia de la Habana, leg. 214–15, causa 285 1902)

The judges were not impressed by the argument that, since the police raid had produced no membership lists or statutes of the supposed association, the defendants had been engaged in a spontaneous reunion in celebration of Cuban independence rather than an association of lasting character. Still, Fernández Larrinaga had put his finger on an important point: his clients were, in effect, tried according to colonial laws whose applicability was rendered patently absurd by the fact that they pertained to the reunions of slaves! Not surprisingly, the prison sentences and hefty fines imposed on all but one of the defendants were overturned in the course of a review by the Cuban Supreme Court. Apart from the unexpected results, however, what must have been the most vexing aspect of the case was that, regardless of whatever connection the "reunion" on May 21 had with the proclamation of the Republic, the evidence left—and, indeed, still leaves—little doubt that it was *also* a ritual gathering of an abakuá group: not only had the police recovered a large number of ritual implements, but at the moment of the arrest three of the accused had worn the *trajes* of *diablitos* (or, more properly, *íremes*): ceremonial body masks transforming their wearers into embodiments of spirits. One of the defendants, the thirty-nine-year-old white sailor Vicente Sosa Sánchez, a man with a police record reaching back to 1878, had only recently returned from the Spanish penal colony of Fernando Poo, to which he had been deported in 1896 under charges of being a member of abakuá in the course of the brutal counterinsurgency measures enacted by Capitán General Valeriano Weyler during the Cuban War of Independence (ANC, Audiencia de la Habana, leg. 214–15, causa 285 1902).[28]

Despite its ironic outcome, the case clearly demonstrated to what extent the Cuban authorities were prepared to contort the law in ignoring the constitutional guarantees of freedom of religion and freedom of association and resurrecting slave law to construct a group of people engaged in African-derived practices into incriminable subjects. That they did not succeed, however, owed less to the inadequacies of the law than to the fact that, as a symbol of Cuban national identity, the constitution *eo ipso* signified the legality of those forms of Afro-Cuban difference that it had come to encompass. Witch-hunters fared even worse in cases where the victims of police raids were legally inscribed associations and—to the dismay of the officers in charge—could usually produce written permission from the municipal government to stage "festivities according to the African custom." In more than one sense, the rule of law—and a curious hybrid of Spanish penal legislation and republican constitutional guarantees at that—thus provides a key to the inability of republican persecutors to achieve their goal of eradicating the traces of "African savagery" in their midst. Inscribed within one and the same legal framework, Afro-Cuban cult groups and the executive organs of the Cuban state were technically constitutive of each other. The Africanity of the one not only mirrored the Westernness of the other. They were deeply implicated in each other. Indeed, from the perspective of the early republican witch-hunter, it was only now becoming clear in what fatal ways Spain had failed to provide for the civilizational progress of its dependencies.

A brief digression on colonial Spanish persecution practices may be in order here. Like all other New World colonizing powers, Spain, too, perceived the religions of their subaltern populations as a potential source of disturbance or seditious motivation. Slave rebellions were repeatedly connected to the incendiary influence of African—or African-style—religious leaders. By and large, however, in the Spanish colonies such perceptions never led to the development of a legal apparatus that consistently targeted African religious manifestations, as similar legal machineries did in—say—the British West Indies. Part of this was due to the lingering effects of the persecutionary technologies imposed on the Spanish overseas possessions by the Holy Inquisition as the arm of a highly rationalized division of imperial labor concerned with maintaining an "order secured through culture"[29] among transplanted Old World populations in the Americas.[30] Owing to the eminent role of the Catholic church within the Spanish colonial enterprise, offenses with a potential connection to religious matters could (at least in theory) be adjudicated by secular authorities only after the regionally responsible clerical authorities had given explicit clearance. Yet, to speak with Franklin (and Strathern, from whom Franklin derives the term), the perspectival technos of the Spanish Inquisition imposed a rather rigid diagnostic regime on those who would target manifestations of African religion in the New World as punishable offenses. Two of the key elements of that regime, codified in the *edictos de fe* were the distinctions between *herejes* and *aberrantes*, and between the offenses of *hechicería* and *brujería*—loosely translatable as "heretics" and "wayward believers" and as "superstitious practices" and "witchcraft," respectively.[31] Both conceptual pairs were long-standing tools in the persecution of European religious deviance but proved ill suited to the construction of non-Western forms of religious practice and ideation as heterodox and, therefore, legitimately punishable in colonial settings (see Rafael 1992).

In sharp contrast to the brutal persecution of metropolitan disbelievers, the ultramarine incarnation of the Holy Office (instituted since 1571) exhibited a considerably more lenient attitude—as well as a remarkable reluctance to use torture—with respect to religious offenses committed by its colonial subjects. Particularly African or African-descended offenders were much more likely to be classified as *aberrants* than as *heretics*, as *hechicheros* than as *brujos*. As Ortiz (1975, 408) argued in his magnificent late work on an epidemic of demonic possession in seventeenth-century Cuba, at a popular remove from canon law, "the problem came into focus from the same traditional point of view as in Spain without considering the exotic contribution of the Africans. The magic and superstitious practices of the blacks blended with those of the whites, and all was called *brujería*." Still, in the eyes of the Inquisition, brujería constituted a highly specific offense that, by definition, differed from *hechicería* in that the author of the latter acted individually while the category *brujería* circumscribed the kind of collective crime emblematically associated with the witches' sabbath—a construct denoting the existence of diabolical sects or anti-Christian conspiracies that had figured prominently in the Inquisition's violent activities in the Basque provinces (see Ballesteros Gaibrois 1955). In the Americas, however, bona fide brujería was conspicuous by its relative absence in the records of the Holy Office. While the New World Inquisition hunted down Protestant heretics whenever it could lay its hands on them and faced a veritable *embarras de richesse* in terms of cases of blasphemy, sexual misconduct, superstitious practices, and other forms of aberration among the white, black, and racially mixed population under its jurisdiction (see Palmer 1976; Ballesteros Gaibrois 1955; Lea 1908; and Ortiz 1975), prevailing interpretations of the African-American behavior inhibited the extension of its legalistic vocabulary to precisely those phenomena that, in the aftermath, might well be judged to have represented instances of African American resistance to Christianization. "The convulsive rites, whether of benevolent or malevolent character," writes Ortiz (1975, 408),

> during which the blacks felt themselves possessed by their gods, and the fact that the most conspicuous forms of collective ritual of the Africans always found expression in vivid dances, songs, and the din of drums, on the one hand inspired only disdain on the part of the whites with their pompous and strict church observances. These were the ludicrous antics of the blacks! On the other hand, this [attitude] motivated them to tolerate [such manifestations of African religion] as mere riotous festivities that allowed the slaves to assuage their nostalgia and suffering by means of the exuberant diversions of their ancestral customs.

Despite a long-standing Iberian tradition of ascribing to Africans a particular affinity for contact with the powers of darkness (see, e.g., Ortiz 1975, 40; Acosta Saignes 1967, 188f.; or Alvarez Nazario 1974, 257), even in regions graced with closer inquisitorial supervision than the pastorally scandalously understaffed Cuba[32] (such as Nueva España and Nueva Granada), the vast majority of cases involving Africans and their descendants entered the record under the rubrics of blasphemy or superstitious practices (Palmer 1976). Although *all* of the offenses of that nature registered by the tribunal of Cartagena in the second half of the seventeenth century had been committed by persons of African descent, only one case of brujería was pinned on a black person (Ballesteros Gaibrois 1955, 14).

Far from effectively preempting the retransformation of African cultural knowledge into viable New World practices, the perspectival technos instituted by the division of religious and secular persecutional responsibilities in the Spanish Empire actually created institutional sites in which New World African religions began to inscribe themselves in an officially sanctioned manner. The best known examples are, of course, the so-called cabildos de nación, church-sponsored corporations endowed with legal rights to hold property and enact regulations governing their ostensibly ethnically organized collective social and political life. Condoned by secular authorities on account of long-standing metropolitan legal precedents and their imputed function of fostering ethnic antagonism within the African population, the cabildos soon mutated into the social "milieux" within which truly Afro-Cuban religious formations germinated and achieved traditionalization (Ortiz 1921; cf. Palmié 1991, 106–66; Palmié 1993).

By the time of the final disestablishment of inquisitorial power in the early years of the nineteenth century, the newly secularized power structure in Spain's remaining American possessions thus found itself faced with the legacy of a policy that, for centuries, had encouraged rather than inhibited the incorporation of forms of African or African-derived cultures within its very institutional structures.[33] Significantly enough, it was not until the Spanish government began to dismantle the legal framework of slavery itself that it found itself willing—and legislatively able—to gradually restrict the activities of the cabildos by submitting them to the general law of associations (Ortiz 1921, 22–23; cf. Scott 1985, 265–68). While this rendered them somewhat more visible to the controlling apparatus of the secular state, it also turned them into civic corporations. The very rule of law now restricted persecutionary measures to a gray zone where the police repeatedly found themselves in the role of lawbreakers, public prosecutors had to resort to contorted legal constructions in order to manufacture incriminating evidence, and courts repeatedly failed to uphold convictions based on the smuggling of slave laws into postemancipation trials or similarly absurd machinations. Quite contrary to official intentions, the measures taken to render Afro-Cuban cult houses transparent to the gaze of the modernizing colonial and early republican state *eo ipso* firmly (re)installed African-derived bodies of knowledge and practices within the institutional structures of that state. Indeed, there are good grounds for arguing, not just that old-style cabildos now came to convert themselves into civic associations, but that several of the most famous casas de santo or ilé ocha[34] still remembered today among practitioners of the Yoruba-influenced regla ocha look back neither on a history reaching far into the colonial period nor

even on direct continuities with the cabildos de nación. They took their origin in precisely this period and under these legal auspices—a fact borne out by both contemporary priestly genealogies (none of which reach back beyond the period of emancipation) and documentary evidence.[35]

Writing in 1921, Ortiz seems to have recognized this strange collusion between the modern state and its African deities. "The government aim—announced in the most optimistic terms—of transforming the cabildos into modern associations failed completely," he lamented.

> The government persists in attacking the external and antiquated forms and does not take care to note the persistence of the internal essence. Thus disappeared the cabildo, together with all its positive features: mutual aid, the insurance against illness, the bases, in short, of a traditional and rigorous mutuality. What disappeared, in part, was the noisy form of drum-accompanied dance, as inoffensive as it is pleasing to the African; what remained, in turn, halfway obscured, was the savage animistic fetishism under a Catholic advocation, and a reglementation adapted to the demands of legal formalism. And the authorities were satisfied. How much better would have been a contrary outcome! How much better would it be if we today had mutualist cabildos and public dances with African drums and not temples of brujería, of clandestine or [openly] tolerated nature! (30)

By the time of his writing, Ortiz was already on his way to a fundamental revaluation of Afro-Cuban culture. In 1929, he had come publicly to denounce the political-economic rather than natural referents of concepts of race. In a no less radical venture, in 1937, he introduced the first stage performance of an Afro-Cuban ceremonial drum orchestra (still legally proscribed at the time) at Havana's Institución Hispanocubana de Cultura as a contribution to the "glory of the national music of Cuba." In 1939, he founded the Sociedad de Estudios Afrocubanos and, after a well-reasoned attack from his student Romulo Lachatañeré,[36] admitted to some of the more obviously problematic aspects of his early work, particularly *Los negros brujos* (Ortiz 1973)—a text that soon after its original publication in 1906 had acquired canonical status within the republican antibrujería campaigns. This is not the place to unravel the complexities of the evolution of Ortiz's thought, riddled as it seems at first glance with unresolved contradictions and intellectual as well as political somersaults (see Palmié 1998b). Still, regardless of the fact that Ortiz radically changed his perspective on the matter in the course of his long scholarly career, it was he who put the legally intractable phantom of brujería on the map of a regime of knowledge geared toward constituting the odious racial and cultural other as an object of scientific elimination.

MICROBES AND OTHER ANIMALS: THE SANITIZING GAZE CAPTURES THE BRUJO

Recalling, in 1937, the beginnings of his research into Afro-Cuban issues, Ortiz noted the parallel nature of the intellectual path that had led the Brazilian scholar Nina Rodrigues and Ortiz himself to ethnographic investigations. "My book *Los Negros Brujos* was published in 1906," he wrote, "and had been written between [the years] 1902 and 1905, of which I passed three in Italy and only one in Havana, where I initiated my direct investigations. It is certain that I, like Dr. Nina Rodrigues somewhat earlier in Brazil, came to the ethnographic study of Cuba from the field of criminal anthropology, to which I had dedicated my most fervent zeal" (85). Ortiz received his doctorate in law from the University of Madrid in 1901 and was keenly aware of new positivistic currents in the sociological study of crime initiated by Spanish scholars such as Manuel Salés y Ferré, Constantino Bernaldo de Quirós, and Rafael Salillas. During his consular service in Genoa, Marseilles, and Paris (1903–5), he became closely associated with the *nuova scuola penale* of Cesare Lombroso and Enrique Ferri and, indeed, published his first three articles on Afro-Cuban topics—black crime, criminal superstitions among Cuban blacks, and black suicide—in Lombroso's *Archivio di psichiatria, scienze penali ed antropologia criminale* (Bremer 1993, 126 nn. 16–19).[37] By that time, Lombroso's positivistic theories of delinquent behavior as a function of physiologically determined (and anatomically detectable) moral atavism—that is, individual regression to biologically "older," animalistic psychological states conflicting with the stage of moral evolution of the delinquent's social milieu—had strongly affected, not only European, but also Latin American thought on the scientific rationalization of social control (see Gould 1981, 122–42). This new criminological idiom—allowing for the establishment of a correlation between delinquency and physiology, on the one hand,[38] and an evolutionary scheme of collective moral progress on the other—paved the way to Nina Rodrigues's and Ortiz's conceptual refiguration of common and longstanding elite constructions of black deviance into scientifically circumscribable indices of Africanity.

If Lombroso's theory of atavisms focused on physiological variants ("stigmata") as symptomatic of *individual* regression to phylogenetically older stages among Europeans (thus producing statistically circumscribable criminal types), its transference to racially conceptualized *collectivities* was already prefigured in the notion of an evolutionary lag characteristic of Africans and their New World descendants.[39] Nina Rodrigues, thus, vigorously attacked the republican Brazilian penal code for making no provisions for the differential culpability of blacks and whites. Given the racial inferiority of Afro-Brazilians—"a phenomenon of perfect natural order, product of the unequal march of human phylogenetic development"—the law had to take account of an "ethnic criminality, product of the coexistence, within the same society, of peoples or races in different phases of moral and juridical evolution" (Nina Rodrigues 1977, 5, 273). For what counted as normalcy within one frame of reference constituted crime in the other. Somewhat more cautiously, Ortiz (1973) proposed that the study of Cuban lowlife held great potential for comparative criminal ethnology because the racially complex character of Cuban society might add valuable data to a "science still in the stage of formation" that had hitherto "almost exclusively occupied itself with the observation of the white criminal" (21). Yet he too stuck to an Americanized version of Lombroso's basic conception of atavism:

> In Cuba a whole race entered into the criminal underworld. At their arrival, the blacks collectively entered into the lowlife of Cuba, not as if they had fallen from a higher level of morality, but as incapable, momentarily at least, of ascending toward it. Their sexual and familial relations, their religion, their politics, their moral norms, in conclusion, were so deficient that they had to remain, in the thinking of the whites, below the same individuals of the lowlife of the latter; for the white underworld did not lack some intimate linkages with the honor-

able masses; their disadaptation was not complete, while that of the unhappy blacks was. (20)

In no uncertain terms Ortiz enumerated the "stigmatic" symptoms of the atavism with which Cuba's black population was afflicted/had been afflicting Cuba:

> In their love life the blacks were exceedingly lascivious, their marriages reached polygamous proportions, prostitution did not merit their repugnance, their families lacked cohesion, their religion goaded them on to human sacrifice, to the violation of graves, cannibalism, and the most brutal superstitions; human life inspired little respect in them. (20)

Nevertheless, he concluded in truly Lombrosian spirit,

> one cannot say in a rigorous manner that the blacks, on entering Cuba, were not honorable and immoral, given the relative character of honorability and morality in sociological perspective. The blacks were honorable with respect to their criteria of morality; they were not insofar as they now had to regulate their behavior in line with the more elevated criteria that the whites had [developed] for themselves and for those they dominated. (20–21)

Hence it was not through massive physical repression but through the scientific policing of the population—so difficult, as Nina Rodrigues (1977, 10) lamented, "in a country governed without statistics"—and through the transposition of conceptions of deviance and crime into an idiom of physiological or psychic abnormality that irruptions of Africanity into the public sphere would become knowable as *racial atavisms* and, therefore, subject to consequent measures of social hygiene.[40] Particularly in the Cuban case, the metaphor of hygiene—with its implications of scientifically enforced cleanliness and transparency—provided a powerful rhetorical tool for the objectification of brujería as a noxious agent, a social pathogen. This was an especially compelling conceptual solution not only because it articulated with an internationalizing discourse on the (at least implicitly sexualized) transgressions by which uncivilized bodies contributed to the degeneration of civilized nations. Rather, the metaphors of sanitation held an additional attraction in the

Cuban case. For the successful eradication of yellow fever through the sanitation campaigns conducted by the U.S. occupation forces between 1900 and 1902 had been based on the Cuban physician Carlos Finlay's earlier discovery of its vectors and could, thus, be claimed as a triumph of Cuban science. Arguing that a "classic dogmatism" marred current penal criteria by focusing on definitions of crime rather than on its human perpetrators, Ortiz (1973) coined what would become a key analogy in the public campaigns against Afro-Cuban religious practices in the first two decades of the twentieth century. Having earlier remarked on the "contagious" effects of African atavisms on the "inferior classes of the white race" (18) in Cuba, Ortiz unraveled his vision of a medical-criminological regime based on positive knowledge:

> One wants to attack brujería, and, in general, delinquency, without studying the brujo and the delinquent, without discovering the factors that determine them. One wanted to extirpate yellow fever without studying the sick or discovering the factors of morbidity. And I make this comparison because nothing other than the total victory over yellow fever that we have achieved in Cuba thanks to the energetic application of medical and hygienic measures in line with the genial Cuban physician Dr. Finlay could better predict the result that will be obtained in the struggle against brujería and, in general, against other forms of lowlife if one pursues with like energy the repressive and preventive procedures (of social therapy and prophylaxis) demanded by current scientific progress. (234)

Hence the scientistic savagery of his therapeutic suggestions and prognostics:

> The first [measure] in the defensive struggle against the brujería has to be to finish off the brujos, to isolate them from their faithful like those afflicted with yellow fever, for the brujería is by its nature contagious, and, while these [i.e., the brujos] enjoy more or less complete liberty to continue their parasitism, it will subsist and will attempt to maintain those who sustain it in the intellectual passivity necessary for that they continue to support it even happily. Once those swindlers are gone, their feasts, dances, and savage rites ended, their temples destroyed, their impotent deities confiscated, all the tentacles of the brujería

that chain its believers to the barbaric bottom of our society cut, then, free of hindrances, they will be able to alleviate their still not de-Africanized minds of the weight of confused superstitions and rise to successive zones of culture. (242)

What is remarkable about these passages is how well they illustrate Foucault's notions about a modern transition from the exercise of the centralized power of the sovereign state (Nina Rodrigues's "unscientific repression," Ortiz's "classic [penal] dogmatism") to diffuse and polymorphous techniques of subjection enacted on the subjects' physical existence through disciplined methodologies of knowledge production and productive, in turn, of "regimes of truth."[41] The complex intertextuality between physiological and moral discourses and the enormous semantic productivity of the metaphoric linkages between ethnography and epidemiology, sanitation and punishment, science and domination, that Ortiz established in *Los negros brujos* immediately affected an amazingly wide discursive field. What is particularly intriguing about this is that Ortiz's positivistic regime of knowledge production initially foisted itself, not on empirical data, but on secondary recensions of atavistic bodies, African customs, and Afro-Cuban practices that he merely systematized and fused into the authoritative product of a truly Cuban contribution to the world of science. While his discovery of the value of Victorian Africanist writing for elucidating the ethnic provenance of Afro-Cuban beliefs and practices may have been a genuine (although—given Nina Rodrigues's precedent—not original) intellectual achievement, the language in which he fashioned linkages between black bodies, African culture, and New World crimes derived in no small measure from the Cuban press at the time of the niña Zoila trial.[42] Nor did he—as he repeatedly admitted—have any firsthand knowledge, at the time, of the beliefs and practices he so eloquently condemned as a social pathogen. "Having been away from Cuba [at the time], I could not have undertaken the necessary investigations and studies," he admitted midway through the second edition of *Los negros brujos* (1973, 103), "to analyze with precision and in all of its aspects the case in question [i.e., the Zoila murder] and had to avail myself exclusively of what the press published at the time and the information that I solicited and received through the amiability of some friends."[43]

Nevertheless, as the public reception of *Los negros brujos* shows, once removed from the genre of reportage to that of science, the veracity of the "data" so produced and the questionable referential functions of the theories built on those data turned into a nonissue—a certainty on which other forms of discourse began to build and that was soon fed back into those genres from which it had, originally, taken off. In an ingenious comparison between the texts of a verdict rendered on the alleged authors—meanwhile lynched (or fusillated in flight, if you will)—of the 1919 killing of "la niña Cecilia" in Matanzas, Chávez Álvarez (1991, 30ff.) has shown in detail how the very wording of the incriminatory document indicates beyond doubt the wholesale transfer of entire passages from *Los negros brujos* to a legal text ostensibly describing a crime that took place fourteen years after the book's first publication. The judges who wrote the verdict in Matanzas in 1919 not only dragged Ortiz's secondhand reconstructions of the Zoila case into the courtroom. They also used the garbled descriptions of objects of ritual and belief that Ortiz had culled from mid- to late-nineteenth-century Africanist texts in order to Africanize a phenomenon that he himself had not yet observed—Afro-Cuban brujería. And, again, their use of such materials, more than a decade later, obeyed a curious logic twice removed from any empirical evidence: to reconstruct the motives of people whom they were trying to incriminate posthumously![44]

More obviously yet, Ortiz's diagnostic and therapeutic suggestions amply fed back into the journalistic discourse from which they had taken their initial departure. Reading about the so-called niño Onelio or niño Cornelio case of 1913 in Havana's Biblioteca Nacional and Ortiz's personal files in the winter of 1994, I was repeatedly jolted from my lecture by powerful *dejá lu* experiences. On July 1, 1913—some two weeks after the boy had gone missing—the *Diario de la Marina* reprinted a letter to the editor of the periodical *El Día*. Signed "X.X.," it suggested the following measures against brujería:

> a) Perpetual deportation for all those who are justifiably considered to be brujos, regardless of sex or race.
> b) Males and females are to be confined separately in different localities so as to render impossible their coming near each other.
> c) The localities to be designated for their deportation could be the

> keys or islets that surround our island or any other territory bought by the state for this purpose, and in these places the vigilance necessary to avoid the escape of the confined will be enacted.
> d) In these banishment territories arable land will be distributed among the confined, who will there be at liberty to, and have access to the means of, work.
>
> In summary: what is needed is to organize colonies of brujos and brujas absolutely and definitively closed off to the outside while giving them freedom within the territory that they inhabit and the means to subsist by labor but impeding them from escape and reproduction.

Although not elaborated in quite as much disgusting detail, the idea of a penal colony had been a brainchild of Ortiz's. Arguing that incarceration would lead only to the infection of other prisoners and that the wholesale deportation of brujos to other countries would be difficult to effect in both legal and practical terms, Ortiz had concluded in *Los negros brujos* that, "if in Cuba there existed a true penal colony, the problem would almost [!] be resolved" (1973, 244). Finding himself in fundamental agreement with "X.X.," the author of the *Diario de la Marina*'s commentary nevertheless saw fit to add the following modifications, strongly reminiscent of Ortiz's more "humanitarian" suggestions about administering educational measures to at least the Cuban born (and, therefore, potentially curable) brujos:

> If one isolates lepers, paupers, and the pestilentially infected from society, it would be logical to remove from it those cancerous in spirit. However, even though under such free deportation the "brujos" must inflict their pestilence upon each other, and infect and consume each other, in the last instance because they are humans, they have the right to regeneration and redemption. Search, if you want to, for an asylum. But that separation and liberty of the asyled should not rule out that the medicines of education and religious sentiments reach them. Everything else would be cruel and sterile. (*Diario de la Marina*, July 1, 1913).

Only three days later, another commentator in *El Día* offered rather more severe variations on a theme by Ortiz. As in the animal kingdom there existed the threefold distinction between "tame," "tamed," and "wild" beasts, he suggested, so humanity divided itself among the "civilized," "civilizable," and "refractory." If, in both cases, the third category universally merited extirpation, Cubans would do well to face up to the example given by the nation whose civilizing efforts they had benefited from so much in the past:

> The Americans, insuperable people insofar as practical sense is concerned, have given to us a good object lesson and grand proof in respect to that problem occupying us now. It is known that [the United States] is the most tolerant country of the world, the great "country of tolerance" par excellence: there all sects—however excitable they may be—are respected. Well then, the so-called Moros of Mindanao and Jolo (in the Philippines) were, are, an equivalent to the Cuban brujos: in their barbarous practices, insofar as they eat children, cut the throats of and mutilate Christian maidens, with which they attain the heavenly reign (of their heavens, that is). And what did the Americans do? Well, they publicly, officially, and without unnecessary qualms gave the order to exterminate them. And General Wood [well-known to Cubans as the head commander during the second occupation] obediently and happily "diminished them" (as the Mexicans say) with gusto. And at this very moment, under the present American administration, we just read the following (fresh off the press), what the *New York Herald* of the twenty-second of the past month of June tells us with respect to those Philippine equivalents to the brujos: "As the government of President Wilson is convinced that the troglodyte crimes of the Moros of Jolo and the septentrional part of Mindanao represent a formidable threat to the civilized natives and resident Americans as well as that any solution given to the Philippine problem has nothing to do with the extirpation of a savagism "immune to Christian teachings," it has been decided in Washington [that it is necessary] to "destroy that which one cannot regulate."[45]

Comparing brujos and Moros to undomesticable animals, the author of the article in *El Día* concluded that Cuba had little choice but to follow the example set by the "greatest and most practical nation of the world" and its "most liberal and democratic institutions"—adding that even "illustrious anthropologists" nowadays maintained that brujería constituted, not a "race," but a "species." As his colleague from the *Diario* had argued the day before, race as such was not the issue in the persecution of brujería, and any attempt to construe the matter in such terms constituted an absurd falsification. "Brujería dishonors the whites as much as the blacks," he wrote. "It is an opprobrium of civilization, humanity, nature" (*Diario de la Marina*, July 1, 1913). Hence the taxonomic finesse of distinguishing between *race* and *species* exhibited by his colleague shortly afterward. The brujos, concluded the latter, have a certain commonality with humanity—just as the ape or orangutan—but are "physiologically animals" (*El Día*, July 4, 1913).

The trajectory of reduction that Ortiz (1973, 248) had suggested in commending "the progressive immunization against the microbe of brujería" had run its full biotic course. In a metaphoric progression running across diverse fields of inquiry, the brujo had evolved from microbiotic to simian incarnations, from feral to indomitable stages, and from republican civic status to that of a product of nature—a different species, noxious, parasitic, and irredeemable. He or she had to go if Cuba was to prosper, and it is surely no accident that the verb *lynchar* entered Cuban Spanish as an American loanword at just that time and in precisely this context.

THE BRUJO'S BODY

On the night of Sunday, June 29, 1919, a mob of several thousand citizens of Matanzas converged in a ghastly candlelight march on the fortress San Severino. There the rural guard and national military were guarding eight "brujos" suspected of the ritual murder of a four-year-old girl who had disappeared on the twenty-first. On the twenty-eighth, one of the accused had been found dead in his cell, and, on the morning of the twenty-ninth, the mutilated body of a child was discovered in the local cemetery. Simultaneously, news had reached the city of the killing of a black Jamaican day laborer in Regla at the hands of a lynch mob the day before. Spurred by the events in Regla, Matanzas's concerned citizens demanded justice. When the commanding officer refused to deliver the brujos up to their hands and denied them entry to the fortress on the grounds that there were also political prisoners in his custody who might flee in the disorder that would ensue, the mob forced the doors open and rushed into the courtyard. The soldiers opened fire on them, killing two members of the crowd and wounding several others. Inside the prison, the guards yanked five of the prisoners from their cells, conducted them to one of the ramps leading to another part of the fortress, and executed them "in attempted flight" (Chávez Álvarez 1991).

Photographs of their bodies taken immediately after the execution are reprinted in Roche Monteagudo (1925, 231) as gruesome trophies of a victory of civilization over barbarism. Himself a seasoned veteran of the cause against brujería, Roche did not mince words when it came to the issue of the physical eradication of "fanatics who merited to suffer the lynch law" (216), particularly since the penal code so insufficiently provided for the wholesale incrimination of brujos. Equivocating on the superficially "religious" character of brujería, the law, not only tied the hands of the police by offering only inadequate definitions of crime, but, in linking penal measures to the establishment of motive, neglected the fact that the intent to "kill and to harm as much as possible" (232) underlay *all* the brujos' activities. Roche's savage strictures against what he called "militant brujería" represent what one might call the right wing of Cuba's republican witch-hunting front. Although he does not explicitly say so, his treatment of the events in Matanzas suggests that, had *the people* not intervened, some or all of the brujos might have "escaped justice" at the hands of the state—as, from such a point of view, indeed, occurred in the case of the two surviving victims who were absolved in court in the spring of 1920 (Chávez Álvarez 1991, 23).

Roche's frustrations with the insufficiently tight net of the law and his open sympathy with popular justice, however, reflected a serious political problem that the district attorney of the Audiencia de Matanzas more explicitly raised in a speech given under similar circumstances in 1913. Reflecting on the understandable desire for vengeance that the child sacrifices by brujos inspired among "every halfway civilized human being," the licenciado Fernández Alvarez nevertheless cautioned that "direct violence by the collectivity" and "executions as are being realized in the South of the United States of North America" would have to be avoided (República de Cuba 1913). The rule of law could not be compromised. Still, in suggesting the liberal extension of existing law to cover all aspects of brujería, including "the gravest penalties for all who in one way [or another] contribute to the perpetuation of these savage idolatrous beliefs," Fernández Alvarez failed to perceive that what effectively guaranteed the perpetuation of brujería was the rule of law itself.

The constitution admitted to no halfway solutions. The law either would have to either discursively capture brujería as crime or leave it alone in order not to compromise its own authority. Thus, in a strange sense, what had occurred in the fortress San Severino that weekend in June 1919 was that the military had seen itself faced with little other choice than "merely" shooting the prisoners down in "attempted flight" if they wanted to preserve the state's legitimate monopoly on organized violence. In either case, the accused would not have lived to stand trial. Had their custodians surrendered them, the mob would have torn them apart. They had to be saved by a military volley. As a consequence, and regardless of whoever killed the child and for what reasons,[46] the incident *did* involve human sacrifice. Only its victims were the imprisoned brujos, its priestly officiants the national military, and the fetish to which they addressed it the republican Cuban state. Their immolation was inevitable, as was the solemn installation of the two other "innocent" victims of the incident, together with the (still insufficiently identified) girl's body, in a pantheon speedily erected in the town cemetery.

These were the snares in which, as Fernando Ortiz had realized as early as 1906, the "classical dogmatism" of "unscientific" criminology and penal jurisdiction entrapped the executive organs of the republican state. In Ortiz's (1973) view, the concentration on abstract legalistic taxonomies of types of crimes had "divided [and] pulverized the repression of brujería, dispersing it in multiple and convoluted directions" (234). Merely providing for the classifiability of certain acts as crimes, legislators had lost sight of the criminal and the factors determining his antisocial inclinations. Hence, the law remained blind to the special factors operative in the brujo's case and failed to go beyond the obvious symptomatology to a differential diagnosis of the underlying etiology. In penal terms, the present system was patently incapable, Ortiz argued, to distinguish "between the murder of a girl to obtain the viscera and benefit from them in the construction of an *embó* and the murder of a girl committed to cover up a case of rape. . . . Thus, just as identical pathological phenomena may obey different causes, so can formally equal crimes be produced by different motives; hence, to combat sickness or crime successfully, it will be necessary to study them through the medium of the individual and in the light of the effective causes [operative within him]."

This, then, was the aim of the kind of criminal anthropology that Ortiz and his self-consciously modern colleagues tried to inject into the antiquated system of Cuban legislation and law enforcement: to penetrate beneath the surface of criminal appearances and develop a regime of knowledge capable of rendering the brujo transparent to the gaze of science. To this end, Ortiz himself developed a set of theories designed to capture the brujo as a specific bioevolutionary and social type, a product of the forced introjection of the savage morality of an evolutionarily arrested race into a civilized ambiente, and rendered noxious owing to the brujo's innate inability to adapt successfully to his progressive surroundings. Unlike the common murderer, Ortiz argued, the brujo acted, not out of vengeance or malice, but in good faith. As the niña Zoila case had shown, his crimes were motivated by the desire to cure.[47] In a way, what Ortiz suggested was a form of ethnography aiming to establish the mental templates on which Cuba's African brujos committed their horrendous crimes. Although the perversity of the enterprise is striking, it shared more than superficial features with the fieldwork methodology that Malinowski was busily perfecting at around the same time in order to "get into the native Trobriander's mind" and that would soon enter into more explicit alliances with colonial regimes for which knowledge of the native other appeared crucial to the project of domination on the cheap.[45]

Ortiz's colleague Israel Castellanos, at the time professor of criminology at the University of Madrid, was to go one step further. In his memoir *La brujería y el ñáñiguismo desde el punto de vista medico-legal*, premiered by the Academía de Ciencias Médicas, Físicas, y Naturales de la Habana and published in 1916 under the motto "Kulturkampf," Castellanos declared the brujo's body the theater in which the nascent science of Cuban criminology would perform its most significant feats. Emulating the taxonomic and procedural regime established by Lombroso and other champions of an anatomy of the criminal body, Castellanos literally attempts to dissect the brujo's physiology in search of typologically salient features, few as they surprisingly turn out to be: the "simian cleavages" of his brain, the smallness of his ears, the asymmetrical implantation of his eyes, the tendency to cover his small (by "racial standards") lower jaw with a beard, his longevity. Meager as these results were for a self-conscious heir of Comte anticipating the future reign of a differentiated "sociological chemistry" (*sic*) (Castellanos 1916, 8) able to predict the reactions of social compounds on the grounds of their constituent elements, for Castellanos they were nonetheless highly significant. What Castellanos's investigations revealed was that the brujo exhibited uncannily normal features—he was of "racially" average height; his fingerprints showed no established signs of primitivity or degeneracy; his thorax did not exhibit the asymmetrical characteristics held to be symptomatic of epileptics; he excelled in terms of neither prognatism, height, weight, nor nasal width. The mismatch with the "stigmata" delineated in the European literature on forensic anatomy was stunning. Yet, for Castellanos, this was precisely the proof of the pudding. For the semiotics of the brujo's body apparently involved a cunning attempt at biotic simulation. Take the width of his forehead. Six of the brujos in Castellanos's sample of seven proved to have neither narrow nor fleeting foreheads. This, however, was not surprising at all, for "in our territories there arrived blacks with wide and bulgy foreheads, as well as with fleeting and narrow ones, in accordance with the frontal type of their respective [African] regions of provenience; among the criminal blacks who have a narrow and fleeting forehead this characteristic is accentuated, as it is in the case of the ñáñigo; and the brujo, whether he is native of the provinces [of Africa] where narrow or wide foreheads predominate, distances himself from estenocrotaphy and always chooses a more ample frontal diameter" (Castellanos 1916, 31).

The mere fact that he "chose" such a forehead, in other words, was enough to distinguish the "born brujo" from other types of criminals as a specific evolutionary type—even if that implicitly rendered Cuba's entire African-descended population potentially identifiable as either common criminals, or ñáñigos, or born brujos. At face value, Castellanos's pompous memoir, in fact, reads like an awkward attempt to prove the physiological normalcy of the handful of convicted brujos who did not escape the calipers of Cuban amateur anthropometrists. Of course, for Castellanos, this somewhat embarrassing fact indicated nothing less than that he was on the right track. The brujo was as polymorphous as the civic status of Cuba's African or African-descended population remained polysemic under the republican regime. And both were in need of fixing. Because of the scandalous lack of anthropological collections in Cuba, a self-conscious pioneer of science like Castellanos had to make do with a single cranium, one brain, four sets of fingerprints, perhaps a dozen photographs of brujos dead or alive, and a handful of previous descriptions of the physique of this scientifically highly important category of offender. The one single issue on which he seemed most authoritatively informed was the tendency of brujos to live to old age (a fact that corroborated their anachronistic conservation of savage mental traits) and their tendency to grow white beards—which was easily interpreted as an attempt, not only to hide their "racially anomalously small chin," but to inculcate the impression of sacerdotal authority among the credulous. In other words, any elderly Afro-Cuban man who chose not to shave closely was either a potential criminal or a potential brujo.

But Castellanos had more to say about the brujo than his meager catalog of features mismatching Lombrosian standards of stigmatism indicated. In the uncanny absence of stigmatizing physiological features (or, rather, the insidious capacity for simulation of normalcy that seemed to be bred into the bones of born brujos), the brujo was sure to be identified by his exaggerated sexual instincts, his social parasitism and disdain of honest work, his misguided altruism based on a savage sense of morality, the crude art he displayed in religious contexts, the language he spoke, the dances he danced, and the names he bore. Science penetrated even the most vexingly average physiological features in detecting the protean brujo under the skin of the ostensibly normal black citizen of the Cuban Republic. Even to have pointed out the inapplicability of European textbook indices of degeneracy or primitivism in the Cuban case was a triumph of Cuban science. Statistics would follow later. What mattered was that the theory they would eventually corroborate was well in place when data would finally begin to pour in in great quantities.

This bizarre exercise in conjuring up a textual simulacrum of the physiologically invisible brujo was not a mere aberration, a quirk of scientistic opportunism. Not only the prize that Castellanos's memoir won from Havana's Academía de Ciencias, but the very heuristics and methodology on which it was based, bespoke the working of a much more widely dispersed regime of knowledge, a form of semiosis that—in reinscribing relations of dominance and inequality on human bodies in the form of relations between civilization and savagery—constantly strove to materialize its object, only to annihilate it. Visualizing the brujo was the first step. Sanitary measures would follow. As a site of both lynch justice (or its "legitimate" last-minute preemption) and criminological science, the brujo's body was little else than a scenario within which a variety of discourses, afloat in early republican Cuba, found or created their reified referents.

In this sense, Castellanos's efforts to "make science" from the stuff of black Cuban bodies bear a striking resemblance to the semiotics of police investigations in the aftermath of raids productive of instruments of brujería. Not surprisingly, officers barging into tenement buildings or private homes often found themselves faced, not only with a multitude of people engaged in activities of unclear portent, but also with a profusion of objects of even stranger aspect. Carted off by the police in vast quantities, duly cataloged, and usually included in legal files and press reports in the form of long descriptive lists, such objects came to perform multiple functions in the making of brujería. On the one hand, and at face value, the catalogs of items confiscated by the police *precisely because* of their strange appearance and ostensibly nonintelligible function reveal a peculiarly archaeological mechanism of interpretation that assigned "ritual" values to what, in fact, were simply ill-understood heaps of decontextualized objects. Although such lists undoubtedly contain what must have been perceived by the victims of the raids as ritual objects, the main purpose was, not to understand their meaning, but to create evidence of something that had no meaning—and, indeed, could have none—in the eyes of their original owners / manipulators: brujería. We might call this the *enunciatory function* of such loot. Yet these sadly jumbled remains of sacred objects and ensembles, reassembled according to a bizarre new logic together with unrelated mundane articles at the hand of cataloging police clerks, underwrote the reification of brujería in still another way. For they not only objectified the presumed existence of the referent of brujería but served as palpable signs of the effectiveness of the reconnaissance strategies with which law-enforcement and scholarly agencies pursued what otherwise seemed to elude them. Not accidentally, many of these objects wound up in the newly founded anthropological museum of the University of Havana, where they underwent yet another set of semantic transformations circling around the idea of brujería under the cataloging direction of Dr. Luis Montané, a former disciple of Broca. Then and there, they assumed their second function as signs, not of brujería, but of the productivity of a science that they served to constitute.[49]

Here we might note a final and rather intriguing parallelism of practices. Part of the catalog of crimes laid at the doorstep of Cuba's brujos was the desecration of graves to obtain human body parts. Bones and dirt from the graves of specific persons do, indeed, play a significant part in the rites of the reglas de congo to this day. As we have seen in the previous chapter, such remnants of the dead serve to animate complex objects—known as ngangas or prendas—by installing the spirit of the dead in a relationship determined by the object's owner's power to feed and manipulate it for his or her own ends. Possession of the remains of a person to this day represents the key to accessing the power of his or her spirit. It is a relation surrounded by sinister images of slavery, wage labor, and dependence. But, just as modern-day brujos constitute their priestly competence on the domination of one or more muertos (spirits of the dead), so did the science practiced by Castellanos and his colleagues in the Museo Antropológico constitute itself on the grounds of possession of the bodily remains of dead brujos. As Castellanos (1916, 22) himself opined, the fact that the brains of the garroted authors of the niña Zoila crime wound up—along with innumerable other objects—in the able hands of the illustrious Dr. Montané was (although not productive of results at the time of Castellanos's writing) a sign of auspicious portent regarding the future of Cuban science. As contemporary priests of palo monte might say, the Museo Antropológico had turned into a giant nganga, animated by the enslaved remains of the powerful dead. Conjuring science out of violated bodies had become a republican drum of affliction.

DR. ORTIZ'S DILEMMAS

The repeated drone of magical incantations about the animality of the brujo to the contrary, priests of Afro-Cuban religions were all but unaware of the terms of the republican social contract that bound them to their ferocious adversaries. Indeed, it comes as a sad irony that some of them, at least, seem to have strongly identified with the new Cuban state. We can only speculate about the motives that had led the members of the abakuá grouping arrested on May 21, 1902 to stage a ceremony on precisely that day. But there is other evidence. Ortiz (1973, 52) thus gives an unwitting hint to another aspect of the process by which Cuban republican modernity and Afro-Cuban tradition were appropriating—co-opting, if you will—each other in describing an Afro-Cuban shrine that prominently featured, not only the skin of a leopard, but the coat of arms of the Republic. Likewise, Roche Monteagudo (1925, 187) refers to a 1906 police raid on a cult house in Guanabacoa that brought to light an exceedingly complex arrangement of animals and objects featuring "roosters, goats, a squalid black cat attached to a cord in moribund condition due to hunger and thirst; turtles, bones of various animals, shells, a great quantity of pots filled with fetid substances, guinea and johnson plaintains hanging from the wall; sacks of bones, goat tails, two great altars with images of Saint Barbara adorned with Spanish flags and crowned by a Cuban one, sixteen cauldrons with concoctions or infusions of herbs, and an infinitude of objects destined for the use and ceremonies practiced by the ñáñigos." The intromission of symbols of modern statehood into such ostensibly savage altars and assemblages tended to elicit either ridicule or a sense of outrage at the "profanation"—as Roche Monteagudo (1925, 79) put it in the case of abakuá ceremonies on Independence Day—of the sacraments of the civil religion that Cubans were supposed to have discovered in their newly won nationhood. Roche's formulation, by itself, was revealing, for only that which has the characteristics of the sacred can be profaned. There is, of course, no question that the kind of statehood that Cuba had acquired under North American guidance was, ultimately, a fetish of a neocolonialist imagination. The pseudo-Republic came into existence through American intervention, and it subsisted—with all its "anticipatory affirmations of prosperity and plenty"—as a subsystem of the economy of the United States. It was Monsieur L'Amérique with whom Madame Terre Cubaine went to bed under the chaperonage of the first Cuban Republic, and we have already seen in which ways U.S. capital interests played into the making of Cuba's black brujería. Yet the fetish of the republican state was tied to its African fetishists in other ways as well, and the agency of the bastard sons and daughters of this pernicious union between U.S. capital and Cuban republican selfhood is not to be dismissed out of hand. Just as the ideologues of republican modernity built Afro-Cuban religion into their version of Cuba, so did "those whom fortune disinherited"[50]—as an Afro-Cuban priest named Fernando Guerra (1915) referred to himself and his religious associates—build the Cuban state into their vision of a self-consciously modern future of their traditions.

The first reference to Guerra and his associates that I found in the documents[51] is in a petition addressed by a "Sociedad de Socorros Mutuous de la Nación Lucumí" to the American military government in 1900. Signed by José Cornelio Delgado and Francisco Roche, the petition concerns the use of African drums in the society's festivities, denied by Havana's municipal governor. It includes the society's *reglamiento* (legal statute), which lists not only the famous African-born babalao (priest of the ifá oracle) Remigio Herrera as the honorary president of the association, but contains the names of such other highly famous first-generation creole babalaos as Eulogio Rodriguez (better known as Tata Gaitán), Bernabé Menocal, Pedro P. Pérez, Luis Pacheco, Esteban Quiñones, Isidoro Somodevilla, and Bonifacio Valdés on its roster of dignitaries. The list further includes two priests named Isidoro Sandrino and Silvestre Erice who were both to play a significant role in the eventful history of this particular association (NA RG 140 Milit. Govt. Cuba, letters received, 1899–1902, 1900:6725–1/2, box 120). As Ortiz surmised in 1921, the association in question was the heir to a "cabildo africano lucumí" "reorganized" by Joaquín Cádiz—another famous (first-generation African) babalao—in the calle Jesus Peregrino 49 in 1891. In 1893, the group adopted a red and white flag, and it legally "reorganized" again in 1905, 1909, and 1912, at which time it had moved its operations to the calle San Nicholás 302 (Ortiz 1921, 26–27).[52]

As his personal papers deposited in Havana's Instituto de Literatura y Lingüistica show, Ortiz spent considerable time scrutinizing the historical record that the cabildos de nación and their successor organizations had left in the Cuban archives. In this case, however, there are good grounds for arguing that his knowledge of the republican career of the cabildo africano lucumí derived from more immediate experience. Among his papers (Fondo Ortiz Carpeta 35 desde 535 a 540) there is a handwritten letter dated March 12, 1911, in which Fernando Guerra, in his office as secretary of the Sociedad de Protección Mutua y Recreo del Culto Africano Lucumí, Sta "Bárbara," announced the following:

> Sir, I notify you by means of the present diploma that you have been nominated in the extraordinary meeting celebrated on the night of the second of March in the calle San Nicholas 302 to be honorary president of the Sociedad de Protección Mutua y Recreo del Culto Africano Lucumí, Sta "Bárbara," which will live satisfied with the utmost glory

> that has befallen the ones whom fortune disinherited [to count among them] the doctor Fernando Ortiz. Therefore I beg the man of the science of good government to give himself the honor to acknowledge the receipt of that which I respectfully offer.[53]

Given Guerra's subsequent correspondence with Ortiz, there is no reason to assume that the latter declined the honor.

We can only speculate about Ortiz's motivation in entering a relationship that for Guerra and his associates must have appeared a strategic alliance between religion and science. It is clear that this man who had been so influential in the forging of a persecutionary regime against African savagery repeatedly visited the society's premises, attended rituals, and corresponded with Guerra. Although Ortiz, at the time, was about to embark on a political career, it seems unlikely that the unveiled slur his former friend Eduardo Varela Zequeira directed against him in 1913 explains his motives. In the course of investigating a child abduction near the town of Corral Falso, Varela had claimed to have been told that, "some time ago, a lawyer from Havana with political ambitions joined a *bembé* ceremony, put on yellow garments with little bells, and participated in the rituals like a believer" (*El Mundo*, May 7, 1913). Apart from impugning Ortiz's sexual preference by indicating that he wore the yellow ritual dress of devotees of the goddess Ochún,[54] Varela was using the "rumor" to launch a vicious tirade against the "scandal" of (near) universal male suffrage—a situation conducive to such unholy alliances between politicians and brujos. But Ortiz probably did not commence his fieldwork in Matanzas until some decades later, and, given his excellent connections to the liberal republican elite, it seems unlikely that he would have gone campaigning among rural Afro-Cubans at the time.

On the other hand, at least as far as his connections to the Sociedad de Protección Mutua y Recreo del Culto Africano Lucumí, Sta "Bárbara," and its sister organization, the "Sociedad Santa Rita de Casia y San Lázaro," are concerned,[55] there is no question that he repeatedly visited their cult houses and observed or participated in ritual activities. In a broadside published and distributed by Guerra ("La verdad en su puesto: Hoja suelta") as a reply to an article in *El Mundo* (December 8, 1914) grossly distorting an interview that Guerra had given to the reporters, Guerra argued that it was not true that the reporters had surprised him and Erice in the act of performing rituals but that he, Guerra, had voluntarily come to the journalists' offices in order to disabuse the public of the false impressions that were being spread about his and his friends' religion. On the contrary, had the reporters been on the premises of the society (as they had written), their presence would be noted by two witnesses beyond reproach. For, at the time they claimed to have been there, the society had been enjoying the honor of a visit by two distinguished scholars, Fernando Ortiz and a colleague from Ireland whom Ortiz had brought along to observe the ceremony that they were staging that day. "The directive of the society," Guerra continued,

> announces to its associates and protectors that Dr. Fernando Ortiz is one of the Cuban men of letters who, for the prestige of his native country, desires to know and conduct studies in the terrain of the Christian lucumí morality [of] everything that is visible under the eyes of god and those of men with clear judgment.
>
> Democrat by nature and by virtue of the noble qualities that adorn him as a native Cuban, [and] without preconceptions in his mind, Dr. Ortiz sat down on a modest chair and watched from there what [the members of the society] sang and played to the sound of *güiros* and *timbales* in accordance with the African lucumí usage.
>
> We repeat that Dr. Ortiz studies the most minute movements in the field of the social life of the Christian lucumí morality, perhaps with the objective of forging all that into a "block" in order to lead it without dirtying his white hands to the repository where the laws are created by the vast wisdom of Cuban knowledge, so that the justice of his native Cuba will not have to lament [its abuse] in facing the justice of the other republican nations of the civilized world. (Guerra 1914)

Regardless of Ortiz's intentions, Guerra and the associates for whom he spoke obviously pursued their own projects. In the aftermath, it seems as if they did so by striking at the root. Like their Brazilian contemporaries, who busily incorporated social scientists into the moral communities of terreiros by initiating them as *ogans* in order to mobilize scholarly discursive authority in their fight against the state (see Dantas Gois 1988), Guerra and his associates seem to have correctly perceived Ortiz as a key player whom they needed to convert to their cause. If modern science reached out to fix African magic, its alter, the republican brujo, likewise strove to capture and entangle the Cuban scientist in a discourse of moral authority and human responsibility. In a strategic, and often antagonistic, dialogue, they each literally inscribed themselves into the projects of the other. Decades later, Ortiz would openly acknowledge his ties to the Regla-based cult groups of Pepa Herrera and Susana Cantero and his indebtedness to the formidable knowledge of their drummers, Trinidad Torregrosa and Pablo Roche. At the same time, there are some indications that he, in return, gave these religious virtuosi access to his collection of Africanist ethnographic literature. By the 1950s, such relations of intellectual reciprocity had engendered a complex set of feedback loops, along which knowledge circulated in an intricate movement whereby science and religion, African tradition and Cuban modernity, engaged each other in mutual self-construction. The results are observable today in the form of both Afro-Cuban religion and Afro-Cuban anthropology (Palmié 1995a).

Yet, although Ortiz mentioned Guerra's group as a "most interesting case" in his 1921 article on the cabildos, he never openly broached the topic of his involvement with the Sociedad de Protección Mutua y Recreo del Culto Africano Lucumí, Sta "Bárbara," or the Sociedad Santa Rita de Casio y San Lázaro. It could be that, at that time, he himself was still too much a part of a world in which, as he later wrote (Ortiz 1945–46, cited in Izuaga 1989: 4), "even to speak of the Negro in public was a dangerous thing that could be done only furtively and confidentially, as if one were dealing with syphilis or with a nefarious sin in the family." But Ortiz's ambivalence may have related not just to a fear of the kind of salacious slander that his former colleague in arms Varela Zequeira directed against him in the summer of 1913. Mere face work was not all there was to it. Having discovered the brujo's humanity in concrete social relations *after* establishing his own scientific reputation by making the black other thinkable as enemy, parasite, and animal, Ortiz's silence on his involvement with Guerra and his group may well bespeak some rather more fundamental ambivalences.

At any rate, Ortiz, it seems, reciprocated. On June 18, 1912, Guerra sent a copy of a letter to Ortiz that he had also expedited to the secretary of the provincial government of Havana, the president of the Cuban Republic, and the director of the Anthropological Museum of the University of Havana, Dr. Luis Montané. Containing a drawing of the three drums constituting a Yoruba-Cuban *batá* ensemble, the letter designated these as *pandereta* 1–3, the heading *pandereta primera* crossed out and *añá* overwritten in a different hand (quite probably Ortiz's), indicating the possibility that he gave legal advice. The term *pandereta* (lit.: "tambourine" rather than "drum"), at least, testified to Guerra's keen understanding of the legal specificities involved in the then frequent confiscation of Afro-Cuban drums, an activity that, in the case of consecrated batá (or, as practitioners today would say, *tambores de fundamento*) constituted the violent and religiously highly problematic severance of an animated object or, rather, objectified being[56] from the only context in which it could fulfill its divine purpose: the Afro-Cuban cult group. The sacred nature of these drums—rather than what Ortiz and other liberal observers saw as their entertaining functions for "the blacks"—was what set the *sociedades* of people like Fernando Guerra at the most obvious odds with the laws of the republic. Hence their repeated moves to have batá legally inscribed as *tambourines* or *African-style tambourines,* underlined by a fortuitous structural similarity between the bell-enclosed upper end of a batá drum with the latter type of idiophone, exempted as it was from legal strictures by its pervasive use in Spanish-derived popular music.

FERNANDO GUERRA AND "LA SALACIÓN CIENTÍFICA"

Guerra's voice would ring out publicly several more times in the years to come, but I will close by focusing on his statements in the context of the so-called niño Cornelio murder of 1913. In this case, a three-year-old boy named Cornelio García had gone missing in mid-June from the "central Socorro" (a sugar plantation) near Jovellanos, Matanzas, where his parents worked. By June 24, the police had arrested a suitable culprit, the fifty-two-year-old creole black day laborer and veteran of the Liberation Army Faustino Baró, who had been denounced for practicing evil magic with a *prenda judía,*[57] which contained bones, earth, and stones, and who—as his accuser and former coworker Severino Jiménez claimed—was in the habit "of eating the blood of people." As Baró's common-law wife Demetria Calello pointed out, she had repeatedly "fed" his "saints" (i.e., deities) with chicken blood during the six months that Baró had earlier spent in prison, but both adamantly protested their innocence (*La Noche,* June 24, 1913; *El Mundo,* June 25, 1913). Days later, journalists and policemen were combing the area for sick African ex-slaves, only to encounter an interesting group of two women and a man who all bore the surname Armas. Benito Armas, a twenty-six-year-old illiterate creole Afro-Cuban working in the provisioning department of the plantation Socorro, proved entirely unrelated to the two women, just as they in turn proved unrelated to each other. As the journalists found out, the two ancient African women were not relatives at all but *carabelas*—they had shared the horrors of the middle passage on the same slave ship and had chosen to bond for life on the basis of this experience, although each continued to practice her own brand of African religion (*El Mundo*, June 26, 1913).

Meanwhile, the authorities in Havana were gearing up for what *El Mundo*, on the thirtieth, called "a crusade against brujería." Foremost among the publicized witch-hunters was Capitán Plácido Hernández, chief of police of station 11 in the sixth district comprising the—then—fairly well-to-do barrio of El Cerro, on the southwestern hills beyond the original barrios extramuros that had grown since the late eighteenth century on the outskirts of Havana's old walled city. Hernández's special target was an explicitly religiously motivated Afro-Cuban mutual aid society named the "Sociedad Santa Rita de Casio y San Lázaro" installed in the calle Ayuntamiento 18 of El Cerro since the turn of the century. It was the group that Silvestre Erice had founded in 1902 and continued to direct. Hernández and Erice repeatedly engaged each other in well-publicized legal as well as paralegal exchanges, a fact that—more effectively than "Papá Silvestre's" reputed ministrations to the white "better classes"—rendered Erice a sort of public celebrity. His very visibility made him a readily available object of journalistic cathexis. It was to his cult house that reporters turned when in need of some firsthand material on brujería in the capital. But it was also there that they—if they were inclined to listen at all—got well-informed lessons about the way in which articles 26, 28, and 37 of the Cuban constitution underwrote what they were observing. Indeed, nothing in Erice's and his friend Guerra's public behavior indicated less than their ability to engage both African deities and the republican fetish state on their own terms.

Two weeks after the niño Cornelio case had first made the headlines, Guerra issued a public manifesto. It was a protest, not just against the vicious slander thrown in their direction by the journalists, but against "the fantastic fact that some Cubans in the field of political studies, in respect to the subject of brujería, propose the installation in the Cuban territory of the moral system of a new slavery" (Guerra 1913). Quite obviously, Guerra knew of the legal niceties arising from the patently hybrid character of the then-reigning penal code. Given the intellectual stature of the man, it need not have been Ortiz who alerted him to this fact. Guerra seems to have closely followed the journalistic coverage of the case and to have been fully aware of the debate on "sanitation" measures. Given the frenetic agitation to which journalists had worked up the public imagination, lynch mobs and sexually segregated labor camps were on the verge of transforming from symbols of a collective fantasy to its concrete manifestations.[58] The same year, Guerra and Erice coauthored a similar broadside entitled "The Truth, with its Face toward the Sun," in which they emphasized that, "aided by the laws of the Republic and the idiosyncrasy of the Cuban people, we sing and dance on festive occasions according to the African lucumí usage without the presence in the ceremonial of a corpse or gravely ill person" (Guerra and Erice 1913), thus forestalling the very argument that Ortiz had initially introduced in the discourse on brujería and that had sent scores of rural policemen in search of ill-looking elderly Africans. "Therefore we see neither the reasons nor the motives," they continued, "for which one should want to deprive us [of our liberties] on the grounds of that which some write on sheets of paper in some newspapers under the guise of information," writings productive of nothing else than the violation of articles 26 and 28 of the constitution and the general "ill-feeling that they sow in the Cuban people."

Erice died on September 15, 1915, and it was, perhaps, no accident that he was eulogized not only in the press that monitored the enormous cortege trailing his coffin to his final resting place in Havana's famous cemetery Colón. His long-term associate, friend, and father-in-law Fernando Guerra and no less a figure than the illustrious Professor Israel Castellanos contributed to "Papá Silvestre" Erice's obsequies—albeit in very different ways. I do not know whether Guerra ever reacted to the painfully condescending and racist remarks with which Castellanos bade farewell to Erice, a man who, by then, may have been one of his favorite foes (if only because the press had written enough on him to give Castellanos an idea—however bizarre—of who he was). In what is the last public statement by Guerra known to me, he issued yet another "manifesto" protesting the irreverent treatment that Erice's death had received in Havana's daily press. In the "name of all those Christians"[59] who belonged to the association that Erice had led and whose head Guerra now had become, he bitterly wrote that he "prayed to the Supreme Being for the happiness and the consolation of all those who, from the columns of some publications such as 'La Marina' would profane the name of he who in life was named SILVESTRE ERISE" (Guerra 1915) and who had more than demonstrated his civic valor in contributing some three hundred pesos to the building of a hospital and five hundred more to the cause of alleviating the situation of Juán Gualberto Gómez (a famous black Cuban politician) during his exile in Spain. Guerra further announced that, not only had the mayor of Havana, but also police captain Hernández been apprised of the festivities in Erice's honor. He closed by extending his greetings to Erice's old enemy Plácido Hernández in the conviction that—for once, we might add—Hernández would uphold republican law in the barrio of El Cerro during the event. Hernández, it seems, at least bowed to this simple plea for human decency—riddled by bitter ironies though it was.

Guerra may never have read the callous and sinister reply that Castellanos launched against him and his associates, whom the famous forensic scientist chose to call the "hijos de Papá Silvestre" in his already-mentioned prize-winning memoir. In fact, Castellanos apparently could not help but include a full quotation of Guerra's 1915 "Manifesto" in this text—and, when I say *could not help it,* I mean that he had latched onto Guerra's manifesto in order to beef up the painfully meager data otherwise at his disposal. The Manifesto is, in fact, the single piece of original evidence in Castellanos's chapter on the "intellect of the brujo," and its inclusion plainly shows what conjuring tricks a self-consciously modern scientist—colonized as he was by a century-old European political magic—was wont to resort to in order to impress his credulous audience.

In part, Castellanos derided the Manifesto's language as orthographically inadequate, repetitious, and containing an imagery indicative of the black brujo's "mental deficiency" and congenital "incapacity of the brain." Castellanos, thus, poured his ridicule on the moving imagery with which Guerra metaphorically evoked Erice's transformation to ancestrality (in terms that would be wholly understandable to contemporary practitioners of regla ocha). "The body of Mr. Erice," wrote Guerra, "will forever cover the earth with his veil of multicolored stones and roots, which [in accordance with the] social laws of nature makes us all equals" (Guerra 1915). For Castellanos, this paragraph branded Guerra as an unredeemed African. For, despite Guerra's Cuban birth, he apparently had not lost the sense of "irresistible attraction" that "everything that glistens . . . that is painted or colored in vivid hues holds for the true son of Africa" (Castellanos 1916, 99). But what particularly seems to have stung the self-declared (and publicly duly acknowledged) scientist was the way in which the other seemed to mimic a language that he had reserved for himself. It is here that we might say with Bhabha (1984) that the language of differentiation on which the project of scientific authority rests is undercut by its own hybrid product, that what Fields (1982, 575) calls "the inherent danger of all 'civilizing' " missions, that is, the estrangement of an authority based on totalizing discriminations by the oxymoronic presence of the "civilized native," finds its equivalent in a breakdown of the distinctions between the brujo's and the scientist's languages. It is not difficult to see why passages such as the following elicited Castellanos's wrath. "It is clear that all humans," Guerra (1915) wrote, "once they are born must of necessity [strive to] preserve themselves and so assimilate themselves to the very [process of the] transmission of life itself, so that the species will reproduce itself in accordance with all the conditions of a complex of health and strength, to the effect that evolution takes the course it must within the laws of biology." Speaking for "those whom fortune had disinherited," Guerra's evocation of evolution and the laws of biology represented more than a demonstration of equal access to an idiom that derived its universalistic authority from the explicit disavowal and denigration of other knowledge. Nor was it merely the self-conscious creation of a hybrid form of discourse by which savagery and religion incorporated modernity and science, thus disturbing the articulation of discriminatory classifications. Rather, I think it is fair to say that Guerra succeeded in submitting science itself to the test of its own enunciations of universality, thus exposing it as yet another system of knowledge and moral artifact—politically authoritative because linked to a historically specific power structure and regime of truth, but in no other respect essentially different from what Guerra, at this point, no longer called "the Christian lucumí morality" but the "African lucumí religious morality."

For Castellanos, this was too much.[60] "As regards the judgment which the intellectual preparation of the author" of such statements merited, he fumed (1916, 60),

> the only fitting formulation must be: *it is deficient, indecisive, and ignorant of the ideas he takes [to represent] the thought of the whites.* The African brain that determined the motor behavior and mechanics of writing, will it know how to explain the paragraph in the Manifesto that says "to the effect that evolution takes the course it must within the laws of biology"? If he [i.e., the author] were able to comprehend [what he wrote], instead of preparing his statement he would have fashioned an *embó* [magical preparation] to sustain his psychosocial unadaptability in the face of the implacable rigor of what to him must seem to be the *scientific salación* of the whites.

If this remarkable formulation says anything about its author, it is that, unlike Guerra, Castellanos was fully ignorant of the thought of the other. Haunted by the phantasm of the brujo, and fired by the arrogant narcissism of power, Castellanos had no idea that his own rhetorical gesture—the very choice of the popular term *salación*—indicated precisely what he and his colleagues were engaged in: a form of witchcraft. As Ortiz (1973, 86) had written, the concept *salación* signified the working of "an enemy's spell or of some supernatural power that delights in mortifying and disgracing a person by all means available, that is to say, without restricting himself to a specific form of harm." It is hard to think of a better translation of Foucault's conception of the "capillary" effects of the dispersal of power in modern forms of domination into the morally far more acute idiom of popular Cuban speech. And it is hard to think of a statement less denunciatory of the witchcraft—call it *moral derailment*, if you will—of the regime of knowledge to which Castellanos referred as *science* than this witting/unwitting giveaway. Foul was fair and fair was foul in the world that Israel Castellanos inhabited. Although this would overstate the case, one might say with hindsight that what Guerra had done was no less than return a spell on its author.

EPILOGUE

Carnal Knowledge

Die ben waar, em ben mi Vleeschmeester, mar mi vleesch no kan verdraag die. (This much is true, he is the master of my flesh, but he cannot withstand [persevere against] my flesh.)—slave saying in the eighteenth-century Danish Virgin Islands reported by the Moravian missionary C. G. A. Oldendorp

In the summer of 1999, I returned to Regla, where I had last done fieldwork in the winter of 1995–96. By then, the old ferry landing near the sanctuary of the Virgin de Regla and patroness of the harbor of Havana had undergone significant changes. The old *embarcadero* building had been closed since the summer of 1994, when young men carrying crates of gasoline-filled beer bottles and a large frosted cake, from which they pulled a revolver once the ferry had left Havana, tried to hijack the ancient, pre-1959 vessel and steer it toward the Florida straits. It was in the midst of the so-called *balsero* crisis of that summer that the revolutionary Fuerzas Armadas Revolucionarias (FAR) had, for the first time since 1959, opened fire on citizens of the Cuban state. No trace of that particular event remained by 1999, unless one wanted to count a large sign posted at the Havana terminal prohibiting bringing beer bottles or cakes onto the ferry as a memorial to recent bloodshed. However, tucked away beside the sanctuary on the road leading away from any spot of obvious tourist interest, one can now see a small marble-framed plaque reading "Regla 1836–1996: to the Africans who in 1836 founded in this town the secret African society." The subtext "Buro Abacua 5.1.97" explains, not only what African society was founded there, but who is doing the remembering. Currently directed by Ángel Fernández, head of a revolutionary catering brigade and high-ranking titleholder in abakuá, the *buro provincial de abacuá* has managed to write its own memory into that of the revolutionary Cuban state. Representing the single Afro-Cuban religious formation that seems ever to have experienced active persecution by the revolutionary Cuban state, this male secret society that once controlled economic life at the docks of Regla and Havana now remembers itself under the marbled aegis of the Revolution.

Still, materially visible but semantically oblique signposts such as the prohibition of beer and cake on the ferry boat or the plaque awaiting the accidental tourist to Regla are not the only symptoms of the violent histories that continue to seep into the Cuban present at the beginning of the twenty-first century. Make no mistake, behind the palm tree–rimmed beaches to which First World tourists flock in steadily increasing numbers lie half-forgotten spaces of death. Under the shadow of rotting agroindustrial machinery, cane stalks continue to sway in the breezes that once swept slave ships across the Atlantic and returned cargoes of sugar, coffee, and tobacco to the sites of value realization where, to paraphrase Marx, the "blood and dirt" clinging to them dissipated into utilitarian oblivion. Lack of gasoline and spare parts and adverse world market conditions have rendered these former sites of agroindustrial production mere sites of waste: of time, of human effort, of hopes invested in a socialist future. At the beach resorts of Varadero—located on a peninsula lying athwart some of the most brutal plantation regions of nineteenth-century Matanzas—an awkward turn of the wind may, from time to time, waft the sour, vomit-like stench of rotting cane toward the beach. It is an old smell, harking back to the beginnings of a violent modernity that once dawned in the very fields that now lie abandoned as inessential to the economic survival of the revolutionary Cuban state. There is also an oil refinery in Varadero's hinterland today, and often it is hard for the tourists to tell exactly which modernity is causing their olfactory distress once the wind turns from a seaward breeze to the multiple stenches exuded by the leeward side of the land.

In part, the restructuring of Caribbean economies in line with the functional requisites of what Orlando Patterson (1987) has called a *West Atlantic system* centered on the United States has added a layer of monumental triviality to the palimpsest of the region's history. Just as the Jamaican "Banana Boat Song" no longer speaks to United Fruit Company price-setting practices when it lilts from the speaker system of cruise ships going to anchor in Port Antonio, so do the lyrics of some of the hotel-bar standards in Havana—from the hauntingly beautiful "Guantanamera" and "Hasta Siempe, Comandante" (both commemorating shattered visions of Cuban national self-determination), to the lively "Alto Songo" (which speaks to the annihilation of a black village during the so-called race war of 1912)—no longer register as pertaining to anything but local colorations of tourist experience. Once headquarters of the "Bronze Titan" Antonio Maceo's Liberation Army, the Hotel Inglaterra at the Parque Central nowadays admits Cubans too dark skinned to be mistaken for foreigners only to a waiting area where the security guards can monitor the eventual validation of their presence by the appearance of "their" tourist.[1] Proceeding at an increasingly rapid pace, the restoration of Habana Vieja directed by Eusebio Leal Spengler under the auspices of Unesco and European finance capital has reached the Alamenda de Paula, where a Bennetton store now occupies a site opposite a former slave pillory.[2] As colorfully painted facades begin to replace the moldy grays and browns of rotting nineteenth-century *solares,* a steady stream of socially unproductive former *vecinos* (inhabitants) is channeled toward decaying concrete suburbs such as the Soviet-built Habana del Este or San Miguel del Padrón, thus rendering the expanding *zona turística* safe for dollarized consumption and sparing its previous population what Western observers might call the *demonstration effects* of rampant commodity fetishism in the midst of an increasingly un-real-existing socialism.

The fortress of San Carlos de la Cabaña, where Aponte spent his last days, may not be open to the public yet, and the crania of dead brujos are no longer on exhibit at the Museo Montané. Yet Havana's Casa de África, located just off the main tourist trail through Habana Vieja and originally intended to affirm Cuba's now irrelevant internationalist commitments to Angola, Mozambique, or Guinea Bissão, exhibits as exemplars of Cuba's African heritage many of the desecrated ritual objects that less than a century earlier had served as criminal evidence of potentially deadly portent. Further afield across the bay, Guanabacoa's ethnographic museum features a life-size exhibit representing an elderly black babalao frozen in the act of manipulating an ifá divining chain. Although the mannequin's face has a benign expression, the visual effect of this tableau is very much that of an oracular ceremony interrupted by the police in search of elderly bearded Africans; and, indeed, on closer reflection, the babalao looks uncannily like Bocourt. Of course, as the friendly guide will tell you, the Revolution has done away with all forms of racist discrimination and religious persecution. Cuba now openly embraces its African cultural heritage, and, for a small fee, he will be happy to arrange a meeting with a genuine priest of Santería, who will explain his shrines and maybe even perform cowrie shell divination for you. But, then again, you might prefer to attend a performance by the Conjunto Folklórico Nacional such as the *sabado de rumba* held weekly in different barrios of Havana. It features beautiful renditions of the African ceremonies, all very well choreographed, and you can bring your camera. Everybody loves it. He may wink and add that you might pick up a pretty muchacha there as well.

Regretfully, I have come to know Cuba only at a historical juncture when the remaining semblances of its socialist order have come to be underwritten by market forces that are not just reconfiguring people's material and moral environments, but inexorably reconstructing their physical and social selves along the lines of purchasing power, pigmentation, and perceived utility in satisfying tourist desire. By the time I first went to Cuba in 1993, the island had begun to relive a past that one might well wish it could have forgotten. Sad as it is that a colleague of mine would be able—and with good reason at that—to teach a course on contemporary Cuban literature subtitled "From Revolution to Prostitution," the present in which I conducted my fieldwork and archival research seemed haunted by specters that must surely be obvious to anyone who has spent an evening in the public cafeteria of the Habana Libre hotel or on the Paseo del Prado in the final years of the twentieth century. But all the crazy historical contingencies of the late twentieth century aside—we may at least ask ourselves if these pasts *should* have been forgotten in the first place. This is a question very much at the heart of the effort I put into writing this book, and—who knows—maybe remembrance is the way to appease those ghosts that arguably haunt, not only Cuba, but all of us today.

Of course, the plight of contemporary Cubans may be of little consequence to any assessment of the "modern condition" (whether conceived as unitary or multiplex, continuing or superseded, factually existent or merely a work of language and power). Still, if I were given my choice of imagery to express the relation between Caribbean pasts and our (often only too self-consciously postmodern) present, I would follow José Antonio Aponte in arguing that there are reasons of history that can make wide spatial and temporal seas appear narrow in the image. These reasons I take to be moral ones, and this is why I think that I owe the reader, my Cuban friends, and, perhaps not least of all, myself a sort of concluding unscientific postscript: one that provisionally and only too tentatively makes narrow in the image what may seem merely consecutive or coincidental according to standard practices of disciplined historical narrative.

REMEMBERING THE FUTURE

In late November 1994, I picked up a copy of *Juventud Rebelde* somewhere on the streets of Centro Habana. Representing, next to *Granma*, one of the last remaining newspapers in paper-starved Cuba, the issue carried a notice pertaining to the upcoming festivities for Santa Bárbara on December 4—a popular occasion for rituals in honor of Changó, a deity widely, if somewhat ambiguously, associated with this saint. Reflecting the current party line on Afro-Cuban religions, the author was at pains to point out that the legends of white children abducted on that day and sacrificed by black wizards to African idols referred not just to a *thing* of the past. Rather, he argued, they harkened back to a previous stage of Cuban society when ideologies of racial otherness still mystified the fundamentals of class antagonism that effectively prevented the members of the Cuban nation from realizing their shared Latin African cultural heritage. The implication was that the specter of African brujería had always been an epiphenomenon of capitalism: an ideological fantasm dividing the Cuban working class along racial lines and securing imperialist domination. Hence its obsolescence in a society where socialism had eradicated the iniquitous economic relations that it had served to mystify and so realigned social thought with material reality.

If so, however, why disabuse a socialist readership—fully thirty-five years after the triumph of the Revolution—of the notion that frightful things might happen on the night of December 4? Should it not have been evident to the readers of *Juventud Rebelde* that the drums echoing throughout the poorer and notably blacker barrios of Havana that evening were nothing but testimony to the revolutionary working class's righteous celebration of the culture of what Comandante Castro called "un país latinoafricano"?[3] Why even point out, in so many words, that there was nothing sinister about such ceremonies or that phenotypically white children need not be locked up at home after dark? For Alejandro, a graduate student and recent convert to Pentecostalism who never failed to strike up a conversation in English with me when we ran into each other on the street, matters were rather more straightforward. "Why," he asked me, aware of the subject of my research, "do you keep going to these witchcraft parties [meaning Afro-Cuban religious ceremonies]? They kill people, you know."

I did not keep the copy of *Juventud Rebelde* and have regretted it ever since. For it is striking to what extent notions of dehumanization—of which the image of child sacrifice is surely only a particularly radical specimen—are of continued salience to a symbolic universe in which foreign currency nowadays exerts functions that are as magical in their everyday effects, as they are hoped to be effective in a sense that development economics (whether of socialist or cryptocapitalist persuasion) would seem to predict. Even more fantastically, perhaps, just as such images once attained their prurient vigor in suggesting the transgression of racial boundaries in the case of the sacrifice of white children by black sorcerers, so does their current equivalent derive its salience from the pervasive cash-mediated coupling between white tourists and commodified black Cuban bodies, a moment driven by the "structural violence" (Farmer 1997) attendant on the incorporation of Cuba into the economy of what U.S. president George Bush—in a triumphant conflation of late-twentieth-century political geography with eighteenth-century Masonic eschatology—called the "new world order": the *novus ordo seclorum* proclaimed under the image of a pyramid topped by an all-seeing eye on the backside of the U.S. dollar bill.

For it is not just a legacy of destruction, of violated bodies and suppressed forms of knowledge, that occasionally flares up—like a rumor of something too hastily forgotten—and irrupts onto the surface of such institutional sites of rationalization as the article in *Juventud Rebelde*. As the bubble of Cuba's Soviet-sponsored socialist development burst in the 1990s, Afro-Cuban gods and the spirits of the dead entered into a new form of dialogue with the Cuban state in which ritual forms of dealing with evil are no longer easily dismissed as mere symptoms of the still insufficiently dispelled mystifications of older modes of production. As Karen Fields (1982, 591) has compellingly argued, socially effective definitions of reality and irreality do not necessarily revolve around shared forms of consciousness. Above all, it is the extent to which moral artifacts such as witchcraft, history, the state, hard currency, or the gods come to structure social praxis that endows them with their capacity to affect people's lives and so, for all practical purposes, to become real. "It is the human predicament," she says, "to be 'captured' physically by ordinary ways of doing what we ordinarily do, and mentally, by a corresponding idiom of thought. We at once create and are captive of a real world whose order is delimited by the moral artifacts of quotidian activity." As in the case of early republican witch-hunters puzzling over the concurrent proliferation of modernity and witchcraft, this point was not lost on the authors of a large-scale state-commissioned study of "the so-called syncretic cults and spiritism" in contemporary Cuba undertaken by the Centro de Investigaciones Psicológicos y Sociológicos.

Contradicting earlier assessments of the impending withering away of the gods,[4] the heads of this inquiry, Aníbal Argüelles and Illeana Hodge (1991), saw themselves forced to concede that "under the conditions of the construction of socialism there exist subjective and objective factors that permit the *reproduction* of religious beliefs and practices in some sectors of the population" (10; emphasis added). However, while in the view of these authors the "determination of such factors constitutes one of the principal aspects of research," this, not surprisingly, posed "one of the most complex questions" (10). In fact, one senses the hesitation with which they confront their own conclusions. The puzzling "increase of the membership of these religious groups," they eventually admit, may be due to the influx of "persons who feel the 'need' of expressing religious beliefs with a mythical-magical-superstitious conception of the world without this necessarily implying their distancing themselves from the revolutionary process" (217). The "so-called syncretic cults," in other words, thrive precisely because they are being joined by people who support the Revolution. But can a revolutionary engaged in the building of socialist society afford to entertain a "mythical-magical-superstitious" outlook? Can a *militante comunista* feel a "need" to express religious beliefs? Can he or she engage in practices oriented toward what he or she must surely know are the fantastic objectifications of an alienated social consciousness? Given that the Fourth Congress of the Cuban Communist Party in 1991 removed "religious beliefs" as an "obstacle" to membership (Reed 1992, 88), could it be that Ché Guevara's "man of the twenty-first century" will turn out to be a devotee of Afro-Cuban gods? A hybrid being impassioned by the Revolution and possessed by African deities the vitality and powers of which are underwritten by "factors" that are part and parcel of the "conditions of the construction of socialism"?

For Cuban social science, Marx's dictum that social being determines social consciousness nowadays comes hurtling back as a powerful boomerang. What an earlier generation of Cuban scholars had to say about the gods whom the Cuban state once was prepared to escort to the historically ordained graveyard for collective representations that had outlived their functions as mystifications of class interests today has acquired a strange purchase on Cuban socialist reality itself. "[In the course] of the believer's quotidian relations with his deities," Jesús Guanche (1983, 399–400) once wrote, both "an objective and a subjective evasion of reality takes place. Objective because the social contract circumscribes it in accordance with the form of religious consciousness above other forms of social consciousness. In this sense, his or her objective essence as a social being remains reduced by his or her religious conscience. And, in the subjective sense, because the logical structure of consciousness remains reduced to and is displaced by a dissociative reaction proper to magical-religious thought." If this be so, and irrespective of the definition of *reality* at stake here, the gods and the socialist state are nowadays very much in the same boat.

In recent years, Cuba has become a place haunted, not only by its past, but by a future that never came to pass. Although still officially predicated on a transition to socialism, Cuba's present is marked by a strangely stagnant form of temporality associated with the phrase *périodo especiál.* In official discourse, it refers to a "special period in times of peace," announced by the Cuban government on the eve of the collapse of the Soviet Union in 1990 and lasting to the present day. Designed to convey a sense of wartime conditions, the phrase *special period* was initially associated with increased military vigilance prompted by the fear of a U.S. invasion in the aftermath of the Soviet Union's withdrawal, which turned the country, as Comandante Castro put it in his closing speech to the

Fourth Congress of the Cuban Communist Party in 1991, into an "island of revolution" (Reed 1992, 193) awash in a politically hostile capitalist sea. What this has come to signify for many Cubans is a fundamental disjunction of experience and expectation, a decentering of the coordinates of normal eventuation that generates the very real possibility of remembering what once was the future.

To speak with Guanche, the sheer cognitive dissonance engendered by day-to-day life in contemporary Havana certainly demands the displacement of logical structures of consciousness by multiple and repeated dissociative reactions. If—as we may well suppose—Robin Horton's formula of "explanation, prediction, and control" of the lived-in world underlies both the ideological claims of the Cuban state and those of Afro-Cuban religions, then the days in which a contributor to *El Militante Comunista* could vaunt that the aim of practitioners of Afro-Cuban religion was "that there subsist, in our Fatherland, in the midst of [a] fullfledged revolutionary process, a horrible and mysterious chunk of fifteenth century equatorial Africa" ("La sociedad secreta abakua" 1968, 45) are decidedly over. As Argüelles Mederos and Hodge Limonta (1991, 218) gingerly admit, "the vitality with which [Afro-Cuban] religious expressions manifest and reproduce themselves in Cuban society casts doubt on whether considering them as 'remnants' is justified." Rather, "they have considerable weight within the field of the struggle of ideas." Indeed, for all the caution that they exercise in drawing attention away from the inevitable conclusion, it is hard to refrain from thinking that one terminus of Cuban socialist modernity may lie in Afro-Cuban tradition. This, however, raises a critical issue. In 1983, Guanche could still claim that the "believer remains limited in his physical and intellectual capacities and cannot deliver to society all the fruits [*frutos*] that the latter demands from him" (400). Nowadays, the situation appears to demand an explanation, not just for why the gods continue to possess their devotees and exact sacrifices from them, but why the state manages to do so, too.

This is not the place for a sustained treatment of the dramatic changes that Cuba has undergone since the collapse of the Soviet Union. Nor do I intend to contribute to the particular genre of First World divination that has predicted the downfall of Fidel Castro for the past forty years (see Fernández Retamar 1996). A few remarks on the sheer extent of the present crisis, however, are in order. Although Cuban-Soviet relations had begun to deteriorate in the late 1980s, by the time the Soviet Union self-destructed in 1991, the island was facing a vertiginous economic downward spiral as an estimated 85 percent of its (subsidized) trade with the Soviet Union and COMECON vanished into the thin political air from which it had initially materialized (Segre, Coyula, and Scarpaci 1997, 141; Font 1997). Cuba's GDP declined fully 25 percent in 1991, 14 percent in 1992, and still 10 percent more in 1993, while the slight growth rates of 1994 and 1995 (a much celebrated 2.5 percent in the latter year) hardly translated back into an improvement of everyday living conditions. On the contrary, in contemporary Havana, the inadequacy of state-guaranteed rations of primary goods, the decriminalization of possession of the U.S. dollar by Cuban citizens in 1993, and the increasing scarcity on the nondollarized market, not just of imported products, but of nonrationed goods have led to a situation where deep social rifts are opening up between emerging segments of the population with access to foreign currency and those who remain restricted to the nondollarized sectors of the economy to meet their daily needs.[5]

At the same time, the range of goods and services available exclusively within the dollarized sector of the Cuban economy rapidly expanded: already in 1993 it included a variety of foods (most importantly cooking fats), all products pertaining to personal hygiene, most types of footwear and clothing, and increasingly also pharmaceutical products. What rendered this segmentation of the consumer market particularly devastating for most Cubans was that the black market value of the U.S. dollar exploded to a staggering 120–125 pesos in 1993 and only slowly declined to 40–45 pesos in 1994 and 35–40 pesos in 1995. Given a salary average of 180 pesos per month in 1995 and maximum salaries for skilled professionals ranging around 400–450 pesos, a quart of vegetable oil sold in the state-operated dollar stores (*tiendas de recaudación de divisas* or, more popularly, *chopins*) for around $2.25–$2.75 factually represented the equivalent value of a full monthly wage for most industrial workers and only slightly less for skilled professionals. Still, an experientially salient assessment of the crisis must take into account that, contrary to most Latin American and Caribbean countries whose economies contracted, often dramatically so, in the 1980s, Cuba was experiencing economic growth during much of this so-called lost decade. Such growth had translated into rising standards of personal consumption on the island. Merely measured in terms of daily caloric supply, in the period between 1988 and 1990, Cuba exceeded the UN standards of daily requirements by 37 percent (Pastor and Zimbalist 1995, 9). It is against this background that one must view the dramatic decline in caloric availability, which, in the case of adult men (the group, according to Garfield and Santana [1997], most affected by food deficits) shrank from 3,100 in 1989 to 1,863 in 1994. More significantly even, between 1989 and 1992, the proportion of all calories derived from consumption of refined sugar nationally increased from 18 percent to 26 percent (Garfield and Santana 1997). For many Cubans, sugar dissolved in water—a historically old hunger killer known as *sopa de gallo*—has returned to its social function as a meal in itself.[6]

After nearly forty years of revolutionary advance (both proclaimed and often honestly imagined) toward an egalitarian society composed of "new" men and women—classless, raceless, and sexually liberated—Cubans thus find themselves stumbling through a dream-like maze of chronic distortions. As the Cuban state has settled into an increasingly programmatic routinization of permanent crisis, daily life in Cuba has become an endlessly prolonged anticipation of warfare by other means, a state of siege, perhaps, but one conducted along ill-defined fronts that crisscross the streets of the nation's capital, lined as they are with collapsed or broken-down buildings—the palpable signs of an invisible war raging "in a time of peace." Pervaded by the social dislocations induced by a dual currency system that generates vastly unequal "exchange entitlements" (Sen 1981) and disrupts previous definitions of moral community and individual worth by blatantly pegging them to relations between commodities, everyday life in Havana reproduces itself as a proliferation of damage: spoiled identities, relationships saturated with distrust and misgivings, bodies deformed by malnutrition and disease or transformed into sites of commoditized services that circulate in Cuba's emerging tourist economy.[7]

ECONOMIES OF DESIRE

Cut off from its former moorings in COMECON, and afflicted with the continuing U.S. embargo, the Cuban state has embarked on a highly problematic course of frantically maximizing marginal utility on the world market by redeveloping its tourist industry as a major generator of foreign exchange. As a result, the island is currently experiencing rapid reincorporation into that vast "dependent, social and geographical realm [surrounding] the great industrialized zones of the world" that Turner and Ash (1976) designate as the "pleasure periphery" of the West.[8] Although the political economy of tourism remains an understudied subject (but, for notable exceptions, see Crick [1989], Hall [1994], and Pattullo [1996]), contemporary leisure travel is not only "comparable in its significance to other flows of capital, labor, coercion, information, knowledge, and value across societal, cultural, linguistic, regional and state boundaries" (Böröcz 1996, 4). Rather, as Fanon (1968, 153–54) argued as early as 1963, there are direct continuities between earlier forms of colonial domination and surplus extraction and the global inequalities perpetuated or produced by tourism-oriented development. These, Crick (1989) suggests, may in many instances be adequately characterized as "the hedonistic face of neocolonialism" (322). There is a cruel irony here. For, as Crick points out, from a political-economic point of view, one "of the rationales for tourism development in the 1960s was export diversification away from reliance on primary products" (319), on which both colonial forms of surplus appropriation and their postcolonial equivalents under the control of North American financial and military power had rested. Yet, as Smith (1998) argues, the provision of tourist services constitutes an export business just as well, and it generates its own forms of dependency, unequal exchange, and foreign control that are structurally not all that dissimilar from those associated with the production of tropical staples.[9]

The specificity of these continuities is highlighted by Pérez (cited in Hall 1994, 123–24), who argues that the

> travel industry in the Caribbean may well represent the latest development in the historical evolution of the neocolonial context of the West Indian socio-economic experience. Through tourism, developed metropolitan centers . . . in collaboration with West Indian élites, have delivered the Caribbean archipelago to another regimen of monoculture. As an industry based on the appropriation of West Indian human and natural resources for the ephemeral pleasure of foreigners, tourism offers the Antilles less opportunity and less immediate likelihood

of modifying the basic constellation of dependent relationships established first in the sixteenth century.

Hall (1994, 127) goes even farther in drawing an explicit analogy between the global determinants of historic Caribbean plantation systems and contemporary tourist economies in the Carribean. For, just like the former, the latter are structured, not just by the movement of foreign investment capital, but by the functional requirements of core economies nowadays increasingly centered "more on the production of needs and consumers than on the production of goods" (Bourdieu 1984, 356). And, in this sense, the Antilles continue to function as an external production site of First World economies—the difference is that what is being produced are, not tangible stables, but services. In a movement that strikingly parallels the externalization of productive activities from labor cost–intensive core regions to the periphery, specific types of consumption activity, too fraught with externalities to be easily realized in the core or involving product characteristics for which no domestic equivalent exists, are similarly peripheralized by moving the consumer to the source of utility.

As elsewhere in the Caribbean (Pruitt and LaFont 1995; Pattullo 1996; Benoit 1999; Kempadoo 1999), this has become blatantly obvious in the growth of a vast (and, until very recently, virtually unregulated) market in sexual services emerging on the fringes of Cuba's formal tourist economy. For the post-Soviet dependency of the Cuban national economy on tourism exports has forced the revolutionary state to accede to a pernicious articulation between its own foreign trade deficit, the very real wants of its citizens, and the demand structure of an international market in pleasure-generating foreign consumption behavior. Although dollar prostitution in Cuba remains "disorganized"—to use O'Connell Davidson's (1996) phrase—and lacks the official recognition as a source of national revenue that it enjoyed in the prerevolutionary period, it is nevertheless mediated by a state-administered shortage economy and the vastly unequal exchange entitlements produced by the legalization of the U.S. dollar as a second currency circulating against the spectacularly devalued, nonconvertible Cuban peso (Elizalde 1996).[10] Indeed, since by reorienting its economy toward tourist sales "Cuba has entered a highly competitive industry with powerful buyers, low brand loyalty, low switching costs, and strict international quality standards" (Martin de Holán and Phillips 1997, 787), the need-induced elasticity of Cuba's supply of sexual services functions as a distinct "country factor advantage" on a global market organized by Western fantasies of self-realization through acts of appropriation. Spellbound by the magic of an alien value form—the currency of the U.S. imperialist class enemy—and irredeemably captive to the capitalist world system (which, as Immanuel Wallerstein never tired of pointing out, *always* had enveloped the Second World), Cuba nowadays lives less on the sugar that it still officially sells than off the *caramelos* (lit. "sweets," but more adequately translated as "favors") that its populace finds itself willing to (or unable not to) make available to powerfully effective foreign demand.[11]

The historical resonances are hard to miss, indeed. As Sombart (1967) was perhaps the first to point out, and as Mintz (1985) has persuasively argued, the transformation of slave-produced tropical luxury goods (many of them of drug-like character) into European social necessities was, not just a decisive moment in the emergence of the capitalist world economy, but also a major factor in the development of Western ideologies of individual self-enhancement through nonessential consumption (Campbell 1987; Sahlins 1996). In criticizing Veblen's reduction of consumption to a semiotics of social commensuration, Sombart thus pinpointed a crucial linkage between what Adam Smith might have called the *productive* consumption of Afro-Caribbean bodies and an economy of desire that drove West Indian plantation economies no less relentlessly than the planters' and merchants' more ostensibly "rational" self-interest—indeed, often cannot easily be distinguished from it (see Beckles 1999, 22ff.). "The most convenient means for gratifying the craving for superiority," Sombart (1967) wrote in 1913, "is the accumulation of things, quantitative luxury: numbers of slaves, size of property or fortune, order of rank, and the like. But if luxury is to become personal, materialistic luxury, it must be predicated on an awakened sensuousness and, above all, on a mode of life which has been influenced decisively by eroticism" (61). To Sombart, this transition was evident in the historically increasing social salience of processes of "objectification" (95), which he described as sensual self-enhancement through consumption, the gradual democratization of which, in Sombart's view, had underwritten the development of Western capitalism since at least the sixteenth century. Strange as it seems (and Hegel would surely have shuddered at the twist such a notion imparts to his theory of subject formation), for Sombart the emergence of the modern world was driven by a sensual alchemy of the creation and release of desire miraculously converting the ephemeral pleasure of consumption into productive capital.

Elsewhere, Sombart (1967, 145) talks about Caribbean slaves as a "vast black army" of commodified workers "mobilized" by the cravings of "the pretty little damsels of Paris and London," thereby revealing how core consumptive practices "not only express[ed] but [made] possible a global structure of imperialist politics and labor relations which racialize[d] consumption as well as production" (Holt 1995, 10). More surprisingly, perhaps, Sombart's—by no means unproblematic—analysis uncannily anticipates the future transformations of the Afro-Caribbean body's global economic functions.[12] To be sure, what global capital mobilizes today is no longer just an army of abject peripheral producers catering to a proliferating metropolitan demand for mood-altering substances (this, of course, takes place as well, and the international drug trade is only a particularly obvious example). Still, the pattern by which planeloads of consumers are nowadays shuttled to the sites of anticipated pleasures evidences the operation of a fundamentally related, perhaps even structurally analogous, logic of First World subject formation: one in which command over the objectified bodies of nonwhite humans, in both economic and sexual terms, confirmed—and continues to confirm—a vision of mastery. This logic is highlighted in O'Connell Davidson and Sanchez Taylor's (1999, 37) observation that contemporary sex tourism to the Caribbean "reflects not so much a wish to engage in any specific sexual practice as a desire for an extraordinary degree of control over the management of self and others as sexual, racialized and engendered beings." Obviously, such fantasies of control are multiply determined and do not yield easily to the kind of facile historical analysis that, as Stoler (1991) charges, conflates medium (sex) with message (domination). Nevertheless, Dayan (1995) and Beckles (1999) provide more than circumstantial evidence for locating the origins of such fantasies in what Beckles (1999, 22) calls the legal and customary fiction of "the slave-holders' right to unrestricted sexual access to slaves as an intrinsic and discrete product" of their investment behavior: a return on capital in an economy that "recognized no clear distinction between the slave-based production of material goods, and the delivery of sexual services," thus perversely transcribing the fetishistic logic of capitalist accumulation into the circulation of commoditized bodies (see Painter 1994).[13]

Nowadays no longer economically relevant as an object of creative destruction, such bodies have mutated into a resource appropriated and consumed in a manner that, in Donna Haraway's (1989, 13) words, "guarantees and refreshes" the power of the First World subject of knowledge to regenerate himself[14] through a therapeutic regime based on a fetishistic disavowal of the global economy of unequal life chances on which it is based. Then as now, the capacity both to exercise effective demand for recreational sex and imaginatively to construct the inability of appropriate erotic objects to exercise choice as sexual voluntarism forms part of a "package of benefits" (as Beckles [1999, 40] puts it) deriving from structural relations and cultural constructions long in the making. Too long, in fact, to be actively understood by those (men or women) whose bodies reenact the "unappealing gyrations" (once more to hijack Sir Trevor Roper's famous canard) by which slaveholders once extracted sexual value from the human things legally at their disposal. The analogies, however, run deeper than this. For, as an object of tourist desire, the contemporary Cuban body is configured not only by its potential fungibility as an object of dollarized consumption, produced as it is by the social effects of a dual currency regime empowering the foreign consumer to an extraordinary degree. Rather, the bodies toward which sex tourists nowadays gravitate are charged by the surplus meanings deriving from what Evelyn Brooks Higginbotham (1992) calls a gendered *metalanguage of race*, redolent with historical associations between social abjection, exotic otherness, and sexual abandon.[15]

Speaking about the new forms of exploitation that have supplanted the crude violence of agroindustrial surplus extraction, Turner and Ash (1976, 176), thus, outline only part of the logic by which the productive value formerly crystallized in enslaved workers has mutated into forms of sexual utility nowadays instantiated in racialized Caribbean bodies: "The idea that black West Indians are superior in the realm of the physical carries with it the strong implication that the physical is the Negro's proper sphere—whether this be cutting sugar cane or serving the sexual needs of the white man or woman." Yet needs, whether sexual or other, are cultural constructs, and Turner and Ash's argument works just as well once its terms are reversed: like hooks (1992), Mercer (1994), and Dominguez (1994), who speak of an increasing "commodification of otherness" and the systematic development of a demand structure centering on "a taste for the other" in late-twentieth-century Western consumer economies, Mullings (1999, 72) draws attention to how the "exoticization of women and men of color and the corresponding desire to experience and consume their bodies" implies a "process of 'Othering,' where these so-called traits [constituting their perceived exoticism] simultaneously serve to confirm their status as inferior human beings and their suitability as commodities for consumption." Their bodies, thus, not only come to constitute sites of sexual release fantasized as particularly effective, but function as "most convenient means for gratifying the craving for superiority" (in Sombart's sense) at one and the same time.[16] As Pérez (1999, 189; emphasis added) puts it, if for American tourists prerevolutionary Cuba may have been "the site of sex with women of *the Other*"—that is, a place where the sexual boundaries of U.S. segregation could be transgressed—their trips, not just reflected primitivist yearnings, but transcribed ideologies of white supremacy and interracial antagonism negotiated through sex into forms of hedonistic consumerism. So it arguably is today. It is not the sheer availability or exotic allure of the othered body as a sexual object that generates its utility. It is the transformative work that it performs in the valorization of white male identity (see hooks 1992).

The consequences of this continuity—across what seem concrete historical divides—of an endemic slippage between economic and sexual discourses about the black body as an instrument of value creation, are well captured by O'Connell Davidson's (1996) account of how the vast purchasing power of the U.S. dollar in contemporary Cuba leads sex tourists to fetishize the effects of their own investment behavior as essential attributes of the people whose bodies they instrumentalize in enacting their fantasies of sexual transgression of the racial etiquette obtaining in their own societies. For tourists eager to satisfy "a sexual appetite for the Other they both despise and desire," she argues,

> Cuba is "paradise" in the sense that here, rather than being challenged, their racism is both implicitly and explicitly affirmed. They meet large numbers of Black women who really *are* sexually available,

and even more delightful for the white racist, [Cuban] people tell him that these Black women are sexually available because the are so "*caliente.*" Combined with the general perception that Cuban culture is sexually permissive (again, an idea that is promulgated by some Cubans as well as by tourists), this stereotype spills over onto "mixed" and white Cuban women, to suggest that all Cuban girls are "racialized" Others who are "hot for it" (so hot, they'll go with you for a bar of soap; so hot, even the 14-year-olds are begging for it; so hot, they don't care how old or obese or unappealing the man is). (46)

By the same token, as Fusco (1998, 155) notes, for Cuban women "to engage in sexwork practically means to assume" a nonwhite identity "by association"—and not just in the minds of foreigners enacting their own primitivist fantasies of erotic authenticity. In an insidious convergence of local and global conceptions of female promiscuity, a complex heritage of Cuban perceptions of nonwhite sexuality and female dishonor—rooted, ultimately, in slavery (Martínez-Alier 1974)—likewise conspires to render female sexual agency, particularly when it is visibly focused on and remunerated by foreign men, a pervasively "racialized practice" (see Fernandez 1999). This is patently obvious with respect to the exuberant growth of racial signifiers surrounding the emerging moral economy of dollarized exchange and consumption in present-day Havana. Owing to tourist demand, the commodification of Cuban sexuality proceeds along an axis defined by racial stereotypes and is consequently experienced by many *habaneros* themselves as linked to conceptions of blackness.[17] In the popular Cuban imagination, the figure epitomizing the emergent forms of dollar prostitution popularly known as *jineterismo* is not the classy mulata—whose body traditionally formed the screen for projections of male Cuban sexual fantasies (see Kutzinski 1993). It is the very dark-skinned girl from the countryside or some solidly black barrio of Havana whose vulgarity and awkward comportment (one stereotype is that she cannot even walk on high heels) immediately give her away as black trash.

Hence one of the cruelest ironies attendant on an increasingly intimate articulation between an economy of desire internal to the First World and one of the last remnants of a Second World command economy. As Cuba's economic orientation has rapidly shifted from its traditional agroindustrial export functions toward tourism exports, not only are the bodies of some of its citizens increasingly coming to function as transfer points of value extracted in the form of competitively priced sexual services and realized in the cultivation of foreign male selves. Rather, Cubans themselves increasingly rephrase the question "to what degree will people individually compromise themselves morally in order to access *el fula* [i.e., the U.S. dollar]" as one about the identity of groups whose imputed low standards of morality, lack of self-control, and lack of civic virtue will predispose them to engage in economies of prostitution and predation (see Palmié 2001). Put bluntly, no less than the modernity that early-twentieth-century witch-hunters envisioned was dependent on the (mirage of) the elderly male black body inescapably ridden with biological tendencies toward wizardry, the modernity that European or Canadian sex tourists to Cuba inhabit today is not just structured

by fantasies about the erotically primitive black female body. On the contrary, it actively produces such bodies.[18]

THE AGENCY OF CAPTIVE FLESH

Of course, the forms of carnal knowledge generated by this logic may seem a far cry from the calculations of bodily endurance underlying the practices of scientific planters, the prose of early-nineteenth-century Spanish colonial counterinsurgency, the tactical calculus of anti-colonial terror, or even the scopic regime envisioned by Dr. Castellanos some eighty years ago. Nevertheless, they unfold on a common matrix. Modern sex tourism in Cuba arguably has its ideological and affective origins in the politically unequal bodily exchange that commenced on the eve of the Conquest or the establishment of slave entrepôts on the West African coast, to pick a convenient frame of time.[19] Whether at home (Stallybrass and White 1986) or abroad (Stoler 1995), mastery over appropriate others and due discipline of the self—whether in economic, political, sexual, or other forms—are two of the major sources of modern senses of selfhood: sources as much of a structure of feeling and regime of knowledge as of a global system of domination. From Francis Bacon's "Masculine Birth of Time" to Hegel's *Phenomenology of the Spirit* and onward to Francis Fukuyama's or Samuel Huntington's pronouncements on the post–cold war human condition, the vision of history as the increasing rational domination over an objectified nature has implied, not only the naturalization of the subject's self-enhancement at the expense of a servile world of things, but also the reification of a division between human subjects and objects as a work of nature, increasingly beyond secular moral considerations.

And yet, the separation is never—perhaps cannot be—complete. As in the case of the Afro-Cuban nganga, the fantasy of total control achieved through instrumentalizing thing-like objects as extensions of the self is a precarious one. To be sure, as Winthrop Jordan (1969, 141) and others have argued, the instrumentalization of enslaved human bodies as means of, not just economic, but sexual production "served as a ritualistic enactment of the daily pattern of social dominance." Yet such performances of mastery were nevertheless irreducibly linked to a discourse on the compulsive force exerted by black sexuality on the white master, draining his power even as he enacted it on his possessions, and hybridizing his subjectivity by rendering the victimizer a victim of his own impassionment by a consuming desire (Spiller 1987). Hence, perhaps, Jordan's (1969, 136) suggestion that, "as a source of tension" in New World slave societies, interracial sex "rivaled the slave revolt"—the undoing, that is, of masterful subjects through the agency of dehumanized possessions. Such tensions, Jordan (1969, 150–63) argues, came to be condensed into savage technologies of genital violation that inscribed white fantasies of control over the boundaries of subject and object and the unwonted circulation of desire between them onto raped and mutilated bodies marked as racially other as much by the conceptual preconditions of violation as by the act itself (see Dowd Hall 1983; Helg 2000). Yet such violence—physical and symbolic—arguably served not just the purpose of producing material signifiers of an order of domination, somatically rendering, as it were, the political identities of master and slave (see Comaroff and Comaroff 1992b, 69–91, 215–33). It always also transformed the body of the other into what Thoden van Velzen (1995) calls a *theater of the emotions*—a site both for exploring fearful or disavowed forms of intimacy and for what Appadurai (1998) calls the enactment of violence as a "folk discovery procedure" designed to "expose, penetrate, and occupy the material form" of the other in order to achieve a sense of certainty through "violent closure" in situations of categorial indeterminacy.

Appadurai is concerned with contemporary genocidal violence that resolves the invariable deceptiveness and hybridity of the ethnic body of both victim and killer by acts of physical effacement and destruction that generate forms of knowledge capable of dispersing prior facts of moral interrelation. And he is certainly right in rejecting current interpretations of such atrocities as a "return of the repressed" or—to put the matter in more palatable terms—a matter of insufficient modernization. For, regardless of the formal differences of violence in Bosnia, Rwanda, Sierra Leone, or elsewhere, writing them into inefficiently controlled primordial propensities is nothing but what Herzfeld (1992) calls a strategic *production of indifference* by dissociation, akin to Malthus's somber warnings about too great a moral investment in the fate of the exploited. Arguably, we once more find ourselves in the terrain of the soothing powers analogously dispensed by enlightened economic theory, Temne divination, and the Lemba cult during the period of the slave trade—healing, as they did, elites on both sides of the Atlantic from the afflictions caused by the wealth that they amassed through the systematic wasting of human lives.

Nor would it seem inappropriate that Lemba and similar cults of affliction entered modern Western knowledge under the rubric *fetish cults*. For, no less than the transactions in human flesh that integrated the transcultural space from which originated that curious transcultural conception of the inappropriate mingling of objects and human intentionalities, economic reason and religious belief, utility and desire, on which Marx and Freud were to elaborate in their theories of "fetishistic substitution" (Pietz 1985, 1987, 1988, 1993), contemporary sex tourism in Cuba revolves around the production of the objective phantasm of a radical separation between subjects and objects of knowledge and embodied desire: a moral artifact as devastating in its practical consequences as it is mystificatory of the—historically old—conditions of its own operation (McClintock 1992; hooks 1992; Dayan 1995). In both cases, hybridity not only played havoc with emerging conceptions of subjectivity. It also triggered violent epistemological operations marking the other as an object beyond all moral bounds: operations that meant to redress the balance but effectively only set in motion new cycles of the incitement and satiation of the "sacred hunger" that a character in Barry Unsworth's (1992) eponymous novel diagnoses as the wellspring of the Atlantic economy from which the modern world emerged. As Young (1995, 181–82) puts it,

> the forms of sexual exchange brought about by colonialism were themselves both mirrors and consequences of the modes of economic exchange that constituted the basis of colonial relations; the extended exchange of property which began with small trading-posts and the visiting slave ships originated, indeed, as much as an exchange of bodies as of goods, or rather of bodies as goods. . . . It was therefore wholly appropriate that sexual exchange, and its miscegenated product, which captures the violent, antagonistic power relations of sexual and cultural diffusion, should become the dominant paradigm through which the passionate economic and political trafficking of colonialism was conceived.

Viewed thus, the evil inevitably attendant on every colonial venture—the emergence of hybrid men and women (not to speak of hybrid forms of knowledge) embodying a colonialist version of the original sin—is (shall we say?) a mere structural transformation of contracting HIV abroad today. As Hegel himself inadvertently suggested in rendering the master-slave relationship the paradigm for modern selfhood, the enactment of mastery inevitably breeds categorial confusion.

Nor does the cult of affliction that global sex tourism arguably represents (see Ryan and Kinder 1996) unfold in the absense of the operation of the kind of subaltern moral analytics with which this book has mainly been concerned. As Porter (1993) suggests, it may be more than an accidental conjuncture that William Harvey's discovery of the circulation of blood coincided with the development of an economic ideology equating the health of the body politic with the opulence growing out of the velocity of commercial transactions. If so, the attributes of the Afro-Cuban goddess Ochún suggest no less of a conjuncture, although they do so from the perspective of a peripheral and ostensibly nonrational heuristic. Associated primarily with the flow of sweet (as opposed to marine) water, Ochún's powers are also felt in movements of circulation, not just of earthly waters, but of blood and money. "La sangre corre en las venas"—blood circulates in the veins—is one of the divination verses associated with her, but her influence manifests no less in the circulation of things and values that make up the stream of social interchanges. Her color of preference is yellow, and the substances associated with her include, not just honey and sugar, but gold and, by implication, money. Mythologically styled as the seductress of various male gods, Ochún further exemplifies, not just a moment of irresistible sexual attraction, but female sterility. Some divination proverbs style her as a divine prostitute, but, more important, perhaps, she stands for "all that is sweet in life," including, not just sexual pleasure, or self-enhancement through wealth, but the treacherous sweetness of sugar.

Ochún, we might say, embodies an Afro-Cuban recension of what Sahlins (1996) calls the *sadness of sweetness,* a view of sugar, money, and commodified pleasure turned back on its rational consumer's impassioned delight. As African tradition and Western rationality merge in the figure of this goddess, the evocatory power of the exclamation "¡azúcar!" in Cuban popular music noted by Coronil (1996, 64) in a related context—coinciding as it does with a Cuban sexual vocabulary deeply encrusted with references to the punishment of slaves[20]—uncovers and displays histories of desire, consumption, domination, and impassionment that stand at the core of the formation and reproduction of Western modernity itself. Although I intend to treat this issue more fully in a separate publication (Palmié 2001), it is worth noting here that the term popularly used in Cuba to designate notionally new forms of tourist prostitution—*jineterismo*—already indicates the contours of an alternative view of the agency performed by objectified others on the alien subject of desire: deriving from *jinete,* a word designating a jockey (or, by implication, a rider's whip), the concept of jineterismo circumscribes a vision of the *jinetera* (i.e., dollar prostitute) rather far removed from Western commonsense notions of the political economy of sex work. In contemporary Cuban understanding, the jinetera is not just a depersonalized object of tourist desire, and her sexuality is not a mere object of commercial exchange. Rather, popular discourse inverts this imagery by casting the person engaging in jineterismo as an agent who literally "whips the money" out of his or (more often) her victim whose desire she has aroused for strictly mercenary reasons, impassioning him (*apasionarle*) literally to *buy* into his own fantasy of sexual domination (see Žižek 1997). It is, thus, the tourist's personhood that is reduced to an objectified source of hard cash, imported clothing, household goods, electronic appliances, high-quality foods, and, last—but by no means least—entertainment in bars, restaurants, or cabarets inaccessible to Cubans without an adequate supply of foreign currency and, increasingly so, without visibly foreign company.

Nor are such popular interpretations of the power exerted by sexual objects on the subject of passion mere rationalizations of the indignity of becoming—as Turner and Ash (1976) phrase it—a nation of waiters and prostitutes. As Nancy Fraser (1997, 233; emphasis added) argues in a critique of Carol Pateman's *The Sexual Contract,* far from implying a solid association in prostitution between masculinity and sexual mastery and between femininity and sexual submission, "what is often sold in late-capitalist societies today is male fantasy of 'male sex-right,' one that implies its precariousness in actuality. Far from acquiring the right of command over the prostitute, what the john gets is the staged representation of such command." "A staged representation of command, however," she continues, "involves a *performative contradiction.* The fantasy of mastery that is sold through prostitution is undermined even as it is enacted." Monsieur Le Capital and Madame Le Corps, it would seem, are always on the verge of decomposing into something else. Internet postings by self-proclaimed sex tourists appear to bear out just this moment.[21] Some of the men engaged in such communications seem to be keenly aware of the danger of losing control over their own definition of the situation. As a correspondent to the *World Sex Guide* website (http://www.paranoia.com/faq/prostitution/cuba_bits.txt.html, November 14, 1997) puts it, "The people [in Cuba] are generally very nice. They are willing to help at any time. Some of the girls never asked for money. Give them something anyway. Bring SOME OLD CLOTHES. SMALL PRESENTS are quite welcomed but if you know where to look for the girls you don't get the pros. Look for the nice girls DURING THE DAY when they have time to talk but be careful not to fall in love with them otherwise you're stuck with them the whole time." "You may not have to pay her any money" reports a similar entry in *Desiree's Guide to Sex in Cuba* (http://www.sexyguide.com/cuba/index.shtml), "but you will have to feed her, and take her on a shopping spree. The Cuban girls seem to need an incredible amount of clothes, and they hardly ever have any clothes when they meet you. Shopping for clothes could easily cost 100 dollars if you are not careful, so whether it is worthwhile for you depends on how often you go shopping and how often you switch girlfriends." "Don't fool yourself," reports another particularly astute "participant-observer" (http://www.paranoia.com/faq/prostitution/Havana.txt.html). "No matter how young or good looking or distinguished you think you appear, the reason you can attract young Cuban women is because you're a foreigner with dollars." For "these women are not whores by choice, nor are they doing it just to buy jewelry. Because they are average women caught in circumstances beyond their control it is all that much easier to fall for them—and even harbor the idea of marrying one of them and bringing her back with you."

Yet, precisely because she is "not a whore by choice" (perhaps not a whore at all by her own, or other people's, definition), the jinetera does not so much propose a sexual contract as seduce the stranger into potentially unwilled forms of emotional experience—a state of *apasionamiento* or at least moral obligation. If the commodity seduces its purchaser into a fiction of individuation through the medium of things, the relation between cause and effect seems reversed here. Consumption of ostensibly commoditized Cuban bodies appears to entail the potential loss of self—a danger that sex tourists seem to sense. This is so because the medium of seduction is not confined to the sheer utility of the jinetera's body as an object promising the more or less effective momentary discharge of pleasure. Rather, an uncanny tendency toward the "singularization" (Kopytoff 1986) of the "emotional work" (Hochschild 1983) accompanying and temporally enveloping the actual moments of sexual consumption seems to play havoc with the definitions of rational self-interest that the consumer brings to the situation. To the extent that the jinetera succeeds in *apasionarle al extranjero*, the fetishistic illusion breaks down, and gorgeous bodies, pretty faces, legs, breasts, and vaginas recompose into persons. "I give her what cash I have in my pocket," another contributor to the *World Sex Guide* (http://www.paranoia.com/faq/prostitution/Cienfuegos.txt.html) describes the inevitable farewell scene at Varadero International Airport: "She gives me something very nice to remember her by, and we said some very fond and close goodbyes. I'm intentionally not publishing her name. I'm in love. I'm pretty convinced she is too (and still two weeks later as I write this after having spoken to her since). Damn. This wasn't supposed to happen! I'll be back. I promised. She promised to be waiting, with the wrapped condom she wanted to keep for me until I came back, even if in her case we don't use them."

As these authors of web postings seem to sense, the consumption of bodies of Cubans engaging in jineterismo takes place not so much within a manifestly contractual relation as in one that aims at generating forms of intimacy and involving the client's moral personhood and self-conception to a degree where he feels motivated, impassioned, or simply obliged to engage in potentially open-ended forms of—ultimately predatory—reciprocity. Of course, this is not to say that such forms of reciprocity preclude varying degrees of mutual personal affection and emotional investment. On the contrary, the ostensibly paradoxical character of jineterismo derives precisely from the ambiguity of a relation in which both parties can (and sometimes do) vacillate between objectifying the other as a mere means and personalizing him or her to a degree where the circulation of sex against money becomes representable as a disinterested exchange of emotionally charged favors. Obviously, a dialectic of fantasizing and dissimulation (including self-deception) plays a constitutive role in the processes by which such realtions—if they attain the duration of even only a few days—begin to cycle through stages of instrumentality and its denial, the exercise of mastery and its breakdown in the hybridized intentionalities experienced by the impassioned subject possessed, not only of uncanny buying power, but by the very commodity that forms the object of his desire.[22]

This may be an appropriate point to return to a point raised earlier on. For, as the image of the slaughter of white female children by male wizards intent on healing elderly ex-slaves suggests, part of the agenda of republican Cuban witch-hunters was to violently disaggregate what was socially no longer divisible: the irreversible inclusion of Africans into the Cuban body politic, a massively racially mixed population, the legal incorporation of Afro-Cuban practices into the nation's public sphere, and the absorption of Western modernity by its declared antithesis, African tradition. In a rather old-fashioned structuralist sense, twentieth-century Cuban witch-hunting was a symbolic purge, an attempt to violently realign what Mary Douglas (1973) once called *grid* and *group*—a struggle to eradicate the hybrids apprehended through or created by self-conscious strategies of purification (Latour 1993), strategies that were, themselves, the hybrids of a larger process articulating local representations of modernity with processes of political-economic domination on a global scale.

What eventually came out of it was—as in so many Latin American situations (see Wade 1997)—a collapse of the categories that had long safeguarded national or protonational prestige into a reactive ideology of demographic *mestizaje* and social *transculturación*—a neologism originally coined by Ortiz in 1940 (see Palmié 1998b) and extensively circulated in Latin American nationalist discourse since midcentury. Nevertheless, despite what Moore (1997) calls a protracted process of the *nationalization of blackness*[23] in Cuba (again, like in other Latin American cases), the dissolution of the old *grid* did not bring forth new definitions of *group* on any other than an ideological level (see Martínez-Echazábal 1998; Pérez Sarduy and Stubbs 2000). Neither did this rerouting of the color sign through narratives of national homogenization (from Martí's vision of a denouement of race in Cuban nationhood to Ché Guevara's *hombre nuevo*) articulate—at least not in more than superficial ways—with what, to paraphrase Lattas (1993), we might call the *political history of the Cuban body* that is at issue here.[24] The results, at any rate, were, and are, by and large, of minimal experiential consequence for those structurally dislocated and culturally marginalized segments of national populations that—along with Fernando Guerra and, indeed, the entire populations of contemporary postcolonial nation-states (Ferguson 1997)—might see themselves as disinherited by the fortunes of modernity. Such a political history of the Cuban body—in the sense of a chronicle of local semantic fluctuations between revulsion and desire, violent domination and romanticization of the "black folk" as articulated with larger transnational political-economic scenarios—must remain beyond the scope of this book. Yet no one who has spent more than a few days in post–cold war Havana will be able to deny that the violence, both symbolic and physical, attendant on mutations in a larger—implicitly Western—economy of desire and encoded in the history of such local shifts and fluctuations arcs forward into the very present.

In 1997, I received a letter from a German man asking my opinion in a matter obviously causing him considerable anguish. During a recent vacation in Havana, he had spent a night with a Cuban women to whom he referred as a *prostitute*. Although he had used a condom, he had also engaged in mutual unprotected oral sex. The next morning he found a garlic clove on the windowsill of his room. Days later, the inside of his mouth broke out in whitish ulcerations, which, at the time of his writing, had not healed despite the application of antimycotic drugs. Would I be able to advise him in this delicate matter? I initially thought about a blasting reply, castigating the man for his nerve in attempting to involve me in his well-deserved predicament. But I eventually decided not to be bothered and never answered the letter. Still, in some ways, the man's choice to address me as an expert on Afro-Cuban religions whose properly disciplined knowledge might help redress or, at least, rationalize his worrisome condition held its lesson. Apparently, his expectation was that such knowledge would either disperse the otherwise unsurprising conjunction of oral *candida alba* (primary or secondary) and paid sex with a garlic clove on a windowsill into a scenario of causal (and moral) nonconnection or reveal the hidden connectivity of a malevolent agenda: some dark scheme of magic, guilt, and bodily harm that bound him to the Cuban woman in ways that transcended, both in a temporal and in a moral sense, the seemingly episodic bodily commerce that he and she had transacted that night.

In the latter sense, an appropriate reply from me might have confirmed what the man seemed to suspect: that what he had initially framed as an episodic and inconsequential bodily encounter now seemed to suggest an ongoing plot driven forward by an alien project. A story within which, as Lattas (1993, 53) puts it in a different context, "the language of sickness and healing" served as a template on which "to think about the embodied nature of evil in a social order which organizes power . . . around perceived bodily differences" that come to define unequal access to the sources of such power. Suggestive as they are of further inquiries into the relation between modern Western subject formation and the dehumanization of objectified others, these analogies must form the subject of a separate analysis. Here, I merely want to note the message that the man's letter held for me. For my initial impulse to write a scathing reply stemmed from the fact that the letter had left me with few alternatives but either to cast myself in the role of someone whose repeated visits to Cuba would lead him to express sympathy for a fellow European man unable to resist the fantastic possibilities for cheap sex with exotic partners or to choose the role of the impartial expert, ethically compelled to bring scientific knowledge to bear on a body notionally under mystical attack. Quite clearly, I was unable to reconcile myself with either option—compassionate male bonding in the face of exposure to unbridled exotic female sexuality or dispensing the healing force of rational science to normalize the threat of casual sex turning into a mystically enhanced predicament of fundamentally moral proportions.

Hence the real problem, the real reason I wanted to lash out verbally against a totally unknown person in a situation of anguish: his plea for help, genuine as it undoubtedly was, invariably placed me in a long genealogy of scientific healers of bodies politic (Cuban or other)—the very modernistic exorcists with whom much of this book has dealt. Although I cannot claim this as a particular moral achievement, my anger derived from the fact that I simply could not face myself belatedly joining their ranks. For, looking back, it seems to me that forms of knowledge—different from, although intimately related to, the academic disciplines on which I have staked parts of my identity—killed those men and women whose spirits still seemed to haunt the minds of the orthodox socialist journalist who, in the fall of 1994, saw a need to deny the existence of black wizards. These forms of knowledge were a science no less focused on the bodies of the oppressed than the one that the panic-stricken letter writer appealed to: not as vectors of viral infections in this instance, but as vectors of forms of thought and practice that a sadistic scientism came to brand as diagnostic of a social morbidity in need of radical cures. No doubt, the article that I read in *Juventud Rebelde* in 1994 had a pedigree going back to at least the fall of 1904. So did, if in a different but related sense, the letter of my ailing countryman.

Of course, we could well try to trace both of them much further back. As I have indicated in the last chapter, the "growth of magic" in Renaissance Europe has its parallel in the growth of "traditional knowledge" (or, as Hobart [1993] would have it, of ignorance) in Europe's colonial and postcolonial periphery. Yet why and by what means, to reiterate Hildred Geertz's question, have we become aware of this? And can we really represent this as a process that proceeds separately from, or external to, not just the formation of the modern, autonomous, rational, civicly religious, maximizing, etc. individual, but the emergence of forms of knowledge that underwrite and dominate the constructions of selfhood on which his or her individuation is based? Did not science's career as a hybrid begin at precisely the moment when Giordano Bruno (or his less well-known hermetic operator contemporaries) was tied to the stake? Were not the forms of economic rationality that underwrote European expansion contingent on a fundamental blurring of the categorial distinctions between humans and things that Western thinkers like Newton and Locke were elaborating all the while engaging—as director of the royal mint and investor in slaving voyages—in the systematic dehumanization of racial others? Was it not the consequences of rational choice—a calculus weighing self-enhancement against the economically "external" transaction costs of purely commercial sex—that produced the body invaded by alien forms of intentionality that the letter writer suffered from?

Once more: is not the line between therapy and violation congruous with that separating what Scarry (1985) calls the *making and unmaking of human sentience* and its counterpart, the unintended animation of willful, even vengeful, objects, intent on the destruction of their maker? Is it not the fantasy of the completely singularized, transcendent subject inscribed—in the last instance, if you will—on the commodified matter of a body that renders subjectification contingent on the gratifying or violating, enhancing or destructive, work of the other on the self? Far from representing the terms of a series or even a sequence, magic, science, and religion, tradition and modernity, self and other, are concepts whose semantic productivity, perhaps, ever emerges only in what Kaplan and Kelley (1994, 129) call *zones of transcourse*—sites of sociality, determined first and foremost by discriminatory practices, but nonetheless undermined by the copresence of a multiplicity of contingent moral authorities. In such fields, the erasure or denigration of the other is never complete. It cannot be. Not just the ghost of Zoila Díaz, but those of the victims of the 1919 fusillade in Matanzas, of José Antonio Aponte, Tata Ezequiel, and Fernando Guerra—and of all "those whom fortune disinherited" for whom Guerra spoke—continue to haunt, not merely Cuba, but all of us to this day.

APPENDIX

Aponte's Library

BOOKS FOUND DURING THE RAIDS

1. Descripción de Historia Natural
2. Arte Nebrija
3. Guía de Forasteros de la Isla de Cuba
4. Maravillas de la Ciudad de Roma
5. Estado Militar de España
6. Sucesos Memorables del Mundo
7. Historia del Conde Saxe
8. Formulario de escribir cartas
9. Catecismo de la Doctrina Cristiana
10. Vida del Sabio Hicsopo
11. Tomo tercero de D. Qijote

IDENTIFICATION

Unless otherwise noted, the identifications derive from Palau y Dulcet (1948–90), Trelles (1965a, 1965b), and Toribio Medina (1962).

1. Descripción de Historia Natural (?)

Antonio Parra, *Descripción de diferentes piezas de Historia Natural, las más del ramo marítimo, representadas en setenta y cinco láminas* (Havana, 1787).

Although the richly illustrated character of this book (200 pages and 75 engravings) might have appealed to Aponte, the fact remains that, of those 75 engravings, 38 depict species of fish indigenous to Cuba, others show corals, shellfish, petrified objects, etc. Only the engravings numbered 71–73 showed another subject: portraits and anatomical studies of the black beggar Domingo Fernández, a native of Havana (Rigol 1982, 136–37). Whether and for what reasons such contents might have appealed to

Aponte, or whether he might, for example, have acquired this book for the sole purpose of augmenting his collection, eludes me. The second problem is, perhaps more interesting: according to Rigol's sources, by 1878 only six copies of this book were known to exist, and it is rather likely that, even by 1812, it was exceedingly rare (Rigol 1982, 137–38).

2. Arte Nebrija

Possibility A

Aelij Antonij Nebrissensis gramatici introductionis latinae explicitae (Salamaca, 1481) (many editions under sometimes rather divergent titles).

Spanish commentaries on this work (the titles of which often refer to the *Arte Nebrija*) are known since 1531. According to Kropfinger–von Kügelen (1973), three different editions of the book itself are documented as having reached the New World via Sevilla by as early as 1586. American editions are documented since 1664 (Mexico).

The problem with possibility A is that Aponte himself admitted to not being able to read Latin, and, when questioned about why he had inscribed the image of the Virgen de Regla on page 46 of the book with "nigra suns" (*sic*) and if he could explain what these words meant, he answered that he had taken the phrase from the "librito de alabanzas a Maria SSma." and that, as he understood them, they meant "ser negra, pero la mas hermosa" (alluding, one wonders, to the Song of Solomon—a text that, likewise, could have reached him only through secondary recensions). Obviously, someone must have explained to him the significance of this phrase deriving from what, for him (as well as many of his contemporaries, black and white), was an incomprehensible ritual language.

Possibility B

Antonio de Nebrija, *Gramatica Castellana* (Salamanca, 1492).

Palau notes: "Es el libro más antiguo en lengua romance de filología y la primera gramática del mundo en lengua vulga." But "cosa singular: de esta obra, que parecía llamada a tener innumerables ediciones, no se conoce ninguna otra impresión a lo largo de los siglos xv, xvi y xvii." It was not until the eighteenth century that a "torpe falsificación de la edición de 1492" appeared, "que al ojo más inexperto se denuncia inmediatamente."

Could Aponte have possessed this (corrupt) edition?

3. Guía de Forasteros de la Isla de Cuba

Guía de forasteros de la siempre fiel isla de Cuba . . . Habana 1794–1884. 16., 8., y 4. con estados, planos y grabados (Palau).

Trelles mentions a reference to the earliest edition of 1780 and gives the following dates of publication for editions documented prior to 1812: 1781, 1793, 1794, 1796, 1804, 1807, 1808, 1810, and 1811.

4. Maravillas de la Ciudad de Roma

Maravillas de Roma: Mirabilia Roma. 8°. prolongado, 132p. Antigvedades de la Civdad de Roma, sacadas y recopiladas brevemente de todos los avctores antigvos y modernos por Andrés Paladio. *En Roma, por Manelfo Manelfi,* MDCXLVII (1647), págs 133 a 182, numerosos grabs. en madera.

Palau also mentions other editions dating from 1620 and 1661 yet does not give any dates except: Roma. In part, at least, Palladio's (originally unillustrated) text was based on a genre of guidebooks to Rome's Christian and pagan monuments known as *mirabilia Romae,* originating in the twelfth century. Versions of Palladio's work remained in print at least until the early eighteenth century. As Peter Murray (1972) puts it, this tradition links "us to the *milordi* of the Grand Tour [who, like Byron, Keats, and Shelley, after all were Aponte's contemporaries], and them to the 12th century." See the collections of such texts in Valentini and Zuchetti (1940–53) and Murray (1972).

5. Estado militar de España

Estado militar de España. Año 1798. Madrid Imp. Real 8°.

Earliest edition listed by Palau.

6. Sucesos Memorables del Mundo (?)

7. Historia del Conde Saxe

Saxe (Conde de), *Historia de Mauricio, conde de Saxe, mariscal de los campos y ejercitos de S.M. Cristianisima* (San Sebastian, 1754) (2 vols.) 8°.

8. Formulario de escribir cartas (?)

9. Catecismo de la Doctrina Cristiana (?)

10. Vida del Sabio Hicsopo (probably a misspelling by the clerk; it should read Hiosopo or Hiesopo)

One of the many editions of the "Vida y fabulas del Sabio Isopo, Esopo, Ysopo, Ysopet etc." (Origin: *Esta es la vida del ysopet con sus fabulas hystoriadas* [Saragossa 1489]).

11. Tomo tercero de D. Qijote [*Don Quixote*] (edition?)

BOOKS MENTIONED DURING THE INTERROGATION

12. Guía de forasteros de Roma
Probably identical with item 4.

13. Un libro historico

14. Noticias de la Historia universal (?)
Possibly identical with item 1 or 6.

15. Libro de la vida de San Antonio Abad
Vida y milagros del príncipe de los anacoretas, padre de los Cenobiarcas Nuestro Padre S. Antonio Abad el Magno, salaca a la luz R. D. Joseph [d.i. José] Navarro. Van añadidas en esta impresión, las grandezas de la Religión de S. Antonio, en las partes de Etiopía y Egypto. . . . Gerona, Por Antonio Oliva 1683, grab. del Santo con orla al boj. 8. 2 h. 260 p. 2 h 700 pts.

Navarro merely translated it from the French. The author is apparently unknown. The Münchner Staatsbibliothek has a copy of an edition published in Barcelona in 1760 that *might* be identical with the one that Aponte perused.

16. Librito de alabanzas a Maria SSma.

NOTES

PROLOGUE

1 At the time, Carlos was earning a living as the supervisor of several laundromats and a part-time private eye (or so he claimed). "Don't even question it," he used to say when talking about matters such as spiritual afflictions. "Most of my clients are far more crazy than you and me put together."

2 On epistemology, language, and "out-there-ness," cf. Rorty (1991), Rorty (1999, 175–89), Needham (1972), and Das (1998). For particularly lucid statements of the problems underlying the long-standing tendency of Western social science to insinuate its own categorial apparatus into life worlds that these very categories cannot but represent as structured by "belief" or other forms of "irrationality," see also Hildred Geertz (1975), MacGaffey (1981), and Clark (1983).

3 "An anachronism," Oakeshott (1933, 114) thus argues, "is not (as is often supposed) a contradiction in a world of past events, it is a contradiction in a present world of experience: it is something which comes to us as a fact, but which fails to establish its factual character on account of the incoherence it introduces into our world of present experience."

4 The inquiring subject's relation to the past is, thus, certainly mediated by empirical operations but cannot be reduced to them. More crucially, as Kuhn (1970) has made unambiguously clear for the—seemingly more transparent—case of the natural sciences, unless it remains confined to an individual's private ruminations, such a relation cannot be but a social one. Following his lead, Shapin and Shaffer (1985) have provided us with a case in which human nature became contingent on a leaky air pump operating—and being debated—in the midst of the English Civil War. Compare Bruno Latour's (1993, 15–32) comments on their findings.

5 It is for this reason that even staunchly secular, nonprovidentialist views of history somehow never quite escape analogies with those classic definitions of religion that do not feature the belief in personalized divinities as a necessary component. Who, e.g., could seriously disagree with a view of historiography as constituting "(1) a set of symbols which acts to (2) establish powerful, pervasive, and long lasting moods and motivations in men by (3) formulating conceptions of a general order of existence and (4) clothing these conceptions with such an aura of factuality that (5) the moods and motivations seem uniquely realistic" (Geertz 1973, 90). Geertz, of course, is not speaking about history here.

6 Of course, this was not always so, and not only because some of our forebears may have believed in ghosts (see, e.g., Thomas 1971, 701–24). In introducing his notion of the *temporalization of history* (*Verzeitlichung der Geschichte*), which he takes as a defining moment of "modernity," Koselleck (1985, 1–20) uses Albrecht Altdorfer's magnificent *Alexanderschlacht* (1529) to illustrate the structure of a "space of historical experience" that systematically deployed, rather than disallowed, what we, today, would be inclined to call *anachronism*, in the service of faithful historical representation. In Altdorfer's painting the battle of Issa and the Turkish siege of Vienna, Alexander and the emperor Maximilian, "merge in an exemplary manner." What is more, the lines between the living and the dead, past, present, and future, appear blurred in an even more literal sense: the banners carried by the opposing regiments bear, not only the number of combatants (as gleaned from historical accounts), but also "the number of dead who remain in the painting among the living, perhaps even bearing the banner under which they are about to fall, mortally wounded" (Koselleck 1985, 4, 3–4).

7 This is particularly clear in cases in which the resulting past relationships are of a traumatic nature. An instructive example is the international debate sparked by the so-called German Historikerstreit about the relative or absolute significance of the Holocaust in German history and, by implication, the history of Western modernity (see the contributions in Friedlander [1992]). Another example is the controversy over the so-called False Memory Syndrome (cf. Hacking 1996).

8 Historians sometimes allow themselves a moment of charity in imaginatively conjuring up such ghosts by means of analogy: What would the life of someone *like* Tomás have been like? What would he have done faced with certain options? How might someone like him have reacted to certain events? As will become clear in the introductory chapter, like White (2000, 74ff.) I do not agree with Spivak (1988a) on the a priori irrecoverability of "subaltern" pasts, but she is certainly right in pointing to the deeply troubling implications of such conjuring acts.

9 Compare here Dori Laub's remarks on the "factually incorrect" recollections of a Holocaust survivor with regard to exactly how many chimneys were blown up during the (politically inconsequential) Auschwitz revolt. "The woman," writes Laub, "testified to an event that broke the all compelling frame of Auschwitz, where Jewish armed revolts just did not happen, and had no place. She testified to the breakage of a framework. That was historical truth" (Felman and Laub 1992, 60). See also Sheriff's (2000) treatment of "silence" as a constituent of historically specific forms of local sociality.

10 On the issue of what one might provisionally call *alternative organizations* of historical realities, see, e.g., Taussig (1987), Alonso (1988), Williams (1990), Peires (1990), McCarthy Brown (1989, 1991), Thoden van Velzen (1995), White (1993a, 1993b, 1995, 2000), Shaw (1997, 2002), Dayan (1995), Hale (1997, Feierman (1999), and Comaroff and Comaroff (1999).

11 As Hale (1997) has argued, this is precisely the mission of similar spirits (the *pretos velhos*) in Brazilian Umbanda: to render accessible to situationally varying inter-

pretations what often are astoundingly detailed biographies of—once judged by the standards of academic historiography—merely "imagined" denizens of the past.

12 The analytic significance of Marx's original expression *ungeheure Warensammlung* has been more than warped by the standard translation as "an immense collection of commodities."

13 It was this moment of historical insulation that Voltaire captured in an episode of *Candide* as early as 1759. Here, the hero, himself displaced to Surinam, encounters a horribly mutilated slave. Explaining how both mill and master systematically dismembered his body, the wretched creature reminds Candide that this is the price at which sugar is eaten in Europe.

14 According to Freud's original formulation, the "uncanny" (*das Unheimliche*) is uncanny, not because it is alien to us, but precisely because it belongs "to that class of the frightening which leads us back to what is known of old and long familiar" (Freud 1955, 620).

15 This is not the occasion to explicate the workings of *ifá* and its subsidiary forms of divination. Suffice it to note that the supreme oracle, *ifá* is, not just a corpus of divinatory verses and techniques, but a personal being (known as *Orunmila*) who was witness to the creation of the world. As a result, *ifá* knows all there was, is now, and ever will be. He is very much like the omniscient narrator of certain types of nineteenth-century fiction who looks down on the mundane or tragic struggles of those subjected to the twists and turns of plot structures that he already knows. *Ifá*, we might say, is the supreme historian—priests specifically dedicated to his cult (*babalaos*) often speak of *ifá* as the ultimate book. *Ifá*, it would seem, knows a story when he sees it, and he does so simply because he understands how it was laid out for its protagonists at the beginning of time. Nevertheless, they are not his creatures—another deity actually made the universe, and yet another created human beings—and the story lines that *ifá*'s oracle reveals are constantly subject to being strained or circumvented by the contingencies of people's failure or willful refusal to achieve the fullness of life in deviating from the paths of destiny laid out for them. Although representing knowledge personified, *ifá*, thus, cannot look down on the world with august detachment, secure in his knowledge of inescapable predestination or even only in his knowledge of the path of the march of time. Humans are volatile creatures—they were, after all, created by *Obatalá* in a state of drunkenness, and it takes patient deities to figure out how people make their own histories—if under conditions not of their choosing.

16 I owe this phrase to Bonno Thoden van Velzen (1995). The afflictions that members of Suriname Maroon matrilines experience from the spirits (*kunu*) of historical individuals wronged by their ascendants is, of course, a paradigmatic case—not just because past wrongdoings define the limits of exogamous kin groups, but also because membership in such communities (imagined on the basis of common uterine descent) brings with it the danger of falling prey to the group's historically

accumulated haunts (from which affines are blissfully exempted). For a concise statement of the mechanisms by which the concept of *kunu,* revolving as it does around the notion that past evil inexorably continues to afflict the present, integrates the lineage structure of the Saramaka maroons, see Price (1973). What Price neglects is that *kunu* also circumscribes a form of historical consciousness in which past relationships vital to the continuity of contemporary social forms explicitly build on re-presentations of the unavenged "sins of the fathers" (or rather, in the case at hand, mother's brothers).

17 Put differently, what this book aims to achieve is not a reconstruction of a particular non-Western or subaltern "tradition" as something that somehow predated Western "modernity" and was merely overwhelmed, marginalized, or distorted by its forces of material and intellectual rationalization. Instead, the premise on which *Wizards and Scientists* builds is that the realities to which such "asymmetrical counterconcepts" (Koselleck 1985) as *modernity* and *tradition* pertain are, not just cut from the same cloth historically, but also unknowable if treated as phenomena or conditions sui generis. How could we know what is modern without a reference to the tradition that it purports to supersede? And, vice versa, is a discourse on tradition even possible in the absence of some sense of change or transcendence (cf. Palmié 1995a)?

18 As will be obvious by now, this distinction runs parallel to the one that Habermas (1987) makes between *system* and *lifeworld.* My differences with his approach—if not already apparent—will become so in the introduction.

19 For example, Marcus and Fisher (1986). The tradition, of course, ultimately dates back to Tacitus's *Germania.* For a powerful critique of some of the assumptions on which attempts at pitting allegedly undomesticated subaltern "counternarratives" against officialized versions of history thrive, see Stoler and Strassler (2000).

20 Celebrated, of late, under the rubric *hybridity.*

21 I am referring here, not merely to conceptual casualties, but to moral shipwrecks. For what such modernizing regimes of categorial purification actively "disappeared" (in the transitive sense well-known from recent Latin American political history) were not just the cultural and historical authenticity of the Caribbean region. In the case at hand, such "unthinkable" hybrids appear in the form of people reduced to the status of things, forms of rationality that beget phantasmagoric levels of violence and destruction, strategies of individuation that thrive on the enslavement and systematic debasement of others, and so forth.

22 For a differently motivated but ultimately concordant critique, see Ahmad (1995).

23 On this issue, see Joseph Gugelberger's (1996) introduction to the problem of the "authentic voice" (and its various mediations) in Latin American "testimonial" literature (cf. Stoler and Strasser 2000). A telling case in point is provided by the acerbic controversy between Michael Zeuske (1997b) and Miguel Barnet (1997) over Barnet's decision to authorize (in both literal and figurative senses) only select parts of Esteban Montejo's recollections in his famous *Biografía de un cimarrón* (Barnet 1984) and to decontextualize them further by eliding Montejo's

activities in the postcolonial period (which, as Zeuske shows, were all but exemplary in terms of the 1960s revolutionary pedagogical goals for which Barnet's text seems to have aimed).

24 The term *nganga complex* glosses a variety of forms of ritual activity centered around complex object assemblages condensing the powers of the spirits of dead humans.

25 Ann Stoler's (1989, 1991, 1992, 1995) work has so far provided the most nuanced guidelines for such an inquiry. For examples specifically concerning the Caribbean, see Dayan (1995) and Beckles (1999). Of course, Fanon (1967) remains a distinguished but rarely acknowledged precursor to such work.

26 No doubt, the communities of interpretation and action that constituted themselves in the course of the struggles with which this book deals defined themselves in accordance with fundamentally gendered notions of identity, morality, and social performance. Putting matters rather crudely, the normative subject of universal history was, of course, little else if not white and male. Just so, we may suppose that Aponte's book contained complexly coded references to gendered forms of historical valor or that the mercenary ethos attributed to palo monte articulates with conceptions of masculine performance, themselves the products of subterranean (or, rather, submarine) histories. To recover these dimensions, however, is a project rather different from excavating similar semantic structures from the copious records constituting the archive of gendered rationality and desire in Western cultures.

27 For might not attempting to redress this imbalance on the last pages of a rather lengthy book imply that the gendered dimension of the confrontations of knowledge that I have been trying to delineate could simply be tagged onto, as it were, a seemingly primary set of issues?

28 Although I attempt to do so elsewhere (see Palmié 2001).

INTRODUCTION

1 Even within disciplines, allocation of expertise does not seem to come easy. Although the mainland regions customarily included under the term *Caribbean* contain large populations speaking Guaraní, Arawak, Maya, or other Native American languages, few specialists on, say, coastal Maya-speaking groups in Yucatán would consider themselves Caribbeanists. Conversely, despite the fact that the existence of remnant populations of Native American descent on, e.g., Dominica is beyond dispute, the disappearance or irrelevance of a Native American factor in Antillean societies after, say, 1700 is a foregone conclusion in virtually all historical and anthropological treatments of the region. By the same token, although the bulk of the population in the area customarily indexed under the rubric *Caribbean* is of African descent, Africanists have rarely ventured a glance across the Atlantic for reasons other than to calculate the quantitative dimensions or local social significance of the population losses that Africa incurred in the direction of this particular New World region. Again, every text-

book on Latin American history includes a chapter or two on the Caribbean dealing with the Columbian moment itself and, perhaps, the institutional legacy that carried over from the initial Caribbean phase of the *conquista* into the later mainland stages. Yet the spaces nowadays designated *Caribbean* tend quickly to pass out of the purview of every Latin American history survey. In recent years, the institutional expansion of North American colonial history, and particularly the study of slavery in colonial British America, has led to the inclusion of *some* of those Caribbean islands (typically Barbados and Jamaica) whose official language remains English—usually as comparative test cases against which to measure "properly continental" variables. Yet excepting the case of Haiti—important because of its ideological impact on the debate on slavery in the republican United States—even among historians who should know better this "new" comparative interest rarely extends across what often are simply language barriers.

2 A massive, topically ordered, and thoroughly ill-conceived compilation of indexed ethnographic descriptions originally produced for purposes of controlled statistical cross-cultural comparison, the HRAF nowadays gathers dust in the reference sections of most major American university libraries as a monument to anthropology's not-so-distant positivist past.

3 Leyburn, one should add in all fairness, would later author a perceptive and still valuable monograph on Haiti. Nor would he have had any doubts about the nonexistence of Czechoslovakian "tribes." Quite obviously, the literature on "ethnographically valid" difference and otherness in that part of the world had grown out of the administrative difficulties that the Austro-Hungarian Empire had experienced—not just with recalcitrant peasants resisting Germanization or Magyarization, but with alienated "ethnic" intellectuals claiming national autonomy for the "peoples" they were in the process of inventing. The potential for "ethnic swarming" never seems to have been far from the minds of Austro-Hungarian administrators.

4 This is not to deny the existence of a vast popular and scholarly literature on "exotic" forms of Haitian otherness that centers—how could it be otherwise?—on the most patently "African" aspects of their folk culture: *vodou*. As Sidney Mintz caustically remarked, "For each anthropological paper on [Haitian] peasant economy . . . there must be at least a hundred on *vodoun*, folklore, music, and dance" (1975, 482 n. 14). The point, however, is that allegations of Haitian proclivities toward "atavistic superstitions" or (to put it in more anthropologically palatable terms) "African ritual and belief" have traditionally been deployed to discredit Haiti's nationhood and trivialize its political predicament (such as in assertions about the elder Duvalier's involvement in *vodou*—as if this explained anything about Haitian political history). They have not led to the uncontroversial definition of Haiti as a bona fide "ethnographic" case.

5 This distinction was moot in the case of—say—the Ilongot of central Luzon, whose "primordial savagery" went unquestioned during the American occupation. It did apply, however, to the "Moros" of Mindanao and Jolo, who not only

were part of recognizably state-like Islamic polities but resisted American encroachment in a systematic way. They clearly represented more than an "ethnographic" problem—and were consequently shunned by anthropologists. If, as Joan Vincent (1990, 286) argues, Redfield's classification of "American Negroes" as "marginal" or "remade folk" renders "an interesting reflection of his view of the place of African-Americans in American society in the 1930s," it equally reflects both on their place within the categorial grid of anthropology and on the place of anthropology within America's political culture.

6 Salvage ethnography, of course, provides the most patent example. It is surely no accident that the institutionalization of ethnographic forms of knowledge dealing with Native Americans in the United States (e.g., in the form of the Bureau of American Ethnology) occurred at the point when most "tribes" were no longer perceived as a political factor of potential relevance to the future history of the United States, but had become simply an administrative problem created by the conjunction of past forms of human development (fading on reservations) with a presumptively overpowering and self-consciously progressive civilization.

7 The patent absurdity of applying the term to "natural" phenomena—plants, animal species, geologic formations—speaks for itself. We have no doubts about Mount Cameroon, but it is hard to imagine on what grounds (other than sheer metaphor) a geologic formation could be called *African American*. Conversely, while it may make some sense to call maize a *New World* ("American") cultigen or swine an *Old World* animal species, to characterize corn bread and chitlins as African American food invariably evokes the work of history and culture. Once we begin critically to attend to the single, seemingly transhistorically operative defining feature of "African Americanness"—racial otherness as construed within historically specific New World local contexts—it begins to slip away into a congeries of strategically deployed technologies of differentiation and boundary maintenance designed to reproduce or challenge certain arrangements of privilege, power, and prestige. See, e.g., Mangum (1940), Mintz (1971), Martínez-Alier (1974), Alexander (1977), Barbara Fields (1982), Novit-Evans and Welch (1983), Hoetink (1985), Dominguez (1986), Stoler (1989, 1992), Wade (1993), and Harrison (1995) as well as the rapidly growing literature on the social phenomenon of "whiteness" (e.g., Hartigan 1997).

8 Here, we might want to recall Marx and Engels's (1967, 83) famous diagnosis of modernity in the *Communist Manifesto:* "Constant revolutionizing of production, uninterrupted disturbance of all social conditions [*Verhältnisse*], everlasting uncertainty and agitation distinguish the bourgeois epoch from all earlier ones. All fixed, fast-frozen relations, with their train of ancient and venerable prejudices and opinions, are swept away, all new-formed ones become antiquated before they can ossify."

9 If only through various kinds of multiplier effects, as economic historians have been keen to point out. Neither has the Williams thesis been explored in relation to the other great colonial powers in the Caribbean—such as France and Spain—

where factors internal to the European context seem to balance or outweigh the role of colonial trade in the accumulation of domestically viable industrial finance capital. For recent assessments of the debate, see the contributions in Solow and Engerman (1987) and Engerman and Inikori (1992).

10 For the pervasiveness of such analogies in contemporary British discourse, see Stedman Jones (1977), Stocking (1987), Stepan (1982), Catherine Hall (1992), and Thorne (1997). Gilman (1985), Linke (1990), and Bailey (1993) provide important clues as to the further elaboration of such metaphoric linkages into scientized forms of knowledge such as criminal ethnography, statistics, and the various disciplines concerned with the deviant body and pathological mind.

11 "Though there were as yet few factories with internal combustion engines in London," Johnson and Grant (1979, 238 n. 9) note, somewhat pedantically, "windmills, watermills, and treadmills were nothing new: Milton's Samson labors 'Eyeless in Gaza at the Mill with slaves.' "

12 As early as 1700, the Barbadian planter Thomas Tryon indicated to what extent Caribbean sugar mills had developed what Giedion (1948, 79) calls the *central preoccupation* of modern industry with continuous production. Characterizing life in the mills as "a perpetual Noise and Hurry," Tryon (cited in Mintz 1985, 47–48) speaks of labor as being "so constant that the Servants [or slaves] night and day stand in Great Boyling Houses, where there are Six or Seven large Coppers or Furnaces kept perpetually Boyling; and from which with heavy Ladles and Scummers they Skim off the excrementious parts of the Canes, till it comes to its perfection and cleanness, while others as Stoakers, Broil as it were alive, in managing the Fires; and one part is constantly at the Mill, to supply it with Canes, night and day, during the whole Season of making Sugar which is about six months of the years." In the fields, the gang system so characteristic of sugar estates displayed "a degree of regimentation and discipline that called forth military or machine metaphors from all who witnessed them" (Berlin and Morgan 1993, 14), again evoking, not only the view of the human body as a machine, but what Frederick Winslow Taylor, by the early twentieth century, was to call the *military type of management* (Giedion 1948, 99). On the stunningly "panoptic" characteristics of the mature Cuban "barracón" (i.e., slave barracks), see Pérez de la Riva (1978, 13–40). For a cogent argument for the "avantgarde" nature of early-nineteenth-century Cuban "scientific management," see Moreno Fraginals (1978, vol. 2, chap. 1).

13 As Thorne (1977, 253–54) puts it in her fine discussion of the interrelation between colonial and internal missions, "Scholarly discussions of the intersections of class and race in colonial discourse have emphasized the many and important ways in which metropolitan ideas about class were transformed in the colonies into a discourse about 'race.' Or, to put it in another way, the primary concern has been to illuminate the ways in which the language of race spoken in the Empire—as well as at home—was 'classed.' The history of evangelical missions . . . ,

however, suggests that the ideas about class that British colonizers brought with them to the Empire might already have been 'raced,' constructed on the basis of a social nomenclature whose primary referent was the colonial encounter."

14 For the British Empire, see, e.g., Williams (1973, esp. chap. 24), Blackburn (1988, 419–71), Comaroff and Comaroff (1992a), Catherine Hall (1992) and esp. Linebaugh (1988) and Linebaugh and Redicker (1991). Marx, of course, remained ambivalent about how to explain the "formal" existence of the archaic (in his view) institution of slavery within capitalist modernity. Nevertheless, he clearly saw a functional relation between New World slavery and one of the key processes in the modernization of Europe: the emergence of an industrial proletariat. "The veiled slavery of the wage-labourers in Europe," he wrote, "needed the unqualified slavery of the New World as its pedestal" (1977, 1:925). Being the quintessential modernist thinker that he was, Marx had more to say about the matter. Commenting on the U.S. abolitionist Cairns's denunciation of the inhumanity of the nineteenth-century slave trade from older North American plantation regions to the newly emerging Cotton Belt, he suggests: "For slave trade read labor market, for Kentucky and Virginia [read] Ireland and the agricultural districts of England, Scotland and Wales" (378). Marx's implicit analogy to the Georgian enclosure movement and other strategies of freeing peasant labor for industrial production illustrates yet another aspect of this process: a seeming loss of continuity between present and past effected by the destruction of previous forms of sociality and identity. If the loss of access to the means of production and the subsequent massive commoditization of labor power has been construed as the initiation of the European worker into an alienated proletarian modernity, then—as several writers have noted (e.g., Lewis 1968; Mintz 1974, 1996; Gilroy 1992; Miller 1994)—the far more radical nature of the African slave's modernization experience of "social death" (Patterson 1982), transcontinental displacement, and ruthless exploitation as a commoditized laborer is obvious.

15 A few years later, the German nationalist poet Heinrich von Kleist would find himself imprisoned under accusation of espionage in a cell of the same fortress, proudly imagining that it might be the one in which Toussaint had once languished, sacrificing his life for the freedom of his people (Schüller 1992). Unlike Wordsworth's romantic praise of the "black Spartacus," however, von Kleist's admiration for Toussaint grew not just out of a politically decontextualized abolitionist sentimentalism. Von Kleist also saw in Touissaint a model of the modern leader of a nation emerging into statehood; a figure that the German-speaking peoples—occupied as their various territorial states were at the time by Napoléon's troops—had yet to bring forth.

16 Part of what is at issue here is a distinction between *modernity* and *modernism* as a self-conscious reflection on the "modern condition." To speak with Bhabha (1997), the impression of "mimicry" registers merely on the screen of the imperial imaginary. For possible explanations for why Haiti's rulers continued to lock its

peasantry into "modern" forms of exploitation in the service of an export economy that literally prefigured the fate of most twentieth-century non-Western nation-states, see Dupuy (1989) and Trouillot (1990).

17 This, arguably, is the subject of Belafonte's perhaps most famous tune, the "Banana Boat Song." Reduced to generic Caribbean Muzak incessantly played in hotel lobbies and on cruise ships to this day, it contains unveiled references to the abuse of peasant labor in northeastern Jamaica by agents of what is easy to identify as the United Fruit Co.

18 A comprehensive history of the appropriation of Christianity into the evolving worldview of nineteenth-century Jamaican freed people remains to be written. But, for partial treatments of the issue, see Curtin (1955), Schuler (1980), Stewart (1992), Chevannes (1994), and Austin-Broos (1997). The most vivid contemporary account is Waddell's (1863).

19 On some of the ideological convolutions characterizing French emancipation, see Blackburn (1988, chap. 12), Mancini (1989), and Drescher (1992).

20 A related point was made by David Brion Davis (1974) in his critique of the heavily psychologistic debate about the origins of American racism waged in the 1960s. "The attention," Davis (1974, 9) argued, "devoted to racial conflict and racial adjustment—problems easily consigned to the realm of group psychology—may well have obscured questions of class, culture, and power that lead to the structural foundations of American society" (cf. Barbara Fields 1982). In a sense, we might say, the debate itself was a continuation of the moment of dispersal that Gilroy denounces.

21 As an analytic category, *gender* provides a useful analogy here. Manhood and womanhood are linked social polarities. But they are so paired, not because of immutable facts of human anatomy, but because they are in every instance part of a single, culturally structured historical field of social relations and discursive practices (cf. Riley 1988; Butler 1990; Mohanty 1991). Although problematic in its own right, Kopytoff and Miers's (1977) argument that Western notions of *individual freedom* are likely to distort African realities, where the antithesis of *slavery* may be, not *freedom*, but *belonging*, points in a similar direction. For more recent treatments of the issue, see Guyer and Belinga (1995) and Piot (1996). For a sophisticated attempt to link both discussions in a Melanesianist reflection on concepts of property and personhood, see Strathern (1988).

22 As we shall see, such conceptions, of course, beg definitions of the boundaries of the self. Where, e.g., lie the limits of alienability pertaining to aspects of bodily performance separable from the self or "moral personhood" as socially construed? The forms of dealing with the dead that I analyze in chap. 2 below are cases in point.

23 It seems striking that a good deal of what Prakash (1992b) calls *postfoundational* criticism appears to result in structural transformations of what Ralph Ellison once called the *white man's dilemma*. "Are American Negroes simply the creations of white men," Ralph Ellison (1966, 301) asked in 1944, "or have they at least

helped to create themselves out of what they found around them? Men have made a life in caves and upon cliffs, why cannot Negroes have made a life upon the horns of the white man's dilemma?" I suspect that Ellison might not have agreed with the position taken by Prakash vis-à-vis the problem of representing subaltern historical subjectivities. "The interpreter's recognition of the limits of historical knowledge," Prakash (1992a, 175) writes, "does not disable criticism but enables the critic to mark the space of the subaltern as *aporetic* that, by resisting a paternalist recovery of the subaltern voice, frustrates our repetition of the imperialist attempt to speak for the colonized subaltern woman." All this is easily pronounced from the position of the academically installed theorist. Limits there are to historical knowledge (and, as the reader shall see, part of the theoretical subtext of chap. 1 deals with the question of how far they can be pushed). But, one might ask, what good does it do the historical "subaltern woman" to have her "subject position" posthumously disclosed as aporetic? If such revelations be our goal, we might as well shut up (cf. Ortner 1995).

24 It may be ironic that Thompson's strictures against a brand of Marxism that would subtract human beings from the structures that they inhabit also enable an argument for the reinstallment of subject positions into a critique of the silences endorsed by recent brands of social theory that negate, not historical subjectivity per se, but the possibilities of its recovery.

25 I am mindful here of Joan Scott's (1991) criticism that appeals to *experience* as a seemingly prediscursive ontological foundation of subject positions (as in *working-class experience*, *women's experience*, or the *black experience*) have troubling implications in that they black box "the operations of the complex and changing discursive processes by which identities are ascribed, resisted, or embraced." I also find myself in fundamental agreement with her earlier strictures (Scott 1988, 68–90) against the (largely unspoken) masculinist subtext underlying much of Thompson's analysis of class formation. Yet I do not see why the uncovering of such processes constituting differentiated subjectivities should not be reconcilable with the study of the effects that they engender on the level of those "linguistic events" (as Scott would have it) that we tend to regard as signifiers of "experience."

26 Despite the fact that Toussaint and his successors explicitly outlawed the practice of vodou in Haiti, Johann Gottfried von Herder and Heinrich von Kleist, somewhat ironically, might have understood the gist of Métraux's statement. The "modernity" into which these German-speaking theorists of (a then decidedly peripheral and not yet effectively politicized) European population were heading had no room for what historically preceded it but was nevertheless in dire ideological need of representations of "tradition." As "all that is solid melts into the air," the past begins to loop into a future to be created in tandem with it. Hence both Wagner's Burgundian epics filtered through Scandinavia and Haitian national historians' dutiful inscription of vodou into the foundational fictions of the very state that tried (albeit unsuccessfully) to eradicate its practice.

27 The problem here is that, since the French and Haitian Revolutions disrupted the process, we will never know whether France might have become even more exemplary for the linkages between colonial slavery and domestic industrial capitalism than England.

28 It is no accident that African slaving would have played a key role in the "articulation of modes of production" episode that caused so much controversy in Marxist quarters in the 1970s. Apart from the fact that the major proponents of French Marxist anthropology—Rey, Meillassoux, and Terray—had worked on African regions long integrated into the Atlantic economy, the paradox of "capitalism without wage labor" was traditionally linked to African slavery in the Americas. For different aspects of the problem, see Foster-Carter (1978) and Mintz (1978).

29 It is not the (debatable) facility with which commodity fetishism as the "custom of the capitalist world economy" translated itself into local discourses that is at issue here but the epistemological problem of stepping "behind," as it were, what Sahlins (1988) calls the emergent *chrematistic pidgin languages,* articulating them in order to reveal the contingencies involved in their local constitution (cf. Austen 1993). A prudent statement of the problem in another context comes from the pen of a demographic historian: speaking about the cultural transformations the Chesapeake region underwent in the seventeenth and eighteenth centuries, Allan Kulikoff (1986, 12–13) argues that such changes were, "neither inevitable, nor completely determined by economic and demographic change." "Chesapeake planters," he continues in a passage worth quoting at length,

> did not *have* to choose to form domestic patriarchies. They could have maintained the relatively egalitarian family system of the seventeenth century. That planters chose to organize patriarchal families almost as soon as they could do so suggests that they may have considered older forms of family life to be less than ideal. Nor did wealthy men *have* to form dynasties just because rising life expectancy gave them that option; they might have continued the policy of rotation in office that ensured that most unrelated men of wealth and a few poorer freeholders served as justices and assemblymen. Wealthy planters probably looked back to England and insisted that class control of politics was the best way to guarantee social peace in the very different slave society of the Chesapeake. And, despite severe constraints, even the slaves made choices. They formed communities from among the extended kindred who lived on large plantations, and they adapted those African forms of child rearing that were compatible with chattel slavery. And while masters determined who would work in each slave gang, slaves themselves set the pace of work.

30 Part of what is apt to disturb us in this case is, of course, the color of that skin and the presumptions about cultural loyalties that we are inclined to think into this particular historical situation.

31 On the problem of relativism and what he calls *sizable differences,* see Latour (1993).

32 The contours of such problems already emerge on an etymological level. To mention but a few random examples, one might think of *magic* (a Persian heresy), *Africa* (a Phoenician slave settlement in Tunisia), *cannibalism* (a habit of the native population of uncolonized Caribbean islands), *Guinea* (a Berber term for slaves, converted into a British coin and a variety of place-names all over the world), or *slave* (a bondsman drawn from Europe's Black Sea slaving [*sic*] frontiers). I will return to this issue in the next chapter.

33 Note here that one of the most impressively playful and creatively synthetic cultural forms to emerge in the twentieth-century Caribbean—Rastafari idiolectal conventions (*I-tesvar*)—is considered by its users as one tool (among several) designed to purge their speech of impure elements and so further their disengagement from Babylon (cf. Breiner 1985–86). As Littlewood (1995) suggests, there may be more than superficial affinities between Rastafari and seventeenth-century radical Puritanism—a similarly omnivorous (shall we say *catholic?*) system of semiotic creativity that likewise understood itself as combating hybridity.

34 Ardener himself gives a particularly powerful example of the kind of logic underlying this incident in a footnote to a paper on witchcraft in the Cameroons. When the first serious military engagement between the Germans and the Bakweri in 1894 left the leader of the expedition, Freiherr von Gravenreuth, dead (possibly by "friendly fire"), the retreating German forces "sought as if by antennas," Ardener writes (1996, 257–58 n. 6), "for the belief system of the Bakweri. The latter, as 'savages,' were expected to prize a victim's head and heart: the Germans spared their leader's body the ignominy of losing those parts to the Bakweri by removing them themselves. Any explanation of the German behavior must be found, then, in German belief, not in the belief of the Bakweri, for whom the events, had they been aware of them (and possibly they were), would merely have suggested (on the contrary) that it was the Germans who prized the heads and hearts of the dead." What Kaplan and Kelley (1994) call *zones of transcourse* seem particularly prolific breeding grounds for such hybrids. A more recent and truly fantastic example concerns the repatriation of the bones of Che Guevara to a country in which he was not born in order to make his handless body speak to Cuba's future.

35 One would want to note here that seven hundred *cacos* pardoned after the breakdown of the rebellion in 1920 found themselves funneled into HASCO's labor force (Heinl and Heinl 1978, 462). For the ways in which foreign-capitalized companies such as HASCO "caused the expropriation and/or ruin of thousands of small peasants," see Dupuy (1989, 136). Richman (1992, 127–64) provides local background information on what she calls "the coming of HASCO to Leogane."

36 For similar examples from the Cameroons, see Ardener (1970) and, more recently, Geschiere (1997).

37 The problem, of course, was that, despite long-standing Dominican traditions of racializing Haitianness, physiological criteria did not adequately "pick up" the difference between Dominican citizens and Haitian others. Eight years later,

Joaquín Balaguer, then Dominican ambassador to Colombia, would justify the slaughter by marshaling a remarkable string of insubstantiable allegations—rumors backed by a violent state. "By 1935," Balaguer argued, "there were 400,000 Haitians in our country, resulting in the corrosion of national solidarity; voodoo, a kind of African animism of the lowest origins became the preferred cult among Dominicans in the border area. The *gourde* replaced the peso. Peasants were learning from the Haitians anti-Christian customs, such as incestuous unions. We were about to be absorbed by Haiti" (cited in Fiehrer 1990, 11). On the context, political and cultural, of the 1937 massacre, see Castor (1987), Fiehrer (1990), or Derby (1994). Lundahl (1992, chap. 13) provides a comparative political-economic perspective on the evolution of predatory states in both Haiti and the Dominican Republic.

38 Speaking about Duala ritual specialists (nganga), de Rosny (1985) notes that initiation "into the functions of a *nganga* consists in opening candidates' eyes to the acts of violence committed around them" (248; emphasis added). De Rosny contrasts such revelatory tactics with the manner in which Western modernity displaces the horrors of such violence as the nganga must consciously engage into ideologies of legitimate force "authorizing manifestations of violence" and "immunizing" the citizen of First World states against the "naked violence, impossible to contain, [that] infiltrates the public life" (250). In contrast, we might say, the nganga's spectral vision reveals the way in which the creative destruction of what George Bataille (1967) called *la part maudite* is constitutive of the order that upholds a semantic economy of normalcy.

39 Again, de Rosny (1985, 288) provides a useful example. Speaking of Duala conceptions of *ekong*, a type of sorcery involving the exploitation of captured and commercially transacted souls, he notes that the "clearest sign of the presence of *ekong* sorcery is for someone to dream of being carried off towards the sea, hands bound." Given the history of the southern Cameroons, de Rosny wonders about the kind of reality that such dreams appear to index. "Is this a phantasmal representation of the memory of the slave trade?" he asks. And he adds: "The appearance of a horse in a dream likewise provokes panic: the German invasion a century ago?"

40 The puzzle is partly resolved by noting that our high priests had been reading Durkheim. Nonetheless, the irony persists. For little could be farther from the classic structural-functionalist position of the concept of *social facts* (including ideological projections thereof) as fundamental constraints on individual moral choice than the kind of conflict sociology at the heart of Marxist theories of social contradictions. I owe this point to Bonno Thoden van Velzen.

41 What I refer to as *classic* is the sense in which Strathern (1992, 48) describes the twentieth-century anthropological consensus that cultures are "artificial creations natural to the human condition." From this perspective, somewhere behind the multifarious facades of kinship systems or gender definitions, e.g., lie the "brute facts" of biological descent and sexual difference. Needless to say, we are nowa-

days no longer so sure if the facts of nature are not, in themselves, to a large extent a cultural creation.

42 Ironically, many an anticolonial revolutionary faced exactly the same problems. Hence, e.g., Fanon's thoroughly misguided reflections on the role of violence in shattering premodern mystifications. "After centuries of unreality," he wrote on one of the most desperately modernistic pages of *The Wretched of the Earth* (1968, 58), "after having wallowed in the most outlandish phantoms, at long last, the native, gun in hand, stands face to face with the only forces which contend for his life—the forces of colonialism. And the youth of a colonized country, growing up in an atmosphere of shot and fire, may well make a mock of, and does not hesitate to pour scorn upon the zombies of his ancestors, the horses with two heads, the dead who rise again, and the djinns who rush into your body while you yawn. The native discovers reality and transforms it into the patterns of his customs, into the practice of violence and into his plan for freedom."

43 "Its most important campaign," Trouillot (1990, 106) adds, "was its participation alongside the Marines in the war against the peasant nationalists led by Charlemagne Péralt and Benoit Battraville, when Marines and *Garde* together killed at least 6,000 peasants. Another 5,500 cultivators died in the forced labor camps that the *Garde* ran for the occupiers." "Domination," Horkheimer and Adorno (1972, 28) write in a different but related context, "is paid for by the alienation of men from the objects dominated" or, to put the matter in terms more appropriate to the issue at hand, by the objectification of the dominated as alienable and, therefore, disposable.

44 Pérez (1990, 1–81) provides a good introduction to the subject. For the development of the Cuban dependency on the U.S. sugar market during the colonial period, see Moreno Fraginals (1978, 2:186–208).

45 Drawing on different estimates, Pérez (1986, 72) agrees that Cuban ownership of land had been reduced to 25 percent of the total holdings on the island.

46 A new type of agroindustrial complex that emerged in the final decades of the nineteenth century from the consolidation of older, privately held plantation properties around single, technologically highly advanced milling and refining plants and under corporate (and increasingly foreign) ownership (cf. Ayala 1999).

47 For a regional study of the growth of the "parastatal" networks of patronage and clientelism that underwrote such trends, see Zeuske (1997a).

48 Excepting the questionable engagement of a disproportionally black (by even Cuban standards) fighting force in Angola, the FAR (Fuerzas Armadas Revolucionarias) so far have seen battle against Cuban citizens only in a brief episode of violence during the chaotic summer of 1994. Nevertheless, the official declaration of a "special period in times of peace" gives new meaning to the large measure of control that the Cuban army exercises over a tourist sector within which the prostitution of civilian sexuality plays a major economic role.

49 This holds true not just for the interior of states. Does the possession of a national airport, postage stamps, an army, border posts, or a seat in the United Nations

make the difference between, e.g., an international labor reserve and a sovereign nation? The fringe states of the South African Republic, Mobuto's Zaire, Biya's Cameroon, and even contemporary Mexico would seem to suggest reason for doubt (Bayart 1993; De Boek 1996; Ferguson 1997).

1. "FOR REASONS OF HISTORY"

1 The bulk of the documentary evidence regarding Aponte's case is found in ANC, Fondo Asuntos Políticos, legajo 12, signatura 16–24, most of which has been transcribed and published by José Luciano Franco (1977).

2 Since St. Domingue had produced roughly 60 percent of all sugar consumed in the Atlantic economy, between 1790 and 1795 world market prices for sugar tripled (Pérez 1988, 71), and Cuba's aspiring planters were ready to jump the breach. Between 1792 and 1806 in the province of Havana alone, the number of sugar mills increased from 237 to 416 (Pérez 1988, 73), and the island's total sugar exports soared from 14,445 to 38,192 metric tons (Moreno Fraginals (1978, 3:43–44).

3 For the extent and astonishing efficiency of the "subterranean" (or, perhaps better, maritime) communication networks through which information about the Haitian Revolution had rapidly spread to slave populations throughout the Atlantic Basin in the early 1790s, see Scott (1986).

4 Philip Foner (1962, 1:92) claims that "two Negroes in Havana" denounced Aponte as the leader of a planned uprising after having been arrested and subjected to torture. The story was, in fact, far more complicated and circumstantial. The individuals to whom Foner seems to be referring were three slave artisans, Cristóbal de Sola and the brothers Pablo and José Benito Valdés, who were in contact with Aponte and Juán Barbier, one of Aponte's close associates. At the same time, however, they were also on good terms with Luis, the black driver of the marqués de Someruelos, who seems to have denounced them to his master. Yet, while Sola was arrested on March 9, and the Valdés brothers only a day later, it was not until March 16 that Aponte was arrested himself, and there seems to be no direct evidence that any of these three slaves implicated him (Franco 1974, 175–76).

5 See Ponte Dominguez (1951, 43–58) and Morales Padrón (1972, 353–57). The participation of black militiamen in the Masonic plot is highly probable. At least three of Aponte's fellow officers in the "Batallón de morenos disciplinados" and one common soldier were charged with being involved and sentenced to deportation and ten years' incarceration in Spanish presidios. Masonic ideas first seemed to have reached Cuba during the British occupation of Havana in 1762–63. Prior to 1810, there had been five lodges in operation in Havana, most of which were affiliated with the French rite.

6 As in the famous case of Guaman Poma's twelve-hundred-page letter *La primera nueva crónica y gouierno*, originally addressed to King Philip III of Spain but

accidentally discovered in the Danish Royal Archive in 1908, Aponte's images may still await revisualization.

7 Aponte's case seems to have made its first appearance in Cuban historiography in Antonio José Valdés's *História de la isla de Cuba y en especial de la Habana* (Valdés 1964), first published privately by Valdés himself in 1813. Valdés applauds Someruelos for putting down Aponte's "conspiracy" and speaks of the affair as an "event that could have disturbed the tranquility of the inhabitants [of Cuba], caused untold damages to agriculture, and especially to the owners of rural plantations, for there the major attacks and ravages would have been committed" (237). But he also includes the "sedition of the Negro Aponte and his followers" among a whole array of local and international turbulences, the portent of which he "as of yet" did not feel confident to predict with "the necessary fullness and clarity" (242).

8 The thesis itself appears to have originated with Monica Schuler (1970), who presented it in a far more moderate form and—perhaps significantly—in a relatively inaccessible Jamaican journal.

9 Having only recently been captured / conscripted in Africa, the Trinidadian mutineers of 1837, we might say, simply were not aware that such an appointment had been made.

10 Greggus (1989) and Trouillot (1995)—albeit for very different reasons—provide notable exceptions.

11 His eldest son, Benito, was twenty-eight years old at the time of his arrest—i.e., had been born in 1784 (Franco 1974, 146). Besides that, Aponte had fought in the American War of Independence (see below).

12 Franco quotes a turn-of-the-twentieth-century novel by Francisco Calcagno in which Aponte is described as a former slave of a white creole planter of Dominican origin named Delmonte who seems to have removed to Cuba. This, however, is not easy to reconcile with Aponte's own testimony to the effect that his paternal grandfather and uncle had served in the battalions of free blacks during the English invasion of Havana in 1762, i.e., around the time of Aponte's birth. On the other hand, although Havana had since its earliest days boasted an unusually large free black population, and although some of Aponte's paternal relatives were undoubtedly free, he could have inherited slave status from his mother, Mariana Poveda, who was listed as a free creole in the records of 1812 but might have been manumitted sometime after Aponte's birth. It is, thus, not improbable that Aponte had, in his youth, been a slave.

13 The social benefits of membership in the black battalions were considerable: apart from the fact that the Afro-Cuban militiamen were removed from the discriminatory civil jurisdiction and placed under the *fuero militar* on equal terms with white soldiers, they enjoyed military *preeminencias* relieving them from certain types of municipal labor levies, taxes, and licenses. Officers such as Aponte received a salary and were expected to live in the district of their companies and to contribute

to unit management and discipline, thus presumably not only gaining social distinction and prestige but being positioned at the nodal points of social networks constituted by the free black militiamen of a given barrio (Kuethe 1986, 43, 74–75, and passim; see also Klein 1966; and Deschamps Chapeaux 1971a). As the case of Ternero suggests (he apparently held the office of *capataz* of a *cabildos de nación*—see below), it may not have been uncommon for such networks to be at least partly coextensive with the membership of these Afro-Cuban ethnic associations (cf. Paquette 1988, 108). On the institution of the cabildos de nación, see Ortiz (1921), Palmié (1991, 1993), Brown (1993), and Howard (1998).

14 See Klein (1967, 194–227) and Deschamps Chapeaux (1971b). As Saco put it in his famous diatribe against the ideology of the *deshonor de trabajo* among Cuba's white population, *Memória sobre la vagancia en la Isla de Cuba* (1830), by that time "it was no longer to be hoped that any white person would dedicate himself to artisanry, for by the singular fact of embracing it, it would seem that he renounced the privileges of his class; thus the practical arts all came to be the exclusive patrimony of the colored people, while literary and maybe two or three other types of careers deemed honorable remained reserved for the whites" (cited in Rigol 1982, 38).

15 For the Cuban situation, see Deschamps Chapeaux (1971a, 1971b), Deschamps Chapeaux and Pérez de la Riva (1974), and Knight (1972, 1977b). For other parts of the Americas, see e.g., Cohen and Greene (1972), Campbell (1976), Heuman (1981), or Neville Hall (1992, 139–56).

16 As Jensen (1988, 38) suggests, de Someruelos's decision to suppress the news about the abolition debates in the Cortes by censoring articles 37 and 38 of its *Diario de sesiones* merely unleashed a stream of rumors of which Aponte would undoubtedly have become aware.

17 We encounter here the plotting devices of a narrative that should be familiar by now. The "progressions" implied by the authors cited above belong to a discourse that systematically mutes and disperses structures of experience and signification "unfit" for inclusion into (because disruptive of) its self-consciously elaborated and self-centered drama of historical transitions toward modernity radiating outward from Europe. As we have already seen, this narrative stands particularly good chances of empirical falsification in the Caribbean.

18 The transplantation of thousands of enslaved Yoruba speakers to Cuba was clearly a function of the transatlantic historical conjuncture between Cuba's extremely late development as a plantation society (dating back, at the very earliest, to the English occupation of Havana in 1762) and the disintegration of the paramount Yoruba state of Oyo between about 1796 and 1836. If the latter events unleashed a half century of continuous warfare ravaging large parts of what is today southwestern Nigeria and the People's Republic of Benin, Cuba's simultaneous economic transformation rendered the island (along with northeastern Brazil) a prime recipient of the vast numbers of captives generated by these

African wars. Yet, despite the somewhat unlikely timing of Aponte's probable birth and the fact that Aponte's father's father had already lived in Cuba, we know from an inventory of cabildos de nación—i.e., officially endorsed associations of Africans organized according to what appears to have been constructions of common ethnicity—compiled in 1755 that, already then, groups of Africans designating their collective identity by the term *lucumí* possessed two assembly houses in Havana (see Palmié 1991, 117–20). We do not, of course, know to what extent this can be taken to evidence the presence of Yoruba speakers in Havana. But we may assume that—whoever they were—individuals regarding themselves as lucumí had managed to build up what one might call an *ethnic infrastructure* in Havana and its immediate environs. If some of Aponte's grandparents had been Africans (which is not unlikely), it is conceivable that they might have spoken what we, today, would recognize as a variant of the language that—owing to the efforts of Protestant missionaries—by the late nineteenth century would become known as Yoruba.

19 Indirect evidence for this can be found in the fact that Changó is worshiped—if only as one of the minor *lwa* (deities)—in the *rada* "pantheon" of Haitian vodou. For it is rather unlikely that the cult of this deity diffused to Haiti after the Revolution put a final stop to all slave importation to this colony in the early 1790s.

20 Examining legal papers relating to several Afro-Cuban cabildos de nación in the early years of the twentieth century, the Cuban scholar Fernando Ortiz uncovered detailed references to the former existence of a "cabildo africano Lucumí" under the Catholic advocation of Santa Barbara in the calle Jesús Peregrino, no. 49 (Ortiz 1921, 26). This association of free and enslaved urban blacks rallying around the representations of an emergent Yoruba-Cuban culture had, according to Ortiz, been on record since 1839, when it underwent reorganization and adopted a flag in red and white—colors symbolic, not only of Santa Barbara, but also of the oricha Changó. By the late 1940s, one of Lydia Cabrera's informants still remembered that, before removing to the "barrio de Jesús María" in the last decades of the nineteenth century, the cabildo Changó Teddún had occupied a house in the calle Jesús Peregrino (Cabrera 1983, 24 n. 1), and even one of my informants who grew up in Jesús María in the 1920s recalled that the famous lucumí cabildo had relocated there from what, by then, had become known as Centro Habana's barrio of Cayo Hueso during his infancy. As David Brown (1989, 20 n. 16) has argued, the name, incidentally, appears to represent a corruption of the Yoruba *oríkì* or praise name *Ṣòngó ti edun:* "Changó who is / is like the thunderstone," i.e., the celts that this royal warrior deity is thought to hurl from the sky when lightning strikes the earth.

21 During the interrogation of one of Aponte's associates, Clemente Chacón, on March 26 we first hear of "dos varas" (i.e., about three feet) of a type of fabric known as "Platilla Nueva" (Franco 1977, 117) that Aponte apparently had received from another member of the putative conspiratorial group, José del Cár-

men Peñalver. Questioned as to the use to which this piece of cloth was to be put, Chacón replied that Aponte had told him that it was destined for a banner (*bandera*) that Aponte had meant to raise at the entrance of his house. Chacón further explained that Aponte had insisted that white cloth was needed for this purpose and that the flag would bear an image of Nuestra Señora de los Remedios (Franco 1977, 118). Aponte himself at first confirmed this, adding that he had instructed Chacón and Peñalver as well as two other of his associates, Francisco Javier Pacheco and Francisco Maroto, to fashion similar banderas. For, as he put it somewhat ambiguously, "from her [i.e., the Virgin of Remedios] protection alone could one hope a successful outcome [*buen acierto*]" (Franco 1977, 120). Momentarily, Aponte's interrogators let go of this line of inquiry, but, during the last examination on March 30, it became clear that they had formed a quite specific opinion about what exactly he had meant by *buen acierto*. Franco (1977, 21), who accepts their interpretation, writes that the raising of a white flag with an image of the Virgen de los Remedios at Aponte's home had been intended as a signal for the conspirators to open the insurrectionary attack. Confronted with this charge, Aponte, who later on referred to himself as a deputy of the Virgin of Remedios (*diputado de la Nuestra Señora de los remedios*) in the context of explaining why he possessed a copy of a Real Cedula pertaining to "congregations, lay brotherhoods, and fraternities [*congregaciones, ermandades y Cofradías*]" (Franco 1977, 170), almost angrily retorted that he would never engage in such a vile thing as harnessing the "means" (lit. *remedios*) of the Santísima to such ends (Franco 1977, 167–68). And it is here that we begin to sense both the complexity of Aponte's thought and the multilayered nature of the dialogue in which he and Nerey engaged. For now this self-declared bearer of a religious commission (we might ask, What kind of religion was he talking about?) begins to elaborate on his involvement in what, in fact, could have been a conspiracy of significant proportions. Yes, he explains, Peñalver, Chacón, and Pacheco did frequently meet at his house, yet, when he overheard them talking about setting fire to the *barrios extramuros* in order to divert the attention of the authorities from their attack on the dragoon barracks and the military post at the Castillo de Atarés, he, Aponte, tried to dissuade them, arguing that they would only hurt their families and friends in the almost exclusively black extramural neighborhoods by doing so. But, as they persisted in their plan and wanted to fashion flags for that purpose, he counseled them to make these flags of white cloth and to implore the help of the Santísima because he felt that the Virgin would not allow such evil to come to pass (Franco 1977, 165). By no means, however—Aponte would continue somewhat later—did he encourage them to implore the Virgin for any nefarious purpose, only for whatever good she would grant to such simple folk as them. Proof of this was to be seen in the color of the flag, for, although such a flag was, in fact, never assembled, its whiteness would have signified peace, thus expressing Aponte's hope that her sovereign patronage would bring to naught all malicious intent, as—he added almost in the manner of an afterthought—indeed had happened

(Franco 1977, 167). The documentary record will never tell us, but one imagines Aponte's voice as tinged with bitter sarcasm.

22 In examining the original records transcribed by Franco, I was unable to locate such materials. For a useful introduction to the history and ritual practices of abakuá, see Sosa Rodríguez (1982).

23 Along with the (apparently much more recent) Vai script, nsibidi represents one of the better-known indigenous African writing systems. See the list of ethnographic sources in Thompson (1983, 298). The Cuban manifestations (*anaforuana*) of nsibidi are discussed briefly in Sosa Rodríguez (1982, app. 5). Cabrera's collection of anaforuana (Cabrera 1975) gives an impression of the amazing complexity of this pictographic system.

24 For a survey and trenchant critique of similar compromise formations in the study of African primary resistance movements, see Ranger (1986).

25 Expectably, Aponte is not the only one given this kind of modernistic workover by well-meaning historians. Speaking about the leaders of the last major slave rebellions in the British Caribbean before emancipation, Craton (1982, 251–52; emphasis added) emphasizes the rationality of their own political aspirations and duly notes how they "relied *cleverly* on millenarian tactics, employing the Bible, preaching, and oaths *to sway a susceptible people,* and used *convenient rumors that they themselves knew to have been untrue, unlikely, or half-truths.* In sum, the rebellions occurred because the leaders were able to mobilize the slaves, harnessing their discontent, exploiting their potential for retaliatory violence, and offering fulfillment for their deepest dreams." How embarrassing, then, to think of such instances as Nat Turner's rebellion, where the leader survived long enough to tell his executors that he had taken on Christ's yoke in fighting the Serpent at the end of days! Nat Turner's riposte to a Southhampton magistrate provides a good antidote to this particular version of what E. P. Thompson (1968) once called *the enormous condescension of posterity:* "I see, sir, you doubt my word" Turner said. And then he continued, "but can you not think" that "the same ideas and strange appearances about this times in the heavens might prompt others, as well as myself, to this undertaking?" (cited in Aptheker 1963, 305–6). What he was referring to was both biblical prophecy and the solar eclipse of February 12, 1831, which had sent him and his followers on their fateful path toward attacking the appropriately named county seat Jerusalem. It is hard indeed to make out the prescient scheming of a crafty folk intellectual in these words.

26 "La primera [pintura] donde se figuran dos exercitos en acción de batallas y haciendo se fuego mesclando en la de la dra. varios Negros: y así mismos en la oja qe. continua a la propria mano se notan soldados blancos, y negros uno de estos a cavallo con la cavesa de uno de aquellos en la punta de una hasta, y otro negro igualmente q. tiene una cavesa cortada arrojando sangre hayandose aquí en citua-ción, de vencidos los 'blancos.' "

27 Chacón may have been telling the truth. Aponte seems to have produced the book only on special occasions, otherwise shielding it from the eyes of those who, like

Chacón, could read but were, perhaps, not meant to be initiated into its secrets or have a share in the power that these images conveyed. As I shall argue below, it seems likely that Aponte invested his book with meanings rather different from those conventionally associated with books as a means of communication.

28 As with the repeatedly mentioned "General Salinas," the scribe present on this occasion apparently still did not grasp the connection of the portrait with the famous Haitian revolutionary leader, for in the document the name appears as "Laubertú" (Franco 1977, 172).

29 I hasten to preface the following remarks with the caveat that, in "reading" Aponte's explanations of his images, I am necessarily moving into alien intellectual terrain. Apart from the general problem of translating his statements back into visual forms, art historians will undoubtedly find my interpretations naive.

30 "En estos se hace presente el autor del libro en su retrato figurando al pecho un Laurel de fidelidad palma pr. victoria de parecer un compas—á la izquierda se advierte el banco de carpintería donde se trabajó el referido Libro manifestándolo el blanco y la infancia representada pr. una figura de niño atada á una columna y en la plana del frente un rostro de anciano qe. significa atarse la infancia recuerdo de antiguedad, se ven igualmente, sobre el banco tintero, regla y botes de pintura—Así á la mano dra. en lo inferior aparecen dos Indios sustentando las almas, la Ciudad de la Havana en la boca del Morro pr. la salida del declarante el año del mil setecientos ochenta y dos qe. se noto arriba pa. la imbación de la isla de providencia qe. se ve pintada a la dra. con sus callos inmediatos Buques conductores de las compañías de morenos qe. saltó en tierra á las ocho de la mañana abriendo un monte como de una legua. pr. el mismo callo y durmiendo aquella noche á la orilla de los arrecifes frente al Pueblo hasta la tarde sigte. qe. pasamos al muelle de la Aduana y se alojaron en el Castillo del Fuerte . . . habiendo procedido á todo esto las Captitulaciones."

31 Strongly reminiscent of the iconography of the vanitas complex that gained increasing popularity in Spain during the *siglo de oro* and may have reached Aponte in various derivative forms.

32 The *Calendario manual y Guía de Forasteros* (1795) mentions a Capitán Antonio Soledad as the commander of the "Batallón de Morenos Libres" of Havana.

33 "Á la izquierda está figurado el dios de los bientos. Esta frente a la boca de Cabañas qe. se haya debajo rotulado con el Ingenio de D. Gonzalo de Herera y el Torreon del Mariel el muelle de tablas en la parte inferior, y el de D. José María Escovar Callo titulado de Pu . . . y algunos barcos de pescadores mas á la dra. La Diosa Velona en su carro tirado de dos cavallos indiciando la ansta, á la batalla dada por el Capn. Joaquín de Aponte abuelo del qw. declara en el Torreon de Marianao á seis sientos hombre y un . . . ton de Ingleses qe. desembarcaron allí mismo quedando prisioneros todos excepto el milor qe. murió y se pinta en esta disposición con bestido encarnado con el pie del mismo Torreon sobre el qual hay una Fragata qe. los condujo á dho. parage. Junto al Torreon y serca del muerto hay algunos soldados morenos qe. le hicieron fuerza y otro a cavallo qe . . . el

Tente. Ermengildo de la Luz mas á la dra. sobre unos arrecifes estan pintados el Sub Tente. José Anto. Escoval y el resto de la Compañía de morenos en demonstración de llebar unos hombres blancos pricioneros qe. fueron los Ingleses los quales entraron en esta Ciudad á las seis de la mañana traidos pr. Nicolas Aponte hijo del nominado su abuelo qe. tambien se ha figurado á cavallo, dho. abuelo serca de una bandera qe. bajo la mano de un León escondido en la mayor parte de su cuerpo dentro de una concabidad."

34 See Rigol (1982, chap. 4). Although we do not possess a pictorial record of this early popular art form, the profusion of such murals in nineteenth-century Havana was remarked on quite frequently by foreign visitors, passing an almost unanimous judgment, not only on their "ludicrous" character and crude execution, but also on their concentration in the largely black "suburbs." See, e.g., Jameson (1821, 62), Abbot (1971, 126), or Ballou (1854, 156–57). That this popular tradition did not exhaust itself with the images of wildlife, domestic activities, or stereotypical figures like *el heroe español* or *el buen amigo* described by these authors but responded sensitively to ideological and political currents is shown by the fact that, in 1812 (the very year of Aponte's arrest!), a Don Vicente Segundo was denounced for having commissioned a mural of seditious content and that, during the Spanish War of Independence against Napoleonic France, "the traditional announcements that covered the walls of Spanish merchants disappeared under the most grotesque manifestations of an exalted patriotism that depicted Maret [i.e., Hugues-Bernard Maret, Napoléon's secretary of state] as having fallen into the claws of the Spanish lion or the imperial [French] eagles as fallen at the feet of Fernando the Beloved" (Evelio Govantes in Rigol 1982, 48–49).

35 In humanistic art theory, *muda metafora* refers to an allegorical or symbolic image lacking a conceit: the *picta poesis* (for discussions of the terminology, see Praz 1964; and Gallego 1972). Aponte probably meant that he intended to turn it into an *impresa* or *emblema* but had not gotten around to devising the epigrammatic text (i.e., the *décima*) that he intended to insert.

36 "El júbilo del Capn. Aponte a Dios al Rey representado en el León con la bandera ó la Patria qe. se figura en una India conducida en brasos de quatro, tambien Indios, otra muger con dos tambores y otros bueltos del frente al Mairel qe. se llamaba así el mismo Indio. El júbilo de Aponte buelve á decir está significado en una décima muda metafora cuya colocación debía ser en el blanco superior tiene diez líneas echas con lápiz; se significa por el arbol puesto abajo en medio de las aguas y florido con llamas qual estas prodijioso . . . ben . . . sobre florido gajo se derrama.—De Aponte al Dios Rey y á la Patria el amor como fuego arde en vivas llamas. Oculto á buestras vistas su ardor rompiendo de las Aguas el fuerte muro respira yamas en humo puro. La pintura qe. sigue arriba con la luna al estremo concluye la alucion del mismo arbol con las armas de la Ciudad de la Havana y un Aguila sobre otro arbol en adorno de la figura."

37 The name recalls the Renaissance genre of humanistic "hieroglyphics," taking its origin, perhaps, from the discovery of the *Hieroglyphica* of Horapollo in 1419 and

their ultimate popularization by Piero Valeriano in his *Hieroglyphica, sive de Sacris Aegyptorum aliarumque Gentium* (1566). Rigol's description of these pictures, however, makes clear that they much rather represented an American version of (the quite closely related forms of) emblematic imagery that had enjoyed an immense popularity in seventeenth-century Spain (as indeed in all of Europe) and seem to have experienced a sort of revival in the late eighteenth century—not the least in the context of the French Revolution (see Praz 1964; Levitine 1959; Gallego 1972; Santiago et al. 1980; and Renouvier 1863). For a detailed analysis of the iconological sources and social context of origin of an example of late-seventeenth-century emblematic mortuary art from Sevilla (Valdés Leal's *Jeroglíficos de nuestras postrimerías* of the Hospital de la Caridad), see Brown (1978). These as well as others of Valdés Leal's famous illustrations of the Renaissance idea of the *ars moriendi* (see Gallego 1972, 24) may—despite their incomparably more complex nature—represent a precursor to or perhaps even a direct source of inspiration for the popular Cuban jeroglíficos.

38 The mortuary celebrations of at least three eminently prominent personages in the course of which the display of jeroglíficos is documented fall within the period during which Aponte seems to have created his libro de pinturas: it is, thus, likely that Aponte personally witnessed the public rites attending the translation of Columbus's ashes in 1796 or the obsequies held in Havana on receipt of the notice of the death of Don Luis de las Casas and the princess of Asturias, Doña María Antonia de Borbón, in 1801 and 1806, respectively (Rigol 1982, 52). (For the probable Spanish sources of the aesthetics of such elite mortuary displays, see Gallego 1972, 161ff.) The following description of the tarjetas fashioned for the memorial service of the former Capitán General Luis de las Casas gives a good clue to the conventions of genre, form, and symbolism within which Aponte framed the "jubilation" of his grandfather described above:

> In the targetas Don Luis appeared in the act of laying the foundations of the Casa de Beneficencia; in another one the deity Minerva led Las Casas to the temple of Glory, [while] the muse Calliope ordered those who marched along to render tribute of reverence while the Nymph Habana sadly sighs:
>
> See the air of sadness and mourning,
> Apollo pays the tribute of moaning
> may the orb fill itself with sorrow, weeping
> Casas, because of your death.
>
> (Fina García Marruz cited in Rigol 1982, 52)

39 See the discussion of ways of defetishizing the object character of works of art by viewing them as one type of resultant (and only one among others) of social practice in Williams (1980, 31–49).

40 Had Aponte's book survived, it might be well worth the effort of an art historian to check its imagery against such standard sources of emblematic design as Piero

Valeriano's *Hieroglyphica* (1st ed., 1556), Juán de Borja's *Empresas Morales* (1st ed., 1581), Hernando de Soto's *Emblemas Moralizadas* (1st ed., 1599), Sebastián de Covarrubias Horozco's *Emblemas Morales* (1st ed., 1610), or Diego de Saavreda Fajardo's *Idea de un príncipe político cristiano* (1st ed. ca. 1640) or, indeed, one of the many Spanish editions of or commentaries on the *Emblemata Alciati* (the first of which appeared in 1549) and Cesare Ripa's *Iconología* (1st ed., 1593). On the significance and editorial history of these works, see Praz (1964), Gallego (1972), and Santiago (1981).

41 This might have been less true had Aponte been a Spaniard of the siglo de oro, when European allegorical conventions had not yet become what Gallego (1972, 186) polemically calls "in effect a universal language, accessible to every *idiot* . . . petrifying at European courts of the eighteenth century"—a fact amply testified to by the frantic efforts of the French revolutionaries during the years I and II to subject this common pictorial language to an ad hoc semantic revaluation (see Hunt 1984). Yet, having produced such images as a free black artisan living in a long-neglected Spanish dependency at least a hundred years after the genre conventions from which he borrowed had consolidated in the metropole, he must be presumed to have, at least partly, authored the system of signification according to which he realigned the figurative and thematic elements that he derived from originally European sources.

42 The following passage summarizes the part of the record of Aponte's interrogation reproduced in Franco (1977, 122–27).

43 "Un carro tirado pr. mugeres qe. significan el día y la noche."

44 "Llamado tanbn. el Preste. Juan." Here, Aponte may have confused (or consciously combined?) two different personages: the mythical "Prester John" and the historical Ethiopian emperor Asnaf Sagad, known to the Europeans as "Claudius."

45 That is, the Order of the Knights of San Antonio, with whom Aponte was familiar from the *Grandezas de la Religion de S. Antonio en las partes de Etiopía, y Egypto*, appended to the *Vida y milagros . . . de San Atonio Abad*, a copy of which (most likely the 1760 ed.) he possessed.

46 "Habiendo los portugueses descubierto o conquistado la indicada parte del Orbe."

47 "Parecen arrollados y destruidos con el fuego."

48 Manuel de Godoy (1767–1851), minister of Spain. Godoy rose from the position of protégé of the queen to the de facto regent after the death of Carlos III. Praised for his role in the conclusion of the peace treaties of Basel (1795), he acquired the popular epithet *principe de la paz* and, in 1801, was awarded the title of *generalisimo.* Favored by Napoléon, he was ousted in the course of the Aranjuez riots in 1808 and forced into exile in France. Incidentally, this reference to Godoy gives us a good clue to the period during which Aponte must be presumed to have created his book.

49 On the analytic problems presented by what he calls the performance of the *parole* upon the *langue* within complex continua of (in this case, visual) discourse, see Pocock (1988, 1–34).

50 The subhead represents a quotation of a statement by a Yoruba seller of popular Hindu prints in Togo recorded by Drewal (1988, 45).

51 Even during its heyday, the Inquisition never seriously bothered to occupy itself with a backwater of the Spanish Empire such as Cuba had been until the late eighteenth century. Yet, as everywhere in the Americas, the French and Haitian Revolution did stir up the clerical as well as secular censorial apparatus. By 1793, Capitán General Luis de las Casas reported an order given in 1791 to prohibit the introduction of French books, and, by 1794, the virrey of Nueva Granada wrote to Spain about an inquiry from Las Casas as to the licit nature of a pamphlet entitled "Desengaños del hombre" (roughly translated as "Humanity disabused") (Driesch 1982, 165). For a general overview of censorship in eighteenth-century Spanish America, see Driesch (1982, 159–99). For a case study of censorship of the Cuban periodical press, see Jensen (1988). For pan-Caribbean attempts to suppress news of the French and Haitian Revolutions, see Scott (1986, 233–94).

52 The title of this book leaves room for fascinating speculations. For, whether Aponte knew as much or not, in all likelihood what he had in front of him was a derivative of the medical genre of guidebooks for pilgrims known as *Mirabilia Urbis Romae*, filtered through the late Renaissance sensibilities of none other than the famous architect Andrea Palladio (1508–80) and, of course, the Spanish translators, editors, and plagiarists who appropriated versions of Palladio's immensely popular text (see the appendix). This is borne out by Aponte's statements concerning precisely those locations and monuments that Palladio mentioned. Descriptions of the churches that Aponte (see below) calls San Esteban de los Indianos and Santa Maria del Pueblo, thus, are found in Palladio's *Descritione de le Chiese di Roma*, while the Colossus of Apollo and the tomb of Caius Sixtus pertain to its companion volume *L'Antichita di Roma*.

53 This could, of course, have been just about any *historia Natural:* a chronicle of the conquista such as Acosta's *Historia natural y moral de las Indias* or Oviedo's *Historia general y natural de las Indias;* a version of the standard texts of early European geography such as Pliny's *Historia Naturalis*, Pomponius Mela's *Cosmographia*, or Solinus Polyhistor's *De mirabilibus mundi;* or even a genuine natural history of the Enlightenment. The title given in the document, however, leaves some ground for speculation about whether it might have been Antonio Parra's *Descripción de diferentes piezas de Historia Natural, las más del ramo marítimo, representadas en setenta y cinco láminas*, published in Havana in 1787. There are, however, at least two specific problems with this identification; these are discussed in the appendix.

54 As is detailed in the appendix, this book presents an intriguing problem. Did *Arte Nebrija* refer (as is most probable) to one of the popular Spanish commentaries to Antonio de Nebrija's *Gramatici introductionis latinae explicitae* (1481–), which are

known to have existed in American editions since at least the second half of the seventeenth century, or to the exceedingly rare *Gramatica Castellana* published in 1492, of which only one other utterly corrupt edition is known to have been published in Spain before the nineteenth century? The first solution is much more likely, yet, as Aponte himself not only testified but amply proved in the course of his interrogation, he did not read Latin. Could it be that he had acquired it in the hope of making sense of, e.g., Latin inscriptions that he encountered in European sacred imagery?

55 If anything, Aponte's literacy itself was exceptional. Jensen (1988, 21) cites estimates setting the general literacy rate in early-nineteenth-century Cuba at 10–12 percent, and notes that the *gente de color* were excluded from primary schools, not to speak of institutions of higher learning.

56 Although in 1812 the first Cuban sugar boom was just about to begin, even then the amount of ostentation displayed by Havana's white elite (see Knight 1977a; Hugh Thomas 1971, chaps. 11, 12) must have been overwhelming for a man like Aponte. We can likewise assume that he was familiar with the strong iconolatric bent of popular Catholic worship in Cuba: since at least the late sixteenth century, the Hispanic complex of the *inventio* of miracle-working images had taken root in Cuba and continued to flourish with only slightly diminished force in the late eighteenth century and the early nineteenth (see Ortiz 1975). (For the Spanish background, see, e.g., Christian [1981].) Moreover, as a *diputado de Nuestra Señora de los Remedios* who preserved copies of royal *cédulas* pertaining to the law of associations, Aponte certainly was aware of the fact that the written word, and especially printed matter issuing from the metropole, could confer power and legitimacy.

57 One of the most intriguing examples of this tendency to endow books with a sense of the extraordinary paraded by Goody, incidentally, is an African American one. Its general theme, furthermore, appears to have been a topos among African writers in eighteenth-century England. Here is Olaudah Equiano's version of his encounter with the "magic" of the printed word: "I had often seen my master and Dick [a fellow slave] employed in reading, and I had a great curiosity to talk to the books as I thought they did, and so to learn how all things had a beginning: for that purpose I have often taken up a book and have talked to it and then put my ears to it, when alone, in hopes it would answer me: and I have been very much concerned when I found it remained silent" (cited in Goody 1968, 206). Aponte was clearly beyond that stage. Yet, although he had realized, not only the basic rationality of the communicative purposes of books, but also their quality as timeless *repositories* of information, it is not altogether unlikely that he perceived the act of *making* a book in a somewhat different, much less rational way. I would further like to draw attention to the fact that Equiano (even if, as Gates [1988, 127–69] argues, his account of the "talking book" may represent an African American literary commonplace) seems to have sensed that books somehow bridged the gap between the present and a potentially significant past: when

expecting to learn "how all things had a beginning" (as Equiano put it), was Aponte perhaps thinking of cosmogonic or etiological explanations for the present state of the strange world into which history had catapulted him? Equiano himself eventually seems to have found such explanations in predestinarian strains of Methodist Christianity. Aponte's taste, it seems, was far more catholic—in both senses of the word.

58 "El treinta y seis indica la edificación de Roma, por Romulo su primer Rey: el campo Marcio con algunos soldados vencedores á las puertas de la Ciudad Casas de los Reyes el coloso de Apolo, puerta de San Pablo y sepulcro de Cayo Sexto. El treinta y siete comensado por la segunda representa al Papa Clemente . . . con un Cardenal y otro religioso de la orden de San Benito ambos morenos, el primero nombrado Jacobo y el segdo. sin nombre y bivliotecario de su Santidad."

59 This reference to the Church of Santo Stefano degli Indiani derives from Andrea Palladio's *Descritione de le Chiese, Indulgenze, & Reliquie de Corpi Santi, che sonno in la Città de Roma* (1554), often published together with his *L'Antichità di Roma* under the title *Le cose maravigliose dell'alma città di Roma* or similar such allusions to the (by then ancient) genre of *Mirabilia Romae* (Howe 1991). Aponte obviously refers to a Spanish version of this very popular book when he speaks of a "Foreigner's Guide to Rome." Yet his use of precisely that name—San Estéban de los Indianos—for this church, located, as Palladio (see Howe 1991, 88) indicated, behind Saint Peter's cathedral in the Borgo Vaticano, presents a remarkable puzzle: as Howe (1991, 156 n. 24) indicates, this church later became known as Santo Stefano degli Abissini or dei Mori! Needless to say, this change in name would no less than confirm Aponte's larger scheme of things. Yet, if the seventeenth-century compilation of Palladio's and other works that he perused reflected this (as would be possible), why would he have used the original name in his interrogation?

60 "Que haviendo venido á esta Ciudad de España un negro cuyo nombre ignora, el qual tenía el libro de la historia gral. y le instruyó a cerca de ambas figuras en razon de hallarse el declarante formando entonces esta pintura: qe. el qe. absuelve ha leydo el libro de la vida de San Antonio Abad, donde hay mucho de lo figurado en este papel: y la guía de forasteros de Roma en que se da noticia del Templo qe. exciste en la misma Ciudad titulada San Esteban de los Yndianos detras de la Catedral de San Pedro lo qual demuestra la parte superior del numero que se explica acia la derecha."

61 "Siguen a la derecha del mismo numero treinty y siete el Padre Pereira Carmelita, el Padre Obiedo Jésuita qe. fue preposito de lengua latina en Abicinia continúa la pintura de un Cardenal deteniendo á los padres Jesuitas Yllescas y Maseo con su conductor, porqe. eran contrarios de los de Abicinia = Sigue una puerta fabricada por el sumo Pontifice Pio quarto y el Templo de Santa María del Pueblo, á cuya puerta estan tres morenos en trage de eclesiasticos."

62 "Preguntado con qe. objeto se pintaron esos con semejantes vestiduras, y si en

Roma donde ha dho. existir el templo los hay, dijo: qe. se colocaron alli como el lugar propio de sacerdotes; y que se persuade los hay de esta condicion por haver oido á los reverendos padres Fray Diego de Soto y Fray Rafael Miranda á su vuelta de Roma referir qe. los vieron en un concilio á que asistieron predicando la Basilica un moreno que traía el Gral. de Abicinia qe. tambien concurrió: con la advertencia de que no oyó el declarante inmediatamente á los Padres Soto y Miranda sino á otros qe. lo conversaban como referido por aquellos."

63 For we might, with considerable justification, say the same of Aponte's contemporary and fellow artisan-intellectual William Blake. Just imagine a scenario in which Blake's exegesis on some of the more obviously counterhegemonic aspects of his work would have reached us only through channels comparable to those that preserved the "tracks" (in Bloch's [1953] sense) of Aponte's thought. Had Blake come to be known to us through his involvement in a major instance of sedition—and there were plenty of them in Blake's London, from the Gordon Riots to the Cato Street Plot—what would we make of the records of his vision uncovered in the course of an inquest trying to prove his guilt on the basis of the *Visions of the Daughters of Albion* or *The Four Zoas?*

64 In many ways, Lewis's case recalls the ambiguous contrasts between pastoral innocence / primitive backwardness and civilization / corruption afforded by emblematic images about country and city that came to structure Western experiences of modernization (Williams 1973).

65 For a spectacular attack on the long-standing tendency to extricate the cultures of San-speaking groups from the history of the wider social field of the Kalahari, see Wilmsen and Denbow (1990).

66 Clearly, sixteenth-century Friulian inquisitors—and one certainly would not envy them for it—had to deal with people whose intellectual pastimes included the casual perusal of copies of Boccaccio and the Qur'an (readily available as it was in Venice, which was also, not incidentally, one of the largest European markets in African slaves by that time). But this is not all: more troubling, perhaps, is the fact that, to their chagrin, the discourse of the "folk" appeared to reverberate with echoes of heresies that had been on the record for centuries. That Menocchio's views seemed to recall the Manichaean heresy or the problems posed by Origines's speculations about the nature of divinity could certainly be due to a case of accidental convergence. But, discounting this very real possibility, it is not necessary to write off the analogies drawn by the inquisitors as mere figments of a literate imagination capable of drawing on an archive of persecution in order to realize that, by the sixteenth century, the distinction between oral and literate, elite and popular discourses had largely become moot in Menocchio's world: what we face in his case are the palimpsest-like results of centuries of transcourse.

67 There was, e.g., on p. 8 or 9 of his book, an image of a young woman holding a scroll reading "Mi hijo la Paz es echa" (My son, peace is made), which he said he had encountered on a fan. The image "appearing accommodable [to his pur-

poses], he cut it from a fan and made it serve in the way it is encountered in his work" ("pareciéndole acomodable . . . la quitó de un abanico y la hiso servir según la encontre á su obra") (Franco 1977, 128).

68 The passages referred to are found in Franco (1977, 155–56).

69 "Por que mescló la destrucción del exercito de senaqueril con la *invacion* de Tarragona no teniendo conexion una y otra" (Franco 1977, 156).

70 "Que aunque no juegan ambos sucesos, puso lo de senaqueril por razon de Historia como todo los demas del libro: y están dibididos los lugares por un mar ancho aun sinembargo de parecer estrecho en la pintura" (Franco 1977, 156; emphasis added).

71 Were we to follow Bernal's (1987) interpretation, this should come as no surprise. For the problem itself may well have been a product of the nineteenth-century racialization of the ancient Mediterranean world.

72 Peel's rough definition—as apparently the Yoruba concept itself—is, of course, vague enough to fit the idea of titled offices in quite a wide variety of African societies.

73 See the classic analyses by Bloch (1961) and Kantorowicz (1957).

74 Reinventing, as they did, classical antiquity within a humanist mold of ideation from received scraps of information. For an example closer to Aponte's day and age, see Parker (1969).

75 Once more, it will not do to situate Aponte's authorship within any clearly delimitable stream of cultural transmission. The Christian tradition of which he availed himself—most clearly through his perusal of the books on the life and miracle of Saint Anthony and Marian adulation—was in itself a centuries-old palimpsest through which Egyptianizing forms of knowledge ranging from late Roman and Byzantine times to the recent present shone brightly: long-standing Isiac elements in Catholic Mariolatry, the veneration of North African saints and church fathers, baroque pictorial conventions fusing the symbolism of Christ, the archangels Michael, Gabriel, and Saint George with Horus-Harpocrates, Thoth, and Anubis—echoes of all this would have reverberated through the pages that Aponte read. The Spanish edition of Palladio's texts on the *Mirabilia Romae* (themselves originally recensions of a medieval genre) could only have amplified this transhistorical consonance of heterogeneous discourses. Although it is impossible to tell what changes the translator introduced, this book quite probably featured at least glimpses (perhaps even in the form of illustrations—which Palladio's original texts lacked) of the Egyptian artifacts in Hadrian's villa, Nilotic scenes in gardens, temples, and mosaics, the Egyptianizing columns in the nave of Santa Maria in Trastévere, the profusion of obelisks, sphinxes, and pyramids. Just as relevant might be the Egyptianizing symbolism reintroduced, along with the mysteries of hieroglyphic writing, into the center of Catholic Christendom by Athanasius Kirchner and like-minded Counter Reformation hermeticists under the pontificates of Innocent X and Alexander VII, or the fantastic architectural visions of Bernini and Piranesi. Finally, although Aponte's links to Masonic

circles are hard to substantiate, there is no question that this Afro-Cuban contemporary of Mozart, Cagliostro, and Mesmer understood the linkages between Solomonic and Isiac mysteries and their importance for instantiating a non-European origin for the powers wielded by the Spanish sovereign. For expositions of the issues involved in tracing the Egyptianist heritage on which Aponte may have drawn, see Iverson (1961), Yates (1964), and Curl (1994).

76 The coming of "la Reyna Sabá" to Jerusalem was depicted on p. 44 of Aponte's book (Franco 1977, 154).

77 The latter incident refers to chap. 19 of the edition of *La vida y milagros . . . de San Antonio* that Aponte may have read.

78 The description of this image on pp. 46 and 57 of the book is found in the records reproduced in Franco (1977, 157–58).

79 Whether this is the biblical King David is questionable, not only because of the title *principe*, but also because Aponte calls him "hijo de Sta. Elena." Much rather, it seems that the figure whom Aponte had in mind here was the Ethiopian emperor Lebna Dengel Dawit I (1382–1411), who of course did claim Solomonic descent. The favorite wife of his youngest son, Zera Yaqob, who succeeded to the throne in 1434, bore the name Elleni (also Helena or Illeni) and was well known to the Europeans for a letter that she wrote to the Portuguese king offering Ethiopian support against the spread of Islam (Prouty and Rosenfeld 1981). Most likely, Aponte's source for these names was the *Vida . . . de San Antonio Abad.*

80 Again, this need not be the biblical Moses but perhaps the Abyssinian church father Moses of the fourth century A.D. (see Snowden 1970, 209ff.).

81 "Pa. no recibir nada con ellos."

82 Again, the most obvious source appears to have been the 1760 edition of the *Vida . . . de San Antonio,* in particular the more martial aspects of the text *Grandezas del principe de los Anacoretas, y Religion de nuestro Padre San Antonio el Magno en las partes de la Etiopia, y Egypto* appended to it.

83 Once more, Calderón's formulations (Curtius 1936, 93) are apposite: when painting "depicts battle, it stimulates [political] undertakings; when incendiaries, it incites anguish of horrors; when storms, it saddens; when good weather, it delights; when ruins, it worries; when [different] countries, it entertains; when gardens, it relaxes; when the postmortal glory of generous heroes, it corroborates their exploits in their portraits and incites the guileless envy of their deeds; when subjects of learning, [it stimulates] the dignified pursuit of their study; when holy men, the glorious imitation of their virtues; and finally, when in reverent pictures, it presents to our eyes the most arcane mysteries of the Faith, which dormant heart would not wake to the quiet sounds of ritual, reverence, and respect?"

84 There is no telling to what extent Aponte was able to form a conception of the incredibly violent processes of surplus appropriation that had begun to devour thousands of Africans in the fields and plantations surrounding Havana while he was composing his book. But we can well imagine him observing the ghastly transactions at the *barracones* of Havana's main slave market that had emerged on

the grounds of the old army barracks constructed between the calle Consulado and calle Alameda in 1779, in fewer than twenty minutes' walking distance from Aponte's house (Torre 1857, 77). Even though the phase of the "grán barbarie" (Castellanos and Castellanos 1988, 130) still lay in the future (annual Cuban slave imports would begin to exceed 20,000 only after Spain removed the final barriers to free trade in 1815), Aponte must have been aware that, after the slump in slave importation through the port of Havana in the troublesome years of 1808 and 1809, more than 6,000 slaves were annually funneled through these barracoons in the course of the last years of his life, and he may have remembered the year 1802 when some 13,800 arrived in Havana (Castellanos and Castellanos 1988:142). At the same time, Aponte would surely have witnessed the increasing ostentation displayed by an emerging merchant and planter elite and may well have come to perceive some of the mechanisms that were beginning to transform Cuba's agricultural sector into a veritable space of death.

85 Erdman (1977, 230ff.). See also Richard and Sally Price's excellent introduction to their edition of Stedman's original 1790 manuscript (Price and Price 1988).

86 Their fears were by no means unfounded: by May 1793, a group of 110 imprisoned republicans (most of them black) from Fort Dauphine was shipped to Havana (Scott 1986, 241–42), and, in 1795, the first largely black insurrectionary movement inspired by the French and Haitian Revolutions, "la conspiración de Morales," was uncovered.

87 According to Morales Padrón (1972, 353–54), the trial records mention at least five black militia officers, one common soldier, and two slaves as having been implicated in the conspiracy. The Bassave, Luz, and Infante group may have been an important source from which information about the slavery-related debates in the Spanish Cortes diffused into the black barrios. On the other hand—as the constitution of the "Republic of Cuba" drafted by Infante (Pichardo 1973, 1:258–59) shows—these Cuban "Jacobins" were all but in favor of emancipation and racial egalitarianism!

88 As the record of the inquest shows, Aponte knew of the American, French, and Haitian Revolutions, the career of Godoy, the Napoleonic wars in Europe, and the political chaos in Spain. It is more than likely that he was aware of the hurried evacuation of Columbus's ashes from Santo Domingo to Havana in 1796 and witnessed the riots directed against the French refugees in 1809 as well as the public execution of Joseph Bonaparte's emissary Manuel Alemán in 1810. Given that the free-press legislation of the exiled Spanish Cortes took effect in Cuba in early 1811, Aponte may well have known of the revolutionary events that had begun to unfold on the Spanish American mainland since the spring of 1810.

89 "Que el venia á conquestar esta tierra pa. la gente de color como lo havian hecho ya en otros muchos."

90 References to this "general negro" appear again and again in the documents of the trials. What they pertained to was the fact that the brigadier Gil Narcisco, another veteran of the Haitian revolutionary wars, and like Jean Francois at least tempo-

rarily in Spanish service against Toussaint's troops, in 1812 was being held in the fortress Casa Blanca. For good reasons, Judge Rendón tried to establish a connection between Aponte's group and this man whose fame and military experience might have helped catalyze the kind of massive popular uprising for which the conspirators seem to have hoped and that the authorities seemed to fear.

91 Mysterious because no one seemed to know where exactly these mountains were. Might they have been the Catalonian Montserrat of Aponte's imagination? A site of Saint Anthony's miraculous activities during his legendary sojourn in Spain?

92 For a perhaps even more striking example, the opening of the royal caskets at Saint Denis in October 1793, see also Kennedy (1989, 206ff.). Is the revolution advanced by such obviously noninstrumental actions as throwing bones in the street? The answer would seem to be yes.

93 He would not have been the first to do so either: two of the leaders of the 1796 revolt in Dutch Curaçao had taken on the names Toussaint and Rigaud (Julius Scott 1991, 47).

94 This is amply borne out in yet another influential formulation designed to solve the vexing relation between instances of individual practice and their presumably collective templates: Bourdieu's (1977) notion of *habitus* as a "generative grammar of behavioral patterns" can, thus, hardly be taken adequately to account for concrete instances of practice in social fields less homogeneous and bounded than that depicted in Bourdieu's account of Kabylia as a thoroughly oversocialized place. Bourdieu (1979, 252–53) himself concedes elsewhere that access to the means by which people in any but what he calls "minimally or undifferentiated" (*sic*) societies ("sociétées peu ou pas différenciées") appropriate their own cultural heritage must be seen as problematic and a potential source of power ("capital culturel," "instrument de domination"). If so, however, the whole conceptual edifice obviously breaks down in the kinds of social worlds with which both Ginzburg and I are concerned (and, one might suspect, elsewhere as well—to wit, e.g., the crucial contributions of feminist criticism to the political anthropology of what used to be called *acephalous societies*). If it seems unrealistic to claim for the sixteenth-century Friuli that individual social performance of the "popular classes" was rooted in a past so ancient, so "equally mastered by all members of the group" (Bourdieu 1979, 253), so encrusted with profoundly mystified endogenous power relationships, and therefore—ultimately—so hegemonic that the cultural models of and for such performance were no longer discursively available for reflection or contestation and alternatives to them inconceivable, then such claims are patently absurd in the case of Aponte's Havana.

95 Even if they be "rooted" as Ginzburg (1983b) asserts following a (questionable) lead by Murray (1921) in *prehistoric* pan-Eurasian (and, in his case, shamanistic) traditions. For a more general critique of such imputations from a Wittgensteinian perspective, see Clark (1983).

96 Given the extremely heterogeneous and changing geographic origins of Cuba's African slave imports (see Morgan 1997), by the early nineteenth century literally

dozens of African languages must have been spoken on the streets of Havana. We do not have any studies comparable to the linguistic inventory produced by the Moravian missionary Oldendorp (1777) in the Danish Virgin Islands in the late 1760s, but, if Oldendorp's estimation that upward of twenty African languages were still spoken by the slaves on St. Thomas may serve as a guide, one would expect a similar situation to obtain in Havana some four decades later. There can be little doubt that for many Africans in early-nineteenth-century Havana—as Paul Lovejoy (1997, 6) puts it—"the African side of the Atlantic continued to have meaning" as a reference point for interpreting their experiences. We have good indications that, by the time of Aponte's birth, tendencies toward forms of ethnic aggregations among Africans in Havana—most vividly expressed in the context of the cabildos de nación—had resulted in the emergence of a variety of what, for lack of a better word, one might call socially differentiated *neo-African* cultural formations (Palmié 1991, 83–150; Palmié 1993; Brown 1993). Since 1792, the cabildos had been forced to relocate to the sprawling barrios extramuros outside the old walled city, and, even though we do not know the extent of Aponte's involvement in the lucumí cabildo Santa Barbara, also known as *Changó Teddún*, its activities would have been no less part of his everyday life in Pueblo Nuevo than his private perusal of the library of European literature and imagery that he had assembled over the years.

97 For one thing, we are not in a position to answer the crucial question of where, if at all, Aponte drew a line between Africa and Europe. The patent Ethiopianism of his oeuvre, thus, derived, not at all incidentally, entirely from European sources and in many ways prefigured the fashion in which (as Breiner [1985–86, 35] puts it) twentieth-century Rastafari perceive the Bible as "a recovered instrument, damaged by misuse"—a "subverted text" that needs to be released from its captivity at the hands of slaveholders and restored to its truthful meaning by strategic countersubversion.

98 See Harrison's (1993, 145–46) comments on the alleged "cultural instability" of Melanesian societies, which, in his words,

> may look [culturally] instable and entropic if we take individual sociocultural groups as our units of analysis, and assume that their fundamental problem was to ensure the continuity of their particular local traditions across the generations. From the viewpoint of any given group, one might indeed see constant discontinuity and change. But if we take *intergroup relations* as our focus, we see groups embedded in systems of trade and exchange and maintaining relations with each other by producing and exchanging a variety of goods including cultural or religious forms. There is no evidence that these regional systems themselves were prone to spirals of entropy.

99 See Pocock (1988, 33), who *really* is talking about the hegemony of Whiggish definitions of reality in eighteenth-century British politics:

Historians who stress, with much justice, the extent to which the Whig regime was a dictatorship by its ruling groups and classes are tempted to see the ruled as repressed and silent; deprived of the means of articulating a radical consciousness, they must accept the speech of their rulers or formulate modes of symbolic and semiotic opposition outside it (hence the debate as to how far crime was a mode of social protest). But this oligarchy was notoriously incompetent at thought control; the nobs and the mobs sometimes shouted and sometimes shot at each other, and we do not have to regard elite and popular culture as incapable of intertraffic.

100 That the police raids had foiled the charting of the potencia *Arupapá* at the last minute, so to speak, is evident from the fact that Blanco had already applied for its registration and a permit "para bailar diablito junto a la Muralla"—i.e., to conduct rites involving the participation of the *íreme* or *diablito,* a masked dancer personifying an ancestral presence.

101 He seems to have been referring to the first tierra or potencia de abakuá, Bakoko Efor, founded in Regla only three years earlier but active in Havana.

102 "Los jóvenes de su clase."

103 "Trataran de 'imitar a los bozales en sus usos y costumbres' " (Deschamps Chapeaux 1964, 101).

104 The majority of historical sources on abakuá use the term *ñáñigos* to refer to members of the society. Today, at least, it is not used by members of the association themselves, and it may always have carried somewhat pejorative connotations.

105 See López Valdés (1966). Moore (1988, 102, 305) claims that, during the 1960s, abakuá allegedly established control over the black market, which seems to have led to repeated clashes with the revolutionary government. I have not been able to corroborate this during my fieldwork on abakuá in Regla. Nevertheless, unlike the other Afro-Cuban religions with whose affairs the Ministério de Cultura is concerned, abakuá is dealt with by the (feared) Ministério del Interiór.

106 As Chailloux Cardona (1945) puts it, fire represented the traditional means of mass eviction. The 1802 fire started simultaneously in different parts of the barrio and came to destroy 1,332 houses, leaving 11,370 people homeless. Nor was it the only time Jesús María went up in flames: similarly suspect incidences of conflagration occurred in 1828 and 1856.

107 Early-nineteenth-century Havana was a spectacularly violent place. But its unsafe nature—much remarked on in both government statements and the reports of visitors to the city—derived as much from the amazing corruption (conceded even by its governors) of the police and military forces as from the activities of its residents (see Ortiz 1986, 192–208).

108 Ortiz's study of the curros first appeared in serial form in 1927 but was republished posthumously in an augmented version in 1986. It is to him that we owe an amazingly thorough (although not always entirely convincing) historical eth-

nography of this peculiar grouping. Apart from this seminal publication, the following remarks draw heavily on David Brown's imaginative interpretation of Ortiz's data (see Brown 1989, 34–39 and passim).

109 For another example, see White (1991, 185–206). Although they lack the local specificity of White's treatment of black urban culture in early republican New York City, Redicker (1988), Prude (1991), and White and White (1995a, 1995b) are useful, too. Tyler (1989) provides an intriguing early-twentieth-century counterpoint for New York City, as do Simpson (1955), Elkins (1977), Hill (1981), and Chevannes (1994, 119–70) in the case of Jamaica.

110 As early as 1621, Spanish legislation directed toward Cartagena de Indias specified that there were "many negroes and mulattoes whose unrest has caused deaths, robberies, crimes, and harms caused by the legal permission given to them to wear arms and knives as favorites or slaves of officers of the Inquisition, governors, judges, the clergy and military estate with whose help they take many liberties harmful to the public peace" (cited in Ortiz 1986, 190). What this ordinance obscured is that free blacks had long played a crucial role in the defense of port cities (a fact borne out by Aponte's own family history). Even though the increasing polarization of Cuban society along the lines of freedom/whiteness and unfreedom/blackness in the course of the island's sugar revolution and in the aftermath of the Haitian Revolution triggered the steady curtailment of the civil rights of free Afro-Cubans, as late as 1827 the municipal ordinances of Havana specified the right of free blacks to carry arms (Ciudad de la Habana 1827, 19).

111 According to Ortiz (1986, 236 n. 1), *mancaperro* designates a small, scaly reptile native to Cuba. Pichardo (1985, 404) gives the meaning of the word as denoting a species of worm or caterpillar (*Spirobolus grandis*) of greenish-black appearance.

112 For a general critique of "creolization" theories, see Mintz (1996). For a treatment of African American bodily signifying practices that dispenses with such troubling analogies, see Hill (1994).

113 On the "discovery procedures" that Ortiz used at the time, see Palmié (1998b).

114 Outrageous, that is, in the eyes of members of participants in the European (and, perhaps, African) source cultures.

115 The adoption of Jamaican musical styles such as ska into the cultural repertoire of otherwise staunchly racist British skinhead groups provides a telling case in point.

2. GENEALOGIES OF MORALITY

1 My use of this terminology is intended to circumvent the reificatory tendencies and presuppositions about orderliness and systematicity implicit in more conventional terms, such as *religion, religious tradition,* or *religious system.* I take it, not only to suggest a spectrum of internal variation in practical religion, but to signify the fundamental heterogeneity of an aggregate of notions and practices the degree of integration of which cannot simply be presumed but must be treated as an empirical problem.

2 Similarly, although perhaps less closely, associated with an indigenous taxonomy of *nanchons.*

3 On the misguided nature of such typologizing ventures, see Larose (1977), Richman (1992), and Costa Lima (1976).

4 Although imaginative and in many ways pathbreaking, Thompson's work (esp. Thompson 1983) epitomizes this tendency.

5 This is by no means a recent development. In both cases, the establishment of symbiotic relationships between priests and ethnographers can be traced back a considerable time—i.e., to the 1940s–1950s in Haiti and to at least the 1930s in Bahia.

6 See Matory (1999, 75), whose elegant case study on the agency of literate post-emancipation Afro-Brazilian returnees to Lagos in the creation of "Yoruba tradition" demonstrates that "the African dispora at times has played a critical role in the making of its own alleged African 'base line' as well."

7 The following speculations are based on assumptions akin to those Richard Price (1976) employed in correlating temporal differences in regional slave-importation patterns with linguistic data on modern maroon societies in order to arrive at a relative chronology of the formation of different maroon cultures. While both ventures must be regarded as highly speculative, the Cuban case presents the additional problem of conscious re-Africanization facilitated by access to ethnographic literature.

8 Oral tradition and some documentary evidence further indicate that the present forms of Yoruba-Cuban religion (i.e., modern regla ocha) consolidated in the late nineteenth century and the early twentieth.

9 Ironically, this very fact makes it easier to control transatlantic comparisons. For, owing to the early and intense contracts between western Central Africa and Europe and the almost continuous presence of missionaries in the region since the early sixteenth century, we are far less dependent on extrapolations from modern ethnographic accounts to gauge what exactly it is that we are comparing with our New World data.

10 Such as, e.g., the notion of "pantheonizable" divinities (*mpungus*) analogous to the gods (oricha) of regla ocha and assimilated into a (somewhat vague) system of equivalences with the individual characteristics of specific oricha.

11 Regionally datable—in my view—to at least the end of the nineteenth century. Although this is by no means unequivocal evidence, one might cite the fact that one of the key figures in the emergence of modern regla ocha, the lucumí priestess Ala Tuán, alias Timotea Albear (active before the turn of the twentieth century), was married to the headman of a *congo cabildo* named Ta Claro whose office may well have included religious functions (Fondo Ortiz, uncataloged file "Negros-Cabildos").

12 Similar to the function of the term *ocha* (or *Santería*) to designate practices related to the Yoruba-derived regla ocha, in contemporary parlance, *palo* (derived from

palo monte, the name of one of the better-known reglas de congo) commonly subsumes a wider range of Bantu-Cuban religious practices. In the following, I will occasionally refer to priests of Bantu-Cuban cults as *paleros*.

13 For comparable patterns of spatializing the distinction between *guinen* and *maji* in Haitian vodun, see Larose (1977).

14 The term derives from Kikongo: *mvumbi*, "corpse."

15 Exemplified, e.g., by lapping up liquids from calabash containers placed on the floor "like a dog" (a description that, not incidentally, relates to the common designation of the possessed person as *mbua*, "dog," in *lengua de congo* or *perro* in Spanish).

16 This notion seems to relate to ideas about the Yoruba-Cuban initiate's body as a vessel that is (or can be) filled with the god's presence. The ritual scarifications inflicted on the initiate into a congo cult would violate the integrity of such "sacred containers." A compromise solution is the so-called *jubilación*, in which a practitioner of regla ocha undergoes an attenuated form of the initiation rituals of palo monte. This may, e.g., be necessary when divination discloses the need to acquire (or the obligation to inherit) a nganga, i.e., a sacred objectivation central to the practices of the reglas de congo.

17 For African analogies to these views, see Verger (1965) and Matory (1991).

18 As I argue elsewhere (Palmié 1991), the discourse about the oricha draws on a highly differentiated set of idioms or modes of representing the relation between the gods and the natural and social world.

19 In practice, this pattern is considerably complicated by the fact that, apart from the main deity into whose cult a person is initiated, he or she simultaneously enters similar relationships with a whole series of oricha (likewise objectified in the receipt of sacred vessels condensing their presence and powers into a material container).

20 In many (if not most) western Central African languages, the term *nganga* and its various cognates signify the incumbent of a priestly role or commission. Why the term for the religious specialist was transferred in Cuba to the object that he (less often she) manipulates in ritual practice is not clear. Wyatt MacGaffey (personal communication) suggests that it may be based in a close, even visually concretized, identification between nkisi and nganga obtaining among the Bakongo.

21 Often, the resulting "compound" reflects, not a single act of creation, but a process of gradual accretion to an already complex "core."

22 Bakongo ethnography reflects varying conceptions of what kinds of spirits inhabit or activate minkisi objects. Laman (e.g., 1962, 67, 17) thought that nkisi spirits are associated with a particularly "old" type of ancestral spirit that has lost all genealogical connection to contemporary humans. Other minkisi (particularly those of the *kula* type) have been described as containing the spirits (*bankuyu*) of deceased sorcerers (*bandoki*) or their victims. For discussions of the problems surrounding the classification of minkisi spirits, see Janzen (1972) and MacGaffey (1977, 1983, 1988).

23 This symbolism of conception, gestation, and birth is carried even further. For it is facilitated by two sets of "parents": the human initiator (*padrino* or *madrina*) and a ritual attendant (*oyugbona*), on the one hand, and, on the other, a pair of differently gendered oricha (*padre* and *madre*) among which figures the deity into whose cult the person is being initiated.

24 The same informant used a spiritist vocabulary to explain why this may be so. Given the notion that spirits progress in the afterlife from "dark," "unclean," "impure," or "earthbound" stages to higher levels, one would necessarily seek out the grave of a person who led a bad life or died a "bad death," for such spirits are thought to actively seek relations with mortals. Remaining close to the earth, such spirits may attach themselves to humans, thereby affecting their lives in a negative manner. Once this is diagnosed by divination or in the course of a spiritist séance, it can be remedied by giving the spirit the kind of attention that will foster his or her progress in the afterlife (e.g., holding spiritist masses for it, lighting candles, etc.). Paleros, however, seek out such spirits of their own accord. Their aim is, not to aid the spirit in its moral progression, but to harness its afflictive potential to their personal goals.

25 This procedure corresponds with Laman's (1962, 74) descriptions of how bankuyu (spirits of dead sorcerers or their victims) are lured and captured for incorporation into nkisi objects: "The bankuyu are found in the burial ground, especially by the grave of a powerful chief or a great nganga. All sorts of tricks are resorted to in order to soften the heart of the nkuyu and entice it, such as putting out appetizing food and palmwine so that a piece of raffia cloth may be thrown over the nkuyu. Thus caught, it can be incorporated into the image or nkisi."

26 An exception are so-called *promesas,* i.e., promises made to the gods that are fulfilled on return of specified "favors" (often revolving around the restoration of health). These, however, are closely modeled on (and sometimes combine with) the cult of the saints in Cuban folk Catholicism.

27 Although usually classed according to more generalized types—e.g., *Siete Rayos, Sarabanda, Tiembla Tierra, Lucero Mundo, Chola Guengue,* and so forth—each nganga is an individually named presence.

28 One (of several) explanations for why menstruating women are not allowed to come into close spatial proximity to a nganga is that the nfumbi would similarly acquire a taste for their blood and begin to feed on them.

29 Compare the following remarks by MacGaffey (1986, 160) with Ortiz's rendering of a homologous insult quoted above: "Nkondi could also be provoked by using as incantation (*ndokolo*) the standard obscenity, *E Nkondi! ngw'aku!* or *Mbimba!* meaning 'eat, lick your mother' and the like."

30 Apparently related to the Kikogo term *nganga ngombo,* "smell diviner" (Laman 1962, 75).

31 The term may relate to the so-called *mfunya* bundles (also called *mbua,* "dog") of *minkisi mi nloko,* i.e., minkisi used for vengeful magic (described by van Wing 1959).

32 There are, unfortunately, good grounds for suspecting that Barnet's authorial role extended further than just editing Montejo's account (see Wentzlaff-Eggebert [1993] and the heated debate between Zeuske [1997b] and Barnet [1997]).

33 In contemporary parlance, *jugar* (lit. "to play") signifies the ritual manipulation of nganga objects. Being a cognate of the name of a modern regla de congo, *mayombe* can be read as a toponym, but it may also relate to the Kikongo terms for forest (*yombe*) and trance (*mayembo*). A third possibility is that the term directly refers to a particularly violent type of nkisi named *mayimbi* (Kikongo for "bird of prey") (MacGaffey 1993, 75).

34 Elsewhere, Montejo is more precise on how the capture of the victim of such rites is performed: "They followed him on a footpath and took the dust on which he stepped. This they kept and put it in the nganga or in a corner. As the sun went down, so would the life of the person diminish. And, at sunset, the person would be a little corpse" (Barnet 1984, 42).

35 Significantly effected by the proscription of the chiefs' right to execute and enslave—forms of depersonalization that, if in transmuted form, the colonial state now reserved for itself.

36 Commonly used as a designation of the colonial state, the term *Bula Matadi* (lit. "the rock breaker") appears to have been a praise name "given to a chief whose accession to the title was opposed by his fellow chiefs but who overcame them by his wealth and aggressiveness." It was "subsequently given to or appropriated by H. M. Stanley, the Free State, and the Belgian Congo as the indigenous term for 'the government'" (MacGaffey 1986, 35).

37 This interpretation would seem to fall in line with Monica Schuler's (1979) hypothesis that certain forms of Jamaican slave resistance—in particular the so-called Myal dance of the 1760s, which, according to contemporary witnesses, was said to protect against death caused by Europeans—may have represented variations on the theme of western Central African antiwitchcraft movements. Whether Schuler's data—deriving largely from postemancipation indentured laborers from Central Africa—can be extrapolated backward into the eighteenth century, however, remains open to question.

38 For a sample of representative sources, see Sandoval (1956, 349, 363), Bastian (1859, 273n), Axelson (1970, 267, 290), and Piersen (1977). MacGaffey (1968, 1972, 1978), Miller (1988, 4–5), Geschiere (1992, 1997), Austen (1993, 1995), Palmié (1995a), and Shaw (1997) provide contemporary assessments of such evidence.

39 On the perversion of African systems of justice in the course of the slave trade, see MacGaffey (1986, 202), Lovejoy (1983, 87, 126–27), and Shaw (1997).

40 Whether Crame's views on the instrumentalization of the enslaved human bodies drew on the ideas of Descartes and de la Mettrie or represented (as Joan Dayan [1995] might argue) a New World discovery of technologies of reducing humans to their embodiment is merely an academic question here, although one should note that Miller (1985, 48) traces the image of Africans as human machines to a

text referring to a New World context (Charlevoix's *Histoire de l'Isle espagnole de Saint-Domingue*, 1730–31).

41 Moreno refers to the decades between 1830 and 1860.

42 Moreno Fraginals's (1978, 2:88) calculations reveal a crude annual deathrate of 63 per thousand for western Cuban plantations during the period 1835–41. Yet, since it is not broken down by crop regime, this figure is hardly representative of the most brutal sector of Cuban agricultural slavery, sugar production. In the 1830s, Domingo del Monte conservatively estimated a deathrate of 80 per thousand for sugar estates and 20 per thousand for coffee plantations. Using the same data, David Turnbull (on the opposite side of the political spectrum) came up with deathrates of 150 per thousand on sugar plantations and 100 per thousand on coffee plantations (Pérez de la Riva 1979, 37).

43 This, of course, is not to deny that slaves also retaliated in ways less difficult to reconcile with Western notions of rationality. In her study of the contradictions that slavery engendered during the first Cuban War of Independence, Robert (1992, 182–83) presents the suggestive case study of a Camagüeyan slave's eight-year fight against an American engineer. After repeated instances of sabotage, arson, and running away, in 1869 the slave, José—well aware of the political situation—finally denounced the engineer, Douglas McGregor, to the Spanish troops as a rebel collaborator. Much to the dismay of everybody involved—excepting, of course, José—McGregor was initially sentenced to death by a Spanish court-martial and pardoned only because of the intervention of the American consul, Horatio Fox. In obvious alarm, Fox wrote to the local Spanish governor asking what political agenda was being served by giving credence to such denunciations: "Are not the Overseers and all the operatives on an estate liable to be tied and taken to the public jail, by these Negros on this very Estate, as Rebels?" (cited in Robert 1992, 183).

44 Extending this insight even further, Thoden van Velzen and van Wetering (1988) demonstrate how the "ethnogenesis" of Suriname's maroon groups may be understood as a process marked by (and in a sense coterminous with) ongoing struggles to "pantheonize" emergent corporate cults into the framework provided by rivaling, but socially more inclusive, "High God cults" or, conversely, to dismiss the disciplinarian regime of centralized priesthoods in favor of more particularistic sources of sacred power and authority.

45 The term clearly derives from Kikongo *mfumo*, "chief."

46 The following examples are drawn from Ortiz's (1956) pioneering—if sketchy—study of the *matiabos*. As will become obvious, my interpretation differs from his.

47 The author presumed that it served as a receptacle for the "ashes of the corpses of Spanish soldiers killed by the insurgent" ("Isla de Cuba" 1875, 2) and that the whitish matter encrusting the front of the object represented "a dead rooster likewise molded from the ashes of Spaniards that were sacrificed to the brutal hatred of the black rebels." This "reading" appears quite unlikely in the light of documented Central African and Afro-Cuban practices. There is little doubt,

however, that the object contained bilongo-type medicines among which may have figured human remains.

48 Like water gazing, possession trance, and other forms of contemporary Bantu-Cuban divination, the mpaka reveals intelligence unavailable to the normal sensory range of its user. It is used, e.g., to monitor the nfumbi's progress when sent out on mystical errands or to enable the tata nganga to see with the spirit's eyes.

49 On this issue, as well as for background information on the following remarks, see Cepero Bonilla (1976), Scott (1985, 47ff.), and Robert (1992) as well as Ferrer (1991) on the so-called Guerra Chiquita following the controversial Peace of Zanjón. Unfortunately—and for quite obvious reasons (a failed war of national liberation does not generate lists of veterans)—no study rivaling Zeuske's (1997a) analysis of Afro-Cuban participation in the region of Las Lajas in the second Cuban War of Independence exists for the so-called Ten Years' War.

50 For a detailed description of the contents of one such object confiscated by the Havana police, see Roche Monteagudo (1925, 198).

51 For a cogent exposition of the multiple connections of these events, see Helg (1995, 109–16) and Helg (2000). These issues are more fully explored in the following chapter.

52 Made all the more suspicious by these authors' reliance on (potentially overgeneralized) versions of the intellectualist arguments presented by Horton and De Craemer, Fox and Vansina.

53 With Herbert Baxter Adams (as cited and deftly reconstructed in Scott [1989, 680–81]), we might say that, in contemporary palo monte, "history is past politics and politics present history."

54 On the ambiguities of a single deity, Ogou, in Haitian religious thought and practice, see McCarthy Brown (1989).

55 The whole question of the so-called *derechos*—rights to reimbursement for ritual services notionally allocated to the gods instead of the priest—represents a touchy issue that deserves further investigation.

56 This is perhaps best exemplified by the so-called *afrocubanismo* movement and its modernistic celebration of the supposed authenticity of the primitive. Yet, while afrocubanista poetry and music may have "sought to define an ideological space that all Cubans, regardless of color and caste, could presumably inhabit on equal terms," afrocubanismo not only remained "the product of a predominantly white intelligentsia" (Kutzinski 1993, 154–55; cf. Morrison 1999) but had little (if anything) to do with contemporary Afro-Cuban cultural forms. The *jitanjafora* (African-sounding but otherwise meaningless phrases) so prominent in afrocubanista poetry are a case in point: Africanity here becomes a pure simulacrum, conjured up in the name of a political project that substitutes its own artistically elevated re-creation of primitive authenticity for the concrete cultural forms and practices from which it supposedly draws inspiration. For we should not forget that the afrocubanismo vogue coincides with massive campaigns against the more

uncivilized aspects of Afro-Cuban folk culture. It is, thus, a classic irony that, just as Moisés Simons's afrocubanist composition "El manisero" (better known as "The Peanut Vendor") was turning into a global hit, street vendors in Havana were coming under attack as a blemish on the capital's image as a modern city (Pérez 1999, 215). As Moore (1997, 146) puts it, the "disseminat[ion] of musical works that depicted Afrocubans as an important part of the nation, even as social reality continued to demonstrate their subjugation and exploitation," served both rhetorically to foreground "the commonalities of Cuban citizens" and to obscure "hierarchies of internal difference."

57 The newer literature on this issue is diverse, uneven, and (perhaps not surprisingly) largely in English. See, e.g., Martínez-Alier (1974), Booth (1976), Moore (1988), Palmié (1989), Kutzinski (1993), Helg (1990, 1995, 2000), Fernández (1996), de la Fuente (1995, 1998), de la Fuente and Glasco (1997), and Pérez Sarduy and Stubbs (2000).

58 Adechina (alias Remigio Herrera), the last African-born babalao (ifá priest) in Cuba, lived in Regla's calle Perdomo from at least 1891 until his death in 1905. The Fondo Ortiz (carpeta 35 "Brujos-Cuba-Historia" pieza 537) includes a remarkable photograph of this man who is nowadays regarded as the founder of ifá in Cuba. Although dressed in a formal suit and bow tie, both of his cheeks show three parallel horizontal scarifications. Nevertheless, what is noteworthy about this photograph may be, less the fact that Adechina's face bore such indelible marks of Africanity, than that the mode of self-representation that he, himself, chose depicts him, not as an African priest, but as a former bricklayer turned respectable property owner and citizen, a man clearly bridging two worlds. His daughter Joseta "Pepa" Herrera was to found one of the most important neotraditional cabildos of regla ocha of Havana in her native Regla in the early 1920s.

59 Irrespective of his defection in the early 1960s, in Regla Chuchu has nowadays assumed the role of a founding figure for twentieth-century abakuá. Elderly titleholders of local potencias told me in 1995 that he had always stayed close to the barracones of Regla to socialize with and acquire new "secrets" from incoming slaves. The problem with these narratives is that Chuchu was born in 1881—only a few years before the end of slavery in Cuba, and at least a decade after the last substantial illegal slave imports into the island. By the same token, however, the anachronism would seem to corroborate Fabelo's judgment, for, among other things, it represents a latter-day rationalization of Chuchu's religious stature.

60 On the founding of the first white potencia of abakuá in 1857, see Trujillo y Monagas (1882), Roche Monteagudo (1925, 4, 137), Ortiz (1952–55, 4:68–69), and Sosa Rodríguez (1982, 142). In the case of ocha, initiations of white Cubans into the priesthood seem to have commenced during the early years of the republican period—at the very latest. As Brown (1989, 124) has shown, the first white babalao (priest of the ifá oracle), Bonifacio Valdés, died in 1933. Although we do not know the date of his initiation into the priesthood, it is possible that Valdés's religious career commenced before the end of the colonial period.

61 Rife as it is with—often all but unreasonable—speculations about the implication of Cuban politicians in forms of generating power exceeding secular means, Cuban folklore has it that the public space resulting from the construction in 1928 of the Parque de la Fraternidad Panamericana on the grounds of the old Campo Marte under the Machado dictatorship (1924–33) possesses minkisi-like qualities: centered on a huge ceiba or silk cotton tree (a tree with strong sacred resonances in all Afro-Cuban religions), the park's monumental core contains portions of the soil of all American republics. Before its centerpiece was finally enclosed by an iron fence, ritual offerings to this objectification of a U.S.-dominated New World order allegedly occurred with frequency. As Romulo Lachatañeré (1992, 14) noted in 1941, the increasingly violent nature of the *machadato* in the aftermath of his so-called reelection in 1928—the year of the park's construction—may not have been lost on practitioners of Afro-Cuban religion. It is, of course, an intriguing historical irony that the powers of North American capital with which Machado so recklessly conjured were no less instrumental in his rise to power than they were in his undoing.

62 A mass migration during which some 125,000 Cubans left the island for the United States within the span of barely four months in the summer of 1980 (see Bach 1987; Palmié 1989).

3. UNE SALACIÓN CIENTÍFICA

1 The term *epidemic of signification* on which this phrase builds is Paula Treichler's (1988).

2 See Geschiere (1997) as well as the Comaroffs' most recent pronouncement (Comaroff and Comaroff 1999) on the fundamentally occult (phenomenologically obscure, morally inscrutable, fearful, as well as irresistible) nature of the global economic forces currently driving the explosion of local economies of the occult (but see also Moore's [1999] critique). Setting up an even taller order, Geschiere, in fact, sees globalization and witchcraft as mutually constitutive, both thriving on a paradoxical relation between local experience and translocal determination of life chances and moral iniquities. I would not disagree. But I would argue against the overextension of an ethnographic concept (problematic as it is to begin with) as the descriptor of an allegedly "global(izing)" condition.

3 For the history of the discursive objectification of "religion" that makes such judgments possible, see Harrison (1990). For the unacknowledged work of such conceptual objects in contemporary anthropology, see Scott (1994).

4 We do not know the precise grounds on which the Holy Inquisition sentenced Bruno to death. But, from a contemporary vantage point, the question of whether his Counter Reformation henchmen regarded Bruno's heliocentrism as more heretical than his reading of the Christian cross as an Egyptian magical signature, perhaps, matters only insofar as it disturbs presentistic sensibilities that leave us ill equipped to deal with the idea of an enchanted science as progenitor of our current rationalities.

5 The etymology of the term *obeah* remains notoriously obscure (see Götz 1995, 11). On what one might call the work of obeah in nineteenth-century British culture, see Richardson (1993).

6 In 1953—i.e., at the height of the short-lived ethnographic interest in the region—the Jamaican legislature set the maximum penalty for the practice of obeah (or for consulting obeahmen) at twelve (six) months of prison with or without forced labor and augmented by or substituted for by corporeal punishment not to exceed twenty-four strokes for males aged sixteen or older (Götz 1995, 146 and n. 8). Since 1898, the composition, publication, and distribution of obeah pamphlets had become subject to incrimination (PRO CO 137/591 # 237), and, to this very day, the possession of magical tracts and compendia of Euro-American origin continues to constitute evidence of the crime of obeah, along with any other (more ostensibly traditional) objects used or intended to be used for purposes of allegedly occult or supernatural character (see Bilby 1999).

7 On the role of magical tracts in the formation of the system of Leonard P. Howell, one of the major founding figures of Rastafari, see Hill (1981).

8 Hill (1981) remains the single serious treatment of such materials. M. G. Smith stumbled across such an expert in "reject knowledge" in the late 1950s. His life history of Norman Paul (Smith 1963) remains an extraordinary (if somewhat unwitting) testimony to the kind of narrative eloquence and genuinely reflexive attitude of the victims of globalization that the Comaroffs (Comaroff and Comaroff 1992c) themselves appear to downplay in their exegesis of the Tswana madman's silence. Peter Wilson (1992) not accidentally chose to subtitle a personal memoir of his relationship with one such figure on Providencia "an inquiry into the nature of sanity." For a more recent and no less fascinating example of Caribbean science expounded by a practitioner, see Beck's (1979) work on Alexander Charles.

9 In a manner similar to the way in which Cohn and Dirks (1988) interpret Corrigan and Sayer's theories about the technologies of power by which European state making proceeded in the creation of metropolitan subject populations as dialectically articulated with the simultaneous creation of an external colonial theater of control and legitimation.

10 Fijian land tenure was probably the first case seriously so studied (e.g., France 1966; Clammer 1973; Thomas 1992), but the 1935 special issue of *Africa* (dedicated to witchcraft) certainly ranks as an important, although confused, predecessor.

11 For different facets of this process in Africa, see Meyer (1992, 1994) and Thornton (1995).

12 Influenced as the latter probably were, at least in part, by Marcus Garvey's Ethiopianist recensions—richly complicated with an exuberance of contradictory references to begin with—of Italian fascist military ritual. On the latter issue, see Gilroy (2000, 231–37).

13 For a detailed summary of the (truncuated but still massive) trial records and the contemporary press coverage, see Helg (1995, 109–11).

14 Literally meaning "harm," *daño* is still prevalently associated with unspeakable violations—such as rape or witchcraft—in Cuban popular speech.

15 An all-black party founded by disgruntled veterans of the Liberation army. On the history of the Partido Independiente de Color and its brutal suppression, see Helg (1995). According to even conservative estimates, the campaign led to the killing of at least three thousand Afro-Cubans in the eastern provinces.

16 The distinction between architectural facade and social content in central Havana's urban landscape was a feature often remarked on by contemporary commentators. As Clark (1902, 745) noted, "The laborers' tenements . . . known locally as *solares* . . . usually present a very respectable appearance from the street . . . not unlike that of a middle class private residence." "The difference," Clark continues, "appears when one passes the main entrance and looks down the long, narrow lane of the interior" and sees a long row of "doors that face each other at 10 or 12 foot intervals." "Behind each door is a room of 12 feet or more, accommodating a family. Fifty or a hundred people," Clark surmised not unrealistically, "live in a single alley of this kind extending back to the end of the lot. There will be but one or possibly two water-closets or privies, and one water faucet for the whole number. Much of the cooking is done in the open air, in the limited space before the dwellings. As the doors are often the only source of light and air, there is absolutely no privacy." For the historical evolution of lower-class housing—the *solares* and the even more infamous *ciudadelas*—in Habana Vieja and the former barrios extramuros, see Chailloux Cardona (1945), Arriaga Mesa and Delgado Valdés (1995), and Segre, Coyula, and Scarpaci (1997).

17 On Afro-Caribbean labor migration to Cuba—illegal according to the U.S.-sponsored immigration laws that excluded persons of color and only post facto legalized in 1913—see Pérez de la Riva (1979), Knight (1985), Lundahl (1992), and McLeod (1998).

18 A feature that already disqualified the case for inclusion in the kind of sequence that Ortiz had apparently hoped to build.

19 To this day, in the Cuban popular imagination, Haitians and their descendants are often cast as potential practitioners of potent forms of black magic—a notion that is particularly strong among practitioners of other Afro-Cuban religions. As contemporary folklore has it, Castro and his companions received strategic supernatural aid when preparing their attack on Batista's forces in the Sierra Maestra (a region settled by many descendants of former Haitian migrant workers in the sugar estates of Oriente Province). On the stigmatization of Haitians as prone to witchcraft, see McLeod (1998). For the general attitude of the early republican black middle classes toward patently African-derived cultural practices, see Morrison (1999, 76–87).

20 Legal segregation in the United States provides the striking exception to the rule in the case of the Americas.

21 This is not to say, however, that social and economic standing can serve as a straightforward indicator of cultural loyalties among Afro-Cubans at the time. On

the contrary, to presume so would be to fall into the trap of a vulgar determinism akin to shorthand deductions of class consciousness from class position. Although there are plenty of other examples, none is perhaps as striking as that of Don Remigio Herrera or Adechina, a native Yoruba born around 1810 who came to Cuba as a slave in the 1820s and ended his life as a wealthy property owner in Regla, where he commanded considerable respect, not only among the local Afro-Cubans, but also among the white population. At the same time, however, Adechina/Herrera was a polygynist whose scrupulously registered plural marriages were simply never detected as bigamous by the Cuban authorities and a man who, by the time of his death in 1905, was widely revered as both one of the founding figures of the cult of ifá in Cuba and the most senior African babalao on the island. Adechina will be the subject of a forthcoming biography by Pedro Cosme Baños who generously shared the above information with me.

22 But see also Kaplan (1993).

23 In the Brazilian case, Skidmore (1990) plausibly ascribes the increasing acceptance of European and North American scientific racism to the ascendance of "liberal cosmopolitan ideology" in the republican period. A similar case could probably be made for Cuba, particularly in the aftermath of the U.S.-aborted War of Independence (see Helg 1995, 92ff.).

24 Herskovits (1948, 471), interestingly, made the same point in discussing why Morgan and other early American evolutionists never wholeheartedly bought into the British idea of survivals. Living in Rochester, N.Y., he argued, Morgan was *physically* too close to the Iroquois to feel comfortable with representing them as an earlier stage in human development. Living in New York City, one might say with hindsight, did not prevent Herskovits from denying temporal coevalness with the Suriname maroons.

25 Indeed, Africanity apparently was so much a part of everyday life in late-nineteenth-century Brazil that Silvio Romero found it necessary to lament the failure of Brazilian scholars to tap what he called a "wellspring for the study of primitive thought." "It is a badge of shame for Brazilian science," Romero wrote,

> that we have dedicated none of our labors to the study of the African languages and religions. When we see men like Bleek, hiding away in the centers of Africa for decades on end just to study a language or collect some myths, we, who have the material in our house, who have Africa in our *kitchens*, just like we have America in our *forests*, and Europe in our *salons*, have produced nothing of the sort! It is a shame. Just as the Portuguese spent two centuries in India and discovered nothing of scientific value there, leaving the glory of revealing Sanskrit and the Brahminical books, so are we thoughtlessly abandoning our Africans to death as useless and leaving to others the study of so many dialects spoken in our slave huts. The black is not only an *economic* machine; above all, and despite his ignorance, he is an object of science. (cited in Nina Rodrigues 1977, 16)

26 At least in Ortiz's case, this statement needs qualification in the light of the considerable transformations that his thinking underwent in the course of his long scholarly career (see Palmié 1998b). There is no telling how Rodrigues's views would have evolved had he not died at age forty-four in 1906 and had important elements of his perspective not been canonized by self-appointed successors such as Artur Ramos.

27 This clearly was only a fraction of the number of cult houses of the various Afro-Cuban religions operating at the time. In all likelihood, the Register of Associations reflects merely those groups that saw their future in legal inscription and possessed the corporate structures and leadership to press legal recognition.

28 The celebration of a *plante* (abakuá ceremony) on Independence Day need not surprise us. Given the ages of the accused, many of them must have been veterans of the Liberation Army. In 1914, a similar arrest of an abakuá grouping apparently in the process of swearing in a new chapter (potencia) took place in Marianao at dawn on Independence Day (Roche Monteagudo 1925, 70–71).

29 The phrase is Karen Fields's (1982).

30 Unlike African slaves, whose (nominal) Christianization was a legal part of the export formalities from Africa under which Spain granted licenses (the so-called *asientos*) to foreign traders to import slaves into her possessions, Native Americans were early on exempted from its jurisdiction (see Palmer 1976, 226 n. 5; Klein 1967, 88ff.).

31 For a definition of the key term "herejía" and its diverse forms of manifestation, see Lea (1908, 1:34ff.).

32 The Holy Office never instituted a separate tribunal in Cuba. It was not until 1623 that the first Cuban victims of the Inquisition—an African slave named Francisco Angola and a mulata named Luisa Sánchez—were handed over to the tribunal in Cartagena de las Indias (Ortiz 1975, 410).

33 See Karasch (1979a, 1987), who draws comparable conclusions in the case of Brazil. Contrary to the long-standing tradition of research into the African or European character of the religions that emerged within such institutional frameworks, it is, perhaps, more apposite to ask in what sense the entire complex of the cabildo de nación—including its supposedly ethnic form of organization and the religious practices produced within it—might not be better approached as a genuine New World phenomenon the fundamental hybridity of which is merely obscured by reading its formal characteristics *as if* they were signs pointing to fixable Old World referents. It might, at least, clear up some of the muddles associated with the term *syncretism* so often cited in this context (see Shaw and Stewart 1994).

34 The type of modern (in all its senses) cult group that exists to this day. It usually consists (minimally) of a senior priest and his or her *ahijados,* i.e., people initiated by him or her and bound together by ties of religious kinship and ritual obligations.

35 Priestly genealogies are recited at the onset of major ritual undertakings in an invocation of the dead of one's religious lineage. Neither of the two great cult houses that traditionally performed the annual public rites for the deity Yemayá in Regla—that of Josefa (Pepa) Herrera and Susana Cantero—stood in an unbroken line of tradition going back to the period of slavery. Originally from Cienfuegos, Cantero established herself in Regla only in 1914, while Herrera, although the child of the famous African-born babalao Adechina alias Remigio Herrera, had left Regla for Havana in 1912 in order to escape the violence unleashed in the course of the suppression of the Partido Independiente de Color, only to return in 1921, the year in which the processions for Yemayá are first recorded (Alberto Pedroso, personal communication). As in the case of the buildup of Regla as a stronghold of abakuá, the liberal-populist mayor of Regla, Dr. Antonio Bosch Martínez (in office from 1920 to 1926), played a considerable role in this. Although Bosch is nowadays officially remembered in Cuba for having dedicated a public park to Lenin's memory and erecting the first monument to labor in the Americas, an advertising card for Bosch's candidacy for the Liberal Party written in the ritual language of abakuá preserved among Fernando Ortiz's papers (Fondo Ortiz, unnumbered item) demonstrates that Bosch (or his aides) was well aware of the importance of the constituency represented by those of Regla's dockworkers among whom abakuá had come to function as a kind of mystically motivated labor organization (see López Valdés 1966). However, Bosch's respect for Afro-Cuban culture went beyond opportunistic maneuvering. His administrative reforms augmenting Regla's municipal autonomy may well have rendered the town a sanctuary for practitioners of Afro-Cuban religions.

36 A young pharmacist of Haitian descent who had taken up ethnographic fieldwork under Ortiz's guidance. For the article that sparked the exchange between Lachatañeré and his mentor, see Lachatañeré (1992, 196–204). Arguably, Lachatañeré was the most brilliant member of the Sociedad de Estudios Afrocubanos. Had he not met an untimely death in a plane crash in 1941, he might have succeeded Ortiz as the foremost ethnographer of Afro-Cuban culture.

37 The first of these, "La criminalità dei negri in Cuba" (Ortiz 1905), quite obviously echoed an almost eponymous publication of Nina Rodrigues's ("Nègres criminel au Brésil") that had appeared in the same journal some ten years earlier.

38 Elaborated in painstaking detail in Lombroso's magnum opus, *L'uomo delinquente* (1876).

39 As Diana Iznaga (1989, 2) notes, Lombroso's entire scheme rested on a good dose of what we might call *colonial knowledge* (see Dirks 1992). For it contrasted the "normal primitivity" of nonwhites with European atavisms, i.e., forms of regression that were decidedly abnormal (and, therefore, needed to be scientifically explained).

40 In a vitriolic polemic against "unscientific" law enforcement, Nina Rodrigues (1977, 247; emphasis added) thus branded the heavy-handed policy of persecu-

tion that the Bahian police was directing against practitioners of candomblé not only as illegal—for it conflicted, in his view, with constitutionally guaranteed rights of freedom of religion—but as criminal violence in its own right: "In which legalities, then, are based the constant interventions into, and violent abuse of, the African temples and terreiros on the part of the police, the destruction of their idols and images, the imprisonment, without legal formalities, of the pais-de-terreiro and directors of the candomblés?" Might such policies—"repulsive to educated spirits"—not "reveal simply a rudimentary state of [the development of] a sense of justice, *deriving directly from the inferior races that settled Brazil and whose blood still flows hot and plentifully in the veins of many of the executors of such violence*"? And did Bahian police activity achieve anything, Nina Rodrigues asked, but to "reproduce with all rigor the blind, impassioned, and violent power of the petty potentates and despots of Africa"?

41 It is rarely remembered today that Ortiz authored a fairly large number of texts on positivistic legal and criminological reform, including the first Latin American monograph on dactyloscopy (1913) and a draft for a full-fledged *Codigo Criminal Cubano* (1926), based on "scientific principles" and containing a multitude of cross-references between epidemiology and crime control. On comparable "sanitation projects" in colonial India, the Philippines, Fiji, and Central Africa and on Central American United Fruit Company plantations, see Arnold (1988), Ileto (1989), Thomas (1990), Vaughan (1992), and Chomsky (1996).

42 On December 2, 1904, *El Mundo,* e.g., featured an editorial describing the girl's killing as the product of a "terrible moral disease" that "corrodes right into the twentieth century the consciousness of a portion of our population that, perhaps because of the wicked law of atavism, sinks into the depths of depravity."

43 Prominent among these friends, one presumes, was the indefatigable witch-hunter Eduardo Varela Zequeira, whom Ortiz cites repeatedly throughout the book.

44 In one sense, the Matanzas judges were the lineal ancestors of those of us who continue assiduously to compare late-nineteenth- or early-twentieth-century Africanist ethnography with New World data in order to arrive at African American cultural history.

45 Ironically, the author's assessment of American policy in the Philippines was quite correct. As Ileto (1989) persuasively argues, there was an almost seamless continuity—on both rhetorical and practical levels—between American counterinsurgency measures between 1899 and 1902 and the stunning callousness and brutality of the anticholera measures enacted in the aftermath of Miguel Malvar's final surrender in 1902. The war against Aguinaldo's nationalist army, as Ileto (1989, 131) puts it, was merely transposed "from the battlefields to the towns" and continued as a struggle "over the control, no longer of territorial sovereignty, but of people's bodies, beliefs and social practices." "It was," Ileto concludes, "in a sense, the old war in a new, more complex setting—complex, since who can argue against the saving of human lives through proper disinfection, isolation, treatment, and disposal of the dead?"

46 A confession was extracted from one of the prisoners shortly before their deaths. Nevertheless, although suitably mutilated, the identity of the body found in the cemetery with that of the missing child was never conclusively established. Chávez Álvarez (1991, 53ff.), who offers an alternative hypothesis to those entertained at the time, points out that, in several other instances of suspected ritual child murder, the children had been killed either by close relatives or in the course of an accident. Their bodies were mutilated after the fact and in the manner established in the Zoila case (including, e.g., the extraction of the heart) in order to simulate ritual murder and deflect the attention of the police from the killer to practitioners of Afro-Cuban religion living in the vicinity.

47 This was another notion that quickly diffused from the pages of *Los negros brujos* into public knowledge. In several (maybe all) cases of child abduction, not just the concerned citizenry, but journalists and the police themselves immediately commenced searches for ill elderly Africans, from whom they tried to press confessions as to the identity of the brujo who was preparing to cure them with the blood or organs of a child.

48 On the striking imagery of the informant as accused, the ethnographer as judge, and the "ethnographic fact" as crime that Marcel Griaulle deployed as late as the 1930s, see Clifford (1983).

49 Some of them are now on display in Havana's Casa de África. Housing as the Casa de África does an otherwise insignificant collection of African objects donated by socialist regimes, the recontextualization effected by their relocation from the Museo Antropológico to the Casa de África once more bespeaks discursive movements in a wider political arena. Ironically, they now serve to underwrite Castro's claim that Cuba is "un país latinoafricano."

50 "Los desheredados de la fortuna."

51 He is not—or at least not among the priests with whom I worked in Havana—remembered in oral tradition. This, however, need not reflect on his religious standing at the time, for oral tradition (and especially the moyuba) tends to preserve only the names of priests who were prolific initiators and are therefore venerated as founders (fundamentos) of religious lineages (ramas).

52 The addresses provide good grounds for speculating that this association was, in fact, none other than a successor organization to the famous old lucumí cabildo Changó Teddún, which had been domiciled precisely at Jesús Peregrino 49 during Aponte's days and later relocated to San Nicolás in the barrio of Jesús María.

53 Sandrino, at this point, served as its director. That the "extraordinary meeting" took place at Guerra's home is surely significant here.

54 At least today, male devotees of female deities, particularly Ochún, are pervasively rumored to be at least latent homosexuals. In the inimitable and untranslatable words of a babalao with whom I worked in Miami, common stereotyping has it that "casi todos son otro way."

55 There were numerous personal ties between them. Silvestre Erice, the founder of the Sociedad Santa Rita y San Lázaro, was Guerra's son-in-law. Erice founded this

society in 1902 but had been among the original *vocales* of the Sociedad Sta Bárbara at the time of the 1900 petition. Around 1910, both men were of advanced age, Guerra probably in his sixties, Erice in his late seventies. When Erice died in 1915, Guerra succeeded him as president of that society.

56 The drum is ritually invested with the presence of a superhuman being, named *añá*, capable of communicating between humans and gods, but dependent on sacrifice performed through human agency.

57 As discussed in chap. 2, *prenda* or *nganga* is a term used today to designate a power object in the so-called reglas de congo. Usually containing—among many other things—some human remains, these objects relate, through a complex and ill-understood historical connection, to the kind of sacred objectivizations known as *minkisi* in western Central Africa. The adjective *judía*—lit. "Jewish"—is meant to indicate its predominant use for nefarious purposes.

58 The term *collective fantasy* is meant in the sense outlined by Thoden van Velzen (1995).

59 Guerra's frequent use of the term *Christian* (*cristiano*) may indicate, less a reference to concrete religious forms or beliefs (although he repeatedly protested that the lucumí believed in God, too), than an attempt to create—deliberately or simply as a matter of common sense—a resonance with the ancient Spanish distinction between *cristianos*, i.e., members of the moral community of Christendom, and unbelievers. Traditionally, a number of labels were available to represent the other excluded from this category, among them *salvaje* (savage), *africano* (African, implying "slave"), or *judío* (meaning jew, but implying connotations of maliciousness or enmity). As noted before, to this day, practitioners of palo monte call ngangas (actually or reputedly) dedicated to black magic *prendas judías*.

60 What may have made Guerra's intervention even more acute was that Castellanos and his European colleagues were themselves struggling to instantiate a perspective on social relations that *did not* correspond to the still-reigning commonsense view of sociality as a moral rather than a natural affair. The scientific reduction to the biotic—as an ultimate instance of the real—was, at the time, by no means a culturally pervasive (or even widely acceptable) foundational strategy. As Nadel (1957, 205) argued in respect to Castellanos's near contemporary Malinowski (who, in fact, befriended Ortiz during the last years of his life), the acknowledgment by the great scientizer of anthropology of the "indispensable pragmatic figments without which civilization cannot exist" was born from the naive arrogance of someone who feels secure enough in his own epistemological position to admit to the work of "noble lies." Castellanos's position, it seems, was far from that. Relativism, to him, was a scandal.

EPILOGUE

1 The Inglaterra is by no means alone in this. To somewhat varying degrees all tourist hotels in Havana are off-limits to regular Cuban citizens. Hence the pattern whereby phenotypically white young Cuban men able to afford foreign-looking

clothes (shorts, sandals, sunglasses, and so forth) try to gain entry to hotel bars and discos by sporting Spanish or Mexican accents.

2 Given the notoriety that Benetton achieved with its controversial advertisements often depicting scenes of explicit violence (at least in Europe—such ads tend to be banned in the United States), one wonders whether this was planned.

3 "If, under capitalism, the bourgeoisie declared the values created by the dominant classes [to be the] cultural patrimony," the Moscow-trained anthropologist Guanche (1983, 475) wrote, "under socialism it is necessary to valorize the creations of the old dominated classes and, with the proletariat in power, to consider as cultural patrimony the totality, positive or identificatory of what is Cuban, in the material and spiritual traditions of the [national] culture."

4 Guanche (1983) can be taken to represent an exemplary text (the Cuban press repeatedly issued similar pronouncements up until the late 1980s). "During the construction of socialism" he writes (450–51), "there survive, like a remnant of the society divided in classes, forms of religious belief permitted within the existing freedom of religion, but their disintegration increases with the changes that have taken place in the economic base and the consequent gradual elimination of the antagonistic contradictions between classes in favor of the emergence of harmonic contradictions that will permit a qualitative leap toward a more fulfilled [state] of society."

5 In 1995, the state-allocated monthly rice ration per person consisted of five pounds, sold at 24 centavos per pound. Black beans were rationed at twenty ounces but were often not available except on the parallel (or black) market, where they sold at prohibitive prices (from 90 centavos to 1.20 pesos, as opposed to the fixed 30 centavos in the state sector).

6 Benjamin, Collins, and Scott (1985) provide a sensitive and fair assessment of Cuban nutrition policy and practices before the onset of the crisis. Today it is sadly ironic to read that, in the mid-1980s, these authors (and Cuban nutritionists) saw *obesity* as a growing health problem in Cuba.

7 For a fuller treatment of the experiential concomitants of the present crisis, see Palmié (2001).

8 While Turner and Ashe's (1976) formulation remains impressionistic, Crush and Wellings (1983) provide a systematic application of the concept to the case of South Africa. On the history of tourism in prerevolutionary Cuba, see Schwartz (1997) and Pérez (1999). According to Espino (1993) and Martin de Holán and Phillips (1997), the number of tourists visiting Cuba more than doubled between 1990 (340,000) and 1995 (750,000). According to the latter authors, the government is projecting a goal of 2.5 million visitors for the year 2000—more than ten times the number that visited Cuba in 1985 (i.e., before the onset of the crisis and the tourism-related policy changes that commenced toward the end of the decade). Still, the Cuban tourist industry leaks a sizable amount of the revenue that it generates through massive hard-currency investments in infrastructural development and imports necessary to maintain international tourist standards. As Font

(1997, 124) observes, of the U.S.$800 million that Cuba grossed in tourism in 1994, it retained a mere U.S.$250 million. Hence Martin de Holán and Phillips's (1997, 790) warning: "If the number of tourists increases fast enough, the short term [hard-currency] leakage could rise to the point where the net contribution to Cuba is close to zero, leaving social and environmental problems as the only remaining impact of the ever growing number of tourists."

9 "The concept of tourism as an export or import may be an unfamiliar one," Smith (1998, 38) argues, yet there are important structural analogies. "Most export commodities are shipped to consumers in another nation; in the case of tourism, consumers travel to the commodity. The issue is not who or what is moved, or the direction of movement; rather it is the fact that for both commodity exports and tourism exports, the producing nation receives money from foreign sources. The same is true, of course, for imports."

10 As late as the mid-1990s, police toleration of street prostitution was blatant, and, even after the major crackdowns in the context of the pope's visit in 1998, to many Cubans it seems clear that the casual sale of sexual services functions to funnel much foreign currency into the national economy. The makeshift bazaar of stalls selling electronics, household appliances, lingerie, and imported food outside the departure lounge of José Martí airport had disappeared after the pope's visit. While it existed, however, it was hard to imagine that it was catering to tourists' needs. Rather, its obvious function was to provide their Cuban *novias* (girlfriends) with a last chance to extract hard currency—and spend it in state-controlled venues, thus repatriating such funds in the formal sector.

11 Make no mistake here: whether one sympathizes with the ideals underlying the current Cuban regime's desperate struggle for survival or not (and I happen to do so, however reluctantly), the site of *la lucha* to build or, in current Party parlance, preserve socialism is not just the world market. That struggle takes place in the minds and bodies of people trying to preserve an individual sense of social dignity and personal satisfaction as well.

12 Uncritically harking back to the powerful ambivalences produced in the nineteenth-century male bourgeois imagination by the apparent feminization of modern mass consumption (Seltzer 1992; Felski 1995), Sombart's troubling imagery nevertheless, not just bespeaks the parasitic character of Western consumption practices, but reveals their gendered and explicitly sexualized nature as well. For the seemingly uncontrollable saccharine yearnings that Sombart attributed to his archetypical consumptive modernizers, i.e., metropolitan courtesans (themselves both subject and objects of consumption), not only found its concrete equivalent in the colonial dehumanization of machine-like enslaved producers, but echoed the ambivalent, indeed anxiety-ridden, eroticization of those objects of domination against (or on) whom masterful forms of modern Western masculinity were historically produced (see Gilman 1985; Dijkstra 1986; hooks 1992; Stoler 1995).

13 This pervasive slippage between economic and erotic value arguably rendered the Caribbean slave plantation a key site for the emergence of forms of masculinity

that are with us to this day: a place where passions and interests became representable as fused into a hyperprofitable economy centering, not only on the accumulative extraction of value from human bodies, but on masterful forms of fulfilling an increasingly biologically rationalized male sexual destiny.

14 A gendered pronoun may not be appropriate to the Caribbean situation as a whole (see Pruitt and Lafont 1995) but appears adequately to characterize the Cuban situation.

15 In his analysis of Jamaican estate manager Thomas Thistlewood's diaries, Beckles (1999, 38–58) thus explicitly contradicts conventional interpretations of the dynamics of interracial sex in New World slave societies, as originating in a shortage or absence of white females. In Beckles's view, Thistlewood's diary, as well as the behavior of his contemporaries, bespeaks, not so much a preference for black bodies in the presence of potential white sexual partners, as a primary preference for enacting the fantasies of control afforded by "enslaved sexuality" (41)—which, under the historical conditions, virtually automatically implied blackness. In confronting the legal fictions conferring property rights in human beings on eighteenth-century masters with contemporary fictional writing on what Poe called *affectionate appropriation,* Dayan (1995, 192 and passim) similarly argues that bondage, rather than (racial) difference, formed the core of the eroticization of blackness in the colonial Caribbean. See also Gilman (1985), Stoler (1995), Jolly and Manderson (1997), and O'Connell Davidson and Sanchez Taylor (1999).

16 This logic, of course, was not lost on my travel companion whose views of these matters I cited at the beginning of this book: for the gesture of opening his shirt to afford me a view of the bite marks that sexually unrestrained nonwhite females left on his body not only evidenced his eagerness to demonstrate the inevitable ravages incurred in the course of such encounters. It also—if inadvertently—commented on a long history in the course of which white men learned to harness structurally disempowered nonwhite female bodies to the production of their own white masculine superiority.

17 For obvious reasons, the social disadvantages confirmed by ascriptions of blackness in contemporary Cuban society remain a seriously understudied subject. As David Booth (1976, 166) puts it, in prerevolutionary Cuba, discriminatory "folk-stereotypes ascribing chronic unreliability to the black male, promiscuity to the dark female, status sensitivity to mulattoes," were based, not so much on sheer antagonistic projection, as on "broadly realistic assumptions about what being a Negro or a dark mulatto, or the spouse or off-spring of one, normally entailed in terms of life chances and social prestige." Yet, as Fernández (1996, 109) notes, the formal equalization of economic opportunity guaranteed by the revolutionary Cuban state has merely led to a recalibration of the operational logic of those discursive processes that render blackness a social liability: "Through a process of social forgetting," she writes, "the historical relations of domination, slavery, and institutional discrimination that form the roots of current race relations and social divisions are overlooked or played down; as this amnesia takes hold, racist con-

ceptions and practices come to be seen as 'logical' and 'natural.' This logic concludes that darker Cubans remain in lower social positions not because they have not been given equal opportunity, but because they have failed, through either lack of interest or lack of ability, to take advantage of them."

18 Perhaps the most tragic and frightening aspect of this is encapsulated in O'Connell Davidson and Sanchez Taylor's (1995, 8 and passim) comments on how—given the official characterization of dollarized prostitution as driven by individual greed and antisocial hedonism (see Elizalde 1996)—child prostitution in Cuba may lead its victims to "internalize their society's view of them as immoral, superficial and worthless."

19 For concrete examples of the formation of social and cultural contexts for interracial sex in the earliest phases of European overseas expansion, see Elbl (1996) and Campbell (1992).

20 As in *dar un cuerazo* (give a whipping) or *dar un bocabajo* (violate a person prostrated on his or her face, i.e., have anal intercourse). See Moreno Fraginals (1978, 2:40 n. 56), who (at least in my understanding) drastically misinterprets the historical references encoded in these terms by literalizing them as fossilized expressions of "pathological sexual obsessions" induced by slavery. For more appropriate, although largely ahistorical, readings of Nicaraguan and Brazilian idioms of sexual violence, see Lancaster (1992 chap. 2 and passim) and Parker (1991).

21 By the mid-1990s, websites such as *Desiree's Guide to Sex in Latin America*, the *World Sex Guide*, or *Travel for the Single Male* had come to include sizable entries on Cuba. Although treating the correspondence posted on these sites as ethnographically valid data presents the methodological problems common to all forms of virtual sociality (e.g., the staging of web personae, issues of representativity, etc.), my assumption is that such communications are freely exchanged between men who consider themselves peers. Put differently, I take these websites to represent simply new loci of a much older homosocial discourse in which white men define themselves and each other through their sexual conquest of nonwhite females.

22 A particularly confessional web posting on a "travel for the single male" site (http://www.tsmtravel.com/mirror/past_posting/Cuba_Guys_lied.htm) illustrates this moment. After having spent a night with a woman who told him she only "comes out" once a month to support her child, the posting's author spots her again at the same location in front of the Hotel Riviera. This is how he describes the situation:

> After a few minutes, I see something that makes me realize that I am a naive idiot and that I have been had. I see the girl from last night that "only comes out once a month." Well time flies doesn't it, but this is ridiculous. I sit there drinking my beer, and the more I think about it the madder I get. I could give a shit if she comes out every day, just don't feed me a line of shit. As you can see

> by now, I prefer the tender ones, the sometimes amateurs who for whatever reason do this. I try to be kind and leave them not feeling used, but who knows if it works?
>
> This place is full of nice girls who have yet to be jaded and hardened by tourists, and I try to leave it just as I found it. But here I am the one who bought a line of crap. We are the ones who usually do that, it's our job! I feel cheap and used! Not really, but I do feel pissed and I think I'll go out and ask her what month it is and hope she chokes.

This he does. As soon as the woman notices him, she embraces him and tells him that she was looking for him because she told her parents what a nice man he was and they in turn insisted that she bring him for dinner. He is shocked and profoundly embarrassed, yet "I sure as hell didn't want to spend my last night [in Cuba] sitting around with a family to stare at me and monitor my every move, but on the other hand it was kind of sweet and I didn't want to disappoint them." So he meets the woman's family, but invents an excuse that allows him to leave after dinner to still be able to pick up women that night, and spirals on into the next fantasized romance.

23 Or, perhaps better, the increasing (commercial) circulation of signs and practices once emblematic of blackness as a substitute for the social empowerment of people to whom blackness is socially ascribed.

24 Nor could it have been otherwise. For the self-conscious essentialization of hybridity in the service of nationalist projects—epitomized in the virtual ban on representations of racial difference in the official discourse of the revolutionary Cuban state—invariably remains captive to what it ostensibly reacted to, thus producing what Lancaster (1992, 230) calls the "presence of racial thinking," perhaps even an obsession with markers of racial difference, "combined with the absence of corporate races." It is probably not overstating the case to say that twentieth-century Cuban nationalist discourse strategically built preexisting categorial ambiguities into conceptions of Cubanness that deflected institutional mechanisms structuring race into informal quotidian practices of reproducing social inequality on the basis of a model *for* social subjection expressed and negotiated as a model *of* individual bodily difference.

REFERENCES

ABBREVIATIONS

AHN Archivo Historico Nacional, Madrid

ANC Archivo Nacional Cubano, Habana

Fondo Ortiz Instituto de Literatura y Lingüistica, Habana, Ortiz Papers

NA U.S. National Archives, College Park, Md.

PRO CO Public Record Office, London, Colonial Office Records

Abbot, Abiel. 1971. *Letters Written in the Interior of Cuba*. 1829. Reprint, Freeport, Maine: Books for Libraries Press.

Abrahams, Roger D. 1983. *The Man of Words in the West Indies*. Baltimore: Johns Hopkins University Press.

Abrams, Philip. 1988. "Notes on the Difficulty of Studying the State." *Journal of Historical Sociology* 1:58–89.

Acosta Saignes, Miguel. 1967. *Vida de los esclavos negros en Venezuela*. Caracas: Hesperides.

Ahmad, Aijaz. 1995. "The Politics of Literary Postcoloniality." *Race and Class* 36:1–20.

Aimes, Hubert. 1967. *A History of Slavery in Cuba, 1511–1868*. 1907. Reprint, New York: Octagon.

Alexander, Jack. 1977. "The Culture of Race in Middle Class Kingston." *American Ethnologist* 4:413–34.

Alonso, Ana Maria. 1988. "The Effects of Truth: Re-Presentations of the Past and the Imagining of Community." *Journal of Historical Sociology* 1:33–57.

Althusser, Louis. 1971. *Lenin and Philosophy and Other Essays*. New York: Monthly Review Press.

Alvarez Nazario, Manuel. 1974. *El elemento afronegroide en el español de Puerto Rico*. San Juan: Instituto de Cultura Puertoriqueña.

Amselle, Jean-Loup. 1993. "Anthropology and Historicity." *History and Theory Beiheft* 32:12–31.

——. 1998. *Mestizo Logics: Anthropology of Identity in Africa and Elsewhere*. Stanford, Calif.: Stanford University Press.

Anderson, Benedict. 1991. *Imagined Communities*. London: Verso.

Appadurai, Arjun. 1981. "The Past as a Scarce Resource." *Man* 16:201–19.

——. 1986. "Theory in Anthropology: Center and Periphery." *Comparative Studies in Society and History* 28:356–61.

——. 1998. "Dead Certainties: Ethnic Violence in the Era of Globalization." *Development and Change* 29:905–25.

Appiah, Anthony Kwame. 1992. *In My Father's House*. New York: Oxford University Press.

Apter, Andrew H. 1987a. "The Historiography of Yoruba Myths and Ritual." *History in Africa* 14:1–25.

——. 1987b. "Rituals of Power: The Politics of Orisa Worship in Yoruba Society." Ph.D. diss., Yale University.

——. 1991. "The Embodiment of Paradox: Yoruba Kingship and Female Power." *Cultural Anthropology* 6:212–29.

——. 1992. *Black Critics and Kings: The Hermeneutics of Power in Yoruba Society*. Chicago: University of Chicago Press.

Aptheker, Herbert. 1963. *American Negro Slave Revolts*. 1943. Reprint, New York: International.

Ardener, Edwin. 1970. "Witchcraft, Economics, and the Continuity of Belief." In *Witchcraft: Confessions and Accusations*, ed. Mary Douglas, 141–60. London: Tavistock.

——. 1989. *The Voice of Prophecy*. Oxford: Blackwell.

——. 1996. *Kingdom on Mount Cameroon*. Providence, R.I.: Berghahn.

Arendt, Hannah. 1968. *Totalitarianism*. New York: Harcourt, Brace, and World.

Argüelles Mederos, Aníbal, and Ileana Hodge Limonta. 1991. *Los llamados cultos sincréticos y el espiritismo*. La Habana: Editorial Academía.

Arnold, David. 1988. "Touching the Body: Perspectives on the Indian Plague, 1896–1900." In *Selected Subaltern Studies*, ed. Ranajit Guha and Gayatri Chakravorti Spivak, 391–426. New York: Oxford University Press.

Arriaga Mesa, Marcos D., and Andrés Delgado Valdés. 1995. "Contribución al estudio de la vivienda pobre en la Habana del siglo XIX: Ciudadelas y accesorias." *Revista de Índias* 55:453–84.

Asad, Talal. 1993. *Genealogies of Religion*. Baltimore: Johns Hopkins University Press.

Austen, Ralph A. 1993. "The Moral Economy of Witchcraft: An Essay in Comparative History." In *Modernity and Its Malcontents*, ed. Jean Comaroff and John Comaroff, 89–110. Chicago: University of Chicago Press.

——. 1995. "Slavery and the Slave Trade on the Atlantic Coast: The Duala of the Littoral." Paideuma 41:127–52.

Austin-Broos, Diane J. 1997. *Jamaica Genesis: Religion and the Politics of Moral Orders*. Chicago: University of Chicago Press.

Axelson, Sigbert. 1970. *Culture Confrontation in the Lower Congo*. Falköping: Gummessons.

Ayala, César J. 1999. *American Sugar Kingdom: The Plantation Economy of the Spanish Caribbean, 1898–1934*. Chapel Hill: University of North Carolina Press.

Bach, Robert L. 1987. "The Cuban Exodus: Political and Economic Motivations." In *The Caribbean Exodus*, ed. Barry B. Levine, 106–30. New York: Praeger.

Bailey, Victor. 1993. "The Fabrication of Deviance: 'Dangerous Classes' and 'Criminal Classes' in Victorian England." In *Protest and Survival,* ed. John Rule and Robert Malcolmson, 221–56. London: Merlin.

Bakhtin, Mikhail M. 1986. *Speech Genres and Other Late Essays.* Austin: University of Texas Press.

Baldwin, James. 1985. *The Evidence of Things Not Seen.* New York: Holt, Rinehart and Winston.

Balibar, Etienne. 1991. "The Nation Form: History and Ideology." In *Race, Nation, Class,* ed. Etienne Balibar and Immanuel Wallerstein, 86–106.

Ballesteros Gaibrois, Manuel. 1955. "Negros en la Nueva Granada." In *Miscelanea de estudios dedicados a Fernando Oritz,* 1:108–23. La Habana: Úcar García.

Ballou, Maturin M. 1854. *History of Cuba; or, Notes of a Traveller in the Tropics.* Boston: Phillips, Sampson.

Barber, Karen. 1987. "Popular Arts in Africa." *African Studies Review* 30:1–78.

——. 1991. *I Could Speak Until Tomorrow: Oriki, Women, and the Past in a Yoruba Town.* Washington, D.C.: Smithsonian Institution Press.

Barnet, Miguel. 1984. *Biografía de un cimarrón.* Madrid: Alfaguara.

——. 1997. "The Untouchable *Cimarrón.*" *New West Indian Guide* 71:281–89.

Barnett, Steve, and Martin G. Silverman. 1979. *Ideology and Everyday Life.* Ann Arbor: University of Michigan Press.

Barth, Fredrik. 1984. "Problems in Conceptualizing Cultural Pluralism, with Illustrations from Sohar, Oman." In *The Prospects for Plural Societies,* ed. David Maybury-Lewis, 77–87. Washington, D.C.: American Ethnological Society.

——. 1989. "The Analysis of Culture in Complex Societies." *Ethnos* 54:120–42.

——. 1990. "The Guru and the Conjurer: Transactions in Knowledge and the Shaping of Culture in Southeast Asia and Melanesia." *Man* 25:640–53.

Bascom, William. 1969. *The Yoruba of Southwestern Nigeria.* New York: Holt, Rinehart and Winston.

Bastian, Adolph. 1859. *Ein Besuch in San Salvador, der Hauptstadt des Königreiches Kongo.* Bremen: Heinrich Strack.

Bastide, Roger. 1978. *The African Religions of Brazil.* Baltimore: Johns Hopkins University Press.

Bataille, Georges. 1967. *La Part maudite.* Paris: Minuit.

Bauer, Helga. 1969. *Der Index Pictorius Calderóns: Untersuchungen zu seiner Malermetaphorik.* Hamburg: Cram, de Gruyter.

Bauman, Zygmunt. 1992. *Modernity and the Holocaust.* Ithaca, N.Y.: Cornell University Press.

——. 1997. *Postmodernism and Its Discontents.* New York: New York University Press.

Bayart, Jean-Francois. 1993. *The State in Africa: The Politics of the Belly.* London: Longman.

Beard, Charles A. 1934. "Written History as an Act of Faith." *American Historical Review* 39:219–29.

Beck, Jane. 1979. *To the Windward of the Land: The Occult World of Alexander Charles.* Bloomington: Indiana University Press.

Becker, Carl. 1932. "Everyman His Own Historian." *American Historical Review* 37:221–36.

——. 1938. "What Is Historiography?" *American Historical Review* 44:20–28.

Beckles, Hilary McD. 1999. *Centering Women: Gender Discourses in Caribbean Slave Society.* Kingston: Ian Randle.

Benjamin, Medea, Joseph Collins, and Michael Scott. 1985. *No Free Lunch: Food and Revolution in Cuba Today.* New York: Grove.

Benjamin, Walter. 1968. *Illuminations.* New York: Harcourt, Brace & World.

Bennett, Gillian. 1986. "Ghost and Witch in the Sixteenth and Seventeenth Centuries." *Folklore* 97:3–14.

Benoit, Catherine. 1999. "Sex, AIDS, Migration, and Prostitution: Human Trafficking in the Caribbean." *New West Indian Guide* 73:27–42.

Berlin, Ira, and Philip D. Morgan. 1993. "Introduction: Labor and the Shaping of Slave Life in the Americas." In *Cultivation and Culture,* ed. Ira Berlin and Philip D. Morgan, 1–45. Charlottesville: University of Virginia Press.

Berman, Marshal. 1982. *All That Is Solid Melts into the Air.* New York: Penguin.

Bernal, Martin. 1987. *Black Athena.* New Brunswick, N.J.: Rutgers University Press.

Besson, Jean. 1992. "Freedom and Community: The British West Indies." In *The Meaning of Freedom,* ed. Frank McGlynn and Seymour Drescher, 183–219. Pittsburgh: University of Pittsburgh Press.

——. 1995. "The Creolization of African-American Slave Kinship in Jamaican Free Villages and Maroon Communities." In *Slave Cultures and the Cultures of Slavery,* ed. Stephan Palmié, 187–209. Knoxville: University of Tennessee Press.

Bhabha, Homi K. 1984. "Signs Taken for Wonders: Questions of Ambivalence and Authority under a Tree outside Delhi, May 1817." In *Europe and Its Others,* ed. Francis Barker, Peter Hulme, Margaret Iverson, and Diana Loxley, 1:89–106. Colchester: University of Essex.

——. 1997. "Of Mimicry and Man: The Ambivalence of Colonial Discourse." In *Tensions of Empire,* ed. Frederick Cooper and Ann Laura Stoler, 152–60. Berkeley and Los Angeles: University of California Press.

Bilby, Kenneth. 1999. "Neither Here nor There: The Place of 'Community' in the Jamaican Religious Imagination." In *Religion, Diaspora, and Cultural Identity,* ed. John Pulis, 311–35. New York: Gordon and Breach.

Blackburn, Robin. 1988. *The Overthrow of Colonial Slavery.* London: Verso.

——. 1997. *The Making of New World Slavery.* London: Verso.

Bloch, Marc. 1953. *The Historian's Craft.* New York: Knopf.

——. 1961. *Les Rois thaumaturges.* 1924. Reprint, Paris: Colin.

Booth, David. 1976. "Cuba, Color, and the Revolution." *Science and Society* 40:129–72.

Böröcz, József. 1996. *Leisure Migration.* New York: Pergamon.

Bourdieu, Pierre. 1977. *Outline of a Theory of Practice.* Cambridge: Cambridge University Press.

——. 1979. *La Distinction: Critique sociale du jugement*. Paris: Minuit.

——. 1984. *Distinction*. London: Routledge.

Bourguignon, Erika. 1959. "The Persistence of Folk Belief: Some Notes on Cannibalism and Zombis in Haiti." *Journal of American Folklore* 72:36–46.

Bowen, T. J. 1968. *Adventures and Missionary Labours in Several Countries in the Interior of Africa from 1849–1856*. 1857. Reprint, London: Frank Cass.

Brathwaite, Edward Kamau. 1977. "Caliban, Ariel, and Unprospero in the Conflict of Creolization: A Study of the Slave Revolt in Jamaica in 1831–32." *Annals of the New York Academy of Sciences* 292:41–62.

Breiner, Laurence A. 1985–86. "The English Bible in Jamaican Rastafarianism." *Journal of Religious Thought* 42:30–43.

Bremer, Thomas. 1993. "The Constitution of Alterity: Fernando Ortiz and the Beginnings of Latin-American Ethnography out of the Spirit of Italian Criminology." In *Alternative Cultures in the Caribbean*, ed. Thomas Bremer and Ulrich Fleischmann, 119–29. Frankfurt: Vervuert.

Brown, David H. 1989. "Garden in the Machine: Afro-Cuban Sacred Art and Performance in Urban New Jersey and New York," Ph.D. diss., Yale University.

——. 1993. "Thrones of the Orichas: Afro-Cuban Altars in New Jersey, New York, and Havana." *African Arts* 26, no. 4:44–59, 85–87.

Brown, Jonathan. 1978. "Hieroglyphs of Death and Salvation: The Decoration of the Hermandad de la Caridad, Seville." In *Images and Ideas in Seventeenth-Century Spanish Painting*, 128–47. Princeton, N.J.: Princeton University Press.

Burns, Alan. 1965. *History of the British West Indies*. London: Allen and Unwin.

Butler, Judith. 1990. *Gender Trouble*. New York: Routledge.

Butterworth, Douglas. 1980. *The People of Buena Ventura*. Urbana: University of Illinois Press.

Cabrera, Lydia. 1958. *La sociedad secreta Abakuá*. La Habana: Colección del Chicherekú.

——. 1975. *Anaforuana*. Madrid: Ediciones R.

——. 1977. *La Regla Kimbisa del Santo Cristo del Buen Viaje*. Miami: Peninsular.

——. 1979. *Reglas de Congo. Palo Monte. Mayombe*. Miami: Colección del Chicherekú.

——. 1983. *El Monte. Igbo Finda. Ewe Orisha. Vititi Nfinda*. 1954. Reprint, Miami: Colección del Chicherekú.

Calendario manual y guía de forasteros de la isla de Cuba: Para al año de 1795. 1795. Havana: Emprenta de la Capitanía General.

Campbell, Colin. 1987. *The Romantic Ethic and the Spirit of Modern Consumerism*. Oxford: Blackwell.

Campbell, Mary B. 1992. "Carnal Knowledge: Fracastoro's *De syphilis* and the Discovery of the New World." In *Crossing Cultures: Essays in the Displacement of Western Civilization*, ed. Daniel Segal, 3–32. Tucson: University of Arizona Press.

Campbell, Mavis C. 1976. *The Dynamics of Change in a Slave Society*. Rutherford, N.J.: Associated Universities Press.

Carlyle, Thomas. 1853. *Occasional Discourse on the Nigger Question.* 1849. Reprint, London: Thomas Bosworth.

Carrier, James G. 1992. "Occidentalism: The World Turned Upside Down." *American Ethnologist* 19:195–212.

——. 1995. *Gifts and Commodities: Exchange and Western Capitalism since 1700.* London: Routledge.

Castellanos, Israel. 1916. *La brujería y el ñáñiguismo en Cuba desde el punto de vista médico-legal.* Habana: Lloredo.

Castellanos, Jorge, and Isabel Castellanos. 1988. *Cultura afrocubana I: El negro en Cuba, 1492–1844.* Miami: Universal.

Castor, Suzy. 1987. *Migración y relaciones internacionales (el caso haitiano-dominicano).* Santo Domingo: UASD.

Céspedes, Benjamín. 1888. *La prostitución en la Ciudad de la Habana.* La Habana: Establecimiento Tipográfico.

Chailloux Cardona, Juan M. 1945. *Síntesis histórica de la vivienda populár: Los horrores del solar habanero.* La Habana: Jesús Montero.

Chakrabarty, Dipesh. 1988. "Conditions for Knowledge of Working-Class Conditions: Employers, Government, and the Jute Workers of Calcutta, 1890–1940." In *Selected Subaltern Studies,* ed. Ranajit Guha and Gayatri Chakravorty Spivak, 179–230. New York: Oxford University Press.

——. 1992. "Postcoloniality and the Artifice of History: Who Speaks for 'Indian' Pasts?" *Representations* 27:1–26.

Castoriadis, Cornelius. 1987. *The Imaginary Institution of Society.* Trans. Kathleen Blamey. Cambridge, Eng.: Polity Press.

Cepero Bonilla, Raúl. 1976. *Azúcar y abolición.* Barcelona: Editorial Critica.

Chávez Álvarez, Ernesto. 1991. *El crímen de la Niña Cecilia.* La Habana: Editorial Ciencias Sociales.

Chevalier, Louis. 1973. *Labouring Classes and Dangerous Classes in Paris during the First Half of the Nineteenth Century.* London: Routledge and Kegan Paul.

Chevannes, Barry. 1994. *Rastafari: Roots and Ideology.* Syracuse: Syracuse University Press.

Childs, Matt D. 1998. " 'A Black French General Arrived to Conquer the Island': Images of the Haitian Revolution in Cuba's 1812 Aponte Rebellion." University of Texas, Austin. Typescript.

Chomsky, Aviva. 1996. *West Indian Workers and the United Fruit Company in Costa Rica, 1870–1940.* Baton Rouge: Louisiana State University Press.

Christian, William, Jr. 1981. *Apparitions in Later Medieval and Renaissance Spain.* Princeton, N.J.: Princeton University Press.

Ciudad de la Habana. 1827. *Ordenanzas municipales de la Habana.* La Habana: Imprenta del Gobierno y Capitán General.

Clammer, John. 1973. "Colonialism and the Perception of Tradition in Fiji." In *Anthropology and the Colonial Encounter,* ed. Talal Asad, 199–220. New York: Humanities.

Clark, Stewart. 1983. "French Historians and Early Modern Popular Culture." *Past and Present*, no. 100:62–99.

Clark, Victor S. 1902. "Labor Conditions in Cuba." *Bulletin of the Department of Labor* 41:663–793.

Clarke, John, Stuart Hall, Tony Jefferson, and Brian Roberts. 1976. "Subcultures, Cultures, and Class." In *Resistance through Rituals*, ed. Stuart Hall and Tony Jefferson, 9–79. London: Hutchinson.

Clifford, James. 1983. "Power and Dialogue in Ethnography: Marcel Griaule's Initiation." In *Observers Observed: Essays on Ethnographic Fieldwork*, ed. George Stocking, 121–56. Madison: University of Wisconsin Press.

——. 1988. *The Predicament of Culture*. Cambridge, Mass.: Harvard University Press.

Cohen, David William. 1994. *The Combing of History*. Chicago: University of Chicago Press.

Cohen, David W., and Jack P. Greene, eds. 1972. *Neither Slave Nor Free*. Baltimore: Johns Hopkins University Press.

Cohn, Bernard. 1981. "Anthropology and History in the 1980s." *Journal of Interdisciplinary History* 12:227–52.

Cohn, Bernard, and Nicholas Dirks. 1988. "Beyond the Fringe: The Nation-State, Colonialism, and the Technologies of Power." *Journal of Historical Sociology* 1:224–29.

Collingwood, R. G. 1994. *The Idea of History*. 1946. Reprint, Oxford: Oxford University Press.

Comaroff, Jean. 1985. *Body of Power, Spirit of Resistance*. Chicago: University of Chicago Press.

Comaroff, Jean, and John Comaroff. 1992a. *Of Revelation and Revolution*. Chicago: University of Chicago Press.

——. 1999. "Occult Economies and the Violence of Abstraction: Notes from the South African Postcolony." *American Ethnologist* 26:279–303.

Comaroff, John. 1987. "Of Totemism and Ethnicity." *Ethnos* 52:301–23.

Comaroff, John, and Jean Comaroff, eds. 1992b. *Ethnography and the Historical Imagination*. Boulder, Colo.: Westview.

——. 1992c. "The Madman and the Migrant." In *Ethnography and the Historical Imagination*, ed. John Comaroff and Jean Comaroff, 127–54. Boulder, Colo.: Westview.

——. 1993. Introduction to *Modernity and Its Malcontents*, ed. John Comaroff and Jean Comaroff, xi–xxxvii. Chicago: University of Chicago Press.

Cooper, Frederick. 1994. "Conflict and Connection: Rethinking Colonial African History." *American Historical Review* 99:1516–45.

——. 1996. "Review Essay: Race, Ideology, and the Perils of Comparative History." *American Historical Review* 87:1124–38.

Cooper, Frederick, and Laura Ann Stoler. 1989. "Tensions of Empire: Colonial Control and Visions of Rule." *American Ethnologist* 16:609–21.

Corbin, Alain. 1987. "Commercial Sexuality in Nineteenth Century France: A System of Images and Regulations." In *The Making of the Modern Body*, ed. Catherine Gallagher and Thomas Laqueur, 209–19. Berkeley and Los Angeles: University of California Press.

Coronil, Fernando. 1996. "Beyond Occidentalism: Toward Nonimperial Geohistorical Categories." *Cultural Anthropology* 11:51–87.

Corrigan, Philip, and Derek Sayer. 1991. *The Great Arch: English State Formation as Cultural Revolution*. Oxford: Blackwell.

Costa Lima, Vivaldo de. 1976. "O conceito de 'naçao' nos Candomblé da Bahia." *Afro-Asia* 12:65–91.

Courlander, Harold. 1990. "Reflections of Haiti in the 1930s and '40s." *African Arts* 23:60–70.

Craton, Michael. 1982. *Testing the Chains*. Ithaca, N.Y.: Cornell University Press.

Crick, Malcolm. 1989. "Representations of International Tourism in the Social Sciences: Sun, Sex, Sights, Savings, and Servility." *Annual Review of Anthropology* 18:307–44.

Crush, Jonathan, and Paul Wellings. 1983. "The Southern African Pleasure Periphery, 1966–83." *Journal of Modern African Studies* 21:673–98.

Curl, James S. 1994. *Egyptomania*. Manchester: Manchester University Press.

Curtin, Philip D. 1955. *Two Jamaicas: The Role of Ideas in a Tropical Colony, 1830–1865*. Cambridge, Mass.: Harvard University Press.

Curtius, Ernst Robert. 1936. "Calderón und die Malerei." *Romanische Forschungen* 50:89–136.

Dantas Gois, Beatriz. 1985. "De feiticeiros a comunistas: Accusaçoes sobre o Candomblé." *Dédalo* 23:97–116.

——. 1988. *Vovo Nagô e Papai Branco*. Rio de Janeiro: Graal.

Danto, Arthur C. 1985. *Narration and Knowledge*. New York: Columbia University Press.

Darnton, Robert. 1968. *Mesmerism and the End of the Enlightenment in France*. Cambridge, Mass.: Harvard University Press.

Das, Veena. 1998. "Wittgenstein and Anthropology." *Annual Reviews of Anthropology* 27:171–95.

Dash, Michael. 1988. *Haiti and the United States: National Stereotypes and the Literary Imagination*. New York: St. Martin's.

Davis, David Brion. 1974. "Slavery and the Post–World War II Historians." *Daedalus* 103, no. 2:1–16.

——. 1975. *The Problem of Slavery in the Age of Revolution*. Ithaca, N.Y.: Cornell University Press.

Dayan, Joan. 1995. *Haiti, History, and the Gods*. Berkeley and Los Angeles: University of California Press.

——. 1996. "Paul Gilroy's Slaves, Ships, and Routes: The Middle Passage as Metaphor." *Research in African Literatures* 27:7–14.

De Boek, Filip. 1996. "Postcolonialism, Power, and Identity: Local and Global Perspectives from Zaire." In *Postcolonial Identities in Africa*, ed. Richard Werbner and Terence Ranger, 75–106. London: Zed.

de Certeau, Michel. 1984. *The Practice of Everyday Life*. Berkeley and Los Angeles: University of California Press.

de la Fuente, Alejandro. 1995. "Race and Inequality in Columbia, 1899–1981." *Journal of Contemporary History* 30:131–68.

——. 1998. "Race, National Discourse, and Politics in Cuba: An Overview." *Latin American Perspectives* 100:43–69.

de la Fuente, Alejandro, and Laurence Glasco. 1997. "Are Blacks 'Getting Out of Control'? Racial Attitudes, Revolution, and Political Transition in Cuba." In *Toward a New Cuba?* ed. Miguel Angel Centeno and Mauricio Font, 53–71. Boulder, Colo.: Lynne Riener.

Derby, Lauren. 1994. "Haitians, Magic, and Money: *Raza* and Society in the Haitian-Dominican Borderlands, 1900 to 1937." *Comparative Studies in Society and History* 36:488–526.

de Rosny, Eric. 1985. *Healers in the Night*. Maryknoll, N.Y.: Orbis.

Derrida, Jacques. 1994. *Specters of Marx*. London: Routledge.

Deschamps Chapeaux, Pedro. 1964. "Margarito Blanco el 'Ocongo de Ultan.'" *Boletín del Instituto de Historia y del Archivo Nacional* 65:97–109.

——. 1971a. "Los batallones de pardos y morenos leales de la Habana." *Unión* 10:104–18.

——. 1971b. *El negro en la economía habanera del siglo XIX*. La Habana: UNEAC.

——. 1983. *Los cimarrones urbanos*. La Habana: Editorial de Ciencias Sociales.

Deschamps Chapeaux, Pedro, and Juan Pérez de la Riva. 1974. *Contribución a la historia de la gente sin historia*. La Habana: Editorial de Ciencias Sociales.

Díaz Fabelo, Teodoro. 1960. *Olórun*. La Habana: Ediciones del Departamento de Folklore del Teatro Nacional de Cuba.

Diedrich, Bernard, and Al Burt. 1969. *Papa Doc: The Truth about Haiti Today*. New York: Avon.

Dijkstra, Bram. 1986. *Idols of Perversity*. New York: Oxford University Press.

Dirks, Nicholas B. 1990. "History as a Sign of the Modern." *Public Culture* 2:25–32.

——. 1992. "Introduction: Colonialism and Culture." In *Colonialism and Culture*, ed. Nicholas B. Dirks, 1–25. Ann Arbor: University of Michigan Press.

Dominguez, Jorge I. 1978. *Cuba: Order and Revolution*. Cambridge, Mass.: Harvard University Press.

Dominguez, Virginia. 1986. *White by Definition*. New Brunswick, N.J.: Rutgers University Press.

——. 1994. "A Taste for 'the Other': Intellectual Complicity in Racializing Practices." *Current Anthropology* 35:333–48.

Douglas, Mary. 1973. *Natural Symbols*. New York: Vintage.

Dowd Hall, Jacquelyn. 1983. "'The Mind That Burns in Each Body': Woman, Rape, and Racial Violence." In *Powers of Desire*, ed. Ann Snitnow, Christine Stansell, and Sharon Thompson, 328–49. New York: Monthly Review Press.

Drescher, Seymour. 1992. "The Ending of the Slave Trade and the Evolution of European Scientific Racism." In *The Atlantic Slave Trade,* ed. Joseph E. Inikori and Stanley L. Engerman, 361–96. Durham, N.C.: Duke University Press.

Drewal, Henry John. 1988. "Mermaids, Mirrors, and Snake Charmers: Igbo Mami Wata Shrines." *African Arts* 21:38–45.

——. 1996. "Mami Wata Shrines: Exotica and the Construction of Self." In *African Material Culture,* ed. Mary Jo Arnoldi, Christraud M. Geary, and Kris L. Hardin, 308–33. Bloomington: Indiana University Press.

Drewal, Henry John, and Margaret Thompson Drewal. 1983. *Gelede: Art and Female Power among the Yoruba.* Bloomington: Indiana University Press.

Driesch, Wilhem von den. 1982. "Staatliche und kirchliche Zensur in Spanien und Spanisch-Amerika im 18. Jahrhundert." Ph.D. diss., University of Hamburg.

Drinnon, Richard. 1980. *Facing West: The Metaphysics of Indian-Hating and Empire-Building.* Minneapolis: University of Minnesota Press.

Du Bois, W. E. B. 1997. *The Souls of Black Folk.* 1903. Reprint, Boston: Bedford.

Dupuy, Alex. 1989. *Haiti in the World Economy.* Boulder, Colo.: Westview.

Durkheim, Emile. 1995. *The Elementary Forms of Religious Life.* New York: Free Press.

Eckstein, Susan Eva. 1994. *Back from the Future.* Princeton, N.J.: Princeton University Press.

Ekholm, Kasja F. 1991. *Catastrophe and Creation.* Chur: Harwood Academic.

Elbl, Ivana. 1996. " 'Men without Wives': Sexual Arrangements in the Early Portuguese Expansion in West Africa." In *Desire and Discipline,* ed. Jacqueline Murray and Konrad Eisenbichler, 61–86. Toronto: University of Toronto Press.

Elizalde, Rosa Miriam. 1996. *Flores Desechables.* La Habana: Abril.

Elkins, F. W. 1977. *Street Preachers, Faith Healers, and Herb Doctors in Jamaica, 1890–1925.* New York: Revisionist.

——. 1986. "William Lauron DeLaurence and Jamaican Folk Religion." *Folklore* 97:215–18.

Ellis, A. B. 1966. *The Yoruba-Speaking Peoples of the Slave Coast of West Africa.* 1894. Reprint, Oosterhout: Anthropological Publications.

Ellison, Ralph. 1966. *Shadow and Act.* New York: Signet.

Eltis, David. 1987. *Economic Growth and the Ending of the Transatlantic Slave Trade.* New York: Oxford University Press.

Engels, Friedrich. 1969. *The Conditions of the Working Class in England.* London: Granada.

Engerman, Stanley L., and Joseph E. Inikori, eds. 1992. *The Atlantic Slave Trade.* Durham, N.C.: Duke University Press.

Entralgo, José Elías. 1953. *La liberación étnica del cubano.* La Habana: Imprenta de la Universidad de la Habana.

Erdman, David V. 1977. *Blake: Prophet against Empire.* New York: Dover.

Erdman, David V., and Donald K. Moore, eds. 1977. *The Notebook of William Blake.* New York: Readex.

Espino, Maria Dolores. 1993. "Tourism in Socialist Cuba." In *Tourism Marketing in the*

Caribbean, ed. Dennis J. Gayle and Jonathan N. Goodrich, 100–110. London: Routledge.

Evans-Pritchard, Edward E. 1937. *Witchcraft, Oracles, and Magic among the Azande.* Oxford: Clarendon.

Fabian, Johannes. 1978. "Popular Culture in Africa: Findings and Conjectures." *Africa* 48:315–34.

——. 1983. *Time and the Other.* New York: Columbia University Press.

——. 1996. *Remembering the Present.* Berkeley and Los Angeles: University of California Press.

Fanon, Franz. 1967. *Black Skin, White Masks.* New York: Grove.

——. 1968. *The Wretched of the Earth.* New York: Grove.

Fardon, Richard. 1990. "Localizing Strategies: The Regionalization of Ethnographic Accounts." In *Localizing Strategies*, ed. Richard Fardon, 1–35. Washington, D.C.: Smithsonian Institution Press.

——. 1995. *Counterworks: Managing the Diversity of Knowledge.* New York: Routledge.

Farmer, Paul. 1997. "On Suffering and Structuring Violence: A View from Below." In *Social Suffering*, ed. Arthur Kleinman, Veena Das, and Margaret Lock. Berkeley and Los Angeles: University of California Press.

Feierman, Steven. 1999. "Colonizers, Scholars, and the Creation of Invisible Histories." In *Beyond the Cultural Turn*, ed. Victoria E. Bonnell and Lynn Hunt, 182–216. Berkeley and Los Angeles: University of California Press.

Feldman, Allen. 1991. *Formations of Violence.* Chicago: University of Chicago Press.

——. 1995. "Ethnographic States of Emergency." In *Fieldwork under Fire*, ed. Carolyn Nordstrom and Antonius C. G. M. Robben, 224–52. Berkeley and Los Angeles: University of California Press.

Felman, Shoshana, and Dori Laub. 1992. *Testimony: Crises of Witnessing in Literature, Psychoanalysis, and History.* London: Routledge.

Felski, Rita. 1995. *The Gender of Modernity.* Cambridge, Mass.: Harvard University Press.

Ferguson, Charles A. 1959. "Diglossia." *Word* 15:325–40.

Ferguson, James. 1997. "Paradoxes of Sovereignty and Independence: 'Real' and 'Pseudo' Nation-States and the Depoliticization of Poverty." In *Siting Culture*, ed. Karen Fog-Olwig and Kirsten Hastrup, 123–41. London: Routledge.

Fernandez, James. 1982. *Bwiti: An Ethnography of the Religious Imagination in Africa.* Princeton, N.J.: Princeton University Press.

Fernandez, Nadine. 1996. "The Color of Love: Young Interracial Couples in Cuba." *Latin American Perspectives* 88:99–117.

——. 1999. "Back to the Future? Women, Race, and Tourism in Cuba." In *Sun, Sex, and Gold: Tourism and Sex Work in the Caribbean*, ed. Kamala Kempadoo, 81–97. Lanham, Md.: Rowman and Littlefield.

Fernández Retamar, Roberto. 1996. "The Enormity of Cuba." *boundary2* 23:165–90.

Ferrer, Ada. 1991. "Social Aspects of Cuban Nationalism: Race, Slavery, and the Guerra Chiquita, 1879–1880." *Cuban Studies* 21:37–55.

Fick, Carolyn E. 1990. *The Making of Haiti.* Knoxville: University of Tennessee Press.

Fiehrer, Thomas. 1990. "Political Violence in the Periphery: The Haitian Massacre of 1937." *Race and Class* 32:1–20.

Fields, Barbara. 1982. "Ideology and Race in American History." In *Region, Race, and Reconstruction,* ed. J. Morgan Kousser and James K. McPherson, 143–77. New York: Oxford University Press.

Fields, Karen. 1982. "Political Contingencies of Witchcraft in Colonial Central Africa: Culture and the State in Marxist Theory." *Revue canadienne des études africaines / Canadian Journal of African Studies* 16:567–93.

——. 1985. *Revival and Rebellion in Colonial Central Africa.* Princeton, N.J.: Princeton University Press.

——. 1994. "What One Cannot Remember Mistakenly." In *History and Memory in African-American Culture,* ed. Geneviève Fabre and Robert O'Mealley, 150–63. Oxford: Oxford University Press.

Finley, Moses I. 1968. "Slavery." In *International Encyclopedia of the Social Sciences,* ed. David Sills, 14:307–13. New York: Macmillan.

Flores Pena, Ysamur, and Roberta Evanchuck. 1994. *Santería Garments and Altars.* Jackson: University of Mississippi Press.

Fogel, Robert. 1989. *Without Consent or Contract: The Rise and Fall of American Slavery.* New York: Norton.

Foner, Philip S. 1962. *A History of Cuba and Its Relations with the United States.* New York: International.

Font, Mauricio. 1997. "Crisis and Reform in Cuba." In *Towards a New Cuba?* ed. Miguel Angel Centeno and Mauricio Font, 109–33. Boulder, Colo.: Lynne Riemer.

Fortes, Meyer, and Edward E. Evans-Pritchard. 1970. Introduction to *African Political Systems* (1940), ed. Meyer Fortes and Edward E. Evans-Pritchard, 1–23. London: Oxford University Press.

Foster-Carter, Aidan. 1978. "The Modes of Production Controversy." *New Left Review* 107:47–77.

Foucault, Michel. 1970. *The Order of Things.* New York: Random House.

——. 1972. *The Archaeology of Knowledge.* New York: Pantheon.

——. 1978. *The History of Sexuality.* Vol. 1, *An Introduction.* New York: Random House.

——. 1980. "Two Lectures." In *Power/Knowledge,* 78–108. New York: Pantheon.

France, Peter. 1966. *The Charter of the Land: Custom and Colonization in Fiji.* Melbourne: Oxford University Press.

Franco, José Luciano. 1973. *Los palenques de los negros cimarrones.* La Habana: Departamiento de Orientación Revolucionaria del Comité Central del Partido Comunista de Cuba.

——. 1974. "La conspiración de Aponte, 1812." In *Ensayos historicos,* ed. José Luciano Franco, 125–90. La Habana: Editorial de Ciencias Sociales.

——. 1977. *Las conspiraciones de 1810 y 1812.* La Habana: Editorial de Ciencias Sociales.

Frank, André Gunder. 1967. *Capitalism and Underdevelopment in Latin America.* New York: Monthly Review Press.

Franklin, Sarah. 1995. "Science as Culture, Cultures of Science." *Annual Reviews of Anthropology* 24:163–84.

Fraser, Nancy. 1997. *Justice Interruptus.* New York: Routledge.

Freud, Sigmund. 1955. "The Uncanny" (1919). In *The Standard Edition of the Complete Psychological Works of Sigmund Freud,* ed. James Strachey, 17:218–56.

Friedlander, Saul, ed. 1992. *Probing the Limits of Representation.* Cambridge, Mass.: Harvard University Press.

Fryer, Peter. 1984. *Staying Power: The History of Black People in Britain.* London: Pluto.

Fukuyama, Francis. 1992. *The End of History and the Last Man.* New York: Free Press.

Fusco, Coco. 1998. "Hustling for Dollars: *Jineterismo* in Cuba." In *Global Sex Workers,* ed. Kamala Kempadoo, 151–66. London: Routledge.

Gallego, J. 1972. *Visión y símbolos en la pintura española del siglo de oro.* Madrid: Aguilar.

Garfield, Richard, and Sarah Santana. 1997. "The Impact of the Economic Crisis and the U.S. Embargo on Health in Cuba." *American Journal of Public Health* 87:15–20.

Gates, Henry Louis, Jr. 1988. *The Signifying Monkey.* New York: Oxford University Press.

Geertz, Clifford. 1973. *The Interpretation of Cultures.* New York: Basic.

———. 1975. *Islam Observed.* Chicago: University of Chicago Press.

———. 1977. "Centers, Kings, and Charisma: Reflections on the Symbolism of Power." In *Culture and Its Creators,* ed. Joseph Ben-David and Terry Nicholas Clark, 150–71. Chicago: University of Chicago Press.

Geertz, Hildred. 1975. "An Anthropology of Religion and Magic, I." *Journal of Interdisciplinary History* 6:71–89.

Geggus, David. 1989. "The French and Haitian Revolutions and a Resistance to Slavery in the Americas: An Overview." *Revue française d'histoire d'outre-mer* 76:107–24.

Genovese, Eugene D. 1971. *The World the Slaveholders Made.* New York: Vintage.

———. 1979. *From Rebellion to Revolution.* Baton Rouge: Louisiana State University Press.

Geschiere, Peter. 1992. "Kinship, Witchcraft, and 'the Market.'" In *Contesting Markets,* ed. Roy Dilley, 159–79. Edinburgh: Edinburgh University Press.

———. 1997. *The Modernity of Witchcraft.* Charlottesville: University of Virginia Press.

Giedion, Siegfried. 1948. *Mechanization Takes Command.* New York: Oxford University Press.

Gilman, Sander. 1985. *Difference and Pathology.* Ithaca, N.Y.: Cornell University Press.

Gilroy, Paul. 1992. *The Black Atlantic: Modernity and Double Consciousness.* Cambridge, Mass.: Harvard University Press.

———. 2000. *Against Race: Imagining Political Culture beyond the Color Line.* Cambridge, Mass.: Harvard University Press.

Ginzburg, Carlo. 1983a. "Clues: Morelli, Freud, and Sherlock Holmes." In *The Sign of Three,* ed. Umberto Eco and Thomas A. Sebeok, 81–118. Bloomington: Indiana University Press.

——. 1983b. *Night Battles.* New York: Penguin.

——. 1992. *The Cheese and the Worms.* Baltimore: Johns Hopkins University Press.

Gleason, Judith. 1987. *Oya: In Praise of the Goddess.* Boston: Shambhala.

Glissant, Edouard. 1989. *Caribbean Discourse.* Charlottesville: University of Virginia Press.

——. 1997. *Poetics of Relation.* Ann Arbor: University of Michigan Press.

Gonzales Huguet, Lydia. 1968. "La casa-templo en la regla de ocha." *Etnología y Folklore* 5:33–57.

Goody, Jack. 1968. "Restricted Literacy in Northern Ghana." In *Literacy in Traditional Societies,* ed. Jack Goody, 199–264. Cambridge: Cambridge University Press.

Goody, Jack, and Ian Watts. 1968. "The Consequences of Literacy." In *Literacy in Traditional Societies,* ed. Jack Goody, 27–68. Cambridge: Cambridge University Press.

Götz, Nicola. 1995. *Obeah—Hexerei in der Karibik—zwischen Macht und Ohnmacht.* Frankfurt: Peter Lang.

Gould, Steven J. 1981. *The Mismeasure of Man.* New York: Norton.

Gramsci, Antonio. 1971. *Selections from the Prison Notebooks.* London: Lawrence and Wishart.

Guanche, Jesús. 1983. *Procesos etnoculturales de Cuba.* La Habana: Editorial Letras Cubanas.

Gudeman, Steven. 1992. "Markets, Models, and Morality." In *Contesting Markets,* ed. Roy Dilley, 279–94. Edinburgh: Edinburgh University Press.

Guerra, Fernando. 1913. Open letter directed at the "autoridades superiores de la República." Havana, 5 July. Fondo Ortiz.

——. 1914. "Hoja suelta: La verdad en su puesto." Broadside published by Imprenta y Sellos Goma, Monte 135. Havana, 8 December. Fondo Ortiz.

——. 1915. "Manifiesto: Somos religiosos y no ateos." Broadside. Havana, 30 September. Fondo Ortiz.

Guerra, Fernando, and Silvestre Erice. 1913. "Manifiesto: ¡La verdad, con cara al sol!" Broadside. Havana, 19 July. Fondo Ortiz.

Gugelberger, Georg M. 1996. "Introduction: Institutionalization of Transgression: Testimonial Discourse and Beyond." In *The Real Thing,* ed. Georg M. Gugelberger. Durham, N.C.: Duke University Press.

Guha, Ranajit. 1983. "The Prose of Counterinsurgency." *Subaltern Studies* 2:1–42.

——. 1989. "Domination without Hegemony and Its Historiography." *Subaltern Studies* 6:210–309.

Guillaumin, Colette. 1995. *Racism, Sexism, Power, and Ideology.* London: Routledge.

Guyer, Jane I., and Samuel M. Eno Belinga. 1995. "Wealth in People as Wealth in Knowledge: Accumulation and Composition in Equatorial Africa." *Journal of African History* 36:91–120.

Habermas, Jürgen. 1987. *The Philosophical Discourse on Modernity.* Cambridge, Mass.: MIT Press.

Hacking, Ian. 1996. "Memory Sciences, Memory Politics." In *Tense Past,* ed. Paul Antze and Michael Lambek, 67–87. London: Routledge.

Hale, Lindsay Lauren. 1997. "Preto Velho: Resistance, Redemption, and Engendered Representations of Slavery in a Brazilian Possession-Trance Religion." *American Ethnologist* 24:392–414.

Hall, Catherine. 1992. "Missionary Stories: Gender and Ethnicity in England in the 1830s and 1840s." In *White, Male, and Middle Class,* ed. Catherine Hall, 205–54. Cambridge, Eng.: Polity.

Hall, Colin Michael. 1994. *Tourism and Politics.* New York: Wiley.

Hall, Gwendolyn Midlo. 1971. *Social Control in Slave Plantation Societies.* Baltimore: Johns Hopkins University Press.

Hall, Neville A. T. 1992. *Slave Society in the Danish West Indies.* Mona: University of the West Indies Press.

Hamilton, Carolyn. 1998. *Terrific Majesty: The Powers of Shaka Zulu and the Limits of Historical Invention.* Cambridge, Mass.: Harvard University Press.

Handler, Richard, and Jocelyn Linnekin. 1984. "Tradition, Genuine and Spurious." *Journal of American Folklore* 97:273–90.

Hannerz, Ulf. 1987. "The World in Creolization." *Africa* 67:546–59.

Haraway, Donna. 1989. *Primate Visions.* London: Routledge.

Harding, Rachel E. 2000. *A Refuge in Thunder: Candomblé and Alternative Spaces of Blackness.* Bloomington: Indiana University Press.

Harrison, Faye. 1995. "The Persistent Power of 'Race' in the Cultural and Political Economy of Racism." *Annual Reviews of Anthropology* 24:47–74.

Harrison, Peter. 1990. *"Religion" and the Religions in the English Enlightenment.* Cambridge: Cambridge University Press.

Harrison, Simon. 1993. "The Commerce of Cultures in Melanesia." *Man* 28:139–58.

Hartigan, John, Jr. 1997. "Establishing the Fact of Whiteness." *American Anthropologist* 99:495–505.

Hartsock, Nancy C. M. 1983. *Money, Sex, and Power.* New York: Longman.

Harvey, Penelope. 1996. *Hybrids of Modernity.* London: Routledge.

Hastrup, Kirsten. 1992. Introduction to *Other Histories,* ed. Kirsten Hastrup, 1–13. London: Routledge.

Hay, Denys. 1968. *Europe: The Emergence of an Idea.* Edinburgh: Edinburgh University Press.

Hayden, Robert M. 1996. "Imagined Communities and Real Victims: Self-Determination and Ethnic Cleansing in Yugoslavia." *American Ethnologist* 23:783–801.

Hebdige, Dick. 1979. *Subculture: The Meaning of Style.* London: Methuen.

Heinl, Robert Debs, Jr. and Nancy Gordon Heinl. 1978. *Written in Blood: The Story of the Haitian People, 1492–1971.* Boston: Houghton Mifflin.

Helg, Aline. 1990. "Fernando Ortiz ou la pseudo-science contre la sorccellerie Africaine à Cuba." In *La pensée métisse: Croyances africaines et rationalité occidentale en questions,* ed. Robin Horton, 241–50. Paris: Presses Universitaires de France.

——. 1995. *Our Rightful Share: The Afro-Cuban Struggle for Equality, 1886–1912.* Chapel Hill: University of North Carolina Press.

——. 1996. "Políticas raciales en Cuba después de la independencia: Represión de la cultura negra y mito de la igualidad racial." *América Negra* 11:63–79.

——. 2000. "Black Men, Racial Stereotyping, and Violence in the U.S. South and Cuba at the Turn of the Century." *Comparative Studies in Society and History* 42:576–604.

Helms, Mary W. 1988. *Ulysses' Sail: An Ethnographic Odyssey of Power, Knowledge, and Geographical Distance.* Princeton, N.J.: Princeton University Press.

Hendrickson, Hildi. 1996. "Bodies and Flags: The Representation of Herrero Identity in Colonial Namibia." In *Clothing and Difference,* ed. Hildi Hendrickson, 213–44. Durham, N.C.: Duke University Press.

Hershatter, Gail. 1997. *Dangerous Pleasures.* Berkeley and Los Angeles: University of California Press.

Herskovits, Melville J. 1941. *The Myth of the Negro Past.* New York: Harper and Row.

——. 1948. *Man and His Works.* New York: Knopf.

——. 1971. *Life in a Haitian Valley.* 1937. Reprint, Garden City, N.Y.: Doubleday.

Herzfeld, Michael. 1992. *The Social Production of Indifference.* New York: Berg.

Heuman, Gad J. 1981. *Between Black and White: Race, Politics, and the Free Coloureds in Jamaican Society, 1792–1865.* Westport, Conn.: Greenwood.

Heusch, Luc de. 1971. *Pourquoi l'épouser? et autres essais.* Paris: Gallimard.

Higginbotham, Evelyn Brooks. 1992. "African-American Women's History and the Metalanguage of Race." *Signs* 17:251–74.

Hill, Christopher. 1986. "Science and Magic." In *The Collected Essays of Christopher Hill,* 3:274–99. Amherst: University of Massachusetts Press.

Hill, Robert A. 1981. "Dread History: Leonard P. Howell and Millenarian Visions in Early Rastafari Religions in Jamaica." *Epoché* 9:30–71.

——. 1994. "Making Noise: Marcus Garvey *Dada,* August 1922." In *Picturing Us: African American Identity in Photography,* ed. Deborah Willis, 181–205. New York: New Press.

Hobart, Mark. 1993. "Introduction: The Growth of Ignorance." In *An Anthropological Critique of Development,* ed. Mark Hobart, 1–30. London: Routledge.

Hocart, A. M. 1969. *Kingship.* 1927. Reprint, Oxford: Oxford University Press.

Hochschild, Arlie R. 1983. *The Managed Heart.* Berkeley and Los Angeles: University of California Press.

Hoetink, Harry. 1985. " 'Race' and Color in the Caribbean." In *Caribbean Contours,* ed. Sidney W. Mintz and Sally Price, 55–84. Baltimore: Johns Hopkins University Press.

Hogg, Donald. 1961. "Magic and 'Science' in Jamaica." *Caribbean Studies* 1:1–5.

Hollis, Martin, and Steven Lukes. 1982. *Rationality and Relativism.* Cambridge, Mass: MIT Press.

Holt, Thomas C. 1992. *The Problem of Freedom: Race, Labor, and Politics in Jamaica and Britain, 1832–1938*. Baltimore: Johns Hopkins University Press.

——. 1995. "Marking: Race, Race-Making, and the Writing of History." *American Historical Review* 100:1–21.

hooks, bell. 1992. *Black Looks: Race and Representation*. Boston: South End.

Horkheimer, Max, and Theodor W. Adorno. 1972. *Dialectic of Enlightenment*. New York: Herder and Herder.

Horton, Robin. 1967. "African Traditional Thought and Western Science." *Africa* 31:50–71, 155–87.

Howard, Philip A. 1998. *Changing History: Afro-Cuban Cabildos and Societies of Color in the Nineteenth Century*. Baton Rouge: Louisiana State University Press.

Howe, Eunice D. 1991. *Andrea Palladio: The Churches of Rome*. Binghamton, N.Y.: Center for Medieval and Early Renaissance Studies.

Huggan, Graham. 1998. "Ghost Stories, Bone Flute, Cannibal Countermemories." In *Cannibalism and the Colonial World*, ed. Francis Barker, Peter Hulme, and Margaret Iversen, 126–41. Cambridge: Cambridge University Press.

Hunt, Lynn. 1984. *Politics, Culture, and Class in the French Revolution*. Berkeley and Los Angeles: University of California Press.

Hutton, Patrick H. 1993. *History as an Art of Memory*. Hanover, N.H.: University Press of New England.

Idowu, E. Bolaji. 1962. *Olodumare: God in Yoruba Belief*. London: Longmans.

Ileto, Reynaldo C. 1989. "Cholera and the Origins of the American Sanitary Order in the Philippines." In *Imperial Medicine and Indigenous Societies*, ed. David Arnold, 125–48. Manchester: Manchester University Press.

"Isla de Cuba—'Matiabo,' ídolo cogido á una partida de insurrectos." 1875. *La Ilustración Española y Americana* 29, no. 30 (15 August): 1–2.

Iverson, Erik. 1961. *The Myth of Egypt and Its Hieroglyphs in European Tradition*. Copenhagen: Gad.

Iznaga, Diana. 1989. *Transculturación en Fernando Ortiz*. La Habana: Editorial de Ciencias Sociales.

Jackson, Michael. 1990. "The Man Who Could Turn into an Elephant: Shape-Shifting among the Kuranko of Sierra Leone." In *Personhood and Agency*, ed. Ivan Karp and Michael Jackson, 59–78. Uppsala: Almqvist and Wiksel.

Jacobson-Widding, Anita. 1979. *Red-White-Black as a Mode of Thought*. Uppsala: Almqvist and Wiksel.

James, C. L. R. 1963. *The Black Jacobins: Toussaint L'Ouverture and the San Domingo Revolution*. 2d ed. New York: Vintage.

Jameson, Robert Francis. 1821. *Letters from the Havana during the Year 1820 containing an Account of the Present State of the Island of Cuba and Observations on the Slave Trade*. London: John Miller.

Janzen, John. 1972. "Laman's Kongo Ethnography: Observations on Sources, Methodology, and Theory." *Africa* 42:316–28.

——. 1983. *Lemba, 1650–1930*. New York: Garland.

Jensen, Larry R. 1988. *Children of Colonial Despotism: Press, Politics, and Culture in Cuba, 1790–1840*. Tampa: University of South Florida Press.

Johnson, Mary Lynn, and John E. Grant. 1979. *Blake's Poetry and Designs*. New York: Norton.

Jolly, Margaret, and Lenore Manderson. 1997. "Introduction: Sites of Desire/Economies of Pleasure in Asia and the Pacific." In *Sites of Desire, Economies of Pleasure*, ed. Lenore Manderson and Margaret Jolly, 1–26. Chicago: University of Chicago Press.

Jordan, Winthrop D. 1969. *White over Black*. Baltimore: Penguin.

Kantorowicz, Ernst H. 1957. *The King's Two Bodies*. Princeton, N.J.: Princeton University Press.

Kaplan, Amy. 1993. "Black and Blue on San Juan Hill." In *Cultures of United States Imperialism*, ed. Amy Kaplan and Donald E. Pease, 219–36. Durham, N.C.: Duke University Press.

Kaplan, Martha, and John D. Kelley. 1994. "Rethinking Resistance: Dialogics of 'Disaffection' in Colonial Fiji." *American Ethnologist* 21:123–51.

Karasch, Mary. 1979a. "Central African Religious Tradition in Rio de Janeiro." *Journal of Latin American Lore* 5:233–53.

——. 1979b. "Commentary One." In *Roots and Branches*, ed. Michael Craton, 138–41. Toronto: Pergamon.

——. 1987. *Slave Life in Rio de Janeiro, 1808–1850*. Princeton, N.J.: Princeton University Press.

Keesing, Roger M. 1987. "Anthropology as an Interpretative Quest." *Current Anthropology* 28:161–76.

Keesing, Roger M., and Robert Tonkinson, eds. 1982. "Reinventing Traditional Culture: The Politics of Kastom in Island Melanesia." Special issue of *Mankind* 13.4.

Kemp, Anthony. 1991. *Estrangement of the Past*. New York: Oxford University Press.

Kempadoo, Kamala, ed. 1999. *Sun, Sex, and Gold: Tourism and Sex Work in the Caribbean*. Lanham, Md.: Rowan & Littlefield.

Kennedy, Emmet. 1989. *A Cultural History of the French Revolution*. New Haven, Conn.: Yale University Press.

Klein, Herbert. 1966. "The Colored Militia of Cuba: 1568–1868." *Caribbean Studies* 6:17–27.

——. 1967. *Slavery in the Americas: A Comparative Study of Virginia and Cuba*. Chicago: University of Chicago Press.

Knight, Franklin. 1970. *Slave Society in Cuba during the Nineteenth Century*. Madison: University of Wisconsin Press.

——. 1972. "Cuba." In *Neither Slave nor Free*, ed. David W. Cohen and Jack P. Greene, 278–308. Baltimore: Johns Hopkins University Press.

——. 1977a. "Origins of Wealth and the Sugar Revolution in Cuba, 1750–1850." *Hispanic American Historical Review* 57:231–53.

——. 1977b. "The Social Structure of Cuban Slave Society in the Nineteenth Century." *Annals of the New York Academy of Sciences* 292:259–66.

——. 1985. "Jamaican Migrants and the Cuban Sugar Industry, 1900–1934." In *Be-*

tween Slavery and Free Labor, ed. Manuel Moreno Fraginals, Frank Moya Pons, and Stanley L. Engerman, 94–114. Baltimore: Johns Hopkins University Press.

Kopytoff, Igor. 1986. "The Cultural Biography of Things: Commoditization as Process." In *The Social Life of Things*, ed. Arjun Appadurai, 64–91. Cambridge: Cambridge University Press.

Kopytoff, Igor, and Suzanne Miers, eds. 1997. *Slavery in Africa: Historical and Anthropological Perspectives.* Madison: University of Wisconsin Press.

Koselleck, Reinhard. 1985. *Futures Past: On the Semantics of Historical Time.* Cambridge, Mass.: MIT Press.

Kramer, Fritz W. 1993. *The Red Fez.* London: Verso.

Kropfinger–von Kügelen, Helga. 1973. *Europäischer Buchexport von Sevilla nach Neuspanien im Jahre 1586.* Wiesbaden: Franz Steiner.

Kuethe, Allan J. 1986. *Cuba, 1753–1815: Crown, Military, and Society.* Knoxville: University of Tennessee Press.

Kuhn, Thomas. 1970. *The Structure of Scientific Revolutions.* 2d ed. Chicago: University of Chicago Press.

Kulikoff, Allan. 1986. *Tobacco and Slaves.* Chapel Hill: University of North Carolina Press.

Kuper, Adam. 1988. *The Invention of Primitive Society.* London: Routledge.

Kuser, John D. 1921. *Haiti: Its Dawn of Progress after Years in a Night of Revolution.* Boston: R. G. Badger.

Kutzinski, Vera M. 1993. *Sugar's Secrets: Race and the Erotics of Cuban Nationalism.* Charlottesville: University of Virginia Press.

Lachatañeré, Romulo. 1992. *El sistema religioso de los afrocubanos.* 1939–46. Reprint, La Habana: Editorial de Ciencias Sociales.

Laman, Karl. 1962. *The Kongo III.* Lund: Hakan Ohlsons Boktryckeri.

Lambek, Michael. 1993. *Knowledge and Practice in Mayotte.* Toronto: University of Toronto Press.

———. 1996. "The Past Imperfect: Remembering as Moral Practice." In *Tense Past*, ed. Paul Antze and Michael Lambek, 235–54. London: Routledge.

Lancaster, Roger N. 1992. *Life Is Hard: Machismo, Danger, and the Intimacy of Power in Nicaragua.* Berkeley and Los Angeles: University of California Press.

Larose, Serge. 1977. "The Meaning of Africa in Haitian Vodu." In *Symbols and Sentiments*, ed. Ioan M. Lewis, 85–116. London: Tavistock.

Latour, Bruno. 1993. *We Have Never Been Modern.* Cambridge, Mass.: Harvard University Press.

Lattas, Andrew. 1993. "Sorcery and Colonialism: Illness, Dreams, and Death as Political Languages in West New Britain." *Man* 28:51–77.

Lawless, Robert. 1992. *Haiti's Bad Press.* Rochester, N.Y.: Schenkman.

Lea, Henry Charles. 1908. *The Inquisition in the Spanish Dependencies.* London: Macmillan.

Leach, Edmund. 1977. *Custom, Law, and Terrorist Violence.* Edinburgh: Edinburgh University Press.

Lévi-Strauss, Claude. 1966. *The Savage Mind*. Chicago: University of Chicago Press.
Levitine, George. 1959. "Some Emblematic Sources of Goya." *Journal of the Warburg and Courtauld Institutes* 22:106–31.
Lewis, Earl. 1995. "To Turn as on a Pivot: Writing African Americans into a History of Overlapping Diasporas." *American Historical Review* 100:765–87.
Lewis, Gordon K. 1968. *The Growth of the Modern West Indies*. New York: Monthly Review Press.
Lewis, Ioan M. 1986. *Religion in Context*. Cambridge: Cambridge University Press.
Leyburn, James. 1931. *Handbook of Ethnography*. New Haven, Conn.: Yale University Press.
Lienhard, Godfrey. 1961. *Divinity and Experience: The Religion of the Dinka*. Oxford: Clarendon.
Linebaugh, Peter. 1988. "All the Atlantic Mountains Shook." In *Reviving the English Revolution*, ed. Geoff Eley and William Hunt, 193–219. London: Verso.
Linebaugh, Peter, and Marcus Rediker. 1991. "The Many-Headed Hydra: Sailors, Slaves, and the Atlantic Working Class in the Eighteenth Century." *Journal of Historical Sociology* 3:225–52.
——. 2000. *The Many-Headed Hydra*. Boston: Beacon.
Linke, Ulli. 1990. "Folklore, Anthropology, and the Government of Social Life." *Comparative Studies in Society and History* 32:117–48.
——. 1997. "Gendered Difference, Violent Imagination: Blood, Race, Nation." *American Anthropologist* 99:559–73.
Littlewood, Roland. 1995. "History, Memory, and Appropriation: Some Problems in the Analysis of Origins." In *Rastafari and Other African-Caribbean Worldviews*, ed. Barry Chevannes, 232–52. The Hague: Institute of Social Studies.
Lombroso, Cesare. 1971. *L'uomo delinquente: In rapporto all'antropologia querisprudenza ed alle discipline carcerarie*. 1876. Reprint, Rome: Napoleone editore.
López, Valdés, Rafael. 1966. "La sociedad secreta 'abakuá' en un grupo de obreros portuarios." *Etnología y Folklore* 2:5–26.
Lorimer, Douglas A. 1978. *Color, Class, and the Victorians*. Bristol: Leicester University Press.
Lovejoy, Paul E. 1983. *Transformations in Slavery*. London: Cambridge University Press.
——. 1997. "The African Diaspora: Revisionist Interpretations of Ethnicity, Culture, and Religion under Slavery." *Studies in the World History of Slavery, Abolition, and Emancipation* 2:1–24.
Lowenthal, Ira. 1987. " 'Marriage Is 20, Children Is 21': The Cultural Construction of Conjugality and the Family in Rural Haiti." Ph.D. diss., Johns Hopkins University.
Lubazs, Heinz. 1992. "Adam Smith and the Invisible Hand—or the Market?" In *Contesting Markets*, ed. Roy Dilley, 37–56. Edinburgh: Edinburgh University Press.
Lukes, Steven. 1973. *Émile Durkheim*. London: Penguin.
Lundahl, Mats. 1983. *The Haitian Economy*. New York: St. Martin's.
——. 1992. *Politics or Markets? Essays on Haitian Underdevelopment*. London: Routledge.

MacFarlane, Alan. 1987. *The Culture of Capitalism*. Oxford: Blackwell.
MacGaffey, Wyatt. 1968. "Kongo and the King of the Americans." *Journal of Modern African Studies* 6:171–81.
——. 1970. "The Religious Commissions of the Bakongo." *Man* 5:27–38.
——. 1972. "The West in Congolese Experience." In *Africa and the West*, ed. Philip D. Curtin, 49–74. Madison: University of Wisconsin Press.
——. 1977. "Fetishism Revisited: Kongo *nkisi* in Sociological Perspective." *Africa* 47:140–52.
——. 1978. "African History, Anthropology, and the Rationality of Natives." *History in Africa* 5:101–20.
——. 1981. "African Ideology and Belief: A Survey." *African Studies Review* 24:227–74.
——. 1983. *Modern Kongo Prophets*. Bloomington: Indiana University Press.
——. 1986. *Religion and Society in Central Africa*. Chicago: University of Chicago Press.
——. 1988. "Complexity, Astonishment, and Power: The Visual Vocabulary of Kongo Minkisi." *Journal of Southern African Studies* 14:188–203.
——. 1991. *Art and Healing of the Bakongo*. Stockholm: Folkens museum-etnografiska.
——. 1993. *Astonishment and Power*. Washington, D.C.: Smithsonian Institution Press.
——. 2000. *Kongo Political Culture*. Bloomington: Indiana University Press.
Mancini, Matthew. 1989. "Political Economy and Cultural Theory in Tocqueville's Abolitionism." *Slavery and Abolition* 10:151–71.
Manderson, Leonore and Margaret Jolly. 1997. "Sites of Desire / Economies of Pleasure in Asia and the Pacific." In *Sites of Desire, Economies of Pleasure*, ed. Leonore Manderson and Margaret Jolly, 1–26. Chicago: University of Chicago Press.
Mangum, Charles S. 1940. *The Legal Status of the Negro*. Chapel Hill: University of North Carolina Press.
Maraval, José Antonio. 1986. *Culture of the Baroque*. Minneapolis: University of Minnesota Press.
Marcus, George, and Michael Fisher. 1986. *Anthropology as Cultural Critique*. Chicago: University of Chicago Press; Minneapolis: University of Minnesota Press.
Marrero, Levi. 1971–88. *Cuba, economía y sociedad*. Madrid: Playor.
Martin de Holán, Pablo, and Nelson Phillips. 1997. "Sun, Sand, and Hard Currency: Tourism in Cuba." *Annals of Tourism Research* 24:777–95.
Martínez, Samuel. 1996. "Indifference within Indignation: Anthropology, Human Rights, and the Haitian Bracero." *American Anthropologist* 98:17–25.
Martínez-Alier, Verena. 1974. *Marriage, Class, and Color in Nineteenth Century Cuba*. Cambridge: Cambridge University Press.
Martínez-Echazábal, Lourdes. 1998. "*Mestizaje* and the Discourse of National / Cultural Identity in Latin America, 1845–1959." *Latin American Perspectives* 25:21–42.
Martínez Fernández, Luis. 1998. *Fighting Slavery in the Caribbean*. Armonk, N.Y.: M. E. Sharpe.

Marx, Karl. 1977. *Capital.* New York: Vintage.

Marx, Karl, and Friedrich Engels. 1967. *The Communist Manifesto.* Harmondsworth: Penguin.

Matory, J. Lorand. 1991. *Sex and the Empire That Is No More.* Minneapolis: University of Minnesota Press.

——. 1999. "The English Professors of Brazil: On the Diasporic Roots of the Yorùbá Nation." *Comparative Studies in Society and History* 41:72–103.

Mbembe, Achille. 1992. "Provisional Notes on the Postcolony." *Africa* 62:3–37.

Mbembe, Achille, and Janet Roitman. 1996. "Figures of the Subject in Times of Crisis." In *The Geography of Identity,* ed. Patricia Yaeger, 153–86. Ann Arbor: University of Michigan Press.

McCarthy Brown, Karen. 1989. "Systematic Remembering, Systematic Forgetting: Ogou in Haiti." In *Africa's Ogun: Old World and New,* ed. Sandra T. Barnes, 65–89. Bloomington: Indiana University Press.

——. 1991. *Mama Lola: A Vodou Priestess in Brooklyn.* Berkeley and Los Angeles: University of California Press.

McClintock, Anne. 1992. "Screwing the System: Sexwork, Race, and the Law." *boundary2* 19:70–95.

McCracken, Grant. 1988. *Culture and Consumption.* Bloomington: Indiana University Press.

McGrane, Bernard. 1989. *Beyond Anthropology: Society and the Other.* New York: Columbia University Press.

McLeod, Marc C. 1998. "Undesirable Aliens: Race, Ethnicity, and Nationalism in the Comparison of Haitian and British West Indian Immigrant Workers in Cuba, 1912–1939." *Journal of Social History* 31:599–623.

Meillassoux, Claude. 1991. *The Anthropology of Slavery.* Chicago: University of Chicago Press.

Meltzer, Francoise. 1994. "For Your Eyes Only: Ghost Citing." In *Questions of Evidence,* ed. James Chandler, Arnold I. Davidson, and Harry Harootunian, 43–49. Chicago: University of Chicago Press.

Méndez Rodenas, Adriana. 1998. *Gender and Nationalism in Colonial Cuba.* Nashville: Vanderbilt University Press.

Mercer, Kobena. 1994. *Welcome to the Jungle.* London: Routledge.

Métraux, Alfred. 1972. *Voodoo in Haiti.* 1959. Reprint, New York: Schocken.

Meyer, Birgit. 1992. " 'If you are a Devil, you are a Witch, if you are a Witch, you are a Devil': The Integration of 'Pagan' Ideas into the Conceptual Universe of Ewe Christians in Southwestern Ghana." *Journal of Religion in Africa* 22:98–132.

——. 1994. "Beyond Syncretism: Translation and Diabolization in the Appropriation of Protestantism in Africa." In *Syncretism/Antisyncretism,* ed. Rosalind Shaw and Charles Stewart, 5–68. London: Routledge.

——. 1995. "Delivered from the Powers of Darkness: Confessions of Satanic Riches in Christian Ghana." *Africa* 65:236–55.

Miles, Robert. 1993. *Racism after "Race Relations."* London: Routledge.

Mill, John Stuart. 1849. *Principles of Political Economy.* London: Routledge.
Miller, Christopher L. 1985. *Blank Darkness: Africanist Discourse in French.* Chicago: University of Chicago Press.
Miller, Daniel. 1994. *Modernity: An Ethnographic Approach.* Oxford: Berg.
Miller, Joseph C. 1980. "Introduction: Listening for the African Past." In *The African Past Speaks,* ed. Joseph C. Miller, 1–59. Folkestone: Dawson.
——. 1988. *Way of Death.* Madison: University of Wisconsin Press.
Mink, Louis. 1978. "Narrative Form as a Cognitive Instrument." In *The Writing of History,* ed. Robert H. Canary and Henry Kozicki, 129–49. Madison: University of Wisconsin Press.
Mintz, Sidney W. 1964. Foreword to *Sugar and Slavery in the Caribbean,* by Ramiro Guerra y Sánchez, xi–xliv. New Haven, Conn.: Yale University Press.
——. 1970. Foreword to *Afro-American Anthropology,* ed. Norman E. Whitten and John F. Szwed, 1–16. New York: Free Press.
——. 1971. "Groups, Group Boundaries, and the Perception of 'Race.'" *Comparative Studies in Society and History* 13:437–50.
——. 1974. *Caribbean Transformations.* Baltimore: Johns Hopkins University Press.
——. 1975. "History and Anthropology: A Brief Reprise." In *Race and Slavery in the Western Hemisphere,* ed. Stanley L. Engerman and Eugene D. Genovese, 477–94. Princeton, N.J.: Princeton University Press.
——. 1977. "The So-Called World System: Local Initiative and Local Response." *Dialectical Anthropology* 2:253–70.
——. 1978. "Was the Plantation Slave a Proletarian?" *Review* 2:81–98.
——. 1985. *Sweetness and Power.* New York: Penguin.
——. 1996. "Enduring Substances, Trying Theories: The Caribbean Region as Oikoumene." *Journal of the Royal Anthropological Institute* 2:289–311.
Mintz, Sidney W., and Richard Price. 1992. *The Birth of African-American Culture.* Boston: Beacon.
Mohanty, Chandra Talpade. 1991. "Under Western Eyes: Feminist Scholarship and Colonial Discourse." In *Third World Women and the Politics of Feminism,* ed. Chandra Talpade Mohanty, Ann Russo, and Lourdes Torres, 51–80. Bloomington: Indiana University Press.
Monteiro, Joachim John. 1968. *Angola and the River Congo.* Vol. 1. 1875. Reprint, London: Frank Cass.
Moore, Carlos. 1988. *Castro, the Blacks, and Africa.* Los Angeles: Center for Afro-American Studies.
Moore, Robin. 1997. *Nationalizing Blackness: Afrocubanismo and Artistic Revolution in Havana, 1920–1940.* Pittsburgh: University of Pittsburgh Press.
Moore, Sally Falk. 1999. "Reflections on the Comaroff Lecture." *American Ethnologist* 26:304–6.
Morales Padrón, Francisco. 1972. "Conspiraciones y masonería en Cuba (1810–1826)." *Anuario de Estudios Americanos* 29:343–77.
Moreno Fraginals, Manuel. 1976. *The Sugarmill.* New York: Monthly Review Press.

——. 1978. *El Ingenio.* La Habana: Editorial de Ciencias Sociales.

——. 1983. *La historia como arma.* Barcelona: Editorial Crítica.

Morgan, Edmund S. 1975. *American Slavery, American Freedom.* New York: Norton.

Morgan, Philip D. 1987. "Three Planters and Their Slaves: Perspectives on Slavery in Virginia, South Carolina, and Jamaica, 1750–1790." In *Race and Family in the Colonial South,* ed. Winthrop D. Jordan and Sheila L. Skemp, 37–79. Jackson: University of Mississippi Press.

——. 1997. "The Cultural Implications of the Atlantic Slave Trade: African Regional Origins, American Destinations, and New World Developments." *Slavery and Abolition* 18:122–45.

Morrison, Karen Y. 1999. "Civilization and Citizenship through the Eyes of Afro-Cuban Intellectuals during the First Constitutional Era, 1902–1940." *Cuban Studies/Estudios Cubanos* 30:76–99.

Mudimbe, V. Y. 1988. *The Invention of Africa: Gnosis, Philosophy, and the Order of Knowledge.* Bloomington: Indiana University Press.

Mullin, Michael. 1992. *Africa in America.* Urbana: University of Illinois Press.

Mullings, Beverley. 1999. "Globalization, Tourism, and the International Sex Trade." In *Sun, Sex, and Gold: Tourism and Sex Work in the Caribbean,* ed. Kamala Kempadoo, 55–80. Lanham, Md.: Rowman and Littlefield.

Murray, Margaret. 1921. *The Witch-Cult in Western Europe.* Oxford: Clarendon.

Murray, Peter. 1972. *Five Early Guides to Rome and Florence.* Farnsborough: Gregg International.

Nadel, Siegfried. 1957. "Malinowski on Magic and Religion." In *Man and Culture: An Evaluation of the Work of Bronislaw Malinowski,* ed. Raymond Firth, 189–208. London: Routledge and Kegan Paul.

Naipaul, V. S. 1977. *The Middle Passage.* 1962. Reprint, New York: Vintage.

——. 2001. *The Mimic Men.* 1967. Reprint, New York: Vintage.

Navarro, Joseph. 1760. *Vida y milagros del príncipe de los Anacoretas, y padre de los Cenobiarcas, nuestro padre S. Antonio Abad, el Magno; traducido del frances al Castellano por un devoto del santo.* Barcelona: Imprenta de María Angela Martí.

Needham, Rodney. 1972. *Belief, Language, and Experience.* Chicago: University of Chicago Press.

Nina Rodrigues, Raimundo. 1977. *Os africanos no Brasil.* 1932. Reprint, Sao Paulo: Edicoes Nacional.

Novick, Peter. 1998. *That Noble Dream: The "Objectivity Question" and the American Historical Profession.* Cambridge: Cambridge University Press.

Novit-Evans, Bette, and Ashton Welch. 1983. "Racial and Ethnic Definitions as Reflections of Public Policy." *Journal of American Studies* 17:417–35.

Oakeshott, Michael. 1933. *Experience and Its Modes.* Cambridge: Cambridge University Press.

O'Connell Davidson, Julia. 1996. "Sex Tourism in Cuba." *Race and Class* 38:39–48.

O'Connell Davidson, Julia, and Jacqueline Sanchez Taylor. 1995. "Child Prostitution and Sex Tourism, 2: Cuba." ECPAT research paper. University of Leicester, Department of Sociology.

——. 1999. "Fantasy Islands: Exploring Demand for Sex Tourism." In *Sun, Sex, and Gold: Tourism and Sex Work in the Caribbean,* ed. Kamala Kempadoo, 37–54. Lanham, Md.: Rowman and Littlefield.

Oldendorp, Christian G. A. 1777. *Geschichte der Mission der evangelischen Brüdergemeine auf den caraibischen Inseln S. Thomas, S. Croix, und S. Jan.* Barby: Christian Friedrich Laux.

O'Malley, Michael. 1994. "Specie and Species: Race and the Money Question in Nineteenth Century America." *American Historical Review* 99:369–95.

Ortiz, Fernando. 1905. "La criminalità dei negri in Cuba." *Archivio di psichiatria, medicina legale ed antropologia criminale* 24:596–600.

——. 1913. *La identificaión dactyloscópica.* La Habana: Imprenta La Universal.

——. 1921. "Los cabildos afrocubanos." *Revista Bimestre Cubana* 16:5–39.

——. 1924. *Glossario de Afronegrismos.* 2d ed. La Habana: Imprenta "El Siglo XX."

——. 1926. *Proyecto de Código Criminal.* La Habana: Librería Cervantes.

Ortiz, Fernando. 1939. "Brujos or santeros." *Estudios Afrocubanos* 3:85–90.

——. 1952–55. *Los instrumentos de la música afrocubana.* La Habana: Ministerio de Educación.

——. 1956. "La secta conga de los 'matiabos' en Cuba." In *Libro jubilar de Alfonso Reyes,* 308–25. México: Dirección General de Difusión Cultural.

——. 1958. "Las 'malas palabras' en los sacriloquios afrocubanos." In *Miscelanea Paul Rivet,* 849–56. México: Universidad Nacional Autónoma de Mexico.

——. 1973. *Los negros brujos.* 1906. Reprint, Miami: Ediciones Universal.

——. 1975. *Historia de una pelea cubana contra los demonios.* La Habana: Editorial de Ciencias Sociales.

——. 1986. *Los negros curros.* La Habana: Editorial de Ciencias Sociales.

——. 1995. *Cuban Counterpoint.* 1947. Reprint, Durham, N.C.: Duke University Press.

Ortner, Sherry S. 1995. "Resistance and the Problem of Ethnographic Refusal." *Comparative Studies in Society and History* 37:173–93.

Painter, Nell Irvin. 1994. "Thinking about the Languages of Money and Race: A Response to Michael O'Malley's 'Specie and Species.'" *American Historical Review* 99:396–404.

Palau y Dulcet, Antonio. 1948–90. *Manual del librero Hispano-Americano.* Barcelona: Editorial Palau y Dulcet.

Palmer, Bryan D. 1990. *Descent into Discourse.* Philadelphia: Temple University Press.

Palmer, Colin A. 1976. *Slaves of the White God: Blacks in Mexico, 1570–1650.* Cambridge, Mass.: Harvard University Press.

Palmié, Stephan. 1989. "Spics or Spades? Racial Classification and Ethnic Conflict in Miami." *Amerikastudien/American Studies* 34:211–21.

——. 1991. *Das Exil der Götter: Geschichte und Vorstellungswelt einer afrokubanischen Religion.* Frankfurt: Peter Lang.

——. 1993. "Ethnogenetic Processes and Cultural Transfer in Afro-American Slave Populations." In *Slavery in the Americas*, ed. Wolfgang Binder, 337–63. Würzburg: Königshausen and Neumann.

——. 1995a. "Against Syncretism: 'Africanizing' and 'Cubanizing' Discourses in North American Òrìsà Worship." In *Counterworks: Managing the Diversity of Knowledge*, ed. Richard Fardon, 73–104. London: Routledge.

——. 1995b. "The Taste of Human Commodities: Experiencing the Atlantic System." In *Slave Cultures and the Cultures of Slavery*, ed. Stephan Palmié, 40–54. Knoxville: University of Tennessee Press.

——. 1996. "Which Center, Whose Margin? Notes Towards an Archaeology of U.S. Supreme Court Case 91-948, 1993." In *Inside and Outside the Law*, ed. Olivia Harris. London: Routledge.

——. 1998a. "Conventionalization, Distortion, and Plagiarism in the Historiography of Afro-Caribbean Religion in New Orleans." In *Creoles and Cajuns*, ed. Wolfgang Binder, 315–44. Frankfurt: Peter Lang.

——. 1998b. "Fernando Ortiz and the Cooking of History." *Ibero-Amerikanisches Archiv* 24:1–21.

——. 2001. "Fascinans or Tremendum? Permutations of the State, the Body, and the Divine in Late Twentieth-Century Cuba." University of Maryland, Department of History. Typescript.

Paquette, Robert L. 1988. *Sugar Is Made with Blood*. Middletown, Conn.: Wesleyan University Press.

Parker, Harold T. 1969. *The Cult of Antiquity and the French Revolutionaries*. 1937. Reprint, New York: Octagon.

Parker, Richard G. 1991. *Bodies, Pleasures, and Passions: Sexual Culture in Brazil*. Boston: Beacon.

Pastor, Manuel, Jr. and Andrew Zimbalist. 1995. "Cuba's Economic Conundrum." *NACLA Report on the Americas* 29:7–12.

Pateman, Carol. 1988. *The Sexual Contract*. Stanford: Stanford University Press.

Patterson, Orlando. 1982. *Slavery and Social Death*. Cambridge, Mass.: Harvard University Press.

——. 1987. "The Emerging West Atlantic System: Migration, Culture, and Underdevelopment in the United States and the Circum-Caribbean Region." In *Population in a Changing World*, ed. William Alonso, 227–60. Cambridge, Mass.: Harvard University Press.

Pattullo, Polly. 1996. *Last Resorts: The Cost of Tourism in the Caribbean*. London: Cassell.

Peel, J. Y. D. 1979–80. "Kings, Titles, and Quarters: A Conjectural History of Ilesha." *History in Africa* 6–7:109–53, 225–55.

——. 1984. "Making History: The Past in the Ijesha Present." *Man* 19:111–32.

——. 1990. "The Pastor and the *Babalawo:* The Interaction of Religions in Nineteenth Century Yorubaland." *Africa* 60:338–69.

Peires, J. B. 1990. "Suicide or Genocide? Xhosa Perceptions on the Nongqawuse Catastrophe." *Radical History Review* 46:47–57.

Pérez, Louis A., Jr. 1986. *Cuba Under the Platt Amendment, 1902–1934*. Pittsburgh: University of Pittsburgh Press.

——. 1988. *Cuba: Between Reform and Revolution*. New York: Oxford University Press.

——. 1990. *Cuba and the United States: Ties of Singular Intimacy*. Athens: University of Georgia Press.

——. 1999. *On Becoming Cuban: Identity, Nationality, and Culture*. Chapel Hill: University of North Carolina Press.

Pérez de la Riva, Juan. 1978. "El barracón de ingenio en la época esclavista." In *El barracón*, 13–40. Barcelona: Editorial Crítica.

——. 1979. "Cuba y la migración antillana, 1900–1931." *Anuario de Estudios Cubanos* 2:1–75.

Pérez-López, Jorge F. 1995. *Cuba's Second Economy*. New Brunswick, N.J.: Transaction.

Pérez Sarduy, Pedro, and Jean Stubbs. 2000. "Introduction: Race and the Politics of Memory in Contemporary Black Cuban Consciousness." In *Afro-Cuban Voices*, ed. Pedro Pérez Sarduy and Jean Stubbs, 1–38. Gainesville: University of Florida Press.

Perinbam, B. Marie. 1982. *Holy Violence: The Revolutionary Thought of Frantz Fanon*. Washington, D.C.: Three Continents.

Peschuel-Loesche, E. 1907. *Volkskunde von Loango*. Stuttgart: Strecker and Schröder.

Phillips, Ulrich B. 1918. *American Negro Slavery*. New York: D. Appleton.

Pichardo, Esteban. 1985. *Diccionario casi razonado de voces y phrases cubanas*. 1875. Reprint, La Habana: Editorial de Ciencias Sociales.

Pichardo, Hortensia. 1973. *Documentos para la historia de Cuba*. La Habana: Editorial de Ciencias Sociales.

Piersen, William D. 1977. "White Cannibals, Black Martyrs: Fear, Depression, and Religious Faith as Causes of Suicide among New Slaves." *Journal of Negro History* 62:147–59.

Pietz, William. 1985. "The Problem of the Fetish, I." *Res* 9:5–17.

——. 1987. "The Problem of the Fetish, II: The Origin of the Fetish." *Res* 13:23–45.

——. 1988. "The Problem of the Fetish, IIIa: Bosman's Guinea and the Enlightenment Theory of Fetishism." *Res* 16:105–23.

——. 1993. "Fetishism and Materialism: The Limits of Theory in Marx." In *Fetishism as Cultural Discourse*, ed. Emily Apter and William Pietz, 119–51. Ithaca, N.Y.: Cornell University Press.

Piot, Charles. 1996. "Of Slaves and the Gift: Kabre Sale of Kin during the Era of Slave Trade." *Journal of African History* 31:31–49.

Pocock, J. G. A. 1962. "The Origins of Study of the Past: A Comparative Approach." *Comparative Studies in Society and History* 4:209–46.

——. 1988. *Virtue, Commerce, and History*. Cambridge: Cambridge University Press.

Ponte Dominguez, Francisco J. 1951. *El delito de la francomasonería en Cuba*. Mexico: D.F.: Editorial Humanidad.

Poovey, Mary. 1994. "Figures of Arithmetic, Figures of Speech: The Discourse of Statistics in the 1830s." In *Questions of Evidence*, ed. James Chandler, Arnold I. Davidson, and Harry Harootunian, 401–21. Chicago: University of Chicago Press.

Porter, Roy. 1993. "Consumption: Disease of the Consumer Society?" In *Consumption and the World of Goods*, ed. John Brewer and Roy Porter, 58–81. London: Routledge.

Prakash, Gyan. 1992a. "Can the 'Subaltern' Ride? A Reply to O'Hanlon and Washbrook." *Comparative Studies in Society and History* 34:168–84.

——. 1992b. "Writing Post-Orientalist Histories of the Third World: Indian Historiography Is Good to Think." In *Colonialism and Culture*, ed. Nicholas Dirks, 353–88. Ann Arbor: University of Michigan Press.

Praz, Mario. 1964. *Studies in Seventeenth Century Imagery*. Roma: Edizioni di Storia e Letteratura.

Price, Richard. 1973. "Avenging Spirits and the Structure of Saramaka Lineages." *Bijdragen tot de Taal-, Land-, en Volkenkunde* 129:86–107.

——. 1975. *Saramaka Social Structure: Analysis of a Maroon Society in Suriname*. Río Piedras: Institute of Caribbean Studies, University of Puerto Rico.

——. 1976. *The Guiana Maroons: A Historical and Bibliographical Introduction*. Baltimore: Johns Hopkins University Press.

Price, Richard, and Sally Price. 1988. Introduction to *Narrative of a Five Years Expedition against the Revolted Negroes of Suriname*, by John Gabriel Stedman, xiii–xcvii. Baltimore: Johns Hopkins University Press.

Prouty, Chris, and Eugene Rosenfeld, eds. 1981. *Historical Dictionary of Ethiopia*. Metuchen, N.J.: Scarecrow.

Prude, Jonathan. 1991. "To Look upon the 'Lower Sort': Runaway Ads and the Appearance of Unfree Laborers in America, 1750–1800." *Journal of American History* 78:124–59.

Pruitt, Deborah, and Suzanne LaFont. 1995. "For Love and Money: Romance Tourism in Jamaica." *Annals of Tourism Research* 22:422–40.

Rafael, Vicente. 1992. "Confession, Conversion, and Reciprocity in Early Tagalog Colonial Society." In *Colonialism and Culture*, ed. Nicholas B. Dirks, 65–88. Ann Arbor: University of Michigan Press.

——. 1993. "White Love: Surveillance and Resistance in the U.S. Colonization of the Philippines." In *Cultures of U.S. Imperialism*, ed. Amy Kaplan and Donald E. Pease, 185–218. Durham, N.C.: Duke University Press.

Ranger, Terence O. 1986. "Religious Movements and Politics in Sub-Saharan Africa." *African Studies Review* 29:1–69.

Redicker, Marcus. 1988. "Good Hands, Stout Heart, and Fast Feet: The History and Culture of Working People in Early America." In *Reviving the English Revolution*, ed. Geoff Eley and William Hunt, 221–49. London: Verso.

Reed, Gail. 1992. *Island in the Storm: The Cuban Communist Party's Fourth Congress*. Melbourne: Ocean.

Reis, Joao José. 1982. "Slave Rebellion in Brazil: The African Muslim Uprising in Bahia, 1835. Ph.D. diss., University of Minnesota.

Reisman, Karl. 1970. "Cultural and Linguistic Ambiguity in a West Indian Village." In *Afro-American Anthropology*, ed. Norman E. Whitten and John F. Szwed, 129–44. New York: Free Press.

Rejali, Darius M. 1991. "How Not to Talk about Torture: Violence, Theory, and the Problem of Explanation." In *Vigilantism and the State in Modern Latin America*, ed. Martha K. Huggins, 127–44. New York: Praeger.

———. 1994. *Torture and Modernity: Self, Society, and State in Modern Iran*. Boulder, Colo.: Westview.

Renouvier, Jules. 1863. *Histoire de l'art pendant la révolution*. Paris: Jules Renouard.

República de Cuba. 1913. *Memória leida por el lcdo. Sr. José Fernández Alvarez, Fiscal de la Audiencia de Matanzas en el Acto de la solemne apertura de las Tribunales e día 10 de Septiembre del Año 1913*. Matanzas: Imprenta de Quiros y Estrada.

Richards, Audrey. 1935. "A Modern Movement of Witchfinders." *Africa* 8:448–61.

Richardson, Alan. 1993. "Romantic Voodoo: Obeah and British Culture, 1797–1807." *Studies in Romanticism* 32:3–28.

Richman, Karen E. 1992. "They Will Remember Me in the House: The *Pwen* of Haitian Transnational Migration." Ph.D. diss., University of Virginia.

Rigol, Jorge. 1982. *Apuntes sobre la pintura y el grabado en Cuba*. La Habana: Editorial Letras Cubanas.

Riley, Denise. 1988. *Am I That Name? Feminism and the Category of "Women" in History*. Minneapolis: University of Minnesota Press.

Roa, Ramon. 1950. *Con la pluma y el machete*. Vol. 1. La Habana: Ministerio de Educación.

Robert, Karen. 1992. "Slavery and Freedom in the Ten Years' War, Cuba, 1868–1878." *Slavery and Abolition* 13:181–200.

Roche Monteagudo, Rafael. 1925. *La policía y sus mistérios*. La Habana: La Moderna Poesía.

Rorty, Richard. 1991. *Objectivity, Relativism, and Truth*. Cambridge: Cambridge University Press.

———. 1999. *Philosophy and Social Hope*. London: Penguin.

Ryan, Chris, and Rachel Kinder. 1996. "Sex, Tourism, and Sex Tourism: Fulfilling Similar Needs?" *Tourism Management* 17:507–18.

Sahlins, Marshall. 1988. "Cosmologies of Capitalism: The Trans-Pacific Sector of the World System." *Proceedings of the British Academy* 84:1–51.

———. 1996. "The Sadness of Sweetness: The Native Anthropology of Western Cosmology." *Current Anthropology* 37:395–428.

Salamone, Frank. 1982. "Chronicles of the Impossible: Notes on Three Indigenous Peruvian Historians." In *From Oral to Written Expression: Native American Chronicles of the Early Colonial Period*, ed. Rolena Adorno, 9–39. Syracuse, N.Y.: Maxwell School of Citizenship and Public Affairs, Syracuse University.

Sandoval, Alonso de. 1956. *De Instauranda Aethiopum Salute*. 1627. Reprint, Bogota: Empresa Nacional de Publicaciones.

Santiago, Sebastián. 1981. *Arte y humanismo*. Madrid: Ediciones Cátedra.

Santiago, Sebastián, M. Concepción García Gainza, and J. Rogelio Buendía. 1980. *El Renacimiento*. Vol. 3 of *La Historia del arte Hispánico*, ed. R. Buendía. Madrid: Editorial Alhambra.

Santner, Eric L. 1992. "History Beyond the Pleasure Principle: Some Thoughts on the Representation of Trauma." In *Probing the Limits of Representation: Nazism and the "Final Solution,"* ed. Saul Friedlander, 143–54. Cambridge, Mass.: Harvard University Press.

Scarry, Elaine. 1985. *The Body in Pain*. New York: Oxford University Press.

Scheper-Hughes, Nancy. 1996. "Theft of Life: The Globalization of Organ Stealing Rumours." *Anthropology Today* 12:3–11.

Schmidt, Hans. 1995. *The United States Occupation of Haiti, 1915–1934*. New Brunswick, N.J.: Rutgers University Press.

Schuler, Monica. 1970. "Akan Slave Rebellions in the British Caribbean." *Savacou* 1:8–31.

——. 1979. "Afro-American Slave Culture." In *Roots and Branches*, ed. Michael Craton, 121–37. New York: Pergamon.

——. 1980. *"Alas, Alas, Kongo": A Social History of Indentured African Immigration into Jamaica, 1841–1865*. Baltimore: Johns Hopkins University Press.

Schüller, Karin. 1992. *Die deutsche Rezeption haitianischer Geschichte in der ersten Hälfte des 19. Jahrhunderts*. Cologne: Böhlau.

Schwartz, Rosalie. 1997. *Pleasure Island: Tourism and Temptation in Cuba*. Lincoln: University of Nebraska Press.

Scott, David. 1991. "That Event, This Memory: Notes on the Anthropology of African Diasporas in the New World." *Diasporas* 1:261–84.

——. 1994. *Formations of Ritual: Colonial and Anthropological Discourses on the Sinhala Yaktovil*. Minneapolis: University of Minnesota Press.

Scott, Joan W. 1988. *Gender and the Politics of History*. New York: Columbia University Press.

——. 1989. "History in Crisis? The Others' Side of the Story." *American Historical Review* 94:680–92.

——. 1991. "The Evidence of Experience." *Critical Inquiry* 17:773–97.

Scott, Julius S. 1986. "The Common Wind: Currents of Afro-American Communication in the Era of the Haitian Revolution. Ph.D. diss., Duke University.

——. 1991. "Afro-American Sailors and the International Communication Network: The Case of Newport Bowers." In *Jack Tar in History*, ed. Colin Howell and Richard J. Twomey, 37–52. Fredericton, N.B.: Acadiensis.

Scott, Rebecca. 1985. *Slave Emancipation in Cuba*. Princeton, N.J.: Princeton University Press.

Seabrook, William B. 1929. *The Magic Island*. New York: Harcourt, Brace.

Segato, Rita Laura. 1998. "The Color-Blind Subject of Myth; or, Where to Find Africa in the Nation." *Annual Review of Anthropology* 27:129–51.

Segre, Roberto, Mario Coyula, and Joseph L. Scarpaci. 1997. *Havana: Two Faces of the Antillean Metropolis*. Chichester: Wiley.

Seltzer, Mark. 1992. *Bodies and Machines*. New York: Routledge.
Sen, Amartya. 1981. *Poverty and Famines*. Oxford: Clarendon.
Sewell, William G. 1861. *The Ordeal of Free Labour in the British West Indies*. New York: Harper and Bros.
Shapin, Steven, and Simon Shaffer. 1985. *Leviathan and the Air-Pump: Hobbes, Boyle, and the Experimental Life*. Princeton, N.J.: Princeton University Press.
Shaw, Rosalind. 1997. "The Production of Witchcraft / Witchcraft as Production: Memory, Modernity, and the Slave Trade in Sierra Leone." *American Ethnologist* 24:856–76.
——. 2002. *Memories of the Slave Trade: Ritual and the Historical Imagination in Sierra Leone*. Chicago: University of Chicago Press.
Shaw, Rosalind, and Charles Stewart. 1994. "Introduction: Problematizing Syncretism." In *Syncretism/Antisyncretism*, ed. Rosalind Shaw and Charles Stewart, 1–26. London: Routledge.
Sheriff, Robert E. 2000. "Exposing Silence as Cultural Censorship: A Brazilian Case." *American Anthropologist* 102:114–32.
Silverman, Bertram. 1971. *Man and Socialism in Cuba*. New York: Atheneum.
Simmel, Georg. "Conflict." 1908. In *The Sociology of Georg Simmel*, trans. and ed. Kurt H. Wolff. Glencoe, Ill.: Free Press, 1950.
——. 1978. *The Philosophy of Money*. 1900. Reprint, London: Routledge and Kegan Paul.
Simpson, George Eaton. 1955. "Political Cultism in West Kingston, Jamaica." *Social and Economic Studies* 4:133–49.
——. 1956. "Jamaican Revivalist Cults." *Social and Economic Studies* 5:321–442.
Sjørslev, Inger. 1989. "The Myth of Myths and the Nature of Ritual." *Folk* 31:105–23.
Skidmore, Thomas E. 1990. "Racial Ideas and Social Policy in Brazil, 1870–1940." In *The Idea of Race in Latin America, 1870–1940*, ed. Richard Graham, 7–36. Austin: University of Texas Press.
Smith, Michael G. 1963. *Dark Puritan*. Kingston: Herald.
——. 1965. *The Plural Society in the British West Indies*. Berkeley: University of California Press.
Smith, Stephen L. J. 1998. "Tourism as an Industry: Debates and Concepts." In *The Economic Geography of the Tourist Industry*, ed. Dimitri Ioannides and Keith G. Debbage, 31–52. London: Routledge.
Snowden, Frank M., Jr. 1970. *Blacks in Antiquity*. Cambridge, Mass.: Harvard University Press.
Sobo, Elisa Janine. 1993. *One Blood: The Jamaican Body*. Albany: SUNY Press.
"La sociedad secreta abakua." *El militante Comunista*, August, 36–45.
Solow, Barbara, and Stanley L. Engerman. 1987. *British Capitalism and Caribbean Slavery: The Legacy of Eric Williams*. Cambridge: Cambridge University Press.
Sombart, Werner. 1967. *Luxury and Capitalism*. 1913. Reprint, Ann Arbor: University of Michigan Press.
Sosa Rodríguez, Enrique. 1982. *Los Ñáñigos*. Habana: Ediciones Casa de las Américas.

Southall, Aidan. 1979. "White Strangers and Their Religion in East Africa and Madagascar." In *Strangers in African Societies*, ed. William A. Shack and Elliot P. Skinner, 211–26. Berkeley and Los Angeles: University of California Press.

Sperber, Dan. 1982. "Apparently Irrational Beliefs." In *Rationality and Relativism*, ed. Martin Hollis and Steven Lukes, 149–80. Cambridge, Mass.: MIT Press.

Spiller, Hortense. 1987. "Mama's Baby, Papa's Maybe: An American Grammar Book." *Diacritics* 17:65–81.

Spivak, Gayatri Chakravorti. 1988a. "Can the Subaltern Speak?" In *Marxism and the Interpretation of Culture*, ed. Cary Nelson and Lawrence Grossberg, 271–313. Urbana: University of Illinois Press.

——. 1988b. "Subaltern Studies: Deconstructing Historiography." In *Selected Subaltern Studies*, ed. Ranajit Guha and Gayatri Chakravorti Spivak. New York: Oxford University Press.

Stallybrass, Peter. 1990. "Marx and Heterogeneity: Thinking the Lumpenproletariat." *Representations* 31:69–95.

Stallybrass, Peter, and Allon White. 1986. *The Politics and Poetics of Transgression*. London: Methuen.

Stedman, John Gabriel. 1988. *Narrative of a Five Years Expedition against the Revolted Negroes of Surinam*. 1796. Baltimore: Johns Hopkins University Press.

Stedman Jones, Gareth. 1971. *Outcast London*. Oxford: Clarendon.

Stein, Robert Louis. 1979. *The French Slave Trade in the Eighteenth Century*. Madison: University of Wisconsin Press.

Stepan, Nancy. 1982. *The Idea of Race in Science*. London: Macmillan.

Stewart, Robert J. 1992. *Religion and Society in Poste-Emancipation Jamaica*. Knoxville: University of Tennessee Press.

Stocking, George. 1987. *Victorian Anthropology*. New York: Free Press.

Stoichita, Victor I. 1995. *Visionary Experience in the Golden Age of Spanish Art*. London: Reaktion.

Stoler, Ann Laura. 1989. "Rethinking Colonial Categories: European Communities and the Boundaries of Rule." *Comparative Studies in Society and History* 13:134–61.

——. 1991. "Carnal Knowledge and Imperial Power: Gender, Race, and Morality in Colonial Asia." In *Gender at the Crossrods of Knowledge*, ed. Micaela Di Leonardo, 51–101. Berkeley and Los Angeles: University of California Press.

——. 1992. "'In Cold Blood': Hierarchies of Credibility and the Politics of Colonial Narratives." *Representations* 37:151–89.

——. 1995. *Race and the Education of Desire*. Durham, N.C.: Duke University Press.

Stoler, Ann Laura, and Karen Strassler. 2000. "Casting for the Colonial: Memory Work in 'New Order' Java." *Comparative Studies in Society and History* 42:4–48.

Strathern, Marilyn. 1988. *The Gender of the Gift*. Berkeley and Los Angeles: University of California Press.

——. 1992. *Reproducing the Future*. New York: Routledge.

Street, Brian V. 1987. "Orality and Literacy as Ideological Constructions: Some Problems in Cross-Cultural Studies." *Culture and History* 2:7–30.

Tambiah, Stanley J. 1990. *Magic, Science, Religion, and the Scope of Rationality*. Cambridge: Cambridge University Press.

Taussig, Michael. 1987. *Shamanism, Colonialism, and the Wild Man*. Chicago: University of Chicago Press.

——. 1991. *Nervous System*. New York: Routledge.

——. 1993. *Mimesis and Alterity*. New York: Routledge.

——. 1997. *The Magic of the State*. New York: Routledge.

Terdiman, Richard. 1993. *Present Past*. Ithaca, N.Y.: Cornell University Press.

Thoden van Velzen, Bonno. 1990. "Social Fetishism among the Surinamese Maroons." *Etnofoor* 3:77–95.

——. 1995. "Revenants that Cannot be Shaken: Collective Fantasies in a Maroon Society." *American Anthropologist* 97:722–32.

Thoden van Velzen, H. U. E., and Wilhelmina van Wetering. 1988. *The Great Father and the Danger*. Dordrecht: Foris.

Thomas, Hugh. 1971. *Cuba: The Pursuit of Freedom*. New York: Harper and Row.

Thomas, Keith. 1971. *Religion and the Decline of Magic*. Harmondsworth: Penguin.

Thomas, Nicholas. 1990. "Sanitation and Seeing: The Creation of State Power in Early Colonial Fiji." *Comparative Studies in Society and History* 32:149–70.

——. 1992. "The Inversion of Tradition." *American Ethnologist* 19:213–32.

Thompson, Edward P. 1968. *The Making of the English Working Class*. 1963. Reprint, Harmondsworth: Penguin.

——. 1971. "Patrician Society, Plebeian Culture." *Journal of Social History* 7:382–405.

——. 1977. "Folklore, Anthropology, and Social History." *Indian Historical Review* 3:247–66.

——. 1978. "The Poverty of Theory; or, An Orrery of Errors." In *The Poverty of Theory and Other Essays*, 1–210. New York: Monthly Review Press.

——. 1991. *Customs in Common*. London: Penguin.

Thompson, Robert Faris. 1983. *Flash of the Spirit*. New York: Random House.

Thorne, Susan. 1997. " 'The Conversion of Englishmen and the Conversion of the World Inseparable': Missionary Imperialism and the Language of Class in Early Industrial Britain." In *Tensions of Empire*, ed. Frederick Cooper and Ann Laura Stoler, 238–62. Berkeley and Los Angeles: University of California Press.

Thornton, Robert. 1995. "The Colonial, the Imperial, and the Creation of the 'European' in Southern Africa." In *Occidentalism*, ed. James G. Carrier, 192–217. Oxford: Clarendon.

Tilly, Charles. 1984. *Big Structures, Large Processes, Huge Comparisons*. New York: Russell Sage Foundation.

Toribio Medina, José. 1962. *Biblioteca Hispano-Americana*. 1896–1907. Reprint, Amsterdam: N. Israel.

Torre, José María de la. 1857. *Lo que fuimos y lo que somos, o la Habana antigua y moderna*. Habana: Spencer.

Torres, Cuevas, Eduardo, and Eusebio Reyes. 1986. *Esclavitud y sociedad*. La Habana: Editorial de Ciencias Sociales.

Treichler, Paula A. 1988. "AIDS, Homophobia, and Biomedical Discourse: An Epidemic of Signification." In *AIDS: Cultural Analysis/Cultural Activism*, ed. Douglas Crimp, 31–70. Cambridge, Mass.: MIT Press.

Trelles, Carlos M. 1965a. *Bibliografía cubana de los siglos XVII y XVIII*. 1927. Reprint, Vaduz: Kraus.

——. 1965b. *Bibliografía cubana del siglo XIX*. 1911. Reprint, Vaduz: Kraus.

Trouillot, Michel-Rolph. 1982. "Motion in the System: Coffee, Color, and Slavery in Eighteenth-Century Saint-Domingue." *Review* 3:331–88.

——. 1984. "Caribbean Peasantries and World Capitalism: An Approach to Micro-Level Studies." *New West Indian Guides* 58:37–59.

——. 1990. *Haiti: State against Nation*. New York: Monthly Review Press.

——. 1991. "Anthropology and the Savage Slot: The Poetics and Politics of Otherness." In *Recapturing Anthropology*, ed. Richard Fox, 17–44. Santa Fe: School of American Research Press.

——. 1992. "The Caribbean Region: An Open Frontier in Anthropological Theory." *Annual Reviews of Anthropology* 21:19–42.

——. 1995. *Silencing the Past*. Boston: Beacon.

Trujillo y Monagas, José. 1882. "Los Ñáñigos: Su historia, sus prácticas, su lenguage." In *Los criminales de Cuba y Don José Trujillo*, ed. Carlos Urrutia y Blanco, 363–74. Barcelona: Establecimiento Tipográfico de Fidel Giró.

Tucker, Robert C. 1978. *The Marx-Engels Reader*. New York: Norton.

Turner, Louis, and John Ash. 1976. *The Golden Hordes: International Tourism and the Pleasure Periphery*. New York: St. Martin's.

Tyler, Bruce M. 1989. "Black Jive and White Repression." *Journal of Ethnic Studies* 16:31–66.

Unsworth, Barry. 1992. *Sacred Hunger*. New York: Norton.

Urry, John. 1990. *The Tourist Gaze*. London: Sage.

Valdés, J. Antonio. 1964. *História de la isla de Cuba y en especial de la Habana*. 1813. Reprint, La Habana: Comisión Nacional Cubana de la UNESCO.

Valentini, Roberto, and Guiseppe Zuchetti. 1940–53. *Codice topografico della città di Roma*. Roma: Tipografia del Senato.

van Wing, Joseph. 1959. *Études Bakongo*. Paris: Desclee de Brouwer.

Vaughan, Megan. 1992. "Syphillis in Colonial East and Central Africa: The Social Construction of an Epidemic." In *Epidemics and Ideas*, ed. Terence O. Ranger and Paul Slack, 269–302. Cambridge: Cambridge University Press.

Verdery, Katherine. 1999. *The Political Lives of Dead Bodies*. New York: Columbia University Press.

Verger, Pierre. 1965. "Grandeur et décadence du culte de Iyámi Osòróngà (ma mère la sorcière) chez les yoruba." *Journal de la Société des Africanistes* 35:141–243.

——. 1981. *Orixas: Deuses Iorubás na Africa e no novo mundo*. Salvador: Editora Corrupio.

Vincent, Joan. 1990. *Anthropology and Politics*. Tucson: University of Arizona Press.

Waddell, Hope M. 1863. *Twenty-nine Years in the West Indies and Central Africa*. London: T. Nelson and Sons.

Wade, Peter. 1993. "'Race,' Nature, and Culture." *Man* 28:17–34.

——. 1997. *Race and Ethnicity in Latin America*. London: Pluto.

Walkowitz, Judith. 1992. *City of Dreadful Delight: Narratives of Sexual Danger in Late-Victorian London*. Chicago: University of Chicago Press.

Wallace, Anthony F. C. 1968. *Culture and Personality*. 1961. Reprint, New York: Random House.

Weber, Eugen. 1969. *Peasants into Frenchmen*. Stanford, Calif.: Stanford University Press.

Wentzlaff-Eggebert, Christian. 1993. "Miguel Barnet's 'Novela-Testimonio' *Biografía de un cimarrón:* Life Story of a Runaway Slave, Ethnological Study, or Manipulation of Public Opinion?" In *Slavery in the Americas*, ed. Wolfgang Binder, 627–47. Würzburg: Königshausen and Neumann.

Werbner, Richard. 1979. "Totemism in History: The Ritual Passage of West African Strangers." *Man* 14:663–83.

Werner, Wolfgang. 1990. "'Playing Soldiers': The Truppenspieler Movements among the Herero of Namibia, 1915–ca. 1945." *Journal of Southern African Studies* 16:476–502.

Wetli, Charles, and Rafael Martinez. 1983. "Brujería: Manifestations of Palo Mayombe in South Florida." *Journal of the Florida Medical Association* 70:629–34.

White, Hayden. 1973. "The Value of Narrativity in the Representation of Reality." *Critical Inquiry* 7:5–29.

White, Louise. 1993a. "Cars Out of Place: Vampires, Technology, and Labour in East and Central Africa." *Representations* 43:27–50.

——. 1993b. "Vampire Priests of Central Africa: African Debate about Labor and Religion in East and Central Africa." *Comparative Studies in Society and History* 35:744–70.

——. 1995. "'They Could Make Their Victims Dull': Gender and Genres, Fantasies and Cures in Colonial Southern Uganda." *American Historical Review* 100:1379–1402.

——. 2000. *Speaking with Vampires: Rumor and History in Colonial Africa*. Berkeley and Los Angeles: University of California Press.

White, Shane. 1991. *Somewhat More Independent: The End of Slavery in New York City, 1770–1810*. Athens: University of Georgia Press.

White, Shane, and Graham White. 1995a. "Slave Clothing and African American Culture in the Eighteenth and Nineteenth Centuries." *Past and Present*, no. 148:149–86.

——. 1995b. "Slave Hair and African American Culture in the Eighteenth and Nineteenth Centuries." *Journal of Southern History* 61:45–76.

Williams, Brackette. 1990. "Dutchman Ghosts and the History Mystery: Ritual, Colonizer, and Colonized Interpretations of the 1763 Berbice Slave Rebellion." *Journal of Historical Sociology* 3:133–65.

Williams, Eric. 1944. *Capitalism and Slavery.* Chapel Hill: University of North Carolina Press.

Williams, Raymond. 1973. *The Country and the City.* New York: Oxford University Press.

——. 1980. *Problems in Materialism and Culture.* London: Verso.

Wilmsen, Edwin M., and James R. Denbow. 1990. "Paradigmatic History of San-Speaking Peoples and Current Attempts at Revision." *Current Anthropology* 31:489–524.

Wilson, Peter. 1969. "Reputation vs. Respectability: A Suggestion for Caribbean Ethnography." *Man* 4:70–84.

——. 1992. *Oscar: An Inquiry into the Nature of Sanity.* 1974. Reprint, Prospect Heights, N.J.: Waveland.

Wind, Edgar. 1968. *Pagan Mysteries in the Renaissance.* London: Faber and Faber.

Wolf, Eric. 1971. "Specific Aspects of Plantation Systems in the New World: Community Sub-Cultures and Social Classes." In *Peoples and Cultures of the Caribbean* (1959), ed. Michael M. Horowitz, 163–78. Garden City, N.J.: Natural History Press.

——. 1982a. *Europe and the People without History.* Berkeley and Los Angeles: University of California Press.

——. 1982b. "The Mills of Inequality." In *Social Inequality,* ed. Gerald D. Berreman, 41–57. New York: Academic.

——. 1988. Inventing Society." *American Ethnologist* 15:752–61.

Wright, Irene A. 1910. *Cuba.* New York: Macmillan.

Yacou, Alain. 1993. "La insurgencia negra en la isla de Cuba en la primera mitad del siglo XIX." *Revista de Índias* 53:23–51.

Yates, Frances. 1964. *Giordano Bruno and the Hermetic Tradition.* London: Routledge and Kegan Paul.

Young, Robert J. C. 1995. *Colonial Desire.* London: Routledge.

Zeuske, Michael. 1997a. "Die diskrete Macht der Sklaven: Zur politischen Partizipation von Afrokubanern während des kubanischen Unabhängigkeitskrieges und der ersten Jahre der Republik (1895–1908)—eine regionale Perspektive." *Comparativ* 7:32–98.

——. 1997b. "The Real Esteban Montejo? A Re-Reading of Miguel Barnet's 'Cimarrón.'" *New West Indian Guide* 71:265–79.

Žižek, Slavoj. 1997. *The Plague of Fantasies.* London: Verso.

PERMISSIONS

The selection from *Cannibalism and the Colonial World*, ed. Francis Barker, Peter Hulme, and Margaret Iverson (1998), is reprinted with permission from Cambridge University Press.

The selection from Michael Craton's *Testing the Chains* (1982) is reprinted with the permission of Cornell University Press.

The selection from David Brion Davis's "Slavery and the Post–World War II Historians" is reprinted with permission from *Daedalus: Journal of the American Academy of Arts and Sciences.* Original publication in *Daedalus*, issue entitled "Slavery, Colonialism, and Racism," 1974, vol. 103, no. 2.

The selection from Robert Fogel's *Without Consent or Contract: The Rise and Fall of American Slavery* (1989) is reprinted with permission from Norton.

The selection from Edouard Glissant's *Poetics of Relation* (1997) is reprinted with permission from the University of Michigan Press.

The selection from Simon Harrison's "The Commerce of Cultures in Melanesia" is reprinted with permission from the Royal Anthropological Institute of Great Britain and Ireland. Original publication in *Man*, vol. 28, pp. 139–58.

The selection from Mary Lynn Johnson and John E. Grant's *Blake's Poetry and Designs* (1979) is reprinted with permission from Norton.

Selections from Reinhard Koselleck's *Futures Past: On the Semantics of Historical Time* (1985) are reprinted with permission from MIT Press.

The selection from Paul E. Lovejoy's *Transformations in Slavery: A History of Slavery in Africa* (1983) is reprinted with the permission of Cambridge University Press.

Selections from Wyatt MacGaffey's *Religion and Society in Central Africa* (1986) are reprinted with permission from the University of Chicago Press.

Selections from Sidney Mintz's "Enduring Substances, Trying Theories: The Caribbean Region as *oikoumene*" (1996) are reprinted with permission from the Royal Anthropological Institute of Great Britain and Ireland. Original publication in the *Journal of the Royal Anthropological Institute*, vol. 2, pp. 289–311.

The selection from Gyan Prakash's "Can the Subaltern Ride? A Reply to O'Hanlon and Washbrook" (1992) is reprinted with the permission of Cambridge University Press.

The selection from John G. A. Pocock's *Virtue, Commerce, and History: Essays on Political Thought and History, Chiefly in the Eighteenth Century* (1988) is reprinted with the permission of Cambridge University Press.

The selection from Nancy Scheper-Hughes's "Theft of Life: The Globalization of Organ Stealing Rumors" is reprinted with permission from the Royal Anthropological Institute of Great Britain and Ireland. Original publication in *Anthropology Today,* vol. 12, pp. 3–11.

The selection from Michel-Rolph Trouillot's "The Caribbean Region: An Open Frontier in Anthropological Theory" is reprinted with permission from the *Annual Reviews of Anthropology,* vol. 21, © 1992, by *Annual Reviews.*

The selection from Werner Sombart's *Luxury and Capitalism* (1967) is reprinted with the permission of the University of Michigan Press.

The selection from Raymond Williams's *The Country and the City* (1973) is reprinted with the permission of Oxford University Press.

INDEX

STEPHAN PALMIÉ is Assistant Professor of History at the University of Maryland at College Park. He is the author of *Das Exil der Götter: Geschichte und Vorstellungswelt einer Afrokubanischen Religion* (1991) and editor of *Slave Cultures and the Cultures of Slavery* (1995).

Library of Congress Cataloging-in-Publication Data
Palmié, Stephan.
Wizards and scientists : explorations in Afro-Cuban modernity and tradition / Stephan Palmié.
p. cm. Includes bibliographical references and index.
ISBN 0-8223-2828-3 (alk. paper)
ISBN 0-8223-2842-9 (pbk. : alk. paper)
1. Blacks—Cuba—Religion. 2. Cuba—Religion.
3. Cuba—Civilization—Western influences. I. Title.
BL2566.C9 P355 2002 306′.097291—dc21 2001040907